VLADIMIR NABOKOV

Modern Critical Interpretations

The Oresteia
Beowulf
The General Prologue to The Canterbury Tales
The Pardoner's Tale
The Knight's Tale
The Divine Comedy
Exodus
Genesis
The Gospels
The Iliad
The Book of Job
Volpone
Doctor Faustus
The Revelation of St. John the Divine
The Song of Songs
Oedipus Rex
The Aeneid
The Duchess of Malfi
Antony and Cleopatra
As You Like It
Coriolanus
Hamlet
Henry IV, Part I
Henry IV, Part II
Henry V
Julius Caesar
King Lear
Macbeth
Measure for Measure
The Merchant of Venice
A Midsummer Night's Dream
Much Ado About Nothing
Othello
Richard II
Richard III
The Sonnets
Taming of the Shrew
The Tempest
Twelfth Night
The Winter's Tale
Emma
Mansfield Park
Pride and Prejudice
The Life of Samuel Johnson
Moll Flanders
Robinson Crusoe
Tom Jones
The Beggar's Opera
Gray's Elegy
Paradise Lost
The Rape of the Lock
Tristram Shandy
Gulliver's Travels
Evelina
The Marriage of Heaven and Hell
Songs of Innocence and Experience
Jane Eyre
Wuthering Heights
Don Juan
The Rime of the Ancient Mariner
Bleak House
David Copperfield
Hard Times
A Tale of Two Cities
Middlemarch
The Mill on the Floss
Jude the Obscure
The Mayor of Casterbridge
The Return of the Native
Tess of the D'Urbervilles
The Odes of Keats
Frankenstein
Vanity Fair
Barchester Towers
The Prelude
The Red Badge of Courage
The Scarlet Letter
The Ambassadors
Daisy Miller, The Turn of the Screw, and Other Tales
The Portrait of a Lady
Billy Budd, Benito Cereno, Bartleby the Scrivener, and Other Tales
Moby-Dick
The Tales of Poe
Walden
Adventures of Huckleberry Finn
The Life of Frederick Douglass
Heart of Darkness
Lord Jim
Nostromo
A Passage to India
Dubliners
A Portrait of the Artist as a Young Man
Ulysses
Kim
The Rainbow
Sons and Lovers
Women in Love
1984
Major Barbara
Man and Superman
Pygmalion
St. Joan
The Playboy of the Western World
The Importance of Being Earnest
Mrs. Dalloway
To the Lighthouse
My Antonia
An American Tragedy
Murder in the Cathedral
The Waste Land
Absalom, Absalom!
Light in August
Sanctuary
The Sound and the Fury
The Great Gatsby
A Farewell to Arms
The Sun Also Rises
Arrowsmith
Lolita
The Iceman Cometh
Long Day's Journey Into Night
The Grapes of Wrath
Miss Lonelyhearts
The Glass Menagerie
A Streetcar Named Desire
Their Eyes Were Watching God
Native Son
Waiting for Godot
Herzog
All My Sons
Death of a Salesman
Gravity's Rainbow
All the King's Men
The Left Hand of Darkness
The Brothers Karamazov
Crime and Punishment
Madame Bovary
The Interpretation of Dreams
The Castle
The Metamorphosis
The Trial
Man's Fate
The Magic Mountain
Montaigne's Essays
Remembrance of Things Past
The Red and the Black
Anna Karenina
War and Peace

These and other titles in preparation

Modern Critical Views

VLADIMIR NABOKOV

Edited and with an introduction by
Harold Bloom
Sterling Professor of the Humanities
Yale University

CHELSEA HOUSE PUBLISHERS ◇ 1987
New York ◇ New Haven ◇ Philadelphia

a division of Chelsea House Educational Communications, Inc.,
95 Madison Avenue, New York, NY 10016
345 Whitney Avenue, New Haven, CT 06511
5014 West Chester Pike, Edgemont, PA 19028

Printed and bound in the United States of America

∞ The paper used in this publication meets the minimum requirements of the American National Standard for Permanence of Paper for Printed Library Materials, Z39.48-1984.

Library of Congress Cataloging-in-Publication Data
Vladimir Nabokov.
(Modern critical views)
Bibliography: p.
Includes index.
Summary: A selection of criticism, arranged in chronological order of publication, devoted to the writings of Vladimir Nabokov.
1. Nabokov, Vladimir Vladimirovich, 1899–1977—Criticism and interpretation. [1. Nabokov, Vladimir Vladimirovich, 1899–1977—Criticism and interpretation. 2. Russian literature—History and criticism. 3. American literature—History and criticism] I. Bloom, Harold. II. Series.
PG3476.N3Z9 1987 813′.54 87-666
ISBN 1-55546-279-0 (alk. paper)

Contents

Editor's Note vii

Introduction 1
Harold Bloom

Nabokov in Time 5
Quentin Anderson

Sebastian Knight: The Oneness of Perception 15
Julia Bader

Vladimir Nabokov: Illusions of Reality and the Reality of Illusions 27
Elizabeth W. Bruss

Consciousness, Real Life, and Fairy-tale Freedom:
King, Queen, Knave 65
Ellen Pifer

Nabokov's *Invitation:* Literature as Execution 83
Dale E. Peterson

Reading Zemblan: The Audience Disappears in Nabokov's *Pale Fire* 101
Alvin B. Kernan

Parody and Authenticity in *Lolita* 127
Thomas R. Frosch

Pnin 143
Lucy Maddox

The Gift 157
David Rampton

Ada, or the Perils of Paradise 175
Robert Alter

Death Bequeathed 191
Garrett Stewart

Nabokov's Passion 209
Edmund White

Look at the Harlequins!: Dementia's Incestuous Children 223
D. Barton Johnson

Stereoscope: Nabokov's *Ada* and *Pale Fire* 235
Michael Seidel

The Person from Porlock: *Bend Sinister* and the Problem of Art 259
David Walker

Chronology 283

Contributors 287

Bibliography 289

Acknowledgments 293

Index 295

Editor's Note

This book gathers together what I judge to be a representative selection of the best criticism yet published upon the writings of Vladimir Nabokov. The critical essays are reprinted here in the chronological order of their original publication.

My introduction centers upon *Lolita,* admiring the novel's stylistic achievement while noting the curious revenge of the Freudian death drive upon Nabokov's Humbert. Quentin Anderson begins the chronological sequence of criticism with his review of *Despair,* one of Nabokov's early Russian novels, a review that prompts him to an overview of most of Nabokov's fiction, *Pnin* being his favorite.

The Real Life of Sebastian Knight is analyzed by Julia Bader as a "search for the precise relationship between perception and imagination." Elizabeth W. Bruss, a severe critic both of literary autobiography and of contemporary criticism, relates Nabokov's own autobiography, *Speak, Memory,* to the author's consciousness of illusion throughout *Lolita.*

King, Queen, Knave is read by Ellen Pifer as an extreme instance, even for Nabokov, of a fairy-tale freedom in storytelling. Dale E. Peterson, studying *Invitation to a Beheading,* finds it to be a valuable "crystalline parable in defense of modernist narrative." The greatest such parable by Nabokov, *Pale Fire,* receives a distinguished tribute in Alvin B. Kernan's essay on the disappearance of the audience in that weirdly wonderful medley of poem and commentary.

Thomas R. Frosch, in the best balanced study of *Lolita,* sees the parodistic element in the novel as shamanistic and so as an authentic instance of magical narrative working itself through. *Pnin,* widely regarded as Nabokov's most ingratiating work, is read by Lucy Maddox as a vision of annotation raised to the authority of authenticity in representation.

Analyzing *The Gift,* David Rampton centers upon the relation between Nabokov and Russian literature. In an account of *Ada,* Robert Alter decides that the novel's intention is to transcend time and evil "by the twinned power of art and love." Garrett Stewart, considering mostly *Transparent Things,* meditates upon styles of dying in Nabokov's novels. In a rather generous estimation, Edmund White praises Nabokov's insight into romantic love, as well as his mastery of English prose.

D. Barton Johnson reads *Look at the Harlequins!,* Nabokov's final novel, as a retrospective summary of the author's lifelong musings upon incest and identity. In a return to *Ada* and *Pale Fire,* Michael Seidel meditates upon the traumas and imaginative opportunities provided for Nabokov by the saga of his own exile from Russia and its culture.

This volume ends strongly, with David Walker's previously unpublished essay on *Bend Sinister,* Nabokov's first American novel. Walker's tribute to the power of Nabokov's art, in this novel that itself broods massively upon the problem of art, may be another overgenerous estimate but nevertheless has its own persuasive power as poetic criticism.

Introduction

I

If Nabokov enjoys a somewhat inflated reputation at this time, at his best he remains a considerable figure. *Pale Fire* can sustain a remarkable number of rereadings. *Lolita,* baroque and subtle, is a book written to be reread, though whether its continued force matches the intricacy of its design seems to me problematic. Little is gained for Nabokov by comparing him to Sterne or to Joyce. Borges, who was essentially a parodist, is an apter parallel to Nabokov. Perhaps parodists are fated to resent Sigmund Freud; certainly Borges and Nabokov are the modern writers who most consistently and ignorantly abuse Freud.

Where Nabokov can hardly be overpraised is in his achievement as a stylist. This is one of the endlessly dazzling paragraphs of *Lolita:*

> So Humbert the Cubus schemed and dreamed—and the red sun of desire and decision (the two things that create a live world) rose higher and higher, while upon a succession of balconies a succession of libertines, sparkling glass in hand, toasted the bliss of past and future nights. Then, figuratively speaking, I shattered the glass, and boldly imagined (for I was drunk on those visions by then and underrated the gentleness of my nature) how eventually I might blackmail—no, that is too strong a word—mauvemail big Haze into letting me consort with little Haze by gently threatening the poor doting Big Dove with desertion if she tried to bar me from playing with my legal stepdaughter. In a word, before such an Amazing Offer, before such a vastness and variety of vistas, I was as helpless as Adam at the preview of early oriental history, miraged in his apple orchard.

It is a grand prose-poem, and the entire book in little. Reading it aloud is a shocking pleasure, and analyzing it yet another pleasure, more inward and enduring. Humbert, more "cubus" than "incubus," casts the red sun of his lustful will over the aptly named Haze females, yet avoids incurring our moral resentment by the exuberance of his language, with its zest for excess. What could be more captivating and memorable than: "While upon a succession of balconies a succession of libertines, sparkling glass in hand, toasted the bliss of past and future nights"? That delicious double "succession" achieves a kind of higher innocence, insouciant and stylized, delighting more in the language than in the actual possibility of sensual bliss. Shattering the sparkling glass, Humbert breaks the vessels of reverie in order to achieve a totally drunken vision of sexual exploitation, indeed like a new Adam overcome by the fumes of the fruit.

What Nabokov offers, in *Ada* as well as *Lolita,* is an almost pure revel in diction, by no means necessarily allied with insight. His loathing of Freud reduces, I think, to a fear of meaning, to a need to defend against overdetermined sense, a sense that would extend to everything. Memory, in Nabokov, fears not so much Oedipal intensities as it does more-than-Oedipal genealogies. Here, Nabokov compares weakly to Proust, his most daunting precursor. *Lolita* gives us Marcel as Humbert and Albertine as Lolita, which is to replace a sublime temporal pathos by a parodistic cunning that unfortunately keeps reminding us how much we have lost when we turn from Proust to Nabokov.

II

Early defenses of *Lolita* by John Hollander and Lionel Trilling centered upon the insistence that it was an authentic love story. Rereading *Lolita* now, when no one would accuse the book of being pornography, I marvel that acute readers could take it as a portrayal of human love, since Humbert and Lolita are hardly representations of human beings. They are deliberate caricatures, as fabulistic as Charlotte Haze and Clare Quilty. Solipsistic nightmares, they wander in the America of highways and motels but would be more at home in *Through the Looking-Glass* or *The Hunting of the Snark*. Poor Lolita indeed is a Snark, who precisely does not turn out to be a Boojum.

Nabokov, like Borges, is the most literary of fantasists and takes from reality only what is already Nabokovian. Jane Austen, a powerful Protestant will, was as interested in social reality as the compulsive Dreiser was, but Nabokov's social reality died forever with the Bolshevik Revolution. Admirers who defend Nabokov's writing as mimesis do him violence. His genius was for distorted self-representation. Whether the Proustian intensities of sexual jealousy lend themselves to the phantasmagoric mode of Gogol is a considerable question, but Nabokov intrepidly did not wait for an answer.

"So what is that queer world, glimpses of which we keep catching through the gaps of the harmless looking sentences. It is in a way the *real* one but it looks wildly absurd to us, accustomed as we are to the stage setting that screens it." That is Nabokov on Gogol, or Nabokov on Nabokov. It is not Humbert on Humbert. Nabokov's uncanny art refuses identification with his protagonist, yet lends the author's voice to the comically desperate pursuer of nymphets. "The science of nympholepsy is a precise science," says Humbert, and we reflect that Nabokov is the scientist, rather than poor Humbert, a reflection that is proved by an even more famous declaration:

> I am not concerned with so-called "sex" at all. Anybody can imagine those elements of animality. A greater endeavor lures me on: to fix once for all the perilous magic of nymphets.

Humbert perhaps knows that "the perilous magic" of eroticism crosses animality with death; Nabokov certainly knows, though he rejects so crassly the greatest of modern knowers, Freud. Rejecting Freud however is not a possible option in our time, and the whole of part two of *Lolita* is an involuntary repetition of *Beyond the Pleasure Principle.* The death drive, fueled by that negative libido Freud once toyed with calling "destrudo," takes over poor Humbert completely, through the agency of his dark double and despoiler, Clare Quilty. Refusing to compound with Freud, who is the greatest and most pervasive of modern imaginations, Nabokov is doomed merely to repeat the Freudian mythology of the dual drives, Eros-Humbert and Thanatos-Quilty. All of part two of *Lolita* becomes, not a parody, but a Freudian allegory, considerably less splendid than the joyous part one.

Humbert's murder of Quilty is at once the most curious and the least persuasive episode in *Lolita.* Each figure is the "familiar and innocuous hallucination" of the other, and Humbert's bungling execution of his double lifts the book momentarily into the category of nightmare. It is no accident that Humbert returns to the slain Quilty (C. Q.) in the novel's closing sentences:

> And do not pity C. Q. One had to choose between him and H. H., and one wanted H. H. to exist at least a couple of months longer, so as to have him make you live in the minds of later generations. I am thinking of aurochs and angels, the secret of

> durable pigments, prophetic sonnets, the refuge of art. And this is the only immortality you and I may share, my Lolita.

That doesn't *sound* to me like Humbert, and rather clearly Nabokov has usurped these closing tonalities, explaining why he did not have Quilty murder Humbert, which I suspect would have made a better end. I don't hear remoteness in this final tone, but rather an attempt to recover something of the aura of part one, so sadly lost in the frenzies of Humbert's later sorrows.

QUENTIN ANDERSON

Nabokov in Time

Nabokov, describing the work of "V. Sirin" (his pseudonym as a Russian émigré novelist) in *Conclusive Evidence,* says, "the real life of his books flowed in his figures of speech," and "his best works are those in which he condemns his people to the solitary confinement of their souls." *Despair,* the sixth of the nine novels Nabokov wrote in Russian, is neatly bracketed by these remarks. He wrote it in 1932, and translated it into English in 1936. But the text now published is a revision of the original—the reader who has no Russian, and no copy of the first translation for comparison is persuaded that important changes have been made by the virtuosity of the concise and resonant English of the present version. Single words carry more weight than they did in Nabokov's first two novels in English, and produce effects of startling distinctness, effects quite beyond the reach of the accomplished author of *The Real Life of Sebastian Knight* (1941) and *Bend Sinister* (1947).

Hermann, the central figure in *Despair,* is a Russian émigré living in Germany. He is entranced by a fantasy which he justifies to his worldly consciousness as an insurance swindle. He will kill the tramp who appears to him to be his double, get his wife, whom he believes to be devoted to him, to collect the insurance on his life, and assume the double's identity. His absorption in the pattern he is creating is complete. He does not notice that his wife is sleeping with her cousin, and in the end he quite overlooks the walking stick the double is carrying at the time of the murder, a stick on which the double has carved his own name, and that of his town.

From *The New Republic* 154, no. 23 (4 June 1966).

Hermann writes this book after having carried out the fantasy. He is waiting for the reviews of his work; that is, for the press reports of the murder to reach the little town in the Pyrenees where he is hiding. While he waits he lets his memory dictate a book of which the title is unknown until the disastrous realization that he has forgotten the walking stick overtakes him. He had thought of calling his book "Crime and Pun" and "The Poet and the Rabble." But *Despair* is the only possibility in the end—and not simply because of the stick. There is a deeper failure. The whole basis of his work of art has been ignored, nobody thinks him dead, nobody has even noticed the resemblance between the murdered man and himself. In the world's eyes he has no double, and the death he will no doubt die for murder will not even have the effect of bringing him into that final juxtaposition with his image which he had imagined while watching a leaf falling into still water as its double swam up toward it. The reader is confronted by various shifts in perspective—the account given of the whole affair by Hermann's "memory" stands for the fullness of event, for "life," while his work of art, a fantasy which he had pursued in the common light of day, has the status of art in that it is a selection of events made to serve a chosen design. Finally, the account given by memory is the work of art of the émigré Russian novelist to whom Hermann proposes to send his manuscript!

Is the book more than a suffocating joke on its central figure and a trip to a mirrored fun house for its reader? It depends on what you think of the language, it depends on "the figures of speech" and how much you prize them. The very qualities which led Mary McCarthy to say that *Pale Fire* was "one of the very great works of art of this century" are here—not, it is true, in the same measure (the book is not so multilayered), but still they are here. For example, an extraordinary passage in which Hermann finds that the town in which he has undertaken to meet his double seems to be almost wholly built out of reminiscences of his own past; he wonders whether Felix can in fact appear there, or whether his very conception of Felix is not the product of an appetite for repetition which is growing in him. The play with resemblances is, of course, very intricate: is Felix a "minus I" in the sense that traces on a blotter are negatives, and can only be read in a mirror? Did Felix have the obstinacy, the stubborn bad taste (from Hermann's viewpoint) to read himself as the positive, Hermann as the negative?

All this is consonant with the patterned games played in certain other Nabokov novels. *The Eye,* a novella, and *The Defense* resemble *Despair* in that their chief figures are condemned as is Hermann to spin a world out of their fatally repetitive inner resources. With some qualifications, *Laughter in the Dark* and *Lolita* belong in this group.

In the light of one common assumption about the novel it would be denied that these were novels at all. In them the recording consciousness is jealous, and won't give up its world to the reader. What we are given is theme and variations, and denied any sense of cumulation or growth. We get experience of the order of a child's memories, experience deprived of temporal dimension. Each of the rendered moments is like a separate raid on the continuum of life which brings back an observation that is rendered with the tang of immediacy and yet serves an exemplary use in the web Nabokov is weaving. The life of his work does in fact lie in his figures of speech. And there is something in it which is wholly inimical to our gross appetite for stories of growth, development, sequential change.

> I confess I do not believe in time. I like to fold my magic carpet after use, in such a way as to superimpose one part of the pattern upon another. Let visitors trip. And the highest enjoyment of timelessness—in a landscape selected at random—is when I stand among rare butterflies and their food plants. This is ecstasy, and behind the ecstasy is something else, which is hard to explain. It's like a momentary vacuum into which rushes all that I love. A sense of oneness with sun and stone. A thrill of gratitude to whom it may concern—to the contrapuntal genius of human fate or to tender ghosts humoring a lucky mortal.
>
> (*Conclusive Evidence*)

Nabokov's prose medium deserves a name, partly a designation, partly frankly incantatory, as is Gerard Manley Hopkins's "sprung rhythm." We might call it the "light anthropomorphic," and find a simple and characteristic instance of it in the sentence, "Let visitors trip." In this medium the interpenetration of humanity by language, language by humanity is, moment by moment, felt as complete. Its range, its horizontal range, is very wide, gallery upon glittering gallery of the tricks by which we betray ourselves in language and language betrays us. But its scale is single; it can only tell us what we do to words and they to us; it cannot tell us what men have done. It appears to deny the possibility of saying *consummatum est* of any human action. It works minutely and reflectively: one little vaudeville of the light anthropomorphic gives way to the next, and so on until the pattern is complete. Here are some "verbal adventures," to steal a Nabokov phrase.

> He felt that he loved his wife sincerely, tenderly—as much in fact as he was capable of loving a human being; and he was perfectly

> frank with her in everything except that secret foolish craving, that dream, that lust burning a hole in his life.
>
> (*Laughter in the Dark*)

> Occasionally, in the middle of a conversation her name would be mentioned, and she would run down the steps of a chance sentence, without turning her head.
>
> ("Spring in Fialta")

> No lover of solitude, Boris Ivanovich would soon begin to get bored, and from his room Fyodor would hear the rustling growth of this boredom, as if the flat were slowly being overgrown with burdocks—which had now grown up to his door. He would pray to fate that something might distract Schyogolev, but (until he got the radio) salvation was not forthcoming. Inevitably came the ominous, tactful knock.
>
> (*The Gift*)

> When at last I reached the summit I found there a few shacks standing awry, a washing line, and on it some pants bloated with the wind's sham life.
>
> (*Despair*)

The effect of these passages is seldom occasional; three of these are particular reflections of the theme of the work in which they appear. Examples, however, cannot suggest the intricate echoic games which are the works themselves.

Everything that threatens the games played in the group of books to which *Despair* belongs is fiercely attacked by Nabokov as if art were unsafe as long as anybody was generalizing about anything in any context. This is Nabokov's public role, and it is the only public role he permits his characters to assume. Historical and cultural judgment, Marx, Freud, politicians and metaphysicians, Dostoyevski, Balzac, Stendhal, Proust, the novelist who is described as "the family doctor of Europe"—Thomas Mann?—anyone who classifies anything except words and butterflies is scorned. A novelist remarks in *Laughter in the Dark,* "Well, when a literature subsists on Life and Lives, it means it is dying. And I don't think much of Freudian novels or novels about the quiet countryside." The young writer of *The Gift* remarks on the unsuitability of a theme: "I would have become enmired involuntarily in a 'deep' social-interest novel with a disgusting Freudian reek." (As one might anticipate, there is quite another view of Joyce, a figure whom Nabokov says he reveres.) John Wain has remarked in these columns that this scorn of Nabokov's appears to be the scorn conventionally attributed to the artist who is asked to write to somebody else's ends, or everybody else's ends. I think it is a symptom of something more than this.

The scornful detachment of the prefaces conceals the fact that in another group of novels Nabokov's art is—in his sense—very impure indeed. *Invitation to a Beheading* and *Bend Sinister* are novels in which all reality and value inhere in the central figure, and the environing world is condemned to act out an imprisoning fantasy which the hero and the reader see through. These novels are occasioned by their times, and reflect Nabokov's response to his sense of the idiocy of Communism and Nazi Germany. They can hardly be defended on the ground on which Nabokov habitually asserts the independence of his art from all ideological and psychological generalities. The human glory of their central figures is dependent on convictions about human worth that the reader must bring to the book, convictions on which Nabokov relies. With these two novels we may associate two more, *The Gift* (1937) and *The Real Life of Sebastian Knight,* in which the recording consciousness is that of a writer, and is quite as authoritative for the reader as are the heroes of the first two novels. I shall come to *Pnin, Lolita,* and *Pale Fire* in a moment; these four novels suffice to make the point that Nabokov has often ignored what he says in *Conclusive Evidence:* "in a first-rate work of fiction the real clash is not between the characters but between the author and the world." There is a quite shameless human glory about Krug in *Bend Sinister,* about the figures of the writer's parents in *The Gift,* about the hero of *Invitation to a Beheading*—with these characters our sympathy is complete. When these persons are placed beside Hermann, Luzhin of *The Defense,* the central figure of *The Eye,* these latter recede into the texture of the works in which they appear, seem mere themes for light anthropomorphic exercises. We are once more outsiders.

Why shouldn't Nabokov have written in two fictional modes, giving now one, now the other, the ascendancy? What is important is the critical significance of the divergence and final confluence of these two kinds in Nabokov's work. What we may call his naturalism is dominant in Nabokov's recorded memories of his childhood and youth in *Conclusive Evidence.* It is a fully peopled world, rather lush, even sentimental, through which move the figures of a father and mother (whose splendid wordly ascendancy is matched by inner grace and strength), a group of attendant persons, first loves, family retainers and so on. This interrelatedness, this sense of an ordered life in common with others does not of course recur in the Nabokov fiction I know. But *The Gift* offers, in the persons of the young writer's parents, characters who survive out of such a time and such a world. These characters are bordered in black, cherished, lonely and doomed, like Krug, and the lepidopterist father of *The Gift,* who has, anticipating John Shade of *Pale Fire,* a relation to cosmic patterns, "A sense of oneness with sun and stone." This strong sense of a lost sunlit world is the hidden positive in Nabokov's work; it is what such glinting constructs as *Despair* operate to hide. We are justified in saying that Nabokov's publicly stated aesthetic theory is equivalent to a historical judgment. He willed time to a stop. Certain lonely figures in his fiction survive the actual holocaust and his aesthetic assertion of its finality. The naturalism survives in his work and reemerges (somewhat attenuated) in the sentimental naturalism of *Pale Fire.* It is as if, having incautiously trusted to the persistence of the rules of the social order which had nourished his first nineteen years, he had determined never again to accept any set of rules from anyone, or write anything which could be subsumed within any order.

I shall not attempt here to deal with the complex interplay of the patterned as against the naturalist strands in Nabokov's work. I have suggested that the human glory of Krug, which is posed against a cruel and mindless society, represents a naturalism which gives way to a more sentimental strain in Nabokov's later work, in fact in the very next novel, *Sebastian Knight.* Knight, unsupported by a sense of the wholeness of a human community of the order we find in *Conclusive Evidence,* makes his lonely assertion of the generically human: "All things belong to the same order of things, for such is the oneness of human perception, the oneness of individuality, the oneness of matter, whatever matter may be. The only real number is one, the rest are mere repetition." To reinforce this we may quote Shade's poem in *Pale Fire:*

> And if my private universe scans
> So does the verse of galaxies divine
> Which I suspect is an iambic line.

A longer passage from *Sebastian Knight,* which, like Shade's poem, is concerned with a solution to the riddle of death, may make Nabokov's movement from a naturalism conditioned by the memory of community to a naturalism founded on a faith in our kinship with the order of nature somewhat plainer. Both seem to have been present from his youth onward, but the ascendancy of the latter grows as the memory of a society in being recedes.

> And the word, the meaning which appears is astounding in its simplicity: the greatest surprise being perhaps that in the course

> of one's earthly existence, with one's brain encompassed by an iron ring, by the close-fitting dream of one's own personality—one had not made by chance that simple mental jerk, which would have set free imprisoned thought and granted it the great understanding. Now the puzzle was solved. "And as the meaning of all things shone through their shapes, many ideas and events which had seemed of the utmost importance dwindled not to insignificance, for nothing could be insignificant now, but to the same size which other ideas and events, once denied any importance, now attained." Thus, such shining giants of our brain as science, art or religion fell out of the familiar scheme of their classification, and joining hands, were mixed and joyfully levelled. Thus, a cherry stone and its tiny shadow which lay on the painted wood of a tired bench, or a bit of torn paper, or any other such trifle out of millions and millions of trifles grew to a wonderful size. Remodelled and re-combined, the world yielded its sense to the soul as naturally as both breathed.

The belief that such an awareness of nature might afford this measure of human fulfillment lies about fifty years behind us in the European consciousness. It stems from an age in which science seemed to authorize wider hopes, rather than pose deeper threats. When we are thinking of Nabokov as a modernist his grounding in a sentimental naturalism must be recalled. The hardness, brightness and echoing intricacy of his patterned fiction is a culturally determined mode of coping with a world which denies the "sense of oneness with sun and stone."

But I have been speaking as if the Nabokov who willed time to a stop had in the process suppressed the world of his childhood, and this is misleading. His delight in exposing "the contrapuntal genius of human fate" is a quite logical extension of that world, or rather of the breakdown of the interpersonal hierarchic order that world represented. Luzhin, Paduk (the Hitler figure of *Bend Sinister*), Humbert, Hermann, are persons in whom the child's absorption in his play is prolonged into adulthood, prisoners rather than makers of patterns. Humbert keeps wooing the ten-year-old girl of the Biarritz beach, and our consciousness of this is the source of our sympathy, which persists together with our awareness that he has become loathsome. Such figures, like Luzhin, who also invites our sympathy, nonetheless fail to respond to the first moral value of the Nabokovian universe, a respect for the singleness of others. The mocking memoir of Chernyshevsky in *The Gift* brims with venom directed at a generation which infected us all—infected Lenin himself—with the horrible smarmy presumption that we were so nearly identical that we could be understood en masse. Hermann's unforgivable spiritual vulgarity is the hunger for a resemblance that amounts to identity—something that can only be attributed to inanimate things, dead things. And *Despair* is, like all the internally echoing works, a struggle with the reader; he is being tested: if he thinks he can assimilate the pattern to his beliefs and expectations he is one more fool who doesn't know the value of singleness.

I have made it plain enough that the works in which everything is subdued to the pattern, while serially brilliant, seem to me as exhaustible in their interest as reported games of chess. The hero of *Invitation to a Beheading,* while describing himself as incapable of writing says that he has an intuition of the way in which words must be combined, "what one must do for a commonplace word to come alive and to share its neighbor's sheen, heat, shadow, while reflecting itself in its neighbor and renewing the neighboring word in the process, so that the whole line is live iridescence." If you find the patterned works delightful it is such effects you delight in. If you are persuaded you are reading a full-fledged novelist you are unaware of the extent of your collaboration. The text under your eye is like a brilliant musical score, but the continuity of the performance is supplied by the reader, who fills in the curve of imagined human action. Of course this is a question of degree. *Lolita,* up to the death of the mother, has no such limitation. Thereafter it falls, on rereading, into fragments, some of which retain their lustre, like the scene in which Humbert sees his married and pregnant love for the last time, while others have lost it altogether, and in fact share with certain of the American social observations in *Pale Fire* the *fade* and dissonant quality of the marzipan hot dogs sold in fake Viennese candy shops. *Pale Fire* is at once more ambitious and less successful than *Lolita,* because, although there is much to be said for the poem, there is less to be said for the sentimental naturalism which informs it—except as a historical artifact—and the trapped and obsessed figure, Kinbote, unpacked in all his awful flatness and spiritual repetitiousness gives the book the flavor of his sterility. It is possible to be very serious, enormously talented, highly witty, and nonetheless to trivialize what seems a proper outgrowth of Nabokov's career, the attempt to bring to a focus the struggle between the patterned figure, Kinbote, and a last beleaguered human being, John Shade.

But there remains one almost perfect work, *Pnin.* What I have rather clumsily described as the "naturalism" is here to be found in the implied character of the narrator, perhaps the most winning of Nabokov's persons, and the book appears to be completely patterned, yet the narrator's scrupulous and tender attention supplies exactly that continuity of human concern that the other patterned works lack. Not that the narrator has an unqualified role. Indeed his dramatic relation to Pnin is brilliantly sustained and developed. As he physically approaches, Pnin must recede, because the narrator is precisely that element within whose ambience Pnin cannot exist. The book is a delight and a minor classic.

Modernism, the period of Proust, Joyce, Kafka, Eliot, is over, and the preoccupations of poets and writers of fiction are now so different that Nabokov has begun to seem remote. He tries to make language the vessel of our humanity, and supports in public the contention that art is its own excuse for being. He gives this contention away in certain works, and it becomes plain that it is actually parasitic on the memory of an ordered community. His assertion of the self-sufficiency of art will come to seem increasingly unintelligible to a generation unaware of the hidden premise of his humanism. He will go into a temporary eclipse. If the world of community were magically to be reborn the influence of the very thing he publicly denies would serve to reinstate him. But the world in which Beckett, Genet, Burroughs, and the nonnovel flourish is a world in which the politics of the soul is primary, and verbal adventure has lost its invisible supporting warp of remembered human solidarity. This, I take it, is the end, so often prematurely announced, of the romantic movement.

JULIA BADER

Sebastian Knight: *The Oneness of Perception*

Sebastian Knight deliberately casts a distorted shadow of its proposed literary projects. The narrator, V., purports to write a biography of his dead half-brother, Sebastian Knight. The product of V.'s search is not the biography but the quest for it; not Sebastian's "real life," but Sebastian's fictional existence. V.'s technique of arranging the events of Sebastian's life is itself artistic: "My quest had developed its own magic and logic . . . it had gradually grown into a dream, that quest, using the pattern of reality for the weaving of its own fancies." The novel might be titled *The Dream Life of Sebastian Knight,* the "pattern of reality" from which it constantly departs consisting of the circumstantial events of Sebastian's life, and the "fancies" being Sebastian's beautiful novels filtered through V.'s narration. It becomes increasingly clear that the "real life" of Sebastian was contained not in external circumstances but in his writings; and since these writings exist for us in V.'s retelling of them, Sebastian lives in V. who has recreated his brother's artistic and personal life in his own imagination. Thus "real" is gradually defined as the living, growing shadow of a life in prose, a shadow which engulfs the factual biography.

Once we realize the inescapable oneness of Sebastian and V., the "literary trick" element of the novel becomes obvious. *Sebastian Knight* leads toward a discovery, and to the superficial eye the discovery is contained in V.'s ingenuously wide-eyed revelation, on the last page of the novel, "that the soul is but a manner of being—not a constant state—that any soul may be yours, if you find and follow its undulations. The hereafter may be the full ability of consciously living in any chosen soul, in any number of souls, all of them unconscious of their interchangeable burden, Thus—I am Sebastian Knight. . . . I am Sebastian, or Sebastian is I, or perhaps we both are someone whom neither of us knows." If we read "art" for "the hereafter," and Vladimir Nabokov for the "someone" whom neither V. nor Sebastian "knows," we have gained an essential insight into the technique of the novel.

But this ending is a "trick" in the sense that it tells us something we have guessed all along, and the more astonishing and central discovery is hidden elsewhere in the book. The merging of Sebastian and V., and their ultimate dissolution in an omniscient authorial presence, is the culmination of one of the two basic thematic strands in the novel: the concern with methods of fictional composition. What all the different methods have in common is the author's "conscious" presence in all the "souls" (i.e., characters) of his novel. *Dead Souls* (one of Nabokov's favorite novels, specifically mentioned by V.) can be literally applied to Nabokovian characters, in the sense that we are constantly reminded that the only existence they possess is given to them by the author, so that they are no more than reflections of the artistic preoccupation with different motifs.

The other strand of *Sebastian Knight,* which gently curves around the concern with methods of fictional composition, is the search for the precise relationship between perception and imagination. The "secret" of this relationship is the real discovery of *Sebastian Knight,* born of the joint mode of two of Sebastian's novels: his first and his last. "Two modes of his life question each other and the answer is his life itself, and that is the nearest one ever can approach a human truth," V. tells us. The modes of Sebastian's life are artistic ones, "the man is the book," and the "human truth" is the anguished vision of beauty sliding into the past, but recoverable through an act of imagination.

The mosaics of *Sebastian Knight* are interlocking; a composition maneuvered by an omniscient author who plants details and characters with delicate but deliberately observable gestures. The "true conflict," Nabokov tells us, is always between author and reader, between the author's unique solutions to "games of his own invention" and the reader's habitual preconceptions about fiction. All of Nabokov's figures in *Sebastian Knight* are nonrealistic, though in varying degrees, and the shadings of their dimensions create a fantasy world where detail reflects on other detail, with the final product mirroring not reality, but itself. "They are, these lives, but commentaries to the main subject," and the main subject is more than a technical problem, or a proper aesthetic solution: it is the combination of literary composition with patterns of human fate, leading to moments of "curiosity, tenderness, kindness, ecstasy." Sebastian's own novels are small clusters of such moments, individual windows to the soul of the total novel. They are beautiful puddles (one of Nabokov's recurrent images) whose reflection is picked up by the mirror of the novel itself, which in turn reflects the author's imagination.

Theme and method often become slightly distorted in this process of multiple mirroring, but the end product is not a statement about the emptiness of illusion. Rather, the collective reflections reinforce the "synthesized spirality" of human perception. Each spiral ascends to a higher plane of imagination. One of the central insights in Nabokov's *Speak, Memory* is that "in the spiral form, the circle, uncoiled, unwound, has ceased to be vicious; it has been set free." I regard each of Sebastian's novels within *The Real Life of Sebastian Knight* as small spirals whose joint effect is to impart a "truth" about the oneness of human perception.

Sebastian's first novel, *The Prismatic Bezel,* is "based cunningly on certain tricks of the literary trade," such as the detective story, the use of a "medley of people in a limited space," "the boarding-house motif," and the "country-house motif." Each of these parodies is employed as a "springboard for leaping into the highest region of serious emotion." *The Prismatic Bezel* parodies different styles and techniques, as well as themes, but exploits the parody as a means of enforcing the shifting and illusory nature of "reality." It is well for us to remember that "bezel" is defined as (1) the sloping edge of a chisel or other cutting tool, (2) the oblique faces of a brilliant-cut gem, and (3) the grooved ring or rim holding a gem or crystal in its setting. Thus "bezel" refers simultaneously to the tool (i.e., method), the gem (i.e., the theme), and that which holds the gem in place (the style).

"The essential oneness" of literary technique is insisted on in all Nabokov novels. Parody, one of Nabokov's favorite methods, serves to startle the reader into an awareness that his comfortable notions of fiction and "reality" are about to be exploded. The theme of the banality of stock characters and situations is only the starting point. The precise, lucid, uniquely glinting style points to the more important theme: that a vision of beauty can be achieved through a freedom from trite preconceptions and ready-made metaphors. The "plot" of *The Prismatic Bezel* demonstrates the progression toward this kind of emotional and intellectual freedom. Starting with a murder in a boardinghouse, "something in the story begins to shift"; all the lodgers are revealed to be connected with each other, and the story is transposed to a country house. In this new setting the technique becomes "realistic," "the lives of the characters shine forth with a real and human significance." But "realism" turns out to be merely an alternate method of composition, and "at the very moment when the reader feels quite safe in an atmosphere of pleasurable reality," the scene shifts again, and the parody of the detective story is resumed. But the corpse has disappeared, and a harmless "passerby" removes his disguise and reveals himself to be the man supposed murdered. His explanation for the masquerade, "one dislikes being murdered," is the statement of the author himself, who refuses to refine himself out of existence, who insists on upsetting the fictional illusion, who appears in order to put literary conventions in a diminished perspective.

The Prismatic Bezel, like all of Nabokov's own novels, is "not the painting of a landscape, but the painting of different ways of painting a certain landscape." The occupation of the man who "dislikes being murdered" is given as "art-dealer." To "deal" in art means to experiment in different manners of presenting fictional "reality." If the soul is but a "manner of being," the creation of different souls is but the artistic projection of various manners of being. V.'s final, highest estimate of *The Doubtful Asphodel,* Sebastian's last novel, is: "I like its manners."

The "certain landscape" of *The Prismatic Bezel* (a man supposed dead, the search for the killer, the shift to the country house, the essential connection between all the characters, and the unmasking of the "art-dealer") is refracted by the overall outline of *Sebastian Knight.* V. searches for his own identity through clues he has about the life of his dead brother. These clues include Sebastian's "first adolescent romance," which V. depicts in terms of an incomplete dramatic scene: "The curtain rises and a Russian summer landscape is disclosed: . . . the painter has not yet filled in the white space [of the girl] except for a thin sunburnt arm." Sebastian's later romance with Clare Bishop is described as "alliterative" and joyful, but finally dead because its edges grew "hazy." The "formula" of "another woman" leads V.'s detective search to a country house where his "manner" changes. But the femme fatale theme peters out, and the summarized details of *The Doubtful Asphodel* stress the fact that all the disparate characters in Sebastian's life are intimately related to each other through being fictional props in the same plot. Finally, the dead man is resurrected ("I am Sebastian") in the narrator, and both are revealed to be aspects of the conjuring art-dealer, Nabokov.

But just as *The Prismatic Bezel* parodies detective stories whose predictable search for the real killer ends in an easily anticipated discovery, *Sebastian Knight* parodies stories of literary detection which conclude with the unmasking of the real author behind the narrator. Although *Sebastian Knight* ostensibly follows this literary trail, the object of the search is not the artist himself, but rather the meaning of his art. As Nabokov warns in the Afterword to *Lolita:* "If you do not watch out, the real murderer may turn out to be, to the fan's disgust, artistic originality." Artistic originality is contained in no single idea or "word," as V. naively expects in his perusal of *The Doubtful Asphodel,* but in the "combination of the parts," in the interwoven phrases, startling images, and teasing details. Sebastian "had no use for ready-made phrases because the things he wanted to say were of an exceptional build and he knew moreover that no real idea can be said to exist without the words made to measure . . . the words lurking afar were not empty shells as they seemed, but were only waiting for the thought they already concealed to set them aflame and in motion."

By parodying prevalent literary conventions the author questions the reader's assumptions about literature, and by using these parodies as "springboards" he surprises and corrects these assumptions by a burst of literary originality. The "manner" of *The Prismatic Bezel* is parodic, that of *The Doubtful Asphodel* one of "serious emotion," and *The Real Life of Sebastian Knight* utilizes both modes. Sebastian's other works suggest alternate methods and themes, other ways of arriving at the "secret" relationship between the words and the thought embodied in them. The discovery of *Sebastian Knight* is that the secret is decipherable; it lurks not behind the author's mask but within the colored spirals of the combinations and recombinations of "the certain landscape" of his style.

Sebastian's second novel, *Success,* is described as one plane "higher" than the first, "for, if his first novel is based on methods of literary composition—the second one deals mainly with methods of human fate." Given the "formula" of two people who meet and live happily "ever after," the novel sets out to examine how the fomula is arrived at. The justification for this task is "the fundamental assumption that an author is able to discover anything he may want to know about his characters, such capacity being limited only by the manner and purpose of his selection insofar as it ought to be not a haphazard jumble of worthless details but a definite and methodical quest." In the course of his research Sebastian concludes that outward circumstances (i.e., objective reality) are not a causal part of human fate, they are no more than "fixed points." He does not tell us what the methods of human fate are, except that these methods succeed (hence the title *Success*) "by such delicate machinations that not the merest click is audible when at last the two are brought together." This suggests the important assumption that "fate" is a result of subtle authorial manipulation, and literary techniques are a means of creating and refining rather than reproducing the patterns of human fate. But only by perfecting the uniqueness and freshness of literary composition can a writer hope to discover his particular relation to circumstance and fate. The methods of fate are open to the artistic sensibility because these methods can be arranged through the "delicate machinations" of fictional creation. For Nabokov, fate lurks in the turns of prose style, revealing the destiny the writer has prepared for his puppets.

The narrator's composition of his half-brother's life is full of details which may seem haphazard at first reading, but fall into a methodical pattern designed to reveal the essence of Sebastian's artistry. For example, Sebastian's next work is a collection of three short stories, "The Funny Mountain," "Albinos in Black," and "The Back of the Moon." While composing "The Funny Mountain," he is interrupted by a "meek little man" who is "waiting" to see him. A paragraph later we are told that "The Back of the Moon" has a "delightful character," a "meek little man waiting for a train," who is the "most alive of Sebastian's creatures." Later, after the narrator has failed to get the names of the women who had a possible connection with Sebastian, "a little man," complete with all the physical characteristics of the fictional character in "The Back of the Moon," appears, procures the names for him, and provides him with advice: " 'You can't see de odder side of de moon. Please don't search de woman.' "

There are numerous other echoes in connection with this character, who is named Siller in Sebastian's story and introduces himself to V. as Silbermann. One of the passages which V. quotes from *The Prismatic Bezel* has two details which seem relevant to Siller: "A policeman passed leading the night on a leash, and then paused to let it sniff at a pillar box," and the conjuror (bald and black-suited like Siller) saying, " 'They don't kinda like my accent, but I guess I'm going to get that turn all the same.' " Silbermann tells V. that he deals in "hound-muzzles," and has been in "de police," and his appearance is perhaps the "turn" the conjuror gets with a revamped accent.

The appearance within the novel of a character depicted in Sebastian's short story serves to remind us that *The Real Life* exists on a receding series of fictional planes; that the action narrated by V. is no more "real" than the character created by Sebastian. The intermingling of various fictional planes, and the repetition of some clues and details in Sebastian's fiction by V.'s narrative, foreshadow the moment when V. declares: "I am Sebastian Knight."

Further mystification is provided by Sebastian's next novel, *Lost Property*, which is a kind of literary "summing up" of the journey of discovery. We are not told of its plot or technique, only of a chapter about an airplane crash in which half a dozen letters are scattered at the site. "Two of these were business letters of great importance; a third was addressed to a woman, but it began: 'Dear Mr. Mortimer, in reply to yours of the 6th inst . . .'; and the last was an envelope directed to a firm of traders with the wrong letter inside, a love letter." These two letters have been mixed up and put in the wrong envelopes, either by Sebastian, who wrote the chapter, or by V., who is telling us about it. But strangely, the "Mr. Mortimer" of the first letter is mentioned in the second one: "I have not been able to clinch the business I was supposed to bring 'to a satisfactory close,' as that ass Mortimer says." The second letter is a farewell to a mistress, and V. quotes it for its probable relevance to Sebastian's relationship with Clare. But the details of the letter ("I shall joke with the chaps at the office," the "business" with Mortimer) correspond to V.'s life; V. works in an office, and his "unsatisfactory" business meeting is recorded in the novel. The question arises whether V. is the writer of both the narrative and the alleged novels of Sebastian, or whether Sebastian has created a letter written by a fictitious V. The shifting and obscuring of identities is in part a joyous game, and ultimately testifies to the imaginative flexibility of the author, whose consciousness encompasses both Sebastian and V. The identity of the narrator, the subject of his project, and the circumstances of their separate lives are placed in a deliberately jumbled design which undermines the "realistic" facade of V.'s tale.

Just as the letter in *Lost Property* is saying goodbye to the mistress who made the writer happy, the outer novel is saying goodbye to Clare, who is now being deserted by the plot. She is sorrowfully but inevitably left for another theme, what the letter refers to as "the damned formula of 'another woman.' " When V. attempts to find the "other woman," her first husband describes her as if she were nothing more than a literary motif: "You may find her in any cheap novel, she's a type, a type"; "a bad dream after seeing a bad cinema film." And V. wonders whether a woman like that could have interested Sebastian, whether her image was not "too obvious," a prototype of "ready-made forms of pleasure and hackneyed forms of distress."

The plausibility of the "other woman" who destroys a man's life is thus being considered from a chiefly literary point of view. Is it worth our while to turn to this trite trail? But *The Real Life of Sebastian Knight* manages to turn the "other woman" motif into an unusual quest; V. meets a woman whose identity is almost as elusive as his own, a woman compounded of "oldish French novels," whimsical, cruel, and banal. The summary of her life dovetails with that of a conventional formula: "The men she liked proved dismal disappointments, all women with few exceptions were nothing but cats, and she spent the best part of her life in trying to be happy in a world which did its best to break her." She embodies all the insipid stereotypes of French romances: a femme fatale, a woman "good as good bread." V.'s involvement with her reminds him of "that breathless phrase in that second-rate Maupassant story: 'I have forgotten a book.' "

But what is no more than a conventional amorous gambit in Maupassant is a reminder for V. and for the reader, that the "other woman" formula leads away from the live center of *Sebastian Knight.* Another false literary lead is thus dropped, and V. is left to confront Sebastian's last novel. This last novel is not a repudiation of hackneyed conventions; in fact, parody plays no part in its technique at all. Having scrutinized and tested literary convention, Sebastian the artist is now disclosing the meaning of his unique vision. The process of this disclosure is itself essential; the "secret" is muted and submerged in its own details to such an extent that even V. seems to bypass it.

The "composition" of the parts, in the sequence in which V. depicts *The Doubtful Asphodel,* is characteristically Nabokovian. I think we are presented with an astonishing and lucid revelation which is the apex of the entire novel. But the revelation is couched in an oblique manner which minimizes the aura of epiphany (Nabokov again declines to employ a popular formula) and almost tricks us into believing that the revelation has not taken place. The theme of "a man dying" is extended to the book:—"The book itself is heaving and dying"; we are given details which have occurred within the action of *The Real Life,* intermingled with other details which belong to *The Doubtful Asphodel* alone. (An "asphodel" is a kind of lily whose elongated stem bears flowers on short stalks in a methodical succession toward the apex of the plant.)

Nabokov here seems to be playing with the microcosm-macrocosm convention, suggesting that Sebastian's last novel may be a reflection of the whole novel we are reading. But, as the title itself indicates, the narcissistic reflection of the lily has a correspondence to the actual flower which is at best "doubtful." V. reminds us that in the case of *The Doubtful Asphodel,* "it is not the parts that matter, it is their combinations." The parts themselves resemble the parts of *The Real Life of Sebastian Knight*—the chess player Schwarz, the fat Bohemian woman, the soft-lipped girl in mourning, all have their slightly distorted counterparts in the macrocosmic plot—but the combinations differ. V's narrative is concerned with both more and less than "a man dying"; and most importantly, the ending of *The Real Life of Sebastian Knight* provides us with a "secret" other than that of *The Doubtful Asphodel.*

The discovery contained in *The Doubtful Asphodel* is a fusion of emotional and artistic "truth" which illuminates an intrinsic pattern similar to that perceived by Shade in *Pale Fire:*

> It was like a traveller realizing that the wild country he surveys is not an accidental assembly of natural phenomena, but the page in a book where these mountains and forests, and fields, and rivers are disposed in such a way as to form a coherent sentence; the vowel of a lake fusing with the consonant of a sibilant slope; . . . Thus the traveller spells the landscape and its sense is disclosed, and likewise, the intricate pattern of human life turns out to be monogrammatic, now quite clear to the inner eye disentangling the interwoven letters.

The pattern of human life is made intelligible by the precise artistic expression of that pattern; methods of composition and methods of fate are disclosed in the fact of literary creation. For the reader they are disclosed in the act of reading, when he is provided with a new "painting" of the landscape of reality. "The answer to all questions of life and death, 'the absolute solution' was written all over the world he had known: . . . the greatest surprise being perhaps that in the course of one's earthly existence, with one's brain encompassed by an iron ring, by the close-fitting dream of one's own personality—one had not made by chance that simple mental jerk, which would have set free imprisoned thought and granted it the great understanding."

Sebastian, the artist, suddenly understands that his life has meaning only in terms of his art; that "the close-fitting dream of his own personality" has restricted him from perceiving the possibilities for a dazzling freedom of the imagination. A "simple mental jerk" frees the artist from the "iron ring" of a single personality, and allows his life to flow into fictional characters who are unlike him. The pleasure and absorption in fictional characters who are distant and dissimilar from us is the great "secret" and discovery of art. The ability to create this sensation of simultaneous distance and absorption is the "solution" to the artist's quest; Sebastian has given us the "truth" to this work of art, to this "problem" of meaning. Thus V.'s final revelation about the interchangeability of souls is really part of the more important disclosure in *The Doubtful Asphodel,* that a "simple mental jerk" can free one from the confines of space and time—in short, from the physical and emotional "reality" of a single personality. This artistic and psychological statement is basic to Nabokov's art: the vision attained through alienation from one's personality, the glimpse of beauty which the perverted Humbert, the exiled Pnin, the mad Kinbote gain through their partial acquisition of imaginary roles.

But the revelations are momentary and ever-changing. Each art work, often even each chapter and paragraph, has its own secret to yield. V., who has just told us about the above-quoted passages in *The Doubtful Asphodel,* seems to be searching for another secret, perhaps a single "word" which is never given because the protagonist dies at a crucial moment. But V.'s sense of a hovering answer remains, and he says of *The Doubtful Asphodel:* "I sometimes feel when I turn the pages of Sebastian's masterpiece that the 'absolute solution' is there, somewhere, concealed in some passage I have read too hastily, or that it is intertwined with other words whose familiar guise deceived me. I don't know any other book that gives one this special sensation, and perhaps this was the author's special intention." The feeling we have as readers—that V. has indeed missed the "solution" by reading hastily or imperceptively—adds to the comic nature of his amateurish quest, but also reminds us that there may be other secrets, other imaginative freedoms, which will solve different problems of artistic composition and illuminate other patterns of human fate.

Another dream quest, again pointing to the solution contained in Sebastian's artistry, occurs in V.'s "singularly unpleasant dream" about his half-brother. Sebastian appears to him, wearing "a black glove on his left hand," which he takes off, spilling "a number of tiny hands," representing the sinister manipulative capacity of the artist. V. misses the chance to hear the solution from Sebastian; he is paralyzed by his own terror and the armor of a single personality, "the sovereignty of daily platitudes over the delicate revelations of a dream." But *The Doubtful Asphodel*'s suggestion of a freedom from such platitudes through the originality of artistic creation is reasserted by the final action of the novel. The "tiny hands" of the author further dramatize the finding of Sebastian's last novel.

We have been told that the theme of *The Doubtful Asphodel,* the partial reflection of *Sebastian Knight,* is that:

> A man is dying: you feel him sinking throughout the book; his thought and memories pervade the whole with greater or lesser distinction. . . . He is the hero of the tale; but whereas the lives of other people in the book seem perfectly realistic (or at least realistic in a Knightian sense), the reader is kept ignorant as to who the dying man is. . . . The man is the book, the book itself is heaving and dying, and drawing up a ghostly knee.

If "the man is the book," then the man, the hero of the novel, contains the "other people" who may be momentarily given an air of reality, but ultimately fade back into the mind of the hero, which in turn is identified as part of the imagination of the author. (The fact that Sebastian was planning to write a fictitious biography, his exclamation that he is not dead, the narcissistic portrait in which he seems to be looking at the reflection of his other self, and the manipulative little hands hint at Sebastian's possible authorship of his own biography. As in *Bend Sinister,* the imaginative circles merge and diverge, the chronology of details is teasingly jumbled, and the autonomy of the fictional artist is suggested but interrupted by a larger consciousness.) One of Sebastian's important findings is that " 'all things belong to the same order of things, for such is the oneness of human perception, the oneness of individuality, the oneness of matter, whatever matter may be. The only real number is one, the rest are mere repetition.' " In terms of artistic technique, this statement means that regardless of the ostensible "point of view" of any given passage, the speaker is always, inescapably, the author. At the end of an interview with Goodman, the slick author of a rival biography of Sebastian, V. "pockets" the "black mask" which Goodman has been wearing, and remarks that "it might come in usefully on some other occasion." This event is another reminder that the parts allotted to various characters in *Sebastian Knight* are only temporary roles involving a "black mask" which is reusable. It is perhaps this same device which V.'s final declaration alludes to: "I cannot get out of my part: Sebastian's mask clings to my face."

"The only real number is one," as a psychological statement, is an essential part of the novel, and embodies the truth about the impact of life and art. We understand experience only through our perception of its personal significance, just as we understand art only when we grasp the nature and fittingness of its arranged details tending toward a completed design. For Nabokov, psychological understanding is "one" with artistic appreciation; when the reader feels that a work of art is meaningful for him, he will see how it has been rendered meaningful. Used in this sense, the word "psychology" is not blasphemous for Nabokov; as he writes in the Foreword to *The Eye:* "A serious psychologist . . . may distinguish through my rain-sparkling cryptograms a world of soul dissolution." In the case of *The Eye,* the hero exists only insofar as he is mirrored by other souls. In *Sebastian Knight,* the life and commentary of V. exist in order to surround Sebastian's works with an illusion of reality. These works in turn reflect the "number one," the author and finally the reader; they are mirrors to perception.

The primacy of the subjective self in assigning meaning to experience is illustrated by two similar incidents in the novel, which act partly as repeated frames to the total work. The first occurs in the beginning of *Sebastian Knight,* and describes Sebastian's visit to a pension where he thinks his adored mother had died thirteen years before. The idea of her presence at the place produces a sense of emotional revelation: "Gradually I worked myself into such a state that for a moment the pink and green seemed to shimmer and float as if seen through a veil of mist." Later he finds out that he had gone to the wrong town. Toward the end of the novel, when V. receives news that Sebastian is dying, he rushes to the sanatorium, and sits by what he had been told is his half-brother's bedside. The emotion he experiences changes his attitude toward Sebastian; for the first time he realizes the "warm flow" of "the wave of love" which transfigures their relationship. Afterwards he is told that it was the wrong bedside, and that Sebastian had died the day before. But in both incidents, it was not the object of emotion which precipitated the change, but rather the psychological predilection of the beholder. Empirical reality was ancillary to emotional illusion. The "secret" which unlocked the feeling lay in the sudden perception of a meaningful pattern. The quest for Sebastian's identity is resolved by V.'s finding and duplicating the artistic process which weaves its own reality. In this duplication V. and Sebastian become one.

ELIZABETH W. BRUSS

Vladimir Nabokov: Illusions of Reality and the Reality of Illusions

Autobiographers as heterogenous as Bunyan, Boswell, and De Quincey have at least the common assumption that their work reflects and transmits something that exists outside the act of composition. The events, objects, and relationships they describe are there whether or not they are written about, even if they are nothing more than memories or fleeting observations, even if they are known only to God or scarcely believed by the writer himself. However much autobiography may deliberately qualify or inadvertently complicate the scope of their identity, despite the new precision it may give to their knowledge of themselves, it remains in essence the record of a self with its own autonomous existence. It is only because of this, in fact, that autobiography can be a mode of discovery or relevation. Even De Quincey accepts this notion of autobiography, although he uses it to disparage the genre for its false worship of empirical truth.

From a twentieth-century point of view, however, this must seem a naive sort of empiricism, assuming as it does a realm of "fact" that is independent of description. Even the sciences now admit to possibilities of "indeterminacy," to the role of the experiment itself in determining the shape of the discovery. The techniques and equipment which both the physicist and the writer bring to bear upon their materials distort—or better, in part constitute—the behavior of the object under study. For a contemporary author like Vladimir Nabokov, a man who is both artist and scientist, a naive faith in facts damages either sort of observation. As he says in de-

From *Autobiographical Acts: The Changing Situation of a Literary Genre.*

scribing the artistic decline of Gogol: "He was in the worst plight that a writer can be in: he had lost the gift of imagining facts and believed that facts may exist by themselves. The trouble is that bare facts do not exist in a state of nature, for they are never really quite bare."

Facts are never "bare": they are the trajectory of the questions with which one began and the needs which initiated the inquiry. It is not simply a matter of impurities. Observation would be impossible without some initial guide for recognizing similarities and significance. Lacking an informing interest or intention, experience is chaotic and data are meaningless. Categories are the prior condition of perception and knowledge, not the natural outgrowth of experience. Nor is Nabokov inclined to ascribe a transcendental status to such categories. Even the Kantian absolutes of time and space are no more than convenient fictions—what he calls elsewhere "our pseudo-physical agreements with ourselves."

But exposing the necessary fiction at the roots of fact and the interests behind disinterested empiricism places autobiography in a difficult position. What is it that autobiography actually captures? How much does it record and how much does it create? Identity can no longer seem impermeable to the conditions and techniques of the autobiographical act. Doubt is cast on the relationship between the nexus of self and character which develops within the text and that which otherwise exists. Perhaps there is no other nexus—De Quincey's lyric prose had already illustrated how perfectly a disembodied voice mimics the accents of passionate experience. Sincerity can offer no guarantee, since it is a creation of will and appearance, and may be as easily feigned or as much a chimera as anything else. Sincerity, moreover, is consciously unconscious of its own effects, ignoring the artificial condition of a self forever being watched and probed. It is no solution but a futile, even laughable evasion.

Nabokov confronts the fictions in autobiography in less general terms as well. His novel *Lolita* explores the quirks and excesses of the genre by means of parody. A parody as thorough and extreme as *Lolita* becomes possible only with long familiarity and the contempt it breeds. Of course, neither Nabokov nor the object of his travesty is unique in the context of modernist literary heterodoxy. Conscious experimentation and deliberate violation of literary codes and models have accelerated the slow and largely accidental process of literary history in this century. This paradoxical convention of the unconventional has naturally touched autobiography as well as poetry and the novel—giving us, along with free verse and the *nouveau roman, Anti-Memoirs* as well. But since Nabokov writes both an autobiography (*Speak, Memory*) and an autobiographical burlesque, there is no question that the genre retains its vitality for him and for the members of his literary community. Its life has, however, been made more subtle, its claims less naive, and the delicate balance between truth and fiction, tradition and possibility, has been brought into sharper focus.

Lolita is the ostensible autobiography of one Humbert Humbert, although there is a good deal of indecision on the part of the autobiographer and his editor, John Ray, Jr., Ph.D., about the status of the completed work. Humbert's manuscript was left behind at his death with two alternate titles: "Lolita," or the "Confession of a White Widowed Male." To his pedantic editor, its "strange pages," while not without artistry, are best regarded as a psychiatric case history or an unwitting sociological record of "dangerous trends" in modern life. During the course of his narrative, Humbert exhausts a string of categories, including "confession" and "trial notes," "case study" and "memoir," "tragic tale" and "novel." The mock-autobiographer apparently cannot see his own disconcerting oscillation between different centers of attention—Lolita and himself—and contradictory genres—fiction and nonfiction, informal notes for his own use and free-standing narrative art. The suggestion that neither Humbert nor Ray can see what he is about is an important aspect of Nabokov's sabotage of his creatures. Humbert Humbert of course richly deserves this kind of merciless exposure, but in many ways he is no worse than the classical autobiographer. Humbert's confessions parallel in ways too numerous for accident the confessions of Jean-Jacques Rousseau. There is the same elegaic sense of childhood lost and the same paranoid suspicions emerging as the work progresses. Nabokov simply gives another turn to the screw of Rousseau's attempt to justify himself and disarm his tormentors by means of absolute and sensational sincerity. He also travesties more technical aspects of the autobiographical act, found not only in the *Confessions* but in almost all conventional representatives of the genre. Humbert Humbert calls attention to the problems of self-representation and self-imaging, and by doing so makes a shambles of the very effects he had hoped to achieve:

> I do not know if in these tragic notes I have sufficiently stressed the peculiar "sending" effect that the writer's good looks—pseudo-Celtic, attractively simian, boyishly manly—had on women of every age and environment. Of course, such announcements made in the first person may sound ridiculous. But every once in a while I have to remind the reader of my appearance much as a novelist, who has given a character of his some mannerism or a dog, has to go on producing that dog or that man-

> nerism every time the character crops up in the course of the book. . . . My gloomy good looks should be kept in the mind's eye if my story is to be properly understood.

Not only does Humbert unwittingly alert us to the essential artificiality of all attempts at representation, he also displays how gross and hackneyed are the fictions he uses in constructing his image of himself. His physique, his character, his charisma are obviously appropriated from conventional portraits of the dark, romantic hero, from *Wuthering Heights* and *Manfred.* An element of the Byronic, or at least the self-dramatic, is frequently a part of classical autobiography. The autobiographer is torn between observing and being himself; his object is forever just beyond his grasp, contemporaneous with the act of composition and undergoing changes even as he writes. Usually the act is terminated at the point, implicit or explicit, where the character merges with the narrator in a solidified and ostensibly permanent personality and role. But to Nabokov, this coincidence and completion is a fiction, and the three-dimensional wholeness of the person thus constituted is a trick of perspective. To identify and unite aspects of being may be artistic, but to accept an artifact, an impersonation, without qualification is either a delusion or a lie. (And in the case of Humbert Humbert, perhaps both.) *Lolita* does achieve an ironic resolution by allowing its narrator to die just as the book ends. The record is complete only because the life is over: with his death, Humbert is reduced to fit exactly the dimensions of the character he created.

One sees through Humbert's ploys more clearly than those of the ordinary autobiography, of course. Nabokov has provided excess of it, and made the twists and changes in self-impersonation visible through their sheer violence. The man that Humbert observes himself to be, with alternate love and loathing, is treated with ostensible distance and dispassion. Of his past self in particular, Humbert speaks in the third person, using titles and even calling himself by name: "What a foolish Hamburg that Hamburg was! Since his supersensitive system was loath to face the actual scene, he thought he could enjoy a secret part of it." But this is a sham objectivity, not so much naming as name-calling. Humbert's self-representation is far from disinterested. By alienating certain moments and certain actions he has performed, he is able to become his own judge, thereby condemning part of himself while he saves another part from condemnation. Both the manipulation of grammatical person and the epithets he chooses become the tools of his selective self-censure. "I have toyed with many pseudonyms for myself before I hit on a particularly apt one. There are in my notes, 'Otto Otto' and

'Mesmer Mesmer' and 'Lambert Lambert,' but for some reason I think my choice expresses the nastiness best."

Humbert's mode of representing himself as "other" is yet another instance of his obsessional Tom-peeping. It would appear that autobiography appeals to him as a way of sustaining what had always been his chief preoccupation: "I used to review the concluded day by checking my own image as it prowled rather than passed before the mind's red eye. I watched dark-and-handsome, not un-Celtic, probably high-church, possibly very high-church, Dr. Humbert see his daughter off to school. I watched him greet with his slow smile and pleasantly arched thick black ad-eyebrows good Mrs. Holigan." The autobiography of a voyeur is itself voyeuristic. Even, or perhaps especially, in relation to himself, Humbert savors his spectator sport, objectifying his self-image for the sake of perverse, narcissistic pleasure, hoping to "enjoy a secret part" just as he did when he returned to the scene of his first seduction to search through old newspapers for a picture of himself on his way to Lolita's hotel room.

Humbert Humbert's hyperbolic flaws as an autobiographer are only a logical extension from what one can observe in actual autobiographies, however. The struggle against unwitting self-revelation—or its encouragement, in the case of Boswell—is a concomitant of the structure of the act. The gaps and incongruities, the continuity and perfection, of the narrative surface become a symptom and a way of reading hidden information. Humbert awkwardly shows himself at every turn, intruding to confess his peculiar difficulties of composition and noting suddenly how his objectives have been transformed without his notice. The story of *Lolita* is as much the story Humbert refuses to impart as anything he manages to say. Nabokov knows this underside of the autobiographical act intimately, not only as a reader of Rousseau but also as a writer of his own autobiography. *Lolita* follows immediately upon the heels of the first version of *Speak, Memory;* according to Alfred Appel's preface to *The Annotated Lolita:* "As a book about the spell exerted by the past, *Lolita* is Nabokov's own parodic answer to his previous book the first edition of *Speak, Memory.*" And subsequent to the writing of *Lolita,* Nabokov returns to *Speak, Memory* to make of it "An Autobiography Revisited."

What are the things, then, that betray Humbert Humbert and how does Nabokov cope with his disillusioned view of autobiography when he returns to his own text? Primarily there is Humbert's refusal or inability to recognize the fruits of his own imagination and to take responsibility for them. Humbert is a literalist of the imagination, willfully clinging to what he knows to be limited perspectives and evanescent realities. Lolita herself is his creation, a nymphet only to his nympholepsy, a deliberate forgery of his lost childhood love. "She was Dolores on the dotted line. But in my arms she was always Lolita. . . . In point of fact, there might have been no Lolita at all had I not loved, one summer, a certain initial girl-child." Humbert's first love was "Annabel Leigh," thus making his obsession with Lolita an illusion of an illusion. Nabokov emphasizes the madness of this by making the memoirist a professional student of American literature, a man who therefore ought to recognize when his own case begins to resemble a famous poem by Edgar Allan Poe. Humbert describes his adventures, before encountering Lolita, at Melville Sound and Pierre Point, without turning a hair. At the climax of his book, when he murders his nympholeptic double and rival for Lolita's charms, Clare Quilty, the scene reduplicates an earlier catalog of Lolita's favorite films: "musicals, underworlders, westerners." The successive stages of Quilty's death agony involve first stopping to sing at his piano, then doing an imitation of an "underworld numbskull," and finally grappling with Humbert hand to hand in "the obligatory scene in the Westerns."

Although he consciously toys with the jargon of psychoanalysis, thus managing to rebut the classical Freudian theories by showing a perfect and lucid awareness of what should be repressed sexual desires, Humbert cannot prevent certain subliminal manifestations of his madness from leaking into his narrative without his notice. These parapraxes diminish his claims to accuracy and flawless deduction, for one is constantly surprising Humbert in the act of chasing and fleeing acknowledged fictions and dubious private phantoms. "Oh, I am quite sure it was not a delusion," he exclaims, destroying credibility as he tries to bolster it by introducing evidence that he and Lolita really were pursued by mystery cars on the final, fateful portion of their journey. The conflict in his soul between desire and disgust shows plainly through erratic structure and the wild and heedless changes in his diction. Aspects of his "slippery self" appear to battle for control as Latinate euphemisms give way to childish monosyllables within a single page. "Here is Virgil who could the nymphet sing in single tone, but probably preferred a lad's perineum." "Humbert Humbert tried hard to be good. Really and truly, he did." At times an open break in the narration juxtaposes one sentence in schizophrenic condemnation of another. "In a princedom by the sea. . . . About as many years before Lolita was born as my age was that summer. You can always count on a murderer for a fancy prose style."

Throughout the manuscript, brief parentheses puncture the most elevated and grandiose expression, deflating formal beauty with crude actuality. "The fatal gesture passed like the tail of a falling star across the blackness of the contemplated crime. . . . But what d'ye know, folks—I just could not make myself do it!" Humbert's narrative seems incapable of sustaining itself in either plot or style. His sentences fall apart, his narrative becomes fragmented and confused, especially when he is recounting painful situations. "This daily headache in the opaque air of this tombal jail is disturbing, but I must persevere. Have written more than a hundred pages and not got anywhere yet. My calendar is getting confused. That must have been around August 15, 1947. Don't think I can go on. Heart, head—everything. Lolita, Lolita, Lolita, Lolita, Lolita, Lolita. Repeat till the page is full, printer." This is actually an entire chapter: chapter 26, book 1. The same kind of confusion overcomes the narrative in chapter 26 of book 2, Humbert again recounting a visit to the small town of Briceland. "I notice that I have somehow mixed up two events, my visit with Rita to Briceland on our way to Cantrip, and our passing through Briceland again on our way back to New York, but such suffusions of swimming colors are not to be disdained by the artist in recollection."

Thus despite all his attempts to create a reasonable, or at least an unassailable case for himself, Humbert is plagued by pathological slips of the pen. He may use performatives which stress judicious probity—"prove," "explain," "analyze," and "itemize"—but the performance itself rarely bears him out. "With the passage of the Children and Young Person Act in 1933, the term 'girl-child' is defined as a 'girl who is over eight but under fourteen years.' . . . Hugh Broughton, a writer of controversy in the reign of James the First, has proved that Rahab was a harlot at ten years of age. This is all very interesting, and I daresay you see me already frothing at the mouth in a fit; but no, I am not; I am just winking happy thoughts into a little tiddle cup." He cannot even fulfill his promise for a "clear, frank account of the itinerary" of his travels with Lolita without becoming distracted in autistic play: "*Nous connûmes* (this is royal fun) the would-be enticements of their repetitious names—all those Sunset Motels." By his casual but overwhelmingly frequent allusions to dreams during his initial infatuation with Lolita and to nightmares during his hopeless attempt to retain her after her seduction, Humbert demonstrates the instability of his perception of events. "Whether or not the realization of a lifelong dream had surpassed all expectation, it had, in a sense, overshot its mark—and plunged into nightmare."

The dividing line between dream and nightmare seems, in fact, to motivate the partition of the manuscript into two parts, the second a grotesque anticlimax to the first, with mania turned into phobia and realistic surfaces distorted by ever more baroque twists of plot and design. Throughout the book, but especially in book 2, the names and even the natures of the characters undergo the metamorphic transformations of a dream, the process culminating in the figure of Humbert's private nemesis, "Detective Trapp," which suddenly dissolves into that of the man responsible for stealing and ultimately ruining Lolita, Clare Quilty.

Humbert's madness is not really a perverse desire for little girls but a willful attempt to copulate with his own dreams and to murder his own nightmares in his vengeful guilt and disappointment. All the women who become involved with him, save only Rita, are ultimately killed by the effects of his attentions, as though he robbed them of vitality by combining them with his fantasies. Both his first wife and, later, Lolita herself, die in childbirth, as though to indicate the essential and murderous sterility of Humbert's love. So confirmed is Humbert in his voyeurism that even in the pit of his most desperate remorse he remains unable to conceive the error of his ways. He still confuses the carnal reality of his beloved with the phantom shapes of photography and film: "No hereafter is acceptable if it does not produce her as she was then, in that Colorado resort between Snow and Elphinstone, with everything right. . . . Idiot, triple idiot! I could have filmed her! I would have had her now with me, before my eyes, in the projection room of my pain and despair." There is some suggestion that the reformation and change of heart which Humbert undergoes while pondering Lolita in his prison (resulting in the transformation of trial notes into a tribute to his love), is merely an exchange of one delusion for another—a willed sacrifice of both lover and beloved for the sake of artistic immortality. Humbert's manuscript is simply another attempt to capture Lolita, with all the lurking ambiguity that term implies, and his famous outburst—"Oh, my Lolita, I have only words to play with!"—echoes dangerously when one recalls his diseased capacity for erotic play. In his memoirs, Humbert hopes to construct a timeless space he may share with his nymphet, a shrine no doubt, but a tomb as well, recalling the necrophiliac closure to the fable with which Humbert began, the tale of Annabel Lee:

> Thus, neither of us is alive when the reader opens this book. . . . I am thinking of aurochs and angels, the secret of durable pigments, prophetic sonnets, the refuge of art. And this is the only immortality you and I may share, my Lolita.
>
> And so, all the night-tide, I lie down by the side
> Of my darling, my darling, my life and my bride
> In her sepulchre there by the sea—
> In her tomb by the sounding sea.

In love with his own demons and unwilling to be awakened from even his worst dreams, Humbert Humbert can be heard pleading, from time to time, to be left alone with his fantasies. And this may be the ultimate purpose of the memoir, to environ himself more firmly in delusion and to defend his shadowy Humberland from intruding realities. Humbert's penchant for Tom-peeping at remote, gauzy windows, his love for a girl-child surnamed Haze, are the emblems of an underlying horror of anything too sharply seen, too stubbornly defined to become the stuff his dreams are made on. "*Mes fenêtres!* . . . grinding my teeth, I would crowd all the demons of desire against the railing of a throbbing balcony . . . whereupon the lighted image would move and Eve would revert to a rib, and there would be nothing in the window but an obese partly clad man reading the paper. Since I sometimes won the race between my fancy and nature's reality, the deception was bearable."

Humbert Humbert cannot bear the recognition of deception, but Nabokov's own autobiography, *Speak, Memory,* is a celebration of the consciousness of illusion. Nabokov prefers flaunting his "dazzling insincerity" to engaging in Humbert's glib confessions, what Appel calls the "solemn introspection . . . the diarist's compulsive egotism, candid but totally self-conscious self-analysis, carefully created 'honesty,' willful irony, and studied self-deprecation." Andrew Field sees more artwork than personal history in *Speak, Memory,* since "the past is not searched out. It is, rather, carefully selected—the changing form may be likened to breathing—and poetically fixed." Each of Nabokov's fifteen chapters carefully evokes a rich and delicately worked chimera of the past, only to shatter it as the chapter ends:

> I witness with pleasure the supreme achievement of memory, which is the masterly use it makes of innate harmonies when gathering to its fold the suspended and wandering tonalities of the past. I like to imagine, in consummation and resolution of those jangling chords, something as enduring, in retrospect, as the long table that on summer birthdays and namedays used to be laid . . . exaggerated, no doubt, by the same faculty of impassioned commemoration. . . . Through a tremulous prism, I distinguish the features of relatives. . . . In the place where my current tutor sits, there is a changeful image, a succession of fade-ins and fade-outs; the pulsation of my thoughts mingles with that of the leaf shadows. . . . And then, suddenly, just when the colors and outlines settle at last to their various duties . . .

> some knob is touched and a torrent of sounds comes to life . . . like a background of wild applause.

The optical tricks, the description of a memory which feeds on and is fed by the imagination—composing rather than resurrecting the setting—and the final "background of applause," leave little doubt about the status of this scene. It will not be forgotten by any reader of these memoirs that the memory summoned by the title's epic invocation is the mother of all the other arts. Nabokov has said as much in an interview: "I would say that imagination is a form of memory. . . . When we speak of a vivid individual recollection we are paying a compliment not to our capacity of retention but to Mnemosyne's mysterious foresight in having stored up this or that element which creative imagination may use when combining it with later recollections and inventions."

Far from characterizing himself as "handsomely simian" or even dwelling on any sort of self-representation, Nabokov fills his autobiography with the portraits of others. There are his parents, his governess and tutors, even the ancestors whom he never knew, but whose existence has somehow contributed to the pattern of family traditions and possessions, of aristocratic codes of conduct and education which have shaped his own life. The most intimate and important private moments in his life, the assassination of his father, the courtship of his wife, are merely hinted at, anticipated, or mentioned only when they have already taken place offstage. He treats his life in exile—the period in which he met and married his wife and had his only child—by focusing upon the chess problems he composed for émigré journals:

> I remember one particular problem I had been trying to compose for months. . . . It was meant for the delectation of the very expert solver . . . (who) would start by falling for an illusory pattern of play . . . which the composer had taken the greatest pains to "plant." . . . Having passed through this "antithetic" inferno the by now ultrasophisticated solver would reach the simple key move (bishop to c2) as somebody on a wild goose chase might go from Albany to New York by way of Vancouver, Eurasia, and the Azores. The pleasant experience of the roundabout route (strange landscapes, gongs, tigers, exotic customs, the thrice-repeated circuit of a newly married couple around the sacred fire of an earthen brazier) would amply reward him for the misery of the deceit.

The chess discussion itself is an "illusory pattern of play," for hidden within it is a masked account of a marriage ceremony, and immediately following this passage one encounters the first reference to Nabokov's wife and son. "All of a sudden, I felt that with the completion of my chess problem a whole period of my life had come to a satisfactory close. . . . Sleeping in the next room were you and our child."

A similar camouflage covers his father's death:

> This final dachshund followed us into exile, and as late as 1930, in a suburb of Prague (where my widowed mother spent her last years . . .) he could still be seen.
>
> On the night of March 22, 1922, around ten o'clock, in the living room where as usual my mother was reclining . . . I had just got to the end of the little poem about Florence . . . and as she was saying over her knitting, "Yes, yes, Florence does look like a *dimniy* iris, how true! I remember—" when the telephone rang.
>
> After 1923, when she moved to Prague. . .

The telephone message reporting that Nabokov senior had been shot is deliberately blotted out, and only the attentive reader who recalls Prague as the site of his mother's widowhood will recognize what has occurred. The agony of Nabokov's loss is never expressed, although it may be inferred from various statements about his father scattered throughout the book. Nabokov refuses to collect this rich scattering of emotion and memory into one convenient category or to turn a father's death (as Humbert turns Lolita's disappearance) into the locus for his own display of grief. Open trickery is less deceitful than the covert manipulations of sincerity.

Of course, this constant magic and stunning sleight of hand requires a magician, and so it is hardly surprising to find the narrator so often intruding on his tale. The interruptions are even more prominent than in *Lolita*—too prominent, in fact, to be experienced as distractions or digressions:

> For one moment, thanks to the sudden radiance of a lone lamp where the station's square ends, a grossly exaggerated shadow races beside the sleigh, climbs a billow of snow and is gone. . . . And let me not leave out the moon—for surely there must be a moon, the full, incredibly clear disc that goes so well with Russian lusty frosts. So there it comes . . . it glazes the runner tracks left on the road. . . . Very lovely, very lonesome. But what am I doing in this stereoscopic dreamland? How did I get here? Some-

> how, the two sleighs have slipped away, leaving behind a passportless spy, standing on the blue-white road in his New England snowboots and stormcoat. The vibration in my ears is no longer their receding bells, but only my old blood singing. All is still, spellbound, enthralled by the moon, fancy's rear-vision mirror. The snow is real, though, and as I bend to it and scoop up a handful, sixty years crumble to glittering frost-dust between my fingers.

Unlike Humbert Humbert, whose life tapers to a neat, fictitious point, an achieved selfhood in which the fruits of the past have ripened (into solid remorse) and from which all alien elements have been winnowed out, Nabokov's own present and his correlative sense of self are as fluid, as ungeneralized and densely patterned as his past: "the evaporation of certain volatiles and the melting of certain metals are still going on in my coils and crucibles."

If the pattern of his life is found within his autobiography, it is not because Nabokov accepts the fiction of an a priori shape, an identity fixed forever by a process of religious conversion or historical necessity or even the "laws" of association. The discovery of pattern is a creative act, involving imagery and careful counterpoise to bring out the design which otherwise might be undetectable. "Neither in environment nor in heredity can I find the exact instrument that fashioned me, the anonymous roller that pressed upon my life a certain intricate watermark whose unique design becomes visible when the lamp of art is made to shine through life's foolscap."

Nabokov's individuality is nothing more or less than the "unique design" of certain recurrent themes of his past and present, thematic repetitions which become discernible only when the isolated and evanescent details of a lifetime are held fast for a moment—as they were not and cannot be in life—within a work of art. His present sense of self is merely the nucleus of the pattern, the central point defined by the continuum, shifting as the pattern itself appears to change:

> In a sense, all poetry is positional: to try to express one's position in regard to the universe embraced by consciousness, is an immemorial urge. The arms of consciousness reach out and grope, and the longer they are the better. . . . Lost in thought, he taps his knee with his wandlike pencil, and at the same instant a car (New York license plate) passes along the road, a child bangs the screen door of a neighboring porch, an old man yawns in a misty

> Turkestan orchard, a granule of cinder-gray sand is rolled by the wind on Venus, a Doctor Jacques Hirsch in Grenoble puts on his reading glasses, and trillions of other such trifles occur—all forming an instantaneous and transparent organism of events, of which the poet (sitting in a lawn chair, at Ithaca, N.Y.) is the nucleus.

This organism of events does not exist without the "wandlike pencil" of the poet, but neither is the poet anything more substantial than a central point within the pattern he unifies within his consciousness. Memory is, of course, a mode of consciousness, and recollection is a way of expanding its purview. Nabokov therefore is materially changing his position as he writes his autobiography, embracing ever-wider contexts of time and place. Whatever the man Vladimir Nabokov "is," his identity cannot be separated from what he is making of himself by means of *Speak, Memory:*

> Although I had been composing these chapters in the erratic sequence reflected by the dates of first publication given above, they had been neatly filling numbered gaps in my mind which followed the present order of chapters. That order had been established in 1936, at the placing of the cornerstone which already held in its hidden hollow various maps, timetables, a collection of matchboxes, a chip of ruby glass, and even—as I now realize—the view from my balcony of Geneva Lake, of its ripples and glades of light, black-dotted today, at teatime, with coots and tufted ducks.

The act of composition appears to contain the self—the present moment, the very perceptions achieved in the act of writing, are only part of a thematic pattern implicit at the inception of the work, some thirty years before. Indeed, Nabokov ends by putting his own name in the index at the back of the book—an index which is a major addition to his "revisited" autobiography: "Nabokov, Valdimir Vladimirovich, 9–16, 19–310, *passim.*" The entry refers the reader to the introduction Nabokov has also added to his revised edition—pages 9–16—subordinating not only remembered experience but his experience as a writer to the overall design of *Speak, Memory.*

Thus, Humbert's pseudo-objectivity is here replaced by something like a true impersonality: "As far back as I remember myself (with interest, with amusement, seldom with admiration or disgust)." Although like Humbert Nabokov frequently discusses his actions in the third person, it is usually the indefinite third person, "one," a pronoun equally applicable to any individual undergoing such an experience or placed in such circumstances. "One would lag back and shuffle and slide a little on the smooth stone floor of the hall, causing the gentle hand at the small of one's back to propel one's reluctant frame by means of indulgent pushes." Nabokov treats himself as a transparency rather than an image, a means of access to experience rather than an actor:

> I can easily refeel the exhilarating change from the thickly padded, knee-length *polushobok,* with the hot beaver collar, to the short navy-blue coat with its anchor-patterned brass buttons. In the open landau I am joined by the valley of a lap rug to the occupants of the more interesting back seat, majestic Mademoiselle, and triumphant, tear-bedabbled Sergey, with whom I have just had a row at home . . . as I look up I can see . . . great, tensely smooth, semi-transparent banners billowing . . . undoubtedly celebrating now in the city of memory, the essence of that spring day, the swish of mud, the beginning of mumps, the ruffled exotic bird with one bloodshot eye on Mademoiselle's hat.

It is the "essence of that spring day"—an essence composed equally of the excitement of the thaw and the personal discomfort of nascent disease—which is dominant in this passage. The figure of the boy gives way and we rush into the vacuum created by his disappearance, taking his sensations for our own.

While Humbert pursues his shadows and delights in an impressionistic haziness more tractable to sexual mirage, Nabokov comments on the clarity of an act of recollection and pays as much attention to the mechanism of perception as to the object it perceives. "In looking at it from my present tower I see myself as a hundred different young men at once. . . . Not only is the experience in question, and the shadows of all those charming ladies useless to me now in recomposing my past, but it creates a bothersome defocalization, and no matter how I worry the screws of memory, I cannot recall the way Tamara and I parted." Nabokov does not limit himself to visual analogies, but employs the full manifold of consciousness—aural, tactile, and even olfactory awareness enters into his autobiographical act. It is significant, in this connection, that Humbert's moment of tragic recognition comes to him when he stands upon a cliff above a city filled with children whom he can hear at play but cannot see. This is the final experience he describes for us, and it is here that both his life and his manuscript end, since he cannot be an aural voyeur. For Humbert "seeing is believing," but for Nabokov it is only one of many available modes of perception, and all of them are part of the artistry of consciousness. In fact he stresses the "ars" of his "ars memoria" by using verbs such as "reconstruct" and "remember" interchangeably. His performatives are often deliberately fantastic; he uses a language drawn from magic—"conjure," "flying carpet"—from theater, and even from gymnastics—"setting," "puppet show," "bicycle act." The act of writing assumes a life of its own, so dense with images does it become. "A large, alabaster-based kerosene lamp is steered into the gloaming. Gently it floats and comes down; the hand of memory, now in a footman's glove, places it in the center of a round table. The flame is nicely adjusted, and a rosy, silk-flounced lamp shade, with inset glimpses of rococo winter sports, crowns the readjusted (cotton wool in Casimir's ear) light. Revealed: a bright, stylish ('Russian Empire') drawing room."

At another point, the process of reconstruction is likened to the creation of a classic nineteenth-century Russian novel: " 'And what about Yaremich?' I asked M. V. Dobushinski, one summer afternoon in the nineteen forties, as we strolled through a beech forest in Vermont. 'Is he remembered?' 'Indeed, he is,' replied Matislav Valerianovich." This is a novelistic dialogue, with a characteristic alternation of last names and first names with patronymic, and it is, moreover, wholly imaginary—which can be ascertained by recalling the description, several pages earlier, of Nabokov's childhood dream of plunging through the picture frame and entering the "enchanted beechwood" of a drawing hanging on his bedroom wall. The conversation with his former drawing teacher never took place, but any way of rendering the "consequences" of the past simplifies them, fictionalizes them; and to this extent autobiography and novel are alike. "When I learned of these later developments, I experienced a queer shock; it was as if life had impinged upon my creative rights by wriggling on beyond the subjective limits so elegantly and economically set by childhood memories that I thought I had signed and sealed."

The "truth" of autobiography comes only with the recognition that "things past" are never captured in their original form: "One is moved to speak more eloquently about these things, about many things that one always hopes might survive captivity in the zoo of words—but the ancient limes crowding close to the house down Mnemosyne's monologue with their creaking and heaving in the restless night." The autobiographical act is inevitably creative, its realities ineluctably unreal. But if one observes the disparities, if one calls attention to the responsibilities undertaken and the temptations which accompany the act, then and only then will a new, no longer naive autobiographical fact emerge. "Have I really salvaged her from fiction? Just before the rhythm I hear falters and fades, I catch myself wondering whether, during the years I knew her, I had not kept utterly missing something."

Humbert Humbert engages in an act which is the inverse of Nabokov's, although he sometimes expresses a queasy doubt of his procedure. "The beastly and beautiful merged at one point, and it is that borderline I would like to fix, and I feel I fail to do so utterly. Why?" Humbert has no answer for his question, but his attentive reader can easily see the inevitability of failure in a writer who confesses "in order to enjoy my phantasms in peace I firmly decided to ignore what I could not help perceiving." His crabbed and frantic pursuit of proof and self-approval leaves him neither opportunity nor inclination to examine his evidence critically. Thus he misses even as he transmits the truth of his condition. Wherever there is an order which is not his own, Humbert sees only chance or the deliberate machinations of a personal enemy. The excerpts and random lists which he mindlessly includes for the sake of verisimilitude—the catalog of the prison library and the class list of Lolita's school, the tour books which have miraculously survived his travels and arrest and a passage from *Who's Who in the Limelight*—are not as haphazard as he might suppose; they actually contain the ciphers of his own destiny. "Like *Who's Who in the Limelight* and the 'cryptogrammic paper chase,' the 'poetic' class list serves as a kind of magical mirror. The list is printed on the back of an unfinished map of the U.S., drawn by Lolita, suggesting the scale of the gameboard on which the action is played. The image of the map secreted in the *Young People's Encyclopedia* prefigures their journeys (on which H. H. will 'finish' the map by showing Lolita the country), just as the class list prefigures and mirrors an extraordinary number of other things" (Alfred Appel Jr., ed., *The Annotated Lolita*).

The pattern extends beyond Humbert's death, touching his manuscript in unexpected ways. Humbert had never planned on an editor, or on his curt prefatory remarks: "For the benefit of old-fashioned readers who wish to follow the destinies of the 'real' people beyond the 'true' story, a few details may be given. . . . Mrs. 'Richard F. Schiller' died in childbed, giving birth to a stillborn girl, on Christmas Day 1952." This information coming from beyond the autobiographer's ken or control guards the approach to Humbert's manuscript. The revelation of Lolita's marriage is already stale when Humbert announces it and his attempt to resolve his autobiography with the heroic gesture of a romantic visionary and prophet is rendered empty, a glaring deceit, however sincere in its intention: "Dolly Schiller will probably survive me by many years. . . . I hope you will love your baby. I hope it will be a boy. . . . I am thinking of aurochs and angels, the secret of durable pigments, prophetic sonnets, the refuge of art." Humbert's highest rhetorical and emotional achievements become low comedy for an audience which knows the twists and turns of fate long before reading a single one of Humbert's words.

The privacy of Humbert's vision is his ruin, both as an autobiographer and as a hero. All the while he is writing, his materials (and certain unknowns in himself) are in revolt against him, forming connections that he does not, in his madness or his cowardice, seem to recognize. The foreword gives the icily succinct account of Lolita's death, listing it among the indifferent destinies of other characters major and minor. But within Humbert's own manuscript there is a curious foreshadowing of editor John Ray's death notice: " 'And *you* know where her grave is,' I said controlling myself, whereupon I named the cemetery—just outside Ramsdale, between the railway tracks and Lakeview Hill. 'Moreover,' I added, 'the tragedy of such an accident is somewhat cheapened by the epithet you saw fit to apply to it. If you really wish to triumph in your mind over the idea of death—' 'Ray,' said Lo for hurray, and languidly left the room." Humbert misconstrues what he has reported, but in giving Lolita's own words, he has naively included yet another thread from the pattern of a fate which surrounds and has always surrounded him. His offer to make Lolita "triumph" over death—an offer he repeats in the concluding apostrophe to his book—is exploded by the subtle interpolation of a painful "actuality" which withstands the power of his fantasies.

Humbert's grim insistence on his *verbatim* record, exactly reproducing conversations long since past (often without aid of notes or memoranda), is itself dubious and is made more so by his own carelessness. " 'Lo,' I said, 'you got it all wrong. I want you to leave your incidental Dick, and this awful hole, and come to live with me and die with me, and everything with me' (words to that effect)." *Speak, Memory,* in contrast, shuns the pretense of direct quotation, rendering instead the mental silence of memory, broken only by a few habitual mannerisms of speech, a few ofttimes repeated, favorite expressions which made themselves memorable. His own diffused character never speaks directly in Nabokov's autobiography, unlike Humbert Humbert's verbose mannequin.

But more important is the way this realistic speech betrays its author, making it possible to construct alternative interpretations and allowing Lolita a place to demonstrate her own vulgar humanity free from Humbert's solipsistic version of her. "My Lolita remarked: 'You know, what's so dreadful about dying is that you are completely on your own'; and it struck me . . . that I simply did not know a thing about my darling's mind and that quite possibly, behind the awful juvenile clichés, there was in her a garden and a twilight, and a palace gate—dim and adorable regions which happened to be lucidly and absolutely forbidden to me." Here, for a moment, the captive transcends her jealous captor, and Dolores Haze emerges as the heroine of the book.

But none of the devices of documentary realism conspire against Humbert as completely and as successfully as his representation of time and space. It is the absence of naturalistic sequence and contiguity which prevents Humbert from seeing any order or meaning in the lists and catalogs he includes. Traveler and would-be escape artist that he is, Humbert's landscapes show a tendency to flatten out, to shrink from three dimensions to two-dimensional illusions. "Parody of a hotel corridor. . . . There was a double bed, a mirror, a double bed in the mirror, a closet door with a mirror, a bathroom door ditto, a blue-dark window, a reflected bed there, the same in the closet mirror." It is in this maze of mirrors, a hotel room in Briceland, that Humbert finally possesses his nymphet, only to discover that he can never possess her fully. As he lies on this bed, a breathless inch from the fulfillment of his most exuberant fantasies, space suddenly warps and the familiar volume of an inhabitable world turns into a floor plan, a map of the hotel: "The clatter of the elevator's gate—some twenty yards northeast of my head but as clearly perceived as if it were inside my left temple . . . immediately east of my left ear (always assuming I lay on my back, not daring to direct my viler side toward the nebulous haunch of my bedmate), the corridor would brim. . . . When *that* stopped a toilet immediately north of my cerebellum took over. . . . Then someone in a southern direction was extravagantly sick . . . the avenue under the window of my insomnia, to the west of my wake . . . degenerated into the despicable haunt of gigantic trucks."

Humbert not only tolerates this strange, collapsible world, he actually depends upon its being so. His favorite vista is the distinct plane of a window—"thus isolated, thus removed, the vision acquired an especially keen charm." He needs the reductive and dehumanizing quality of the second dimension to make the universe a screen for his own projected lusts. Looking at American geography, he sees a "crazy quilt," a melange of private associations, literary allusions, fairy settlements—in much the same way that he sees the form of Clare Quilty in the scraps of his frustrated and miserable experience. The memoirist is even capable of seeing the implications of such a warped perspective, while failing utterly to see that it is the same viewpoint behind his own memoirs. "The stark, stiff, lurid rhymes correspond very exactly to certain perspectiveless and terrible landscapes and figures, and magnified parts of landscapes and figures, as drawn by psychopaths."

And yet, though Humbert claims he has "safely solipsized" Lolita and bends all his physical and narrative efforts to confining her to the private kingdom of his dreams, it is clear, as the book progresses, that Humberland itself is circumscribed, as it increasingly becomes an object in alien phenomenal fields. "She had entered my world, umber and black Humberland, with rash curiosity; she surveyed it with a shrug of amused distaste, and it seemed to me now that she was ready to turn away from it with something akin to plain repulsion." From the spider who weaves his strategems around his victim, Humbert declines into the helpless postulant who pleads with Lolita "in the most abject manner for clarification, no matter how meretricious of the slow awfulness enveloping me." In the second half of the story, it is Lolita and not Humbert who is the center of orientation, the pole for measuring how all movement "comes" and "goes." When Humbert finally realizes, dimly, transiently, his true situation within a larger destiny, he gives the culminating expression to this hidden force magnetizing his text: "I stood listening to that musical vibration from my lofty slope, to those flashes of separate cries with a kind of demure murmur for background, and then I knew that the hopelessly poignant thing was not Lolita's absence from my side, but the absence of her voice from that concord."

Humbert cannot perceive this gradual reorientation because of his ignorance and evasion of another variable. Time. A world without time is necessarily two-dimensional, since there is no continuum, nothing to connect isolated points in space. As a professional of his perversion, Humbert is at war with mutability and writing to sustain his own never-never land of ageless children.

"In fact, I would have the reader see 'nine' and 'fourteen' as the boundaries—the mirrory beaches and rosy rocks—of an enchanted island haunted by those nymphets of mine . . . insidious charm . . . separates the nymphet from such coevals of hers as are incomparably more dependent on the spatial world of synchronous phenomena than on that intangible island of entranced time where Lolita plays with her likes." But what the memoirist would have is decidedly not what he gets. His recorded adventures are continuously foiled by disguised appearances of time. For example, lured on by the promise of a visit to "Our Glass Lake"—what beaches could be more "mirrory"? what better chance for a solitary idyll with little Lo?—Humbert finds himself instead suddenly entangled in the matrimonial schemes of Lolita's decaying mother. When he ultimately visits the lake in Mrs. Haze's amorous company, Humbert discovers it to be not an exemplar of wonderland and solipsism, but the domain of time itself, "Hour Glass Lake." It is the memory of this lake which returns to haunt him at the climax of the book, when Lolita reveals to him the long-sought name of his rival. Although there are several reasons why Humbert might associate the name of Quilty with an earlier lakeside conversation concerning Quilty's uncle, it is significant that the word which springs to Humbert's mind—"waterproof"—was originally a reference to his wristwatch, a timepiece which could not be stopped even by the enchanted waters of "Our Glass Lake."

Fighting to suppress every trace of time, even avoiding terms like "remember," Humbert is more easily taken by surprise when its passage overtakes him while he writes his manuscript. "When I started, fifty-six days ago, to write *Lolita*. . . . I thought I would use these notes in toto at my trial. . . . In mid-composition, however, I realized that I could not parade the living Lolita. I still may use parts of this memoir in hermetic sessions, but publication is to be deferred." The tenseless opening of his text (which is also situated at the zero-point of space, within Humbert's very body) is a collection of lyric ejaculations and verbless sentence fragments, a grammar meant to leave him free of a commitment to time: "Lolita, light of my life, fire of my loins. My sin, my soul. Lo-lee-ta: the tip of the tongue taking a trip of three steps down the palate to tap, at three, on the teeth. Lo. Lee. Ta." Yet it is a grammar he cannot long sustain, and most of his manuscript is in the imperfect past. Only at the very end does Humbert reach out to touch Lolita and his past, to bridge the temporal distance which like spatial distance is required to preserve the purity of anticipation, the "great rose-gray never-to-be-had" which is the perfection of desire. "Furthermore, since the idea of time plays such a magic part in the matter, the student should not be surprised to learn that there must be a gap of several years . . . between maiden and man to enable the latter to come under a nymphet's spell . . . a certain distance that the inner eye thrills to surmount." In his memoirs, Humbert simply reverses his position, looking backward at his illusions instead of looking forward, but the angle of his lust remains unchanged. Time is coterminous with his very consciousness. It accompanies him even as he hopelessly strives to flee it, in his ceaseless travels with a captive whose nymphet days are mortally numbered, in the remorseful writing of his tale. Time creates and time destroys the phenomena of memory and nympholepsy—and time is the basis of that pattern in which Humbert is too enmeshed to see his own entrapment.

The whole of Humberland collapses if his readers catch a slight calendrical clue. According to the preface, Humbert Humbert died in his cell on November 16, 1952. Humbert himself mentions that his work on his memoirs has taken him fifty-six days, dating the first day of composition no later than September 21, 1952. Yet the fateful letter from Lolita, the letter which reunites them after her disappearance and allows Humbert to learn the name of his fiend-rival (and eventually to gain his murderous revenge) is said to have arrived on September 22, 1952. One could take Humbert's remark about the time of composition as an error or a rough estimate, or there might be a mistake in the date he has assigned to his receipt of Lolita's letter. It is also possible that his editor is wrong about the date of Humbert's death. But it seems more likely that this series of random errors is yet another instance of the contrapuntal pattern undercutting the autobiography. A supernatural explanation is still possible; the composition of *Lolita* may somehow be the feat of Humbert's afterlife. Certainly the enigmatic words near the conclusion of his tale could bear out this interpretation: "And do not pity C. Q. One had to choose between him and H. H. and one wanted H. H. to exist at least a couple of months longer, so as to have him make you live in the minds of later generations." But even if Humbert Humbert is the phoenix of his confrontation with Clare Quilty, he does not thereby gain any greater insight into the difference between delusion and reality, for, as he tells Quilty during the murder scene: "The hereafter for all we know may be an eternal state of excruciating insanity."

The alternative conclusion we may draw is that Humbert Humbert does indeed compose his memoirs between the dates of September 21, and November 16, and that all the incidents reported as occurring after the twenty-first—receiving Lolita's letter, recovering and ultimately losing her, and killing off Clare Quilty—are therefore purely fictitious. Perhaps the writing of *Lolita* is itself the surrogate for the final parting scene, Humbert's only opportunity to assert his sense of love and loss, to communicate his guilt and his remorse to Lolita, and to provide for her future as he tries to do when he gives her money in the Coalmont meeting. The murder of Quilty may also take place only within and by means of Humbert's autobiography. In the hindsight of his manuscript, he does succeed in piecing together the grotesque character of a foe whose menacing presence constantly attended him, interfering with the fulfillment of his desires and intruding upon his private paradise. The analogy between the corpse of his murdered rival and his own manuscript is implicitly acknowledged by the memoirist:

> I could not bring myself to touch him in order to make sure he was really dead. He looked it: a quarter of his face gone, and two

> flies beside themselves with a dawning sense of unbelievable luck.
>
> This then is my story. I have reread it. It has bits of marrow sticking to it, and blood, and beautiful bright-green flies.

In grappling with the nature of his enemy, seeking in prose if not in action for the fiend whose machinations have despoiled and poisoned all his dreams of bliss, Humbert actually does commit a murder. But the man he succeeds in destroying is himself, by torturing himself with memories of his own guilt and failure. In the process of writing, and ever more prominently in book 2, Humbert's probings into the past are turned into the spasms of his diseased heart. If he cannot bear to do it consciously, he has at least subliminally sought and found the source of his defeat and the monster who destroyed Lolita's youth; he has revenged himself upon that monster in himself.

The "eternality of art," Humbert's final hope of refuge, turns out to be just one more in the series of his hopeless illusions, for composing his book has taken time, and time has aged and killed him. The temporal distance between him and his beloved only grows greater as he writes. Although he is symbolically joined to her in his final declaration of love, the process of time goes on, moving within his words. "I am thinking of aurochs and angels"—the progressive aspect mocks his claim to have discovered the "secret of durable pigments." One cannot take literal refuge within art as Humbert strives to do. As a result, the world of appearances, the temporal universe of "becoming"—the only life or even afterlife that Humbert will accept—is never left behind.

Humbert refuses to engage in conscious recollection or take the responsibility of art, autobiographical flaws which are overcome in *Speak, Memory*. Nabokov is the most conscious and the most responsible of autobiographical artists, carefully exposing the unnatural qualities of his re-created creatures and countrysides. "We shall go still further back, to a morning in May 1934, and plot with respect to this fixed point the graph of a section of Berlin." This void and abstraction is far removed from the comfortable and decidedly corporal immortality Humbert imagines he can create. Humbert is trapped within a world of time and space because he is unwilling to surrender his mundane perception of himself and his nymphet love; his need to know carnally and possess physically wars against his desire for another, timeless mode of being. *Speak, Memory* achieves this place outside of time, but only while showing how irrevocably both the pleasures and the pains of the third dimension must be left behind. In the sixth chapter of the autobiography, Nabokov takes the reader on a butterfly hunt which begins in the Russian countryside of 1910 and gradually, wordlessly, changes until—we realize with a start—it is now 1943, in the American Rockies. The author ends this metamorphosis by stating: "I confess I do not believe in time. I like to fold my magic carpet, after use, in such a way as to superimpose one part of the pattern on another. Let visitors trip. And the highest enjoyment of timelessness—in a landscape selected at random—is when I stand among rare butterflies and their food plants. This is ecstasy. . . . It is like a momentary vacuum into which rushes all that I love." Ecstasy it may be, but it is an acquired taste, one far beyond the emotional and imaginative capacities of Humbert Humbert, who, natural man that he is, abhors a vacuum.

Speak, Memory looks down from above on Nabokov's life as it has been lived in the third dimension, manipulating time and space at will. Temporal order is only one of many possible orders, and the least interesting one at that. It has therefore little of the trite suspense Humbert Humbert gives his memoirs. (For all his horror of time, Humbert cannot break the habit of linear plots in which incident follows incident in a neat progression toward the inevitable climax—which climax is usually frustrated, however, as events again conspire against him as they did in his interrupted coitus with little Annabel. The multi-murder of Clare Quilty, who refuses to die dramatically and must be shot again and again, is a case in point.) While each chapter of Nabokov's autobiography begins at a successively later date in his life, exposition within the chapter wanders crazily from place to place and from history into the present moment of composition. The book is constructed according to superimposed patterns, arbitrary coincidences of detail are given the same weight as "real" coordinates of time and space. Recognizing the conventionality of all measurements allows one to treat any moment as if it were the present and all places—even the far-off shores of Russia—as if they were here: "our ground-floor telephone, the number of which was 24–43. . . . I wonder by the way, what would happen if I put in a long-distance call from my desk right now? No answer? No such number? No such country? Or the voice of Ustin saying '*moyo pochtenietse*!' (the ingratiating diminutive of 'my respects')? There exist, after all, well-publicized Slavs and Kurds who are well over one hundred and fifty."

The coalescing patterns allow Nabokov to move in two dimensions at once, creating what he himself calls, in a masked appraisal of his style, "the mirrorlike angles of his clear but weirdly misleading sentences." "I reread that passage in the course of correcting the proofs of the various editions, until finally I made a great effort, and the arbitrary spectacles (which

Mnemosyne must have needed more than anybody else) were metamorphosed into a clearly recalled oyster-shell-shaped cigarette case, gleaming in the wet grass at the foot of an aspen on the Chemin du Pendu, where I found on that June day in 1907 a hawkmoth rarely met with so far west, and where a quarter of a century earlier, my father had netted a Peacock butterfly very scarce in our northern woodlands." The autobiographical act, with its spectacles and metamorphoses, overlaps with the objects recollected and represented in the wet grass, and at the same time, another pattern suggests itself, as two generations of Nabokov lepidopterists coincide around that spot at the foot of the aspen.

Since the pattern is all one weave, an unbroken thread (despite ornamental detours and circumstantial differences in time and setting) which is still being woven into the present moment of writing, there is a continuity of tense in Nabokov's own autobiography that is lacking in his parody. Humbert believes—deludes himself into believing—that he has escaped his past and that what he now does and now is as an autobiographer is a wholly different matter. Nabokov treats his present and his past as equally proximate and equally distant from the point of view of the pattern as a whole. "As far back as I remember myself . . . I have been subject to mild hallucinations. Some are aural, others are optical, and by none have I profited much." Nabokov characteristically begins and ends his chapters in the present tense, often arriving back in the present through a series of dizzying last-minute shifts in tense and aspect:

> Thrice, to the mighty heave-ho of his invisible tossers, he would fly up in this fashion, and the second time he would go higher than the first and then there he would be, on his last and loftiest flight, reclining, as if for good, against the cobalt blue of the summer noon, like one of those paradisiac personages who comfortably soar, with such a wealth of folds in their garments, on the vaulted ceiling of a church, while below, one by one, the wax tapers in mortal hands light up to make a swarm of minute flames in the mist of incense, and the priest chants of eternal repose, and funeral lilies conceal the face of whoever lies there, among the swimming lights, in the open coffin.

This passage, in which his father is tossed up into the air by a blanket held by some grateful peasants, also contains the premonition of his father's death—the two are simultaneous, superimposed as the iterative past merges with the habitual present in the timeless architecture of the text. Unlike Humbert Humbert's linear, ongoing process of writing, Nabokov's own act is most often suspended, still, perfective. Each moment connects to all other moments, each is a creative and created nucleus from which the spiraling design of all space and time spreads out, freed from linear necessity. "I have to have all space and all time participate in my emotion, in my mortal love, so that the edge of its mortality is taken off, thus helping me to fight the utter degradation, ridicule, and horror of having developed an infinity of sensation and thought within a finite existence."

A "global perspective" on one's life can be achieved only by abandoning the illusion of reality for the reality of illusion. One cannot see the true pattern without simultaneously attending to one's own point of vantage. Late in his autobiography, Nabokov attacks positivism for its superstitious idolatry of naked fact, its failure to see the medium and mechanisms of knowledge which go along with the objects of knowledge: "the outside of the inside, the whereabouts of the curvature; for every dimension presupposes a medium within which it can act, and if, in the spiral unwinding of things, space warps into something akin to time, and time, in its turn, warps into something akin to thought, then, surely, another dimension follows—a special Space maybe, not the old one, we trust, unless spirals become vicious circles again." Getting out of the vicious circle, Humbert's circle of obsession, is the goal of *Speak, Memory,* and it is also the story it tells. With its fifteen chapters clustering into groups of five, the autobiography becomes an enactment of the spiraling "triadic series" Nabokov so frequently invokes. The overall design of the work seems to reduplicate precisely the progressive movement from space to time to thought, and so on to the fourth dimension.

The first five chapters, beginning not with Nabokov's birth but with the first moment of his self-awareness, cover themes connected with ancestry and infancy. Nabokov plays with primeval allusions and heraldic metaphor in these early sections of his book. "To fix correctly, in terms of time, some of my childhood recollections, I have to go by comets and eclipses, as historians do when they tackle the fragments of a saga." The focus of these chapters is on the estates and servants, the life-style into which Nabokov was born. The individuals who cared for him and who gave him his earliest instructions are depicted, and although the history of these persons—his mother, his uncle, his Swiss governess—is given in entirety, it is still the primary association that is stressed. Each chapter ends upon a note of childish defenselessness and innocent trust. "I see again my school room in Vyra, the blue roses of the wallpaper, the open window. Its reflection fills the oval mirror above the leathern couch where my uncle sits, gloating over a tattered book. A sense of security, of well-being, of summer warmth pervades my memory. That robust reality makes a ghost of the present. The mirror brims with brightness; a bumblebee has entered the room and bumps against the ceiling. Everything is as it should be, nothing will ever change, nobody will ever die."

A natural termination of this opening section seems to be reached with the departure, in chapter five, of the last of his governesses, whom he and his entire family have outgrown. In chapter six there begins a series of adventures—butterfly hunting, "puppy love," school encounters, and the first serious pangs of sexual unrest—which show Nabokov as a young man rather than a protected infant. It is in this setting that Nabokov places his portrait of his father, as though to stress his new relationship with his family, one no longer based on dependence and maternal care. There is also a change in the manner in which inevitable fatalities are brought into focus at the close of a chapter. "Ten years were to pass before a certain night in 1922, at a public lecture in Berlin, when my father shielded the lecturer (his old friend Milyukov) from the bullets of two Russian Fascists and, while vigorously knocking down one of the assassins, was fatally shot by the other. But no shadow was cast by that future event upon the bright stars of our St. Petersburg house; the large, cool hand resting on my head did not quaver, and several lines of play in a difficult chess composition were not blended yet on the board." This moment of temporary security (created by the discovery that his father would not be forced to fight a threatened duel) cannot be extricated from the increasingly complex patterns of life which open up around the adolescent. This period of expectancy and frustration is brought to its poetic closure in chapter ten: "There it lay in wait, a family of serene clouds in miniature, an accumulation of brilliant convolutions, anachronistic in their creaminess and extremely remote; remote but perfect in every detail; fantastically reduced but faultlessly shaped; my marvelous tomorrow ready to be delivered to me."

Into the five chapters which follow, the last chapters of the book, are crowded all the events of Nabokov's maturity before his emigration to the United States. Beginning with the composition of his first poem and the seduction of his first love (whose pseudonym, "Tamara," is perhaps a pun on the dream of a "marvelous tomorrow" which ended the previous chapter), this section is dominated by Nabokov's life in exile. He at first adopts an elegaic stance toward his lost youth, his lost country, his lost first love—but this is only a preliminary, "antithetic" response to the experience of exile. Nabokov quickly modulates nostalgia into something more sophisticated:

> Tamara, Russia, the wildwood grading into old gardens, my northern birches and firs, the sight of my mother getting down on her hands and knees to kiss the earth every time we came back to the country from town for the summer . . . these are the things that fate one day bundled up pell-mell and tossed into the sea, completely severing me from my boyhood. I wonder, however, whether there is really much to be said for more anesthetic destinies, for, let us say, a smooth, safe, small-town continuity of time, with its primitive absence of perspective. . . . The break in my own destiny affords me in retrospect a syncopal kick that I would not have missed for worlds. . . . What it would be actually to see again my former surroundings, I can hardly imagine. Sometimes I fancy myself revisiting them with a false passport, under an assumed name. It could be done.
>
> But I do not think I shall ever do it. I have been dreaming of it too idly and too long.

The separation between what can be dreamed in the fourth dimension and what can be physically sought and held in the first three becomes explicit in this passage. Loss is transcended by a simultaneous gain in insight and even the pattern of a painful destiny can be appreciated aesthetically, for its "perspective" and "syncopation." The last five chapters of *Speak, Memory* are at once the story of Nabokov's departure from all that he had ever known and valued and of his achievement of a new kind of knowledge and a new way of evaluating his world through the twin processes of creation and procreation. The autobiography ends with the birth of his son, in whose nascent experience he is able to see something of his own past, but in a form unavailable to him then. This is a dialectical return and not a mere repetition; it follows the pattern of "Hegel's triadic series" as Nabokov himself has described it. "Three stages may be distinguished . . . corresponding to those of the triad: We can call "thetic" the small curve or arc that initiates the the convolution centrally; "antithetic" the larger arc that faces the first in the process of continuing it; and "synthetic" the still ampler arc that continues the second while following the first along the outer side."

Elegy, nostalgia, the remorseful and wishful thinking of Humbert Humbert, are merely antithetic extensions of the past. In attempting to wrestle with his fate, Humbert is unconsciously "continuing" the destiny he tries to overcome. But by perceving the perceptions of his own "creation"—his son—Nabokov steps outside his own condition and achieves a level of awareness impossible for Humbert. The primordial allusions which appeared in the first chapter of the autobiography reappear in the last, and the birth of consciousness, the genesis of a world, with which *Speak, Memory* began occurs again: "an infant's first journey into the next dimension, the newly established nexus between eye and reachable object, which the career boys in biometrics or in the rat-maze racket think they can explain. It occurs to me that the closest reproduction of the mind's birth obtainable is the stab of wonder that accompanies the precise moment when, gazing at a tangle of twigs and leaves, one suddenly realizes that what had seemed a natural component of that tangle is a marvelously disguised insect or bird." Consciousness constitutes and then transforms the world, creating new patterns with every stage of awareness. Consciousness thus transforms the past, as a new level of perception makes a new configuration accessible. Even at its most remedial level, it is a kind of art, constructing a universe around itself out of whatever relationships it registers. The final words of the autobiography catch consciousness in the act, performing one of its amazing transformations as it penetrates to the "marvelously disguised" ship which is to take Nabokov to America. "There, in front of us . . . where the eye encountered all sorts of strategems, such as pale-blue and pink underwear cakewalking on a clothesline, or a lady's bicycle and a striped cat oddly sharing a rudimentary balcony of cast iron, it was most satisfying to make out among the jumbled angles of roofs and walls, a splended ship's funnel, showing from behind the clothesline as something in a scrambled picture—Find What the Sailor Has Hidden—that the finder cannot unsee once it has been seen." That ship's funnel is as buried in the sentence pattern which holds it as its original could ever have been buried in balconies and clotheslines. The "stab of wonder" which accompanies our recognition of it here is indeed the "closest reproduction of the mind's birth obtainable." But it is obtainable only through art.

There follows this passage, in the revised edition, an index which redistributes all the various themes and preoccupations of the autobiography into various categories. One can see how themes are in fact recirculated through chapter after chapter, through the listing and cross-listing Nabokov here provides. In *Lolita* lists and catalogs provide ironic counterpoint to Humbert's own slavishly sequential plot, but the final rendering of themes at the end of *Speak, Memory,* following as it does immediately upon the passage cited above, appears to be the culmination of Nabokov's autobiographical method. Here we have the gestalt design, hidden and scattered through the pages of the text, gathered together in a final configuration which cannot be "unseen." One is told at the outset, in the foreword to the revised autobiography, that "Through the window of that index / Climbs a rose," and one is thus alerted for the clues to the text's overall design which are to be found there. Three interlocking terms reveal themselves: "pavilion," "stained glass," and "jewels." There is a naturalistic explanation for this cross-indexing, since the pavilion Nabokov writes about does have stained-glass windows, windows where "the sun breaks into geometrical gems." But if one examines the description of this pavilion more closely, one uncovers the following additional bit of evidence: "the pavilion rising midway like a coagulated rainbow, was as slippery as if it had been coated with some dark and in a sense magic ointment. Etymologically, 'pavilion' and 'papilio' are closely related."

This etymological remark is dropped rather obtrusively into the middle of a paragraph with which it apparently has nothing to do. But in conjunction with the index, and in view of the secondary association between the magical, slippery covering of the pavilion and the silken cocoon in which the butterfly accomplishes its metamorphosis a hidden pattern does begin to emerge. Especially if one matches Nabokov's etymological clue with further dictionary research: "*pavilion.* n. (OF *paveillon,* fr. L *papilio* a butterfly . . .) . . . 3. The lower faceted part of a brilliant . . . 5. *Arch.* A light, ornamented building in a park, garden, or the like." Thus the relationship the index suggests between "pavilion," "jewels," and (faceted) "stained glass" is firmly established, and the connecting link is the artful transformation of the butterfly. When we turn back to the text with the full configuration in mind, its architecture comes clearly into view and the crucial balance points in the spiral of consciousness are revealed. In the opening chapter, for example, we find a jewel associated with the birth of consciousness: "a certain beautiful, delightfully solid, garnet-dark crystal egg. . . . I used to chew a corner of the bedsheet until it was thoroughly soaked and then wrap the egg in it tightly, so as to admire and re-lick, the warm, ruddy glitter of the snugly enveloped facets that came seeping through with a miraculous completeness of glow and color. But that was not yet the closest I got to feeding upon beauty."

The jewel-egg is linked with the most primitive form of infant consciousness, the tactile awareness of a "reachable object" which, as Nabokov later informs us on the basis of his observations of his own infant son, is "an infant's first journey into the next dimension." Then in chapter six, initiating the next stage of the autobiography, we encounter Nabokov's first concentrated awareness and pursuit of butterflies. Once again there is an implied reaching out of consciousness, as Nabokov's pursuit of lepidopteral beauty takes him out of space and into time. "My Swallowtail, with a mighty rustle, flew into her face, then made for the open window, and presently was but a golden fleck dipping and dodging eastward, where it lost a tail . . . across Alaska to Dawson, and southward along the Rocky Mountains—to be finally overtaken and captured after a forty-year race, on an immigrant dandelion under an endemic aspen near Boulder."

In chapter eleven, another and final section of the autobiography opens on a view of the pavilion and on Nabokov's first experience of the "numb fury of verse-making." The quest for beauty now turns from pursuit and possession to creation, the effort of a mind to make "that whereby it rejoices." Although his first attempts at poetry are dismal failures, they open for him at least a dim awareness of another dimension of being. "The instant it all took to happen seemed to me not so much a fraction of time as a fissure in it, a missed heartbeat . . . the shock of wonder I had experienced when for a moment heart and leaf had been one." Time and space, the separation between subject and object, "heart and leaf,"—all are obliterated in this instant. Consciousness becomes conscious of itself: "I was richly, serenely aware of my own manifold awareness." Art thus provides the medium, the "special Space" within which thought and memory may act and simultaneously see themselves acting.

The index of Nabokov's autobiography is itself an aesthetic object as well as an aid for recognizing the artwork of the text. In describing the significance of his pavilion, he seems to be describing the principles behind all of *Speak, Memory,* down to its most trivial detail: "I dream of my pavilion at least twice a year. As a rule, it appears in my dreams quite independently of their subject matter, which, of course, may be anything, from abduction to zoolatry. It hangs around, so to speak, with the unobtrusiveness of an artist's signature. I find it clinging to a corner of the dream canvas or cunningly worked into some ornamental part of the picture." Even a simple index turns out to be complex, with the pavilion "cunningly worked into" it, the artist's signature concealed beneath the artless alphabet.

Of course, Humbert Humbert has also left his signature—one might almost say his fingerprints—on the pages of his memoirs, but it is hardly the signature of an artist. Despite the way he constantly calls attention to his own "bon mot" and pauses to congratulate himself on his triumphs as an author, his position is clearly false. "I gently grade my story" he remarks, ostensibly displaying his control, only to have his story take a sudden, grotesque hop or stumble into anticlimax. He shows himself possessed instead of self-possessed, as he "lingers gratefully in that gauze-gray room of memory" reenacting rather than analyzing his obsessions. He has no control over the magic of his tale; he is the enchanted instead of the enchanter, "lured on" by his need "to fix once and for all the perilous magic of nymphets." Traces of his thralldom are everywhere. He writes under a mysterious obligation: "I have to tread carefully. I have to speak in a whisper." His autobiography, like his captive, seems to have escaped him, to act out its own designs, to seek its own protagonist and punish its own villain. "And I have still other smothered memories, now unfolding themselves into limbless monsters of pain." Humbert's claims to omniscience and omnipotence as an author only exacerbate the incongruity, an incongruity that remains even in the final words he writes—"And this is the only immortality you and I may share, my Lolita"—the tentative quality of which, the expressed need for permission, give the lie to their prophetic finery. Moreover, in this final paragraph, Humbert abandons (or is abandoned by) the egomaniacal first person; the narrator is no longer "I" but "one": "one wanted H. H. to exist at least a couple of months longer, so as to have him make you live."

Here at least one sees the naked expression of Humbert's authorial role. Up until the final passage of his manuscript, Humbert has maintained a variety of postures—"sensualist," "reporter," "poet"—which in spite of their disparity at least share the common implication that Humbert is the source and not the instrument of his text. His vacillation between various titles for himself does do great damage to his proposed defense: "But I am no poet. I am only a very conscientious recorder." "Emphatically, no killers are we. Poets never kill." But whether he chooses one or many of these titles, he must have his incarnation, his book must be the extension of his failing heart and his hot breath: "Only in the tritest terms . . . can I describe Lo's features . . . oh, that I were a lady writer who could have her pose naked in a naked light!"

Humbert's final noble gesture, in which he abandons himself to his fate and asks only to be an eternal artifact, a canonized exemplar of romantic love, is ostensibly an act of contrition, even of courage. But it is really only another of his characteristic ploys for the evasion of responsibility, one more failure or refusal to come to terms with the complexity of his situation. "At this or that twist of it I feel my slippery self eluding me, gliding into deeper and darker waters than I care to probe." Humbert continues to accept a simplification of his condition, invoking it with his dying breath. He is always a character in his own eyes, whether as the hero of his own story or the author of his own autobiography. Rather than abandon his sense of personal identity, he surrenders his role as an autobiographer and fictionalizes himself.

Humbert is a carnal travesty, an inversion of the autobiographical performance Nabokov gives us in his own work. While it is true that

Nabokov emphasizes his capacity as a narrator, what he "can" or "could" do, it is an emergent capacity which could not exist without the aid of art. "And now a delightful thing happens. The process of recreating that penholder and the microcosm in its eyelet stimulates my memory to a last effort. I try again to recall the name of Colette's dog—and triumphantly, along those remote beaches, over the glossy evening sands of the past, where each footprint slowly fills up with sunset water, here it comes, here it comes, echoing and vibrating: Floss, Floss, Floss!" This is a peculiarly impersonal achievement. Creation is a new form of consciousness, transcending the limits of individual experience and personal memory even as it uses them. Nabokov describes the way notions of self shattered in the composition of his first poem: "Looking into my own eyes, I had the shocking sensation of finding the mere dregs of my usual self, odds and ends of an evaporated identity which it took my reason quite an effort to gather again in the glass."

As he becomes the narrator of his autobiography, the same process of evaporation seems to occur. "Peasant girls . . . stark naked in shallow water, romped and yelled, heeding me as little as if I were the discarnate carrier of my present reminiscences." The most common words for his narrative identity are spectral—"ghost," "invisible spy." There are also anagrams which rearrange the elements of his worldly identity and leave behind only the mask of a speaker or viewer totally subordinated to his immediate task: "Vivian Bloodmark, a philosophical friend of mine, in later years, used to say that while the scientist sees everything that happens in one point of space, the poet feels everything that happens in one point of time." "Vivian Bloodmark" is of course Vladimir Nabokov—the same anagrammatic signature worked into the canvas of *Lolita*—but it is equally a transformation of Nabokov into an impersonation and an impersonalization. In fact, Nabokov's authorial first person is exchanged freely for the impersonal pronoun: "Mnemosyne, one must admit, has shown herself a very careless girl." "I" is frequently only a position in a pattern. "I still seem to be holding that wisp of iridescence, not knowing exactly where to fit it, while she runs with her hoop ever faster around me and finally dissolves among the slender shadows cast on the graveled path by the interlaced arches of its low looped fence." Just as frequently, there is no actor named at all: "Certain tight parentheses have been opened and allowed to spill their still active contents."

The agent, in figurative terms, behind the autobiographical act is memory, the force of inspiration summoned by the title. "I find the pattern curiously clear, and the images of those tutors appear within memory's luminous disc as so many magic-lantern projections." The narrator does not form the pattern but "finds" it already implicit in memory, playing the same role of "finder" which appears so prominently at the conclusion of the book. The autobiographical act, then, is a transaction between memory and the perception of that memory. At least two levels of awareness are necessary to escape Humbert Humbert's circular obsession with the past; perception must be perceived and memory must be understood. In order to achieve this trick of "manifold awareness," there must be a perfect fit between the material of the text and the act of the autobiographer. Nabokov's creative contribution is not something he claims, like Humbert, to control but rather something he experiences. "The hush of pure memory that (except, perhaps for some chance tinnitus due to the pressure of my own tired blood) I have left undisturbed, and humbly listened to, from the beginning." By constantly and consciously exposing the quality of this, his autobiographical experience, its emotional and perceptual flavor, Nabokov effects a merger between the original moment of cognition and its present recognition. By seeing what he does rather than searching for who he is—an image which could only be his own creation, after all—he establishes a purely epistemological and aesthetic continuity, a coincidence of pattern which is the only version of "recaptured time" he will allow.

As a memoirist, Humbert attempts to reify what Nabokov struggles to evaporate. One of his chief devices for this is the manipulation of his audience. Even if he himself cannot fully believe in his dreamy characterizations of his "movie star handsome" self, perhaps others can be gulled into accepting them and their gullibility in turn will shore up his failing confidence. The style of his interaction with his readers, however, would undo him even if nothing else in his manuscript did. The glance with which he fixes his readers, the alternate accusations and supplications which reach out to us from his pages, are unhealthy, symptomatic of everything he would deny about himself. For example, there is the way he confuses his audience with his own hallucinations. "Humbert Humbert, sweating in the fierce white light, and howled at, and trodden upon by sweating policemen, is now ready to make a further 'statement' (quel mot!)."

Like hallucinations, Humbert's audience is subject to sudden and irrational transformations, from plural to singular, from distant to intimate, from vindictive to disinterested: "Mid-twentieth century ideas concerning child-parent relationship have been considerably tainted by the scholastic rigamarole and standardized symbols of the psychoanalytic racket, but I hope I am addressing myself to unbiased readers." But the intermittent indications of control on Humbert's part are no less disquieting when one observes that it is tyranny rather than self-control that is his aim. When

Humbert describes his audience, rationally and realistically, providing them with facial features, occupations, and preoccupations, he is in fact trying to treat them as characters he has created: "my learned reader (whose eyebrows, I suspect, have by now traveled all the way to the back of his bald head)." Whether he calls to the "winged seraphs of Heaven"—seeing himself surrounded by the envious angels in "Annabel Lee"—or more discretely addresses his prospective mortal jury, Humbert is still engaged in "solipsizing" whomever he encounters. The reader who accepts these titles and fictional characterizations of himself becomes just another lifeless mirage, subject to Humbert's usual treatment of mirages—murder and seduction. We can see Humbert trying to win over the female members of his jury with the same "fatal charm" he has used on all the other women in his life: "Gentlewomen of the jury! Bear with me! Allow me to take just a tiny bit of your precious time!" When, on the other hand, he addresses his masculine readers as "Bruder," we are reminded less of Baudelaire than of Clare Quilty, Humbert's double and his murder victim, whom he also addresses with this term.

Thus, despite the stunning change in Humbert's relation to Lolita, when he ceases writing about her and begins writing to her toward the close of his manuscript we are not—or should not be—convinced:

> And I looked and looked at her, and knew as clearly as I know I am to die, that I loved her more than anything I had ever seen or imagined on earth, or hope for anywhere else. She was only the faint violet whiff and dead leaf echo of the nymphet I had rolled myself upon . . . but thank God it was not that echo alone that I worshipped . . . even if those eyes of hers would fade to myopic fish, and her nipples swell and crack, and her lovely young velvety delicate delta be tainted and torn—even then I would go mad with tenderness at the mere sight of your dear wan face, at the mere sound of your raucous young voice, my Lolita.

Certainly there is more humanity in this address than in all his stylized apostrophes to Lolita elsewhere in the book. But this evocation and the endearments it arouses are connected with the Coalmont scene—a scene which, as I have suggested above, may not have occurred. Moreover, in the pages following this tender exchange with his beloved, Humbert also tries to stage a conversation with his car: "I was soon to be taken out of the car (Hi, Melmoth, thanks a lot, old fellow)." All of Humbert's proposed readers are imaginary, fantasies with whom he can communicate in ways otherwise impossible for him. His address to Lolita is an attempt to make her live, to make her share with him a love she could not participate in as the inert object of his lust; but she remains his projection to the last. "But while the blood still throbs through my writing hand, you are still as much a part of blessed matter as I am, and I can still talk to you from here to Alaska."

Humbert's machinations are defeated by his editor, who quickly countermands all of Humbert's patient and impatient instructions for the reading of his tale:

> Please, reader: no matter your exasperation with the tender-hearted, morbidly sensitive, infinitely circumspect hero of my book, do not skip these essential pages! Imagine me; I shall not exist if you do not imagine me; try to discern the doe in me, trembling in the forest of my own iniquity; let's even smile a little.

> In this poignant personal study there lurks a general lesson; the wayward child, the egotistic mother, the panting maniac—these are not only vivid characters in a unique story: they warn us of dangerous trends.

Humbert's labor of love is lost upon Ray's "serious readers" who despise aesthetics and imaginative details, who search out the "ethical impact the book should have" and skim for the "general lesson" alone. Humbert Humbert will not be imagined and he will therefore cease to exist.

But perhaps Ray and other serious readers have fallen into Humbert's trap, after all. He had pleaded at the start of his manuscript: "Ah, leave me alone in my pubescent park, in my mossy garden. Let them play around me forever. Never grow up." Observers like editor John Ray are not unfamiliar in Humbert's world; he has learned how to fulfill their expectations while simultaneously pursuing his own ends. "I discovered there was an endless source of robust enjoyment in trifling with psychiatrists: cunningly leading them on; never letting them see that you know all the tricks of the trade, inventing for them elaborate dreams, pure classics in style . . . and never allowing them the slightest glimpse of one's real sexual predicament." Thus when Humbert claims that he has found "the secret of durable pigments," one is reminded of his earlier allusion to pigments: "what twists of lust you might see from your impeccable highways if Kumfy Kabins were suddenly drained of their pigments." His paints are meant to obscure rather than communicate his vision, and his "refuge of art" is simply a visionary asylum, a metaphysical repetition of all those psychiatric retreats which give him the privacy he needs for perfecting his delusions rather than being cured of them.

But if Humbert has managed to wall any intruders out of Humberland, he remains uneasy and insecure with his solitude. As the process of his writing goes on, his attempt to put questions into his readers' mouths gives way to his own anxious need to question. Humbert is forced to inquire of his audience, whose will and perception he has earlier attempted to destroy, what his own failing memory can no longer tell him. "Did I ever mention that her bare arm bore the 8 of vaccination? That I loved her hopelessly? That she was only fourteen?" There are over a hundred instances in Humbert's manuscript in which he calls out hysterically to the reader, to the God he does not believe in, to his dead love, and over fifty occasions when he begs for the solution to his dilemma from the very alien intelligences he had hoped to dupe. In the end, he ceases to "prove" anything to his jury, and wistfully dreams that they will save him from the consequences of his own ineluctable ratiocination: "Unless it can be proven to me—to me as I am now, today, with my heart and my beard, and my putrefaction—that in the infinite run it does not matter a jot that a North American girl-child named Dolores Haze had been deprived of her childhood by a maniac, unless this can be proven (and if it can, then life is a joke), I see nothing for the treatment of my misery." Once again Humbert has come to believe in his own fantasies; the audience which he began by creating must now sustain him. But such an audience cannot outlive its creator and must perish, like Lolita, when the book has ended, bringing down Humbert's visionary world and his dream of immortality through art.

Nabokov rejects the notion of a private art. For art there must be two stages, first the fabrication and then the recognition of what has been made—two distinct but intertwined dimensions of awareness. There must therefore be an autonomous audience in whose perception the pattern is recreated and authenticated. The art of autobiography lies not in vain attempts to repossess the past or to secure a miserly hold upon one's own experience, but in freely "turning over" one's life to another: "I did not know then (as I know perfectly well now) what to do with such things—how to get rid of them, how to transform them into something that can be turned over to the reader in printed characters to have *him* cope with the blessed shiver." Only interaction perfects vision and makes seeing and remembering into "what has been seen." There is thus a division of labor between the text of *Speak, Memory* and its ultimate audience, repeating on another level the converging efforts of narrator and memory. Appreciation must transcend what it recognizes—Nabokov therefore does not make characters of his readers.

Indeed, the only persons represented in the book are dead or seen in guises they have now outgrown (the infancy of his son, for example). Nabokov's wife, Vera, is not a character at all but the principal addressee of the text, the "you" with whom the revelations of memory are so often shared. Unlike Lolita, Nabokov's love is never reduced to an object, something to be written about. Her presence is marked only by a pronoun, each occurrence of which is credited to her in the autobiography's index. But the reading public stands at a further remove. They do not share in his experiences or relish his preoccupations uncritically. Their dispassionate view in fact receives his wry encouragement: "I had found last spring a dark aberration of Siever's Carmelite (just another gray moth to the reader). In the ditch, under the bridgelet, a bright-yellow Silvius Skipper hobnobbed with a dragonfly (just a blue libellula to me)."

Nabokov does not allow this audience immediate participant status. There are no attempts to call on them directly, and only rarely does he use the first-person plural in its inclusive sense. Rather than Humbert's commandments, his badgering or mocking questions, the reader of *Speak, Memory* is given only oblique clues, disguised directions which he must decode for himself. "Let visitors trip." Whereas Humbert rises to tyrannize his readers, making them the objects or the victims of his autobiographical act, Nabokov makes beneficiaries out of each member of his variegated public. "The following passage is not for the general reader, but for the particular idiot who, because he lost a fortune in some crash, thinks he understands me." Even his disdain is treated as something acted out for the benefit of his reader, and not something he inflicts upon him.

The magical space between artificer and audience also means that Nabokov cannot predict, as Humbert believes he can, the actions of his audience or prescribe their responses as John Ray, Jr., might. Only vulgar readers have predictable responses. "To avoid hurting the living or distressing the dead, certain proper names have been changed. These are set off by quotation marks in the index. Its main purpose is to list for my convenience some of the people and themes connected with my past years. Its presence will annoy the vulgar but may please the discerning." The index, of course, does contain keys to understanding the formal pattern of his text, but these are keys to be discovered and not thrust rudely into unwilling hands.

Since the transactional nature of the autobiographical act requires that Nabokov himself take up the role of an observer and an auditor, a member of memory's audience, many of the infrequent imperatives and questions which appear in the text are directed by the autobiographer to himself, or to the source of his own inspiration. "And let me not leave out the moon—

for surely there must be a moon." "How readily Mr. Cummings would sit down on a stool, part behind with both hands his—what? was he wearing a frock coat? I see only the gesture—and proceed to open the black tin paintbox." Most of the remaining questions, orders, exclamations, are in fact chameleons, requests for information which turn magically into acts of creation, effecting the very thing they purport to doubt. "There our child kneeled motionless to be photographed . . . against the scintillation of the sea . . . silvery blue, with great patches of purple-blue farther out, caused by warm currents in collaboration with and corroboration of (hear the pebbles rolled by the withdrawing wave?) eloquent old poets and their smiling similes." Proclamations turn inward on themselves before they ever reach the reader: "The curse of battle and toil leads man back to the boar, to the grunting beast's crazy obsession with the search for food. . . . Toilers of the world, disband! Old books are wrong. The world was made on a Sunday."

It is only by means of such disguise that the role of the audience can become a pure potentiality, a part which may be taken up by any willing imagination, including the autobiographer's. Nabokov imposes no limitations on who may play his game; the act of discovery may take place for anyone, at any time or place. Any reader of *Speak, Memory* may become a "finder," and in doing so achieve a position that is the intellectual and aesthetic equivalent of Nabokov's own. There can be no condescension, no giving away of secrets, if the reader is to have what alone derives from an autonomous act of creation—"the stab of wonder that accompanies the precise moment" when one penetrates "a marvelous disguise." This alone will turn life into a pattern, impervious to time and transcending personal identity, something to be found again by each and every attentive reader of the autobiography. "Now and then, shed by a blossoming tree, a petal would come down, down, down, and with the odd feeling of seeing something neither worshipper nor casual spectator ought to see, one would manage to glimpse its reflection which swiftly—more swiftly than the petal fell—rose to meet it; and for the fraction of a second, one feared that the trick would not work . . . but every time the delicate union did take place, with the magic precision of a poet's word meeting halfway his, or a reader's recollection."

ELLEN PIFER

Consciousness, Real Life, and Fairy-tale Freedom: King, Queen, Knave

In the foreword to the 1968 English translation of *King, Queen, Knave,* first published in Russian in 1928, Nabokov wrote: "Of all my novels this bright brute is the gayest. Expatriation, destitution, nostalgia had no effect on its elaborate and rapturous composition." At this time, Nabokov said, he was dissatisfied with the " 'human humidity,' *chelovecheskaya vlazhnost*', permeating [his] first novel *Mashen'ka,*" published in 1926. If novels, as E. M. Forster remarked, are "sogged with humanity," then Nabokov apparently set out to cure his second novel of this chronic condition. For *King, Queen, Knave* he chose "a set of exclusively German characters," although he claimed he "spoke no German, had no German friends, had not read a single German novel either in the original, or in translation." In art as well as nature, Nabokov pointed out, such "a glaring disadvantage may turn out to be a subtle protective device." From what dangers, we may ask, did the young writer find it necessary to protect his fiction? Ought we to assume, like those who regard Nabokov as exclusively an aesthete, that the emotional detachment sought in *King, Queen, Knave* is an early sign of his indifference to human psychology or "reality" as a subject for art?

The term "human humidity" suggests the novel's extraordinary capacity for creating sentimental effects, for moving its readers to tears. We are frequently "carried away" by novels, which draw us, unconscious and uncritical, into the web of their expansive worlds. The reader experiences an immediate and unchallenged identification with the fictional characters, en-

From *Nabokov and the Novel.* © 1980 by the President and Fellows of Harvard College. Harvard University Press, 1980.

tangled in the familiar conflicts and circumstances of daily life. Existence may be ultimately mysterious to us, but the daily, concrete living out of our existence becomes so familiar in its repetition that it ends by appearing inevitable and even predictable most of the time. The novel, containing more of life in its everyday, repetitive aspect than any other literary form, has the same power to present itself as something familiar and natural. For this reason, I believe, Nabokov saw a connection between the excessive "humidity" of his first novel and its quotidian familiarity: "The émigré characters I had collected in that display box [*Mashen'ka*] were so transparent to the eye of the era that one could easily make out the labels behind them" (foreword). The novel's "human humidity" and the reader's uncritical identification with literary characters both thrive on the generally accepted ideas that circulate among people living in a particular historical era. To those buffeted by the tremendous social and political storms of the early twentieth century, and especially to the Russian émigré population scattered throughout Europe, the influence of history on the individual's immediate life threatened to be overwhelming. By creating characters with whom he had, "ethnopsychically," nothing in common, Nabokov elected to distance himself in *King, Queen, Knave* from the émigrés natural preoccupation with social reality. Here it is important to understand that a lack of social identification with his characters does not necessarily signal Nabokov's shrinking interest in human psychology. His impatience with social "labels" reveals, on the contrary, a desire to create character in a new way. Nabokov's break was not with humanity or the human predicament but with the novelist's traditional regard for historical process as the modern form of fate.

Political revolutions, technological innovations, and social conditions have been grist for generations of novelists. As Mary McCarthy has said, novels are obliged to "carry the news." She adds: "We do really (I think) expect a novel to be true, not only true to itself, like a poem, or a statue, but true to actual life. . . . We not only make believe we believe a novel, but we do substantially believe it, as being continuous with real life . . . and the presence of fact in fiction, of dates and times and distances, is a kind of reassurance—a guarantee of credibility." Denying such guarantees from the outset, Nabokov said of his second novel, "I might have staged *KQKn* in Rumania or Holland [instead of Berlin]" (foreword). With studied detachment he rejects the diligent pursuit of "credibility" engaged in by novelists from Cervantes to Tolstoy. Challenging "the accepted notion of a 'modern world' continuously flowing around us," Nabokov found such historical postulations to belong "to the same type of abstraction as say, the 'quaternary period' of paleontology." In opposition to these abstract historical classifications he posited the more penetrating reality of specific imagination: "What I feel to be the real modern world is the world the artist creates . . . by the very act of his shedding, as it were, the age he lives in."

Nabokov's account of the artist "shedding" the age he lives in, like a reptile emerging from a dead skin, calls for no withdrawal from the world but a renewed confrontation with it. The artist conceives reality afresh only after he has deliberately separated himself from the apparent world formulated every day by those who direct the current interests and affairs of society. A novelist who aims, in Mary McCarthy's words, to "carry the news" of this world winds up dragging the carapace of social-historical formulation along with him. In *King, Queen, Knave,* on the other hand, Nabokov deliberately estranged himself from the generalizing influences and historical postulations of his era. His discovery of the "fairytale freedom" inherent in treating "an unknown milieu" led to his "gradual inner disentanglement" from the immediate pressures and assumptions of émigré life and, as a consequence, from the novelist's inherited obligations to social reality. By disowning the pursuit of literal "credibility," regarded as essential by generations of novelists, Nabokov was able, moreover, to challenge those preconceptions of reality which, consciously or not, most novelists disseminate with the very "news" they seek to carry. Turning our attention to *King, Queen, Knave,* the first of Nabokov's flagrantly artificial worlds, we shall begin to examine the terms of this challenge.

Nabokov's declared detachment from his characters in *King, Queen, Knave* signals, as I have suggested, a break with formal tradition. Critics, noting this detachment and taking into account the novel's title, have found its characters to be mere "cardboard figures." Such labels only serve to obscure the provocative nature of Nabokov's methods of character depiction in this novel. Franz, for example, the young knave, is far too intensely rendered a character to be dismissed, at the outset, as a paper figure. He becomes, in Nabokov's hands, a most ironic representative of *l'homme moyen sensuel*—that recurrent subject and special pride of the nineteenth-century novelist. The stereotypical notion of the average man, whose existence we regard as primarily *sensuel* and carnal rather than psychic or spiritual, is exploded by Nabokov's radical depiction of "physical Franz." Existence for Franz, it is true, consists almost entirely of physical sensations, but those sensations crowd into a void where refining and synthesizing human consciousness ought vigorously to operate. Franz is perpetually afraid of existence because his perception is clogged with indiscriminate sensory data that threaten, at any time, to overwhelm his psyche and set up a tyranny of hateful impressions. Any new, unsavory impression impinging on Franz's cowardly consciousness may unlock a psychic "chamber of horrors," may flood his mind with disgusting images of random physical life. Involuntarily, and much to his horror, Franz may vividly recall a dog he has seen vomiting, a child sucking on "a filthy thing resembling a baby's pacifier," or an old man in a streetcar firing "a clot of mucus into the ticket collector's hand." When such images well up in Franz's victimized psyche, he is overcome by nausea. In Franz's case, predominantly carnal existence is shown to be neither normal nor average. "Physical Franz" is psychically ill.

Franz's moments of well-being also originate in physical sensation: "Warm, warmly flowing happiness filled physical Franz to the brim, pulsated in wrist and temple, pounded in his breast, and issued from his finger in a ruby drop when he pricked himself accidentally at the store." In this description, Nabokov cleverly subverts, while making use of, a familiar cliché. Human happiness is described as "brimming over" or "filling" the one who is happy. Based on a worn metaphor, the cliché locates the ephemeral state of happiness in the physical sensations that mental joy triggers in the body. Thus happiness is identified as physically warm and expansive, like the play of an excited pulse and mounting blood pressure. But Franz's experience of happiness is, quite literally, exposed as sheer physical sensation. Happiness *is* the "warmly flowing" blood that courses through his body, concretely issuing in a bright red drop.

In similar fashion, Franz's memory and imagination prove to be mere instruments of involuntary, quite painful sensation. "His recollections of school seemed always to be dodging away from possible, impossible, contacts with the grubby, pimply, slippery skin of some companion or other pressing him to join in a game or eager to impart some spitterish secret." Franz's memory "dodges" from contact with memories that oppress him like bodies. For him even a secret, that exclusively human form of intimate communication, is a "spitterish" physical thing.

A more violent assault on Franz's senses takes place at the opening of the novel. He is comfortably seated in the third-class compartment of a moving train when a man with a disfigured face suddenly enters from the corridor. As soon as Franz sees the passenger's face, he is overcome by dread and nausea. The stranger's abnormal features reduce "physical Franz" to a state of sickening fear: "Most of the nose had gone or had never grown. To what remained of its bridge the pale parchment-like skin adhered with a sickening tightness; the nostrils had lost all sense of decency and faced the flinching spectator like two sudden holes, black and asymmetrical." The flawed face is a terrible apparition of the confounding physical reality that tyrannizes Franz. Those "black" and "sudden holes"—in place of ordinary features—suggest the black unknown yawning beneath the apparently arbitrary flux of physical phenomena. A flaw in the fabric of reality, the freakish face opens a chink through which Franz glimpses something terrifying. Characteristically, his fear takes the form of acute and painful physical sensation: "His tongue felt repulsively alive; his palate nastily moist. His memory opened its gallery of waxworks, and . . . at its far end somewhere a chamber of horrors awaited him." The gross ironies and accidents of carnal existence—like the old man spitting mucus into the conductor's hand and the child innocently sucking on what appears to be a discarded prophylactic—fill Franz with insane horror. In terms of our creatural existence, all human beings are ultimately as helpless as the old man and the unwitting child. We are easily made the fools of life's little jokes. Franz, a virtual prisoner of wayward physical life, is in this sense as in others the fool, or knave, of the novel.

While Franz shudders in repulsion at the hateful apparition of this monstrous face, the other passengers in the compartment are singularly unaffected: "And worst of all, the old ladies ignoring their foul neighbor [the noseless man] munched their sandwiches and sucked on fuzzy sections of orange." Repulsed even by the texture of the fruit, Franz propels himself into the second-class compartment of a wealthy businessman and his attractive wife. Dreyer, the businessman (who turns out, by Nabokov's design, to be Franz's uncle), eventually leaves the car in search of a newspaper; returning, he passes by the man with the deformed nose whose face has terrified Franz: "Glancing at him as he passed, Dreyer saw the grinning face of a grown man with the nose of a baby monkey. 'Curious,' thought Dreyer, 'ought to get such a dummy to display something funny.' " Where Franz perceives a foul and terrifying monster, Dreyer sees just a funny nose. Both Franz and Dreyer encounter the passenger within the same temporal and spatial dimensions; yet the contrasting effects his deformity has on these two characters makes the stranger an oddly relative phenomenon. He terrifies no one but Franz; in fact, the other passengers hardly notice him. Dreyer, on the other hand, is amused by the freakish nose and promptly considers the possibilities such a funny face has as a display model in his department store. One man's torture is another man's toy, and the reader is left with the job of assessing the problematical "objective" reality of this monster-clown, so dramatically metamorphosed by the contrary perceptions of Franz and his uncle Dreyer.

Many of Nabokov's critics, I am sure, would regard the noseless man's appearance in the novel as compromised, an obvious manifestation of the author's preference for manipulated artifice rather than convincing characterization. Disdaining the novelist's traditional regard for causal laws and verisimilitude, the author arbitrarily introduces the noseless passenger into the text. He merely contrives a handy coincidence so that Franz may join the Dreyers in their second-class compartment and get on with the plot. Nabokov, however, would have us assess the significance of his literary arrangements according to different criteria. Like everything else in his fiction, Nabokov's characters are overt creations of their author. Born of his perception, figured forth in words, assigned their own characteristic perceptions—their status is literary in a radical sense. They live not as reflections of a social-historical era but as representatives of human consciousness and its laws. For Nabokov, our "being aware of being aware of being" defines the essence of human existence and distinguishes man's life from the beast's. The universe we inhabit is not an objectively measured Cartesian machine but a "universe embraced by consciousness." In Nabokov's view, consciousness—and not the dynamics of planetary bodies or historical evolution—"is the only real thing in the world and the greatest mystery of all."

Because language is the primary medium of consciousness, literature is in a special position to explore the nature of conscious life. In literature all representations of matter are distillations of perception; the only reality is that which has been created through acts of imaginative invention. Exploiting this fact of literary life, Nabokov examines the process by which individual consciousness creates the character of the perceived world. This is, of course, a radical inversion of the methods of formal realism, whereby fiction seeks authenticity by approximating our general notions of reality; such fiction may not deviate too far from what we recognize as familiar and plausible. In Nabokov's world, on the other hand, Franz, Dreyer, and the reader may all agree that the noseless man's face is deformed—lacking the ordinary configuration of bridge and nostrils. Beyond this, however, Nabokov does not labor to convince us of the probable appearance of the noseless man in an objective universe; rather, he is interested in the specific life that flows from the operation of uniquely delineated perception. Authenticity does not derive from Nabokov's convincing us of the probable existence of such noseless freaks, although he might have arranged things in this way. (Trains and buses are likely places for a novelist's characters to encounter the bizarre flotsam and jetsam of humanity.) In *King, Queen, Knave,* the noseless man's appearance is rendered incongruous, not natural. Rather than offer an explanation for his appearance in the novel, Nabokov heightens our awareness of the artifice, intentionally undermining the realistic illusion of causality and normalcy. The author shows his hand, but what it holds remains a mystery. He focuses his art at the point where general explanations for reality dissolve. Reality presents itself at the point where Franz's and Dreyer's perceptions diverge, not where they converge. If consciousness is "the only real thing in the world," then the novelist's obligations to reality are going to be radically defined. Nabokov strives to demonstrate how each of his characters particularizes and in a sense "makes strange" the general, familiar world men agree on for the sake of ontological comfort or social expediency. The "only real, authentic worlds," he once said, are "those that seem unusual." Reality is not what appears so inevitable and familiar that we may easily identify with a literary character and his perceptions.

In a well-known essay, "Art as Device" ("Iskusstvo, kak priem"), Viktor Shklovsky, the Russian Formalist critic, examines the "general laws of perception," finding that "as one's actions grow habitual, they become automatic." To illustrate this process, Shklovsky cites the following passage from Tolstoy's diary:

> I was dusting a room and, walking around, approached the divan and couldn't remember whether or not I had dusted it. Since these movements are habitual and unconscious, I could not remember and felt that it was already impossible to remember; so that, if I had dusted and forgotten—that is, had acted unconsciously, then it was the same as if I had not. If someone conscious had been looking on, then the fact could be established. If, however, no one was looking, or was looking on unconsciously, if the whole complex life of many people proceeds unconsciously, then it is as though this life had never been.

Commenting on Tolstoy's observations, Shklovsky remarks: "What is called art exists to restore the sensation of life, to make one feel things, to make the stone stony. The purpose of art is to impart the sensation of things as a form of perception rather than knowledge. The device of art is to make things 'strange,' to make form difficult—which increases the difficulty and duration of perception, since in art the process of perceiving is an end in itself and should be prolonged."

The "difficult" nature of Nabokov's highly wrought artifices, the demands they make on the reader's perceptions, obviously fulfill Shklovsky's requirements for art. Less obvious, perhaps, is the fact that Nabokov, like Tolstoy, regarded the vital "process of perceiving" as fundamental to *life* as well as art. What Shklovsky identifies as the process of *ostranenie*, commonly translated "defamiliarization," operates within Nabokov's fiction as a psychological and epistemological principle. Artifice, rather than opposing life, is deployed by Nabokov to renew the reader's perception of reality—by estranging that perception from habitual formulations. As the act of perception becomes, in Nabokov's fiction, the focal point for examining reality, the general world, whose existence we automatically assume, tends to fade into the relatively unreal. From this vantage point, we can see how misleading it is to exempt Nabokov's characters from reality because they are deprived of apparent autonomy or of a seemingly objective social environment. The specific life or reality of Nabokov's characters depends, first and foremost, on the peculiar nature and quality of their rendered perceptions.

As I have already noted in the case of Franz and his uncle Dreyer, the characters of *King, Queen, Knave* have widely divergent perceptions and responses to their environment. Further events in the novel are, like the noseless man's appearance on the train, arranged by Nabokov to demonstrate the primary role of human consciousness in shaping reality. At one point, for example, Dreyer, his wife, Martha, and Franz, now Martha's clandestine lover, all attend a variety show together. Japanese trapeze artists, a juggler, and a performing seal regale the audience; then, after the intermission, a female violinist dressed "in silver shoes and a spangled evening dress" plays on a "luminous" violin with a "star-flashing bow." For the duration of the song, the violinist, her clothes, and the enlisted musical instrument are flooded by the alternating pink and green of busy spotlights. Martha and Franz quickly lose themselves in a swoon of sentimental music and sexual longing, but Dreyer abruptly interrupts them with a disgusted exclamation:

> [The violinist's] playing was languorous and really delicious and suffused Martha with such excitement, such exquisite sadness that she half-closed her eyes and found Franz's hand in the darkness; and he experienced the same sensation—a poignant rapture in harmony with their love. The musical phantasmagoria (as that item was listed) sparkled and swooned, the violin sang and moaned, the pink and green were joined by blue and violet—and then Dreyer could stand it no longer.
>
> "I have my eyes and ears closed," he said in a weepy whisper, "let me know when this obscene abomination is over."

For a startled moment the swooning lovers fear they have been discovered—only to realize that the "obscene abomination" offending Dreyer's sensibilities is not their adulterous performance (to which he remains blind) but the trashy one occurring on stage. The amplification of banal effects by the changing floodlights betrays a form of degraded consciousness, employing technical means to simulate the magic of imagination. For Dreyer, the violinist's performance is a travesty of human sensibility. Like all sham art, the light show lulls or deadens consciousness with its effects. Appetite and instinct may be aroused in this way, but never imagination. Disgusted as he is, Dreyer does not recognize the full implications of the violinist's banal performance. He does not sense the adulterers' "poignant rapture" nor the lust whetted in them by the sickly music.

The concluding entertainment at the variety show is a movie, in which agile chimpanzees ludicrously mimic human behavior: "On the flickering screen . . . a chimpanzee in degrading human clothes performed human actions degrading to an animal. Martha laughed heartily, remarking: 'Just look how smart he is!' Franz clucked his tongue in amazement, and insisted in all seriousness that it was a dwarf in disguise." As Nabokov's language here indicates, both man and beast are degraded by the circus imitation of one by the other. The mechanical reproduction of human gestures and activity does not begin to approximate the essential quality of human existence. That essence resides in consciousness, which cannot be simulated by beast or machine. Taking delight in this bumbling parody, Martha and Franz reveal themselves to be dangerously complacent about their own humanity. Franz's knavish contention that the bicycling chimp must be a dwarf in disguise bespeaks his own meager conception of the human.

Degraded sensibility like Franz's is unable to assign proper priority to human consciousness. Franz's terror of existence partly arises from his having relinquished consciousness as a source of order, knowledge, and transcendence in the world. Franz lives in dread of the "chamber of horrors" that threatens to release, at any moment, a flood of involuntary images in his captive mind. By contrast, the creative exercise of consciousness signals a triumph of human imagination over the forces of darkness: "The bright mental image . . . conjured up by a wing-stroke of the will; *that* is one of the bravest movements a human spirit can make," avows Nabokov in *Speak, Memory*. Franz's passive submission to Martha's domineering will, even when she devises a scheme to murder his uncle, is simply another aspect of his cowardly perception. True consciousness is a gift realized by its operation—not by mere possession; lacking exercise, the faculty atrophies. In Nabokov's view, human beings may forfeit their humanity out of torpor, sloth, or lack of will. As he once said, "Brains must work the hard way or else lose their calling and rank."

What Nabokov seeks to depict, above all, is the process by which a character's consciousness establishes its own "rank" as an image of psychic existence. An example of Nabokov's techniques for accomplishing this occurs in a passage describing Martha's adultery with Franz. Alluding to his literary predecessors, Flaubert and Tolstoy, who also wrote about adulteresses, the narrator points out that Martha is "no Emma and no Anna. In the course of her conjugal life she had grown accustomed to grant her favors to her wealthy protector [Dreyer, her husband] with such skill, with such calculation, with such efficient habits of physical practice, that she who thought herself ripe for adultery had long grown ready for harlotry." Here Nabokov's editorial comments demonstrate that the laws he is concerned with do not pertain to society but to human consciousness. In terms of these internal laws—as opposed to the public sphere of social convention—Martha's conjugal practices have already descended to a level of experience far baser than that of adultery. Nabokov's emphasis here is on the spirit rather than the letter (or social "label") of Martha's actions. Her marital status does not exempt her from "harlotry"; quite the opposite, Martha's relations with Dreyer are an even bolder form of barter. While the prostitute sells her body with indifference, Martha actively loathes the man whose attentions *she* endures for the sake of material comfort.

A generous, easy-going, totally self-absorbed man, Dreyer has inspired Martha's disgust long before she becomes involved with Franz. Dreyer's behavior, his very existence seem to threaten the tidy blueprint of reality Martha has forged in her mind. Everything about Dreyer offends her rigid sense of propriety. He unsettles the deadly order of her world with "freakish twists" of surprising life. The unexpected, the unusual—hence unique and real—is to Martha an aberration. On the train, for example, she looks on in vexation while Dreyer is reading a book of poetry: "Life should proceed according to plan, straight and strict, without freakish twists and wiggles. An elegant book is all right on a drawing-room table. . . . But to imbibe and relish . . . poems, if you please . . . in an expensive binding . . . a person who calls himself a businessman cannot, must not, dare not act like that." A moment earlier, briefly distracted from his reading, Dreyer gazes at the outside world which "avidly, like a playful dog waiting for that moment, darted up to him with a bright bound. But pushing Tom away affectionately, Dreyer again immersed himself in his anthology of verse." For Martha, meanwhile, "that frolicsome radiance was simply the stuffy air in a swaying railway car. It is supposed to be stuffy in a car: that is customary and therefore good." Here, indeed, is a radical inversion of the realist's convincingly rendered, putatively objective environment. Both Dreyer's and Martha's versions of reality are shown to be constructs, or fusions, of mind and matter. The material properties of the compartment are ultimately psychic in nature, taking shape in the consciousness that endows them with personal significance.

In contrast to Martha's dull blueprint, Dreyer's world is as bright and gay as an affectionate puppy. His active perception quickly transforms the outside world into a "playful dog" that he affectionately pushes away. In short order metaphorical Tom will actually materialize in the form of Dreyer's pet Alsatian, whose irrepressible spirits meet with as much disapproval from Martha as Dreyer's own. In the succeeding chapter, Tom will emerge "with a bound from the sunny haze, becoming alive, warm, active, and nearly knocking [Franz] off his chair." Tom's association with Dreyer's sunny and warm disposition continues throughout the novel until Martha, mistakenly anticipating the death of her husband, has the gardener do away with his dog. Like Tom, Dreyer's world is a highly personal metaphor, something intimate and gay, which he has fused from his own loving, if self-centered, attention. Martha's world is no metaphor but a dreary composite drawn from the most accessible and acceptable versions of reality provided by convention. In the railway car Martha is excluded from the "frolicsome radiance" that charms Dreyer in his world; she suffers, instead, the discomfort she expects. To find anything *but* stuffy air in the train's close quarters would constitute a threat to her mental security. According to the same self-defeating principle, Martha is duly irritated by the weather: " 'Autumn, rain,' said Martha slamming her handbag shut. 'Oh, just a drizzle,' Dreyer corrected her softly."

Employing self-conscious artifice to break with the novelist's traditional obligations to reality, Nabokov challenges the "half-hearted materialist" who conceives a split between mind and matter, between consciousness and the allegedly real world of objective fact. He deemed himself an "indivisible monist," and explained the term in this way: "Monism, which implies a oneness of basic reality, is seen to be divisible when, say, 'mind' sneakily splits away from 'matter' in the reasoning of a muddled monist or half-hearted materialist." Because true reality, in Nabokov's view, is the essentially unique re-creation of the world through individual perception, his characters are made accountable for the quality of their reality. True, they are confined within the patterns of literary artifice: the fiction itself is a fusion of the author's individual consciousness and the "matter" it has shaped. Despite the strictures of artifice, however, Nabokov's creatures are shown to possess a certain autonomy with respect to reality that the formal realist may not grant. As the realist labors to create a convincing illusion of objective reality, his tendency is to emphasize the overwhelming historical and social forces that engulf the individual's life. Mary McCarthy's description of *War and Peace* reflects this emphasis: "Indeed, it could be said that the real plot of *War and Peace* is the struggle of the characters not to be immersed, engulfed, swallowed up by the landscape of fact and 'history' in which they, like all human beings, have been placed: freedom (the subjective) is in the fiction, and necessity is in the fact." By demonstrating that each man's world—that privately created construct—is more "subjective" than we commonly think, Nabokov, the alleged literary despot, affords his "galley slaves" a potential freedom that is inaccessible to the characters of formal realism. In the case of Martha and Dreyer, for example, we note that Martha receives from the "anthropomorphic deity" impersonated by Nabokov both the rain and the stuffy air she warrants. These elements of her environment take shape from her character, or psyche, and are part of her fate. Nabokov scrupulously refrains from inflicting them on Dreyer.

In the vastly different landscapes men create for themselves, they may be prisoners or kings. "Physical Franz" is a victim of every passing impression threatening to unleash the "horrors" that lurk in the depths of his passive psyche. Martha is a prisoner in a different sense. While Franz is the slave of claustrophobic sensation, Martha is afflicted by death. As she gazes through the train window at the scenery outside, Martha finds not only Dreyer but the "flicker of woods in the window" highly "irksome." Her bored and loveless spirit creates a virtual prison of her surroundings: "The sun penetrated her eyelids with solid scarlet, across which luminous stripes moved in succession (the ghostly negative of the passing forest), and a replica of her husband's cheerful face, as if slowly rotating toward her, got mixed up in this barred redness, and she opened her eyes with a start." The play of light and shadow here creates "luminous stripes" that suggest the bars of a prison cell. As many critics have pointed out, reflecting surfaces—mirrors, windows, water—frequently signal the operation of consciousness in Nabokov's fiction. The world we perceive is a reflection, made up of images formed by the lens of the eye, conveyed to the retina, and registered in the mind of the observer. The "ghostly negative of the passing forest" reflected on the underside of Martha's lids suggests the deadly world created in her dormant consciousness. Even more striking is the image of Dreyer's "cheerful face" whirling through this "barred redness." As it gets "mixed up" in the ghostly landscape, the face—like a luminous red sun in a Magritte painting—startles Martha out of semi-sleep with its disturbing life. The image later recurs in transmuted form, but with the same disturbing impact, in Franz's myopic and drunken perception: "Dreyer, slowly rotating before him like a flaming wheel with human arms for spokes, began discussing the job awaiting Franz." Even before they have any motive to murder Dreyer, Martha and Franz struggle with the mysterious source of energy that emanates from his vital being.

Dreyer has a lively internal life that remains vexingly inaccessible to Martha's despotic will. Hating him for eluding the strictures of her world as he "removes himself" with a book, Martha initially projects her destructive impulses on the book itself: "How nice it would be to pluck that book out of his hands and lock it up in a suitcase." As Nabokov later demonstrates in *Invitation to a Beheading,* all prison guards partake of Martha's prison mentality; they want to lock up things and people. After she meets Franz, Martha's impulse to get rid of Dreyer's book quickly mushrooms into an obsession to be rid of its reader. Both thing and person become hateful objects, obstacles to her program for existence. With psychological acumen, Nabokov illustrates the murderer's degraded form of logic and its origin in dehumanizing thought. The first stage of murder is always an act of psychological, rather than physical, violence. The murderer's initial assault on his victim takes the form of deadly mental abstraction: "He now stood in her path, in her plain, straight path, like a solid obstacle, that ought somehow to be removed to let her resume her plain straight existence. How dared he enforce upon her the complications of adultery?" Hoping to get rid of this obstacle, Martha mentally reduces her husband to "the thing called Dreyer."

Unaware that his wife is mentally extracting the life from him, Dreyer is preoccupied with more speculative questions concerning life and death. He hires an ingenious Inventor to create lifelike automannequins for his department store. Ultimately, however, the banality of the results leaves him disenchanted with such mechanical reproductions. Dummies prove to be just that: "This time the woman [dummy] drifted past on slow roller skates, . . . her legs rigid, her profile like that of a skull, her décolleté revealing a tricot smudged by the hasty hands of her maker. . . . Dreyer wondered what aberration of mind had ever made him accept, let alone admire, those tipsy dummies." For Dreyer, the dummies are hopelessly inert approximations of human vitality. The mystery of creation eludes the mechanical techniques of the Inventor, who "ran into some trouble [with the female dummy], a rib failed to function properly." To Dreyer he quips, "After all, I need more time than God did, Mr. Director." The Inventor attempts to rival God's creation, and fails. Paradoxically, his lackluster female dummy is a striking correlative for Martha's mechanical consciousness—only a shallow approximation of the human.

Despite its mechanical qualities, dehumanized consciousness has an inverse effect on Martha's animal spirits. As her hatred for Dreyer intensifies, Martha's appetite for Franz grows voracious: "She leaned toward him, took the glossy-headed half-bared [chicken] bone out of his hand . . . began gnawing at it with relish . . . her lips growing fuller and brighter." She kisses Franz "as if she were about to give him a gentle bite" and "[takes] possession of his lips." She says to him, "I can certainly touch you, and nibble you, and even swallow you whole if I want." Graphically feeding on Franz's sexual organs, Martha pits their "life" against her husband's. Seated on the bed with naked Franz, she says of Dreyer: "And you know lately he's been so terribly alive. Is he stronger than we? Is he more alive than this, and this, and *this*?" In the course of the novel, Martha becomes a kind of vampire, and "physical Franz" her ghoulish food: "Without his obedient lips and young body she could not live more than a single day."

Whether feeding on her lover's feeble life or devising ways to rid Dreyer of his, Martha is gradually overtaken by the predatory forces of death. Dreyer, meanwhile, continues to relish the abundant signs of life all around him. On his way to view the Inventor's automannequins, he enjoys a walk in the sunlight, exclaiming to himself, "What fun it was to be alive." For him, life is rich in possibility, mystery, and delight: "All those people in the street scurrying by, waiting at streetcar stops: what a bunch of secrets, astonishing professions, incredible recollections." As the murder plot thickens, Martha's strenuous effort to turn Dreyer into a dummy only dramatize his infinite and inimitable life: "Dreyer was spreading out monstrously before her, like a conflagration in a cinema picture. Human life, like fire, was dangerous and difficult to extinguish; but, as in the case of fire, there must be, there simply must be, some universally accepted, natural method of quenching a man's fierce life. . . . Dreyer filled the whole bedroom, the whole house, the whole world."

Before the murderer's shrinking humanity, the vitality of the victim appears to expand limitlessly. Their relationship is, as Charles Kinbote notes in *Pale Fire,* strictly "anti-Darwinian": "The one who kills is *always* his victim's inferior." By depriving his victim of life, the murderer paradoxically forfeits his own powers of vital existence. Gazing at the photographs of numerous murderers, Dreyer notes their "pasty faces" and "the puffy faces of their victims who in death came to resemble them." The victim's corpse is the murderer's true twin, a palpable reflection of his deathly condition. Illustrating this "anti-Darwinian" rule of consciousness, Dreyer, the intended victim, survives the plot while his would-be assassins perish. Martha dies of pneumonia at the end of the novel; long before this, Franz has become a mere automaton: "Vertigo became a habitual and pleasurable state, an automaton's somnambulic languor, the law of his existence."

By consigning his consciousness to Martha's murderous will, Franz does become a kind of puppet, remaining so until Martha's death at the end of the novel. But to regard Franz as a puppet, or "cardboard figure," from the outset—just because he is Nabokov's character, confined to a world of artifice—only blurs the distinctions Nabokov makes throughout the novel between real and simulated human life. Those distinctions are emphasized in the following passage, where Franz thinks to himself:

> There was the dangerous irksome Dreyer who walked, spoke, tormented him, guffawed; and there was a second, purely schematic Dreyer, who had become detached from the first—a stylized playing card, a heraldic design—and it was this that had to be destroyed. Whatever method of annihilation was mentioned, it applied precisely to this schematic image. This Dreyer number two was very convenient to manipulate. He was two-dimensional and immobile.

Here, in tracing the process of Franz's thoughts, Nabokov clearly suggests that *murder,* not artifice, is the deadly design, the game of deathly abstraction by which Martha and Franz dehumanize Dreyer and, as a result, destroy their own humanity.

While the work of artifice demands the exercise of imagination, murder is, in Nabokov's view, a matter of cliché. When devising her scheme to kill Dreyer, Martha rehearses "the details of elaborate and nonsensical shootings described in trashy novelettes, . . . thereby plagiarizing villainy (an act which after all had been avoided only by Cain)." Murder is derivative and, when compared to the creative acts of consciousness, "essentially boring": Dreyer "was thinking what a talentless person one must be, what a poor thinker or hysterical fool, to murder one's neighbor. . . . How much those simpletons were missing! Missing . . . the simple pleasure of existence." In Nabokov's view, the murder-thriller is as banal a literary form as the brutal act on which it depends for its meager effects. In *King, Queen, Knave,* Nabokov exposes the psychological realities of murder that are ignored and falsified in the conventional thriller and, Nabokov might have added, even in celebrated works of fiction like Dostoyevski's *Crime and Punishment.* On more than one occasion Nabokov expressed his impatience with Dostoyevski's "sensitive murderers and soulful prostitutes." One may not agree with Nabokov's dismissal of Dostoyevski, but the principle operating behind his mockery is a serious one. To Nabokov, any writer who encourages the reader's identification with the murderer's psychology is a misguided thinker and a poor artist. In *King, Queen, Knave,* therefore, Nabokov deploys the strategies of artifice to distance the reader from Martha's murderous intentions and, at the same time, to distinguish between the murderer's stock notions and the creative qualities of true consciousness. . . .

While Nabokov's character Dreyer may, in some ways, resemble an artist or an artist *manqué,* there is no mistaking his inadequacy as the author's purported "mask" or stand-in. Nor are the limitations of Dreyer's vision and insight to be considered as signs of his author's arrogance toward human beings. Dreyer's inferiority to his creator is, quite simply, a truthful reflection of the laws of all creation. While each man is the partial author of his private world—creating and recreating the landscape from his consciousness *of* it—he is not the Author of the entire universe he shares with others. Nabokov and his readers are privy, therefore, to secrets that escape his characters' active but limited perceptions. Dreyer remains ignorant of the essential nature of his wife, his nephew, and the plot arranged between them. Meanwhile, in the foreword to the American edition of *King, Queen, Knave,* the author identifies the characters who are his true representatives in the novel. In the final chapters of the book, Nabokov points out, he and his wife make "visits of inspection" to the seaside resort where the novel's dénouement occurs. There, on the beach, Franz is appropriately discomfited by the sensation that this foreign couple knows "absolutely everything about his predicament."

Self-conscious artifice, I hope it is clear, does not eliminate reality from Nabokov's novels but reveals it in new ways. Because consciousness is "the only real thing in the world and the greatest mystery of all," Nabokov's artifice reflects not the world so much as the process by which men call it into being. That process is both psychic in nature and psychologically revealing. "All novelists of any worth," Nabokov said, "are psychological novelists," because "the shifts of levels, the interpenetration of successive impressions . . . belong of course to psychology—psychology at its best." Here, certainly, Nabokov gives no indication that his protagonists are meant to serve as mere masks for the artist who created them. In his fiction, as well, Nabokov's emphasis is not on the exclusive enterprise of the artist but on the essentially *creative* processes of consciousness—psychology in action and "at its best." Human reality is a construct, an incomplete but wholly significant fusion of individual perception with the phenomenological world. By drawing attention to the frame of his fiction, Nabokov does more than remind us we are reading a book. He reminds us that *reading* the world is the central preoccupation, and prerogative, of human beings. It is only in the realm of "articulate art," to borrow Humbert's phrase, that we mortals can hope to transcend the partial vision of our own psychic landscape—to contemplate, and share with the author, the lucid design of an entire universe. Here the novelist is godlike, ready to present to his readers the whole story of his creation. We are given to recognize how everything in this delightfully artificial universe has been thoroughly imagined, crafted, and imbued with the values of consciousness. The origins and mysteries of such a world are made accessible to the reader who exerts himself. Articulation—the strategies of composition—demands the vigilant exercise of consciousness, which in turn requires vigilant perception to be grasped. In Nabokov's view, good art is always difficult, unnatural, and strange. By celebrating, and affirming, the highest aspirations of conscious life, good art will always disturb or elude minds that are ready to accept and be ruled by the reflexes of habit.

DALE E. PETERSON

Nabokov's Invitation: *Literature as Execution*

Nabokov drafted the Russian original of *Invitation to a Beheading* in 1934, "in one fortnight of wonderful excitement and sustained inspiration"; the English translation of 1959 initiated the now famous series of "recastings" of Nabokov's Russian writings personally supervised by the author, and it displays the fewest traces of tampering and alteration of all his converted literary gems. Yet, despite the fondness Nabokov publicly lavished on the Russian-born book he most esteemed, readers and critics have failed to reciprocate the author's strong pride in this particular literary brainchild. What has gone wrong, so far as I can judge, is that the daring quirkiness of the narrative has driven its distracted "explicators" to reduce the work to an intellectually manageable allegory of one sort or another.

If Nabokov's *Invitation* is, as [Iris] Murdoch would have it, a "crystalline, quasi-allegorical" modernist work, it is a multifaceted and intellectually opaque creation, rather than a lucid reflection of a single reality. Most of the Russian émigré readers who first confronted the novel were sorely tempted to see Cincinnatus C.'s writhings and wrigglings inside a callously mismanaged detention center as Nabokov's disguised commentary on coping with totalitarianism in the twentieth century. But the logic of the book, when stripped down to a transparent political scenario, leads to conclusions that are maddening. It looks as if Nabokov, although himself a refugee from tyranny, can actually be irresponsible enough to advocate imaginative escapism as an adequate response to police states. If we read *Invitation* as

From *PMLA* 96, no. 5 (October 1981).

political allegory, we have to invent a Nabokov who can make light of totalitarian threats by suggesting that acts of individual imaginative noncompliance and transcendence can dismantle them. Critics capable of inventing such a Nabokov have, understandably, never forgiven him his inhuman solipsism. "It is as if he has nothing to do with anything," observes one of these critics. "He nourishes himself; he attends to himself. He would sooner have visions than think, would sooner look into the specters he has created than what actually surrounds him." Since the earliest reviews of his works, critics have assumed that Nabokov invites his readers to believe that imagination can rise above everything and anything, redeeming mundane hurts and losses. This is a claim that careful readers will look into.

A few of Nabokov's Russian reviewers and many of his avid readers who know his work only in English look at *Invitation to a Beheading* as a camouflaged fable about the trials and tribulations of the artist in our insensitive, literal-minded mass societies. One brilliant article in particular, by the Russian poet Khodasevich, has, with strategic reprintings, virtually established the current orthodoxy that "the life of the artist and the life of a device in the consciousness of the artist" is Nabokov's basic, obsessive theme. If there is to be a conventional wisdom about how to read Nabokov beyond the surface, it had better encourage readers to look for an artistic dilemma, not a social problem, behind the motley costuming of his extravagant fictions. But this approach, in effect, substitutes a more sophisticated style of allegorical reading for the more flat-footed, socially concerned interpretations we find in early critical attempts to take Nabokov seriously. By 1959, in the first of his remarkably aggressive, reader-twitting forewords, Nabokov had learned how to frighten away relevance seekers who might try to treat him like "G. H. Orwell or other popular purveyors of illustrated ideas and publicistic fiction." Ironically, Nabokov seems never to have suspected that his subtle art might suffer trivialization from a different quarter—from enthusiasts who would make an academic cult of all his works. There is a form of "vulgar aestheticism" that reduces Nabokov to the narrow profile of an artist whose every word is about artists attempting to make art or to make a place for art in the world. Only a badly impoverished understanding of Nabokov would read all his fictions as transparent celebrations of pattern-making minds whose "art" establishes a safe sanctuary for the free play of imagination. Fortunately, the actual dimensions of Nabokov's "crystalline" structures are broader. And if there is a trick to appreciating Nabokov's deep implications, it has to do with a willingness to stay attentive and honest to the plainly visible twists and turns that resist being simplified to the contours of straight allegory. Nowhere can we find a better example of Nabokov's deliberate intensification of "reading awareness" than in the puzzles that waylay us in *Invitation to a Beheading.*

The bold block letters that proclaim (in Russian as in English) Nabokov's startling book title also advertise something else—the complicity of anyone who has accepted an INVITATION TO A BEHEADING. To hold the book open for reading is thus to expose oneself to being *announced* as a sensation seeker, an armchair executioner. Of course, not all readers will think to read their own conduct in this way. But they will try to enter into the promised action of this invitingly titled novel. And they will be confronted with a very strange spectacle, a seemingly alien set of juridical norms: "In accordance with the law the death sentence was announced to Cincinnatus C. in a whisper. All rose, exchanging smiles." How curious! What necessitates this concealment of a verdict that is a foreknown conclusion? The prisoner in the dock, as we learn from the framelike structure of chapter 1, has undergone a ritual sentence of condemnation; the defense counsel (required by law to be from the same womb as the prosecutor) has argued in precisely allotted words for "classic decapitation"; and the whispered legal formula delivered to Cincinnatus states that the execution occurs "with the gracious consent of the audience." What, then, is this charade of justice, this mock secrecy that consigns an improbably named victim (who vaguely evokes Roman virtue) to an improbably designed machinery of confinement (to a fairy-tale or operatic fortress) for the purpose of an arbitrary liquidation? The first paragraph is itself sufficient to induce a crisis of interpretation: what sort of world is this? why have we been placed in it? can anything "serious" be accomplished in, or taken from, such a fabulous world?

In the original Russian text, when we are literally at the turning point of the first page, we find one of the most extraordinary exposés of hidden literary pleasure in the whole self-conscious tradition of "modernist" writing:

> So we are nearing the end. The right-hand, still untasted part of the novel, which, during our delectable reading, we would lightly feel, mechanically testing whether there were still plenty left (and our fingers were always gladdened by the placid, faithful thickness) has suddenly, for no reason at all, become quite meager: a few minutes of quick reading, already downhill, and—O horrible!

The text catches us in a pretty tangle here. It makes public the secrets of our own entanglements with fiction, as if an eavesdropper had discovered us thrilling to the private knowledge that we can measure the vitality of persons and places by the flick of a thumb's thickness of pages and print. Yes, we do feel a certain power as we assist inevitability by thinning the fat right-hand text, slicing it away one razor-thin page at a time. Yet this elaborate situation is apparently raised to mind only as a metaphor for the sickening sensation that any victim of a vulgar tyranny might feel. Besides, this particular victim is not close to the end—or we are not—to judge by the remarkably full right-hand cluster of pages left to go. Still, this reassurance does not fully reassure. However prolonged the execution of Cincinnatus's fate seems from the perspective of page 2, however rich his symbolic identity promises to be, he *is* a character in a novel. That would seem inescapable.

Much of the rest of chapter 1, like the entire novel, explores the limits of an absurd confinement and the resources and recourses available to one who seems inescapably confined. Nabokov's exceptionally tricky narrative succeeds in making the seriousness of the confinement as problematic as the seriousness of the various escapes. Although what holds Cincinnatus imprisoned seems finally insubstantial and implausible and although various escape routes seem accessible, Nabokov's sober design requires him to keep both Cincinnatus and us on the hooks of insoluble dilemmas. Within the first chapter alone, the structure that claims to hold Cincinnatus prisoner sometimes looks as sketchy as a rough draft by an incompetent novelist, sometimes as thick as a replica of a repressive bureaucratic regime. It is, of course, hard to tell the two structures apart; in each, characters are interchangeable and gross errors are erased from the record with no one held accountable. There is an analogy between a captive in the clutches of an autocratic power and a character in the meshes of a fictive plot, and Nabokov's writing makes us feel the terror of being subject to arbitrary revisions and reruns inside an announced plan of execution.

Cincinnatus C. offers us the spectacle of a prisoner or a character not yet dehumanized despite a verdict that offers him no choice but to collaborate in the obligatory steps toward his own extinction. That spectacle requires us to follow, chapter after chapter, a Chaplinesque pratfall comedy of endlessly attempted escapes and escapisms. The measure of Cincinnatus's humanness is in his indomitable, often ineffectual will to be elsewhere than in his ordained confinement. In no chapter is Cincinnatus, although imprisoned, fully "with it." Consider, from just the first chapter, the variety of his foiled departures: the waltz with the jailer beyond the cell in a "swoon's friendly embrace"; the "evening illumination" in which optical illusion transforms the posted prison rules, in fiery sunset, into a "reckless colorist's painting"; the extraordinary visit, on the wings of an imaginative parenthesis, to the romantic recesses of those "Tamara Gardens" where our prisoner met (and invented) the love of his life. Since Cincinnatus will succeed in making return flights to Tamara Gardens, it is worth hearing (in Russian) what sounds accompany his transport there: "Tam . . . Tam . . . Zelyónoye, muravchátoye Tam, támoshniye kholmý, tamléniye prudóv, tamtatám dalyókovo orkéstra. . . ." "There . . . There . . . The green, turfy There, thence its local hills, the languid thrumming of its ponds, the tum-ta-tum of a distant band. . . ." Even the translation of this passage shows that Cincinnatus has soared into the realm of faerie. But when one considers that the Russian *tam* is the poetic equivalent of the French *là,* it is clear that the prisoner's unaided imaginative ecstasy has carried him to the borders of that Baudelairean "beyond" whence come all emanations of bliss and perfection. Even on the first day of his confinement, Cincinnatus C. has learned to exercise that fragile human release of being more "there" than "here."

For all the multiple imaginative avenues that seem to conduct Cincinnatus "out of it," each chapter rings to a close with a more or less effective restoration of the humiliating and absurd confinement. The difficulty of achieving genuine escape is compounded in the Russian text by the cruel pun on the term *zaklyuchenie,* which all-inclusively evokes a "lock up" in the sense of both a "confinement" and a "conclusion." Wherever Cincinnatus turns, however he turns, an authority's (or an author's) foregone conclusion encompasses him. Yet there is one other "out," one other defense that is left to the prisoner:

> On the table glistened a clean sheet of paper and, distinctly outlined against this whiteness, lay a beautiful sharpened pencil, as long as the life of any man except Cincinnatus. . . . An enlightened descendant of the index finger. Cincinnatus wrote: "In spite of everything, I am comparatively . . ."

The prisoner is granted the fetching opportunity of transcribing his identity. The privilege of writing offers any prisoner, any character, the chance to translate his existence into another dimension, and this would seem a marvelous emancipation indeed. Yet this instrument of escape has a double edge. Nabokov's language playfully recognizes the latent executive powers of the as yet unwielded pencil—in Russian, it is the promising regal extension of the "pointing" or "dictating" finger (*ukazatel'nyi perst'*). But who or what commands those powers of execution? Why is every man's life (except Cincinnatus's) as long as the offered pencil? Who controls the public articulations of prisoners and characters? We readers are invited to think on such subjects.

If we give serious contemplation to the plot that encompasses Cincinnatus, we can appreciate the complexity of Nabokov's crystalline parable. The closer we look at Cincinnatus's entrapment, the better we can see that it is simultaneously political, philosophical, marital—and, of course, ineluctably fictional. Nabokov's captive has been apprehended and condemned for the sin of "gnostical turpitude"—he will be executed "with the gracious consent of the audience" although, as he is fully aware, he has been "fashioned so painstakingly." Cincinnatus's fatal offense is that he is opaque; unlike the better-suited residents of the "habitus" he finds himself in, he cannot be seen through at first glance, he cannot be understood at the first word. He is, unforgivably, a character who is hard to read. The society that incarcerates Cincinnatus has shown its true colors to him in a dusty little museum on Second Boulevard:

> There was a collection of rare, marvelous objects, but all the townsmen except Cincinnatus found them just as limited and transparent as they did each other. *That which does not have a name does not exist.* Unfortunately everything had a name.

Cincinnatus is trapped by a society that only respects and responds to what is labeled; he is romantically attached to a wife who extends her favors to any named need—"Little Marthe did it again today. . . . it's such a small thing, and it's such a relief to a man." The name of his public defender, the one who advocates a clear-cut "classic decapitation," is Roman Vissarionovich—a sly allusion (Novel, the son of Vissarion) to Vissarion Belinsky, the first critic-propagandist for a social-minded realism in Russian literature. Cincinnatus seems designed to serve as the perfect fall guy for a tyranny of vulgar practicality.

But there are weaknesses in the structure that holds Cincinnatus captive. Well before the prisoner suspects that he resides in a "hastily assembled and painted world," we are puzzling over the propped-up domain that contains and surrounds Cincinnatus. The scenes in the courtroom and in the jail are transparently made up of makeup and stage sets; the judge's mouth looks as though it has to be unglued from the prisoner's ear, and we later look on as the ungluing of a red beard and a leather apron transforms Rodion, the jailer, into Rodrig, the prison director. We notice that both of these "Rods" move with suspicious stiffness, literally accompanied by creaking joints and squeaking backs. Besides the telltale traces of costuming and special effects that weaken the solidity of this imprisoning world, Cincinnatus also observes that his society is in a state of entropic decline. An age of gravity-defying levitation and aspiration has passed; airplanes and even automobiles can only be glimpsed in sideshows or back copies of glossy magazines. Clearly, past accomplishments dwarf present realities. Cincinnatus is held in thralldom by the mental and technological equivalent of Toyland, by a company of strutting players leaping aboard little electric "wagonets" or spring-powered two-seat "clocklets." Finally, it would seem that this pathetically patched, outmoded society cannot finish off its prisoners properly without their genial collaboration. No execution is complete without a ritual embrace, a public collusion between victim and "fatemate." Gradually Cincinnatus and the reader alike come to understand that the beheading has been postponed so that the performer of the execution, M'sieur Pierre, can play at being a fellow prisoner who empathizes with the condemned victim. But this charade of amity is so flawed that a proper execution continues to be delayed. Given the obvious fraud and naiveté that mar the effectiveness of the confining society, what keeps Cincinnatus so long enthralled?

The imagination of Cincinnatus C., despite its better intimations, remains attached to a conceivably improved version of the given world. Like so many earlier and later Nabokov amphibians, half in and half out of mundane reality, Cincinnatus suffers the torment and dislocation of an agnostic Gnostic. He cannot quite bring himself to shake off the blandishments of tangible pleasures, even though his own intellectual conclusions restrict reliable joys to an uncarnal, disembodied realm. The prisoner's entrapment, against his own better judgment, is announced in his first interview with the defense counsel:

> I am surrounded by some sort of wretched specters. . . . They torment me as can torment only senseless visions, bad dreams, dregs of delirium, the drivel of nightmares and everything that passes down here for real life. In theory one would wish to wake up. But wake up I cannot without outside help.

Imprisoned in a claptrap world and yearning, naturally enough, for a "physically feasible freedom," Cincinnatus's gifted imagination plays tricks on him:

> Instantly he imagined, with such sensuous clarity as though it all was a fluctuating corona emanating from him, the town beyond the shallowed river, the town, from every point of which one could see—now in this vista, now in that, now in crayon, now in ink—the tall fortress within which he was. . . . In the confining phenomena of life his reason sought out a possible trail, some

> kind of vision danced before his eyes. . . . and, even though in reality everything in this city was always quite dead and awful by comparison with the secret life of Cincinnatus and his guilty flame, even though he knew this perfectly well and knew also that there was no hope, yet at this moment he still longed to be on those bright familiar streets.

Goaded on by his futile, foredoomed hope for a *literal* escape within the confines of the here and now, this prisoner, this character, falls for all the cheap literary and vicarious resolutions by which the imagination tries to buy time or achieve release:

> Involuntarily yielding to the temptation of logical development, involuntarily (be careful, Cincinnatus!) forging into a chain all the things that were quite harmless as long as they remained unlinked, he inspired the meaningless with meaning, and the lifeless with life.

In this behavior, be it noted, Cincinnatus strongly resembles the unwary reader of serious books. The paths of intellect and the streets the imagination stalks are just as vivid as any given path or street, but they do exist in a different dimension altogether.

It should come as no surprise that Cincinnatus comes closest to escaping his vulgar fate and the "banal senseless dreams of escape" it encourages when he accepts the seemingly useless diversion of writing. Writing becomes the occasion for Cincinnatus to transport his consciousness into communion with that other self which freely wanders in a realm of pure potentiality. Through writing, Cincinnatus can both claim and grant himself an irrevocable furlough from his involuntary servitude to the tyranny of the evident: "part of my thoughts is always crowding around the invisible umbilical cord that joins this world to something." Writing, in its expression of an intelligence free of the burden of immediate time and space, promises to become an actual vehicle of emancipation large enough to transport all us characters and prisoners *there* (*tam, là*) where supple form is given to all the patterns it has been our pleasure vaguely to preconceive. In practice, though, writing is, for Cincinnatus, a "criminal exercise" in an ironic way: it is as much a reminder of his prison bars as it is a ticket to liberation. Cincinnatus cannot invest full confidence in writing as his surest exit from entrapment; he never knows whether he will have time or talent enough to combine commonplace words into whole lines of "live iridescence." Worse yet, his nontransparent, opaque prose has literally no place in his given society, and it is hard to write without "at least the theoretical possibility of having a reader." But the worst failure of self-expression as a way out of confinement finally becomes apparent in one of the prisoner's last jottings:

> My words all mill about in one spot. . . . Envious of poets. How wonderful it must be to speed along a page and, right from the page, where only a shadow continues to run, to take off into the blue. The untidiness, sloppiness of an execution, of all the manipulations, before and after. How cold the blade, how smooth the ax's grip. With emery paper. I suppose the pain of parting will be red and loud. The thought, when written down, becomes less oppressive, but some thoughts are like a cancerous tumor: you express it, you excise it, and it grows back worse than before.

This admission is sinister in at least two ways. It announces the inescapable truth that while writing may freely objectify any conception, it always responds to the dictates of a consciousness dominated by its own felt compulsions. The passage also suggests the lethal finality of all successful executions, physical and poetic, corporal and verbal.

Nabokov sees to it that Cincinnatus's writing expresses a painful vacillation between departures "there" and returns "here." The poetic rhythms that transport Cincinnatus's being into residence in the "unreal estate" of *tam* and Tamara Gardens are continually interrupted by a different, rougher music, the countersound of *tūt* (with ū pronounced "oo," as in *toot*), the here and now: "Tūpóyeh tūt, podpyórtoyeh i zápertoyeh chetóyū 'tvyérduh,' tyómnaya tyūr'má, v kotóruyū zaklyuchyón neūyómnuh voyūshchee ūzhas . . ." "The dense 'dead-end,' propped up and locked up by its pair of *d*'s, a dark dungeon in which an unconstrainedly howling horror is confined." Cincinnatus's ability to waver between here and there teases the reader unmercifully. Yet it is profoundly right that we should be hard pressed to place this character. Had we but known, we could have found the novel's maddening, tricky conclusion foreshadowed in Cincinnatus's first long self-communing passage:

> Our vaunted waking life . . . is semi-sleep, an evil drowsiness into which penetrate in grotesque disguise the sounds and sights of the real world, flowing beyond the periphery of the mind—as when you hear during sleep a dreadful insidious tale because a branch is scraping on the pane. . . . But how I fear awakening! How I fear that second, or rather split second, already cut short

> then, when, with a lumberjack's grunt—But what is there to fear? Will it not be for me simply the shadow of an ax, and shall I not hear the downward vigorous grunt with the ear of a different world? Still I am afraid! One cannot write it off so easily.

Perhaps a poetic sensibility can translate all experience into a different dimension of extended, purer meanings. But, as the writer's treacherous pun suggests, to write off given details as metaphors for something else might only be possible inside texts.

Even as Cincinnatus struggles to express his extradimensional being, Nabokov has him note: "I am trembling over the paper, chewing the pencil through to the lead, hunching over to conceal myself from the door through which a piercing eye stings me in the nape." The reference is, of course, to the unremitting peephole observation that is one of the basic terms of the prisoner's confinement. But only the most literal-minded readers will imagine that the only pair of eyes peering in are those of the red-bearded Rodion, personifying Red Russian totalitarianism. And even such readers, one would hope, would have to see more after the thought-jarring narrative interruption Nabokov hurls into the eleventh chapter:

> The subject will now be the precious quality of Cincinnatus; his fleshy incompleteness; the fact that the greater part of him was in a quite different place, while only an insignificant portion of it was wandering, perplexed, here. . . . Cincinnatus's face . . . with gliding eyes, eerie eyes of changeable shade, was, in regard to its expression, something absolutely inadmissible by the standards of his surroundings . . . the light outline of his lips, seemingly not quite fully drawn but touched by a master of masters . . . the fluttering movements of his empty, not-yet-shaded-in hands. . . . all of this, analyzed and studied, still could not fully explain Cincinnatus. . . . and all this so teased the observer as to make him long to tear apart, cut to shreds, destroy utterly this brazen elusive flesh, and all that it implied and expressed, all that impossible, dazzling freedom—enough, enough—do not walk anymore, Cincinnatus, lie down on your cot, so you will not arouse, will not irritate.

Surely the long-frustrated, much-teased lover of "realistic" character at last recognizes his own eyes, blazing with ire, reflected in this cleverly rendered peek at Cincinnatus's enraged and nameless "observer"? After all, neither prisoners nor "realistic" characters are rightly entitled to the privacy that could protect them from a penetrating understanding of their motivations and behavior. They should be transparent examples to us all.

There is, to put it mildly, a remarkable coincidence between the implications of the passage just quoted and the brilliant thesis expounded in a few paragraphs in Walter Benjamin's essay of 1936 on the Russian storyteller Nikolai Leskov:

> In this solitude of his, the reader of a novel seizes upon his material more jealously than anyone else. He is ready to make it completely his own, to devour it, as it were. Indeed, he destroys, he swallows up the material as the fire devours logs in the fireplace. . . . The nature of the character in a novel . . . says that the "meaning" of his life is revealed only in his death. . . . The reader of a novel actually does look for human beings from whom he derives the "meaning of life." Therefore he must, no matter what, know in advance that he will share their experience of death: if need be their figurative death—the end of the novel—but preferably their actual one. How do the characters make him understand that death is already waiting for them? . . . That is the question which feeds the reader's consuming interest in the events of the novel.
>
> (*Illuminations*)

For Benjamin, the reader of the nineteenth-century novel, or "book of life," has quite literally become a consumer who feeds on the vitality offered by sacrificed characters; for Nabokov, the observer of character is always in essence a predator who needs to expose the vital parts of a maddeningly elusive, opaque prey. Both the reading of novels and the analysis of character are acts of cannibalism at a metaphoric level; the ultimate aim of the activity is to suck the final marrow of meaning from the perfectly exposed innards of a perfectly executed figure.

The prisoner Cincinnatus, with Nabokov's full complicity, comes to understand the lethal design behind the arbitrary confinement he suffers. He and we are given the chance to see viciousness and buffoonery combined in the valedictory speech delivered by pudgy, chummy M'sieur Pierre, the plot's hatchet man:

> Kind gentlemen, first of all and before anything else, allow me to outline by means of a few deft strokes [!] what has already been accomplished by me. . . .

> You gentlemen are of course aware of the reasons for the amusing mystification that is required by the tradition of our craft. After all, how would it be if I had announced myself right at the start and offered my friendship to Cincinnatus C.? This, gentlemen, would have certainly resulted in repelling him, frightening him, antagonizing him—in short, I would have committed a fatal blunder.
>
> I need not explain how precious to the success of our common undertaking [!] is that atmosphere of warm camaraderie which, with the help of patience and kindness, is gradually created between the sentenced and the executor of the sentence. . . .
>
> . . . Sometimes, in peaceful silence, we would sit side by side, almost with our arms about each other, each thinking his own twilight thoughts, and the thoughts of both of us would flow together like rivers when we opened our lips to speak. . . . The results are before you. We grew to love each other, and the structure of Cincinnatus's soul is as well known to me as the structure of his neck. Thus it will be not an unfamiliar, terrible somebody but a tender friend that will help him mount the crimson steps, and he will surrender himself to me without fear—forever, for all death. Let the will of the public be carried out!

This speech uncovers the subhuman vulgarity of the scheme of execution that has been clamped around Cincinnatus. Through it, Nabokov perpetrates a monstrous, double-headed parody. The executioner's pretense of all-knowing intimacy is peculiar to totalitarian regimes—and to the authors of realistic novels. However one looks at Cincinnatus—as political prisoner, unawakened Gnostic, or fictional character—he seems inextricably trapped, even though what victimizes him is a grossly inept and transparently fraudulent tyranny of appearances. The ultimate drama of Nabokov's book is Cincinnatus's struggle to stay the promised end and, through his foreknowledge of the fraudulent omniscience of the confining system, thwart the will to execute a design in which he is tempted to believe. Can a novelist, even one as ingenious as Nabokov, liberate characters from the cannibalism of consumers and free prisoners from the designs of tyrants?

We are nearing the novel's controversial ending. Before the author springs it on us, the prisoner becomes better schooled and skilled in certain "criminal exercises" that obliterate the bars and stripes of confining appearances. When the very thick of the Tamara Gardens stands revealed as a fool's paradise concocted by a tourist-trapping city management, Cincinnatus discovers that his endlessly regenerative imagination cannot be divested of its original shares of bliss: "exploring the surroundings with a diligent eye, he easily removed the murky film of night from the familiar lawns and also erased from them the superfluous lunar dusting, so as to make them exactly as they were in his memory." Even when we can see the perfect forms of elsewhere as optical rearrangements of the here and now, they need not lose their permanent imaginative validity. A little later, a strategically timed bit of escape artistry by nature's own Houdini, an elusive, erratic moth, also strengthens the prisoner's confidence in successful flight. This glorious moth is—by no accident—the most alive character in the book; described with Nabokov's unerring eye for naturalistic detail, its majestic visionary wings with their "perpetually open eyes" elude entrapment by the snares of this world—"But to me your daytime is dark, why did you disturb my slumber?" It is immediately after the moth evades the jailer that Cincinnatus formulates his own worst failure and best hope. He has fallen into "the dead end of this life" (*tūpik tūtoshnei zhizni*) by letting the specious logic of daylight realism close in on him: "I should not have sought salvation within its confines. . . . [I was] like a man grieving because he has recently lost in his dreams some thing that he never had had in reality, or hoping that tomorrow he would dream he had found it again." What Cincinnatus should have realized from the first days of his confinement or conclusion was that he was a captive of his own trust in semblances and verisimilitude. Like all Nabokov's exiled dreamers, he is a "prisoner of Zembla."

It finally happens, inescapably, that we turn the last page. Our leading character is on the block finally about to be executed, as promised, to have his unacceptable opaqueness ended. Here is what occurs:

> One Cincinnatus was counting, but the other Cincinnatus had already stopped heeding the sound of the unnecessary count which was fading away in the distance; and, with a clarity he had never experienced before—at first almost painful, so suddenly did it come, but then suffusing him with joy, he reflected: why am I here? Why am I lying like this? And, having asked himself these simple questions, he answered them by getting up and looking around.
>
> . . . Everything was coming apart. Everything was falling. A spinning wind was picking up and whirling: dust, rags, chips of painted wood, bits of gilded plaster, pasteboard bricks, posters; and arid gloom fleeted; and amidst the dust, and the falling

> things, and the flapping scenery, Cincinnatus made his way in that direction where, to judge by the voices, stood beings akin to him.

What has happened here? Has a character been executed? Are we to believe that this character has escaped execution?

Some will protest this trick ending and will condemn the author for trying to get away with double-talk. Some will decide for themselves what really has happened and will resolve any confusion by reaching their own conclusions. Perhaps some dyed-in-the-wool "modernists" will appreciate the trickery for trickery's sake. But what we all have to cope with, for as long as we face it, is the absolutely unhidden duplicity of this novel's ending. Two Cincinnatuses are present at the novel's close, and it is clearly possible to see either as dominant. In one reading, the basic Cincinnatus is the mortal, "existential" one (the one who counts); like Tolstoy's Ivan Ilyich he achieves a sudden, painful, joyous clarity as the ax falls, leaving us the burden of his posthumous, unlived wisdom. In another view, the basic Cincinnatus is the deathless "metaphysical" one, whose punning, dualistic consciousness ("why am I *here?* Why am I *lying* like this?") awakens itself from a needless collusion with vulgar appearances. The novelist is obviously letting us have it both ways, even as he pulls down the props of a fiction that has so well housed such ambiguous significance. The novelist blatantly refuses to assume responsibility for providing a credible, conclusive ending. Quite understandably, this deliberately staged lack of finish makes us nervous.

Last words, whether or not they become famous, receive the attention true conclusions deserve, and not even Nabokov's artful dodging can forestall the tendency to draw conclusions from endings. So, when Cincinnatus leaves the staging that was to execute him and makes his final turn toward an offstage dimension where kindred beings seem to lurk, it is natural to feel the author's full force pushing open an escape clause. In the Russian, those murky beings toward whom Cincinnatus makes his way are literally his "similars," perhaps the equivalent of Baudelaire's *semblables,* and thus hypocritical readers. Cincinnatus seems about to join whatever posterity literary characters enjoy or, possibly, to blend into the company of us readers, his Baudelairean brethren in the crime of opaqueness. In any case, Nabokov startles us into thinking about a direction in which characters and victims can achieve liberation. Nabokov characteristically springs his variously trapped characters loose at the end of his novels. He invites us readers to executions that he then shows to be literary frauds; he is not a writer who wants us to believe that characters can have their heads entirely or lose them cleanly. Literary characters, like the hopelessly imprisoned victims of any tyranny, cannot escape crude, inhuman execution unless they can survive in a richly imagined afterlife beyond the text's last word. Human vitality is opaque; it shimmers with the aura of a multivariable dimensionality that is impossible to catch in the commonplace mirrors of daylight realism. Thus we return by a long route to the argument that started this discussion: what shape should "moral fiction" take?

Among its many virtues, Nabokov's *Invitation* remains valuable as a crystalline parable in defense of modernist narrative; insofar as Cincinnatus is the victim of a conspiracy to penetrate his privacy and reduce him to a "realized" character, his story is an ethical counterstatement to the mode and manners of conventional literary realism. By a curious twist, Nabokov's Cincinnatus exists to endorse the same standard Iris Murdoch advocates in her manifesto for a return to narratives that reproduce the density of people and events: "Our current picture of freedom encourages a dream-like facility; whereas what we require is a renewed sense of the difficulty and complexity of the moral life and the opacity of persons." Literature ought to foster an alertness to, and even a reverence for, the messiness and mystery of real existence—on that proposition Murdoch and Nabokov can agree. But *how* literary form fosters a respect for life's complication was a matter of great and consistent ethical interest to Nabokov; he cared enough to declare conscientious objection to all forms of the illusion that serious art could duplicate reality.

Some may find it convenient to believe that rampant exhibitionism motivates those writers who remind us that their characters and events are actually lively words in sequence. For Nabokov, however, such reminders of literature's patterned simulation of experience are essential to decent relations with one's reader. The issue is a matter of philosophical integrity and professional ethics; moral fiction is fiction that makes no pretense of being identical with given reality, or even a substitute for it. With his extraordinary gift for minute observation and remembering, Nabokov could have been a master illusionist of literary realism. But his choice was always to spoil the illusion of lifelike narrative so that the reader would become conscious of the true chasm between lived experience and imaginative activity.

In "Pushkin, or Verity and Verisimilitude," an important untranslated article that appeared in a Parisian literary journal just before the publication of *Invitation to a Beheading,* Nabokov confirmed the moral seriousness implicit in his self-imposed fictiveness:

> Is it possible to imagine in its full reality the life of another, to relive it oneself and transfer it intact onto paper? I doubt it; in fact, it makes one tempted to believe that thought itself, in fixing its beam on the life history of a person, inevitably deforms it. Thus, it can only be the verisimilar, and not the veritable truth, that the mind perceives. . . . And yet what rapture for a day-dreaming Russian to depart into Pushkin's world! These visions are probably fraudulent and the real Pushkin would not recognize himself in them, but if I invest in them a bit of that same love I experience in reading his poems, won't what I make of this imaginary life be something resembling the poet's works, if not himself? . . . Thus one would like to think that what we call art is, in essence, truth's picture window; one has to know how to frame it, that's all.
>
> (*La Nouvelle Revue Française* 48[1937]:362–78)

This statement proclaims a mature sense of the necessary relations between factuality, art, and conscience. Actual experience is inimitable and evanescent. Even accounts of one's own experience are always facsimiles of permanently lost vital facts. We can only put our bliss into safekeeping or retard the moment-by-moment extinction of our personal and cultural estate by creating consciously aesthetic corollaries to the losses we mourn and dimly recall. The only permanence we perceive is artificial; the only character we possess we have ourselves fashioned. And the only responsible art is a moral fiction that lets us know we are contemplating a stand-in, a parody version, of an opaque actuality that can never be articulated conclusively. It is because Cincinnatus C. is so very sketchy and so very metaphorical that he can retain some semblance of our true humanity within the execution chamber of literature. It is true to Nabokov's ethical form to employ a coup de grace to assert that the character most read-about and read-into has an unpredictable vitality that eludes the narrative's reach. In the end, Nabokov helps his characters leap into a different dimension of existence; there is, after all, a posttextual life that authors can do nothing about.

The epigraph to *Invitation to a Beheading* is a riddle worth contemplating:

> Comme un fou se croit Dieu
> nous nous croyons mortels
>
> Delalande, *Discours sur les ombres*

Trying to unpack all that wit into English is a challenge, but it might unravel as a passage from *A Discourse on Shades,* by "A. Farland," to the effect that we believe we are mortal just as a madman believes he is God. Delalande, Nabokov's "favorite writer," is himself an invented, apparently Gnostic, sage, and the shades he discusses bring to mind *hombres* as much as Platonic images of supernal forms. Whatever the facts of the case (and they are all shadowy), the wisdom hinted at the beginning of Nabokov's great experimental novel whispers the radical, subversive, antirealistic news that we all inhabit, ultimately, a world constructed of similes and syllogisms, analogies and metaphors. The word from A. Farland to the wise among us recommends that we have the humility and the hard sense to recognize that the real world always escapes us. The extended parable Nabokov introduces with that wisdom encourages a breakthrough beyond the confines of an absurd and humorless "realism" that accepts likely facsimiles for actual truths. The novelist has designed the visible duplicity of *Invitation to a Beheading* to liberate present and future victims from the drab prison houses of authoritarian language. Here again, as in so much else, the wit and wisdom of Nabokov resemble (in an unforeseen coincidence he would have relished) the good-humored, philosophically sophisticated modernism of Wallace Stevens:

> From time immemorial the philosophers and other sane painters have daubed the sky with dazzle paint. But it all comes down to the proverbial six feet of earth in the end. . . . Why not fill the sky with scaffolds and stairs, and go about like genuine realists?
>
> (*Letters of Wallace Stevens*)

ALVIN B. KERNAN

Reading Zemblan: The Audience Disappears in Nabokov's Pale Fire

Literature gained its audience in the modern world, it seems fair to say, at the price of allowing the logic of the university to shape in many ways the definition of what literature is and does. To many this seemed, and continues to seem, a reasonable exchange of at least some degree of romantic autonomy and freedom for a place in the world which enabled literature to prosper and to make reason and the will of God prevail, at least in the minds of the younger generation. But now that audience is disappearing. It is actually disappearing from the classroom as enrollments in literature courses across America continue to drop sharply, and as the "literacy crisis" gives us students who are unfamiliar and uneasy with literature's central means of communication with its readers, the printed word. At the same time the audience is also disappearing on the philosophical and psychological levels as well. Critical pluralism, an increasing body of widely different readings of the same text, interpretation based on misprision, and various types of subjective or reader-response theories all deconstruct the old assumed literary audience into a number of random, individual consciousnesses. The disappearance of the university audience on all these different levels is the subject of Vladimir Nabokov's *Pale Fire.*

Nabokov sets his novel of the failure of literary communication in a university, and his major characters are college teachers, resident poets, and scholars. Wordsmith University—a thinly disguised version of Cornell, where Nabokov himself taught—is a fictional representation of the essential

---

From *The Imaginary Library: An Essay on Literature and Society.*

elements of the academic world where the traditional assumptions about the fixed meaning of the text, its ability to communicate with readers, and its positive effect on them have been most thoroughly institutionalized. The entire literary teaching enterprise is the primary objectification of the extension of Arnoldian principles that what literature has to say has great value in the formation of civilized minds, that there are demonstrably right and wrong ways of reading a text, that a correct methodology of interpretation can be developed and taught, and that a true understanding of the canonical works will eventually improve society. *Pale Fire* realizes the importance of the academy in maintaining these central literary tenets, dramatizes their gradual decay, and extends the process to a *reductio ad absurdum* in which a very precise and pedantic scholar, probably mad, sits in an isolated cabin and edits a long poem written by one of his colleagues, using the opportunity the notes provide to tell the story, probably fictional, of his own life. On the most immediate level in this fable of the radical failure of the university to enable poetry to communicate, misprision results from all the petty jealousies, the distorting pedantry, the academic vanity which imposes its own readings on texts, the lack of accurate knowledge, the sloppy workmanship, and the departmental rivalries which plague, as Nabokov well knew, all teaching and scholarly institutions. These are the ordinary human and professional failings which make it difficult, impossible, or even undesired for one man to read and understand what another has written, and they raise very real doubts about the possibility of communication. But below this surface of academic small-mindedness, Nabokov opens up more profound depths of misunderstanding which focus most of the critical, philosophical, linguistic, and existential doubts of our century about the possibility of full communication or comprehension. Our growing fears of solipsism, the inability to validate our interpretations in events outside themselves, the endless ambiguity of language, the desperate necessity of imposing our own self-justifying systems of meaning on the other—these are for Nabokov, as they are for our time, the problems undermining the old confident beliefs which are the foundation of the teaching of literature in universities: that the poet can know something, can embody that knowledge in a perfectly wrought poem, and can, along with the teacher, through this medium transmit an exact meaning to a reader. The difficulties of literature in the university at the present time are not, in the Nabokovian view, mere academic critical squabbles or the swirlings of departmental politics, but are ultimately the expression of the severe epistemological questions of our age.

Pale Fire consists of an autobiographical poem in heroic couplets, "Pale

Fire," in four cantos and 999 lines, by the distinguished American poet John Shade, with an introduction and notes to the poem, many times as long as the poem itself, by the scholar-teacher Charles Kinbote. Although Kinbote recommends reading his notes before the poem in order to get the context the poem needs to make it meaningful, let us, in good Zemblan fashion, reverse the process and look at the poem first of all. During the course of his poem, Shade mentions a television program on "The Cause of Poetry," in which his name "Was mentioned twice, as usual just behind (one oozy footstep) Frost" (ll. 425–26), and the Frostian tone dominates "Pale Fire": regular metrical system, rhyme, a plain, almost folksy note, a mixture of everyday trivia with sudden terrors lying below the surface, and a search for metaphysical meanings in the ordinary. Nabokov does not, however, entirely suppress his own signature, and the Frostian tone is complicated by a good deal of light mockery, burlesque, and ironic self awareness. But Nabokov's is not the only other poetic voice we hear, for though Frost's style dominates, Shade's style and subject matter are a literary conglomerate containing, among many other poetic echoes, the mock-epic tones and heroic couplets of Pope, Wordsworthian spots of time and a sense of identity with nature, the lyricism of Goethe, the somnambulistic sounds of Poe, touches of Browning's monologues, the linguistic dandyism of Stevens, the rhythms of Yeats, and Eliot's sinister sounding banalities of ordinary speech, such as,

> "If you're not sleeping, let's turn on the light.
> I hate that wind! Let's play some chess." "All right."
> (ll. 655–56)

The elaborate intertextuality of the poem allows Nabokov to concentrate in it a history of poetry and the literary canon. Shade is almost a parody version of what Harold Bloom has called the "weak" poet, the belated writer who has no authentic voice of his own but merely echoes earlier stronger writers, and "Pale Fire" can be read as an extended and amusing spoof on romantic and modern poetry, particularly on Frost. Certainly there are many points in the poem where the pat rhymes, jingling rhythms, and the mixture of high style and ordinary subject matter drop the poem into bathos:

> Jane's fiancé
> Would then take all of them in his new car
> A score of miles to a Hawaiian bar.
> (ll. 386–88)

Both the poet and the poem have been completely absorbed into the isolated world of university literary studies where the poet has become a quiet English professor, who writes criticism as well as poetry, and the poem has become a pastiche of the meters, styles, verse forms, and motifs of other poems. "Pale Fire" is a university poem made to be taught, as it frequently is, by teachers who can demonstrate for admiring students its enormous range of literary echoes; its cunning reference to other poems such as *Paradise Lost* where line 999—the number of lines in "Pale Fire"—of book 9 is the point of the fall; its use of poetic lore like Housman's definition of poetry—"Over the skin a triple ripple send / Making the little hairs all stand on end" (ll. 919–20)—its employment of poetic myths of Daedalus and the Cumaean Sibyl; its symbols of mountain and fountain; and its dense weave of bird and butterfly imagery. The teacher can also point out that "Pale Fire" is that most characteristic type of romantic poem, the autobiographical quest, and demonstrate in great detail the ways in which it corresponds to the archetypical poem of that genre, *The Prelude,* where Wordsworth, in the face of a too-busy world, also seeks some certainty of his poetic election and knowledge of metaphysical certainties which will legitimate his poetry.

Shade's quest is motivated by his desire to escape from solipsism, of being from birth, as he puts it, "most artistically caged" (l. 114). His parents died when he was very young, and though he frequently tries to evoke them, "Sadly they Dissolve in their own virtues and recede" (ll. 74–75), diminishing at last to a pair of medical terms, "bad heart" and "cancer of the pancreas." As a child, he was "asthmatic, lame, and fat," and therefore cut off, except in dreams, from play with other children. Appropriately enough for one so emotionally isolated from others, he was raised by an Aunt Maud, a poet and painter who reflects her own alienation from the world in paintings of "realistic objects interlaced / With grotesque growths and images of doom" (ll. 88–89).

But Shade's family and social isolation only prefigure a deeper exile, a sense of metaphysical immuration in which nature surrounds him with opaque objects, and the sounds of the world from an enclosing wall. All books and people seem to conspire to keep some great truth hidden from him:

> Space is a swarming in the eyes; and time,
> A singing in the ears. In this hive I'm
> Locked up.
>
> (ll. 215–17)

These intimations of mortality, of life as a prison house in which the self lives in perpetual solitary confinement, are occasionally broken open for Shade by visions, Wordsworthian spots of time, which provide him with brief glimpses of the possibility of a life beyond the present one and of some meaning in and Orderer of the universe. In childhood, while playing with a wind-up tin wheelbarrow pushed by a mechanical boy, he had an epileptic fit in which he escaped enclosure and achieved his intimation of immortality in the form of the oceanic sense:

> There was a sudden sunburst in my head.
> And then black night. That blackness was sublime.
> I felt distributed through space and time:
> One foot upon a mountaintop, one hand
> Under the pebbles of a panting strand,
> One ear in Italy, one eye in Spain,
> In caves, my blood, and in the stars, my brain.
> (ll. 146–52)

Much later in life, while lecturing at Wordsmith University, where he teaches, to the Crashaw Club, named after another mystic poet who also had visions, Shade has a heart attack, and feels that he has actually died. As blackness overwhelms him, he sees playing distinctly against the darkness "a tall white fountain" (l. 707). While he is unable to interpret the symbol, it nonetheless "reeked the truth," and seemed to him to have an absolute reality which promised some form of existence beyond the immediate sensory world.

Shade, the good gray poet, old, dumpy, disheveled, a teacher of literature, uxorious, more than a little dull and ordinary, is, in that surprising American way of Emerson and Thoreau, also a mystic and a visionary, irreligious but persuaded that beyond this seen world there is another unseen, and that life here is but a step on the way to a transcendental beyond. But despite his firmly believed intimations of immortality he remains trapped through most of his life in the triviality of daily things and in the prison house of the self. Deeply attached to an only daughter, he is unable to communicate with her or find any way to ease the heavy pain of life for an ugly, lumpish, unpopular child. While the girl walks out on the ice of a nearby lake to drown herself after a crushing humiliation on a date in the Hawaiian bar, Shade, unaware of what is happening, turns the television dial from one awful banality to another. Aunt Maud dies in the isolation of a sanitarium, sitting in the sun, a fly upon her wrist, unable to control her brain well enough to put together a coherent sentence which can communicate her thoughts to Shade. Despite Shade's deep and powerful love for his wife Sibyl, and her warm concern for him, their life together is difficult, and she always retains the mysterious distance of another self from him, the indecipherability suggested by her name.

In an effort to break out of the self, to communicate with the other, to verify the farther reality, Shade becomes involved in such ludicrous activities as I.P.H., the Institute of the Preparation for the Hereafter, where men are taught how to coast into death gradually, how to deal with transmigrations of the soul into such undesirable forms as a toad, and how to manage the awkwardness that is likely to arise when one meets after death the ghosts of two, or more, former wives. A more serious and hopeful attempt to break the walls of the self and know with certainty of the hereafter comes when Shade visits a woman who has died and been brought back to life by a surgeon kneading her heart. In a ghost-written article describing what she experienced in what she tritely calls the "Land Beyond the Veil," Shade reads that she too has seen "a tall white fountain." Believing that here at last is the ultimate verification of the reality of his own transcendental symbol, he drives many miles to see her, only to find that they really have nothing to talk about, and that the word "fountain" in the article was a misprint for "mountain." "Pale Fire" opens with an image of a small bird which has been deceived by the reflection of the sky in the picture window of Shade's house and has died flying into the hard barrier of the image which promises freedom but only reflects the world it is already in. This ultimate image of solipsism prefigures Shade's fate, and he acknowledges in the opening lines of the poem his identity with his Daedalian waxwing bird:

> I was the shadow of the waxwing slain
> By the false azure in the windowpane;
> I was the smudge of ashen fluff—and I
> Lived on, flew on, in the reflected sky.

Kinbote, the editor of the poem, argues that the first line was intended also to be the last line of the poem, and that if Shade had lived he would have used it to round off the 999 lines to 1000 lines. There is no evidence for this editorial dictum, which would end the poem where it began, but Kinbote's suggested emendation is in keeping with the circular patterns of "Pale Fire" as a whole in which every attempt to break out of the self into some identification with and knowledge of something beyond the self ends in failure and death. Baffled in every attempt to communicate with the other and thus validate the self, Shade turns at last, even as poetry itself has, to his poetic art and text as at least a possible guarantee of an order in the universe corresponding to an order of the poetic mind and its language:

> I feel I understand
> Existence, or at least a minute part
> Of my existence, only through my art,
> In terms of combinational delight;
> And if my private universe scans right,
> So does the verse of galaxies divine,
> Which I suspect is an iambic line.
> (ll. 970–76)

But this "suspicion" is immediately undercut by his own sudden accidental death shortly after the poem is finished, and the poem itself falls into the hands of an editor-reader to whom it communicates almost nothing.

"Pale Fire" realizes the failure to communicate with the other which had haunted romantic poetry from its beginnings. Shade's failure, like Humboldt and Lesser's, is an exemplary instance of the inability of the modern poet any longer to believe in the face of the world's evidence to the contrary in the power of his imagination and his art to create the images of desire and make them true. And in this failure Wordsmith University, though it cannot be considered the cause, plays a part, for by removing the poet and his poetry from the world into an academic setting where the context of every poem becomes only the rest of poetry, the university has encouraged the solipsism which has been the chief fear of the poets and the social problem of poetry. In Nabokov's novel this crisis of belief extends beyond poet and poem to include the critic and reader in their uncertainty and inability to communicate with the other. Criticism did not originate in the universities, but it is there that it has flourished in the last century and grown to such prodigious size as to threaten to overwhelm the literature it was designed to interpret and validate. It is this movement toward critical excess and independence from the poetic text that Nabokov satirizes in *Pale Fire,* and Wordsmith University includes, inevitably, not only the poet John Shade but that remarkable scholar-critic, the lecturer in Zemblan, Charles Kinbote, whose extensive commentary on Shade's poem, many times longer than the poem itself, makes up the rest of Nabokov's novel; and makes of it a latter-day version of Pope's *Variorum Dunciad.* Kinbote is an academic politician of the nastier variety, skillful at infighting with his peers, sycophantic to his superiors, sensitive to the nuances of departmental hierarchies, and, above all, aware that the improvement of his tenuous, not tenured, appointment lies in "owning" a poet. To this end he attaches himself to John Shade, moving in next door to him and trying to move into his life, holding long conversations with him, trying to feed him the subject of the poem "Pale Fire," and in general making himself into the "Shade expert." Invidious comparisons to Boswell and Johnson are frequently made. When Shade is killed, providentially on Kinbote's doorstep, Kinbote gathers up the manuscript of the poem—written on notecards—extracts permission to edit from a momentarily distraught widow, contracts for publication, and departs to an isolated cabin in a western state where he produces the edition of the poem which is the novel *Pale Fire*. The professors of the Wordsmith English department and the now recovered and thoroughly alarmed widow, Sibyl, try unsuccessfully to find Kinbote and block what they have reason to fear will be a catastrophically unsatisfactory edition of a great poet's last work.

As an editor Kinbote combines all the worst qualities of pedant and metacritic, and the edition he produces is something like a mixture of *The Variorum Shakespeare* and *The Birth of Tragedy*. His primary critical stance, however, is that of the scrupulous scholar and scientific bibliographer, and parading his scholarship, he provides the reader with a foreword, lengthy explanatory notes to individual passages and words, commentary on possible variant readings, and an index to poem and notes. Kinbote's precise, scholarly, haughtily pedantic manner—in tone not unlike Nabokov's in his edition of *Eugene Onegin*—is, however, only a Scriblerian cover for fundamental carelessness, sloppiness in detail, failure to check and quote original sources, simple error of fact, difficulties with translation and idiomatic English, and various kinds of howlers. When, for example, Shade says that as a child he "never bounced a ball or swung a bat" (l. 130), the Zemblan commentator, thinking to establish full identification with his author, remarks that he too "never excelled in soccer and cricket" (n. 130). So untrustworthy is Kinbote as a scholar that when he refers, as he frequently does, to canceled variant readings of different lines, there is a strong suspicion that these may be simply his own invention. But the real joke, and the real point, of Kinbote's deficiencies as a scholar, come in the long interpretive critical notes he supplies to Shade's poem.

There are those in New Wye, where Wordsmith College is located and Shade teaches English and Kinbote is a visiting lecturer in Zemblan, who believe that Kinbote is insane. We shall return to this question in a moment, but for now let us say simply that he is a melodramatic figure who insists that he is the deposed king of Zembla, who after ruling his remarkable fairy-tale kingdom for more than twenty years was overthrown by a socialist revolution and forced to flee for his life, and is now in hiding disguised as a bearded teacher in this obscure American college town. The extremist party of Zembla is, however, determined to track him down and murder him, and he lives in constant terror of the day when the assassin will arrive in New Wye. In his final notes on Shade's poem, Kinbote tells us that the murderer did arrive, just as he and Shade were about to celebrate the conclusion of the writing of the poem "Pale Fire," but that the murderer missed the king and killed poor Shade instead, despite Kinbote's efforts to intervene.

Kinbote reads Shade's poem entirely out of his own radical differences from Shade, and as a result gives us in his commentary not so much a misreading of "Pale Fire" as a new poem or novel which has, at least immediately, very little resemblance to Shade's poem as a more conventional reader is likely to interpret it. During his short time in New Wye, the second term of the college year and part of the summer, Kinbote has carefully fed Shade the melodramatic story of his kingship and deposition with the firm hope that the poet will make it the subject of his next poem. But immediately he sees the completed poem Shade has written between July 1 and July 21, 1959, Kinbote knows that it is not the Zemblan epic which "would recreate in a poem the dazzling Zembla burning in my brain" (n. 42), and realizes that the poem "in its pale and diaphanous final phase, cannot be regarded as a direct echo of my narrative." He reaffirms his awareness that "Nothing of it was there" in his note to the non-existent line number 1000 and states that what is there is "An autobiographical, eminently Appalachian, rather old-fashioned narrative in a neo-Popian prosodic style—beautifully written of course—. . . but void of my magic, of that special rich streak of magical madness which I was sure would run through it and make it transcend its time." Nevertheless, Kinbote continues to believe that the "sunset glow" of his Zemblan story "acted as a catalytic agent upon the very process of the sustained creative effervescence that enabled Shade to produce a 1000-line poem in three weeks" (n. 42), and that more of the original story still resides in the cancelled variants, some of which he reprints in the notes with, he says, great care, and in the "echoes and wavelets of fire, and pale phosphorescent hints" in the text proper which retain "subliminal debts" to the tale of old Zembla. Acting on the belief that his story ultimately underlies Shade's poem he produces in his extensive commentary not a literal interpretation of Shade's text, but the very thing he denies that he wishes to do: "I have no desire to twist and batter an unambiguous *apparatus criticus* into the monstrous semblance of a novel" (ll. 47–48).

The gap which opens between poem and reader-critic as a result of inattention, carelessness, and linguistic and social differences widens into an abyss because of the reader-critic's intense subjectivity, his obsessive interest in his own psychic life and his own Zemblan inconography. A single word in Shade's poem such as "often" will provide Kinbote with an opening to talk about his own life: "Often, almost nightly, throughout the spring of 1959, I had feared for my life" (n. 62). Shade's reference to his father provides the springboard for Kinbote to launch into several pages on his own father, the aviator king of Zembla, Alfin the Vague (1873–1918). Shade's reference to games leads to a remembrance of the toys of the editor's own royal childhood and the way they led him to a secret underground passage between the Zemblan palace and the National Theater. A word of considerable consequence in the poem, "mountain," sets off a long detailed description in the commentary of how the deposed king of Zembla escaped from the revolutionary government over Mount Glitterntin to the Gulf of Surprise. The notes provide almost a handbook of the patterns of association by which the human mind gets from one thing to another, but all the roads ultimately lead from the other to the self, and the image we are finally left with is a commentator as completely locked in his own private consciousness as the poet Shade felt himself to be locked into the world.

Nabokov has constructed, at least at this level of reading, a grotesque, ingenious, and hilarious satire on the situation of literature in the university. The university poet is only a shade of his great romantic predecessors; his poem, in both theme and form, completely cut off from the mainstream of life, turned inward, and composed only of fragments of other poems and poetic styles; the imagination blocked and ruefully aware that its own desires are doomed to failure and bathos. There is a considerable poignancy in all this—it is so close to where we have actually arrived, an ironic poem about the impossibility of poetry—but the editor-critic, and the academic criticism he is a parody of, elicit little sympathy. His arrogance, pettiness, and pedantry are revealed as mere forms of professional aggression and academic one-upmanship. Worse still, his reading of the poetic text in his notes is so far-fetched as to be insane, has nothing to do with what the poet desperately tried to say, and everything to do with what the critic wants to say about himself. Criticism, in this view, is not only parasitic on poetry in the usual sense, it now goes beyond this kind of piggybacking to use the poem to tell its own idiotic story, which could not get a hearing unless it were attached to the poem and concealed as interpretation.

This is Nabokov's utterly savage portrayal of literature and its attendant criticism in the university, a type of criticism totally at odds, it should be added, with the responsible readings of his own recently published lectures on the modern European novel. Although the university is the setting for this comedy of misprision and therefore responsible to some degree for the solipsism of the poetry and the excesses of the criticism written there, its tendency to isolate literature from the world only intensifies to the point of satiric visibility a far more extensive and profound social breakdown in communication. . . .

It is this increasing doubt about the possibility of communication and therefore of an established meaning of a text which underlies the ghastly literary events in Wordsmith University, and Nabokov dramatizes the impermeable barrier between the one who writes and the one who reads by making the editor and commentator, Charles Kinbote, in almost every way imaginable the exact opposite of the poet Shade. Where Shade is short and rotund, Kinbote is unusually tall and muscular; where Shade is an uxorious heterosexual, Kinbote is a solitary homosexual; where Shade is careless and ordinary of dress, Kinbote loves such finery as velvet jackets and bright lilac slacks. The differences mount steadily as the book proceeds, and we learn that Kinbote differs radically from the "fireside poet" in his reactionary politics, social snobbery, outré gestures, self-dramatization, vegetarianism, and pious orthodoxy in religious matters. All these differences are summed up in the fact that Kinbote is, or at least thinks or says he is, an alien, a native of the vaguely middle-European Graustarkian country of Zembla, a word whose root meaning in Zemblan is "mirror." These sharp differences between poet and critic reflect what our century has learned about human difference and the isolation of the individual in the lonely crowd, but they are only the surface of far more profound psychological differences, which gradually deepen in *Pale Fire* into an awesome and frightening—all the more frightening because so ludicrous—display of the total lack of communication between man and man. Even a poem, that most carefully structured attempt to convey precisely the most intense experiences, fails to penetrate the barrier between individuals, leaving Kinbote sitting, spinning out his own story, utterly deaf to Shade's expressions of his most private fears and hopes, his love for his wife, his agony over the death of his daughter, his mystic experiences, his shattering disappointment when "fountain" turns to "mountain."

Kinbote's story continues to evolve like a butterfly, and as the commentary grows it gradually acquires an interest of its own, as Kinbote constructs in the notes the incredibly detailed fictional world of Zembla, complete with history, topography, religion, social structure, economy, art, language, and political system. He is himself, of course, the hero of this fascinating little world, the last of its royal kings, sophisticated and intelligent, forced from the throne by thuggish revolutionaries, separated from his beautiful queen, by his sexual tastes as well as by events, saved in a melodramatic way by fiercely loyal subjects, parachuting into the United States, and at last hiding out in disguise in an Appalachian college town. The story, though it is told in fragments and in a chronologically disordered fashion, finally has all the intricacy of detail and the internal coherence—it is, as we say, "airtight"—of such fictional microcosms as Yoknapatawpha County, or the cathedral close of Barchester, or the world of the Hobbits. It also has the completeness and absolute mad logic of such great insanities as that of Freud's psychotic Doctor Schreber.

Much of the criticism of *Pale Fire* has approached it as a detective story in which the object of the game is to judge whether Kinbote is mad or sane. There is a great deal of evidence to suggest that the story he tells of Zembla is simply a delusory fiction constructed to justify his own megalomania, explain his paranoid fears, and give concrete form to his schizophrenic personality in the characters of King Charles of Zembla and Charles Kinbote, despised and mocked academic lecturer. Peeping through his commentary are a number of incidents, duly reported by Kinbote but interpreted in his own way, which suggest to the outside eye an entirely different reading of the story he tells about himself. In this version of events, which seems to be shared by almost everyone in New Wye except, just possibly, Shade himself, Kinbote is not only a remarkably malicious, snobbish busybody and a most aggressive and indiscreet homosexual, but is insane as well, a classic paranoid-schizophrenic with delusions of former grandeur and present persecution. The remarkable world of Zembla is, according to this version of affairs, entirely Kinbote's invention, which he has the misfortune, or impudence, to believe, while the death of poor Shade, far from being an attempt to assassinate a former king, is a dreadful case of mistaken identity in which a man who had been sentenced to an asylum escapes, returns to New Wye and shoots Shade, thinking he is the judge who sentenced him to prison. In this version Kinbote, who has rented the judge's house, is only an innocent, and perhaps a cowardly, bystander.

But, on the other hand, the fantastic story could be simply though improbably true. Zembla certainly hangs together well, providing a possible if not a probable explanation for all that happens, and there is a good deal of internal evidence which tends to validate Zembla, such as Kinbote's apparently real ignorance of certain American customs and idiom. The people of New Wye, however, continue to regard Kinbote as mad and his story, insofar as they know it, merely a self-justifying delusion; and everything that happens can be as well explained in their terms as in Kinbote's. Indeed, the story of Zembla is so fantastic, and Kinbote so clearly neurotic, at the least, that the tendency of any ordinary reader is to accept his madness as a fact, and then to pursue the many clues the novel offers for evidence of inconsistency, statements contrary to facts as established by other statements, and distortion of events on the narrator's part. There is plenty of evidence of this kind, and Kinbote regularly seems to misread events, seeing kindness and affection where there would seem to be dislike and even hatred, finding social triumph where he has achieved only in making himself ludicrous, and translating chance events into well-laid plots. Once Kinbote's madness is posited, the detective-critic will follow the Sherlockian clues that wind through the narrative, discovering that the events of the story have their source not in Zemblan reality but in some happening or object of everyday life which Kinbote's imagination has elaborated and fitted into his fantasy. Moving in this direction, to take a small example, the Browning automatic pistol with which Kinbote says, with his usual specificity, Shade was killed by the assassin Gradus, can be traced back to Shade's use in his poem of the Browningesque form of the dramatic monologue, and to Shade's reference to Browning's "My Last Duchess" ("Notice Neptune, though, / Taming a sea-horse") in the title of his book of critical essays, *The Untamed Seahorse*. For those who like more elaborate trails of clues, it is possible to trace a long series of unpleasant associations with the color "green"—the revolutionaries who pursue King Charles often wear green coats, while his friends aid his escape by wearing red—to a young instructor at Wordsmith named Gerald Emerald, who gives Kinbote a good deal of trouble, and whom he dislikes intensely. It is Emerald who, according to Kinbote, finally drives the murderer to Kinbote's door, thus enabling him to kill Shade.

But though literary and psychoanalytic detectives will follow these trails for years to come, they ultimately are circular and lead the reader back only to the image of his own values and assumptions. The name Zembla is, after all, a form "of Semberland, a land of reflections, of 'resemblers' " (n. 894), and Nabokov has so contrived it that everything in the story of Zembla can be read in at least two ways. If Kinbote dressed his fictional villains in green because he disliked Gerald Emerald, then it could be equally true that he disliked Emerald because the revolutionists of Zembla at whose hands he had suffered so much had favored green coats. The decision about which way the trail leads will always in this novel depend on your presuppositions, your own private views, for the trail itself is like the tracks of the pheasant in the snow described in Shade's poem.

> A dot, an arrow pointing back; repeat:
> Dot, arrow pointing back . . . A pheasant's feet!
> (ll. 23–24)

Or the tracks of the great detective who put his shoes on backward as he walked in "The Final Problem" away from the Reichenbach Falls and his encounter with Professor Moriarity:

> Was he in *Sherlock Holmes,* the fellow whose
> Tracks pointed back when he reversed his shoes?
> (ll. 27–28)

In trying to decide the truth about Kinbote and Zembla even the more objective reader-critic, like the people of New Wye, like Shade and Kinbote, finds at last only the isolation of his own subjectivity, for the evidence is infinitely ambiguous, even though it constantly teases us with the possibility of absolute meanings if only we could follow and assemble the myriad of resemblances which look like clues to an absolute meaning. Each effort to reach absolute reality, to find the truth of things and discover whether Kinbote is sane or insane, is an effort to confirm our own reading of the evidence by relating it to or showing it to be in conformity with some truth outside the circle of our own subjectivity, even as Shade tried to verify his intimations of an afterlife by linking the image of the white fountain he had seen in the unconscious darkness after his heart attack with the independent evidence of the similar vision of the woman whose heart had been massaged back to life by the surgeon. But just as there had been finally no corroborating evidence, only a white mountain seen by a rather ordinary woman, so in our reading of the novel each attempt to reach a validated truth by getting outside our own responses ends in failure. The dense Nabokovian weave of coincidences, themes, images, recurrences, and developing patterns in which one thing shifts into another and another, teases us with the constant possibility of a grand and absolute scheme, the truth most books try to deliver, but here we always are left at the end of the track with the puzzled knowledge that it could have gone the other way, that, in the largest terms, Kinbote might as well be sane as insane. Thus, the reader recreates in himself the feeling of the possibility of meaning but the baffled inability to pin it down, which is Shade's experience of life itself as summed up in some of those suspect canceled lines of his poem:

> There are events, strange happenings, that strike
> The mind as emblematic. They are like
> Lost similies adrift without a string,
> Attached to nothing.
>
> (n. 70)

And so the solipsistic circle comes to seem complete: as Shade cannot communicate with those he loves most dearly or with the other world, so Kinbote cannot understand Shade, the people of New Wye cannot understand him, and we the readers cannot really understand their stories. "Life is a message scribbled in the dark" (l. 235), says Shade's poem, and the novel offers an image of an absurd life with each of us listening to the tales of others, their attempt to make sense of their lives, but translating the story into our own terms which are as grotesque a travesty of the original as Conmal's Zemblan translations of Shakespeare, or Kinbote's translation of Shade into Zemblan.

The romantics and moderns posited that the poetic text, like Keats's Grecian urn or Malraux's voices of silence, could stand free of the world, permanently unverified by any human context, telling men all they need to know on earth of truth and beauty. But Nabokov reveals the contemporary reality of poetry, of a text endlessly ambiguous in itself and involved in an endlessly complex and bizarre context of contingencies. "Pale Fire" falls into the hands of Kinbote and is interpreted according to his necessities, and *Pale Fire* falls into our hands and our necessities. Understanding of the kind on which the Imaginary Library has depended would seem to be totally blocked; but neither Shade, nor Kinbote, nor we the readers, nor perhaps, though I am not sure, Nabokov, can quite accept total solipsism.

When Shade returns from visiting the woman who seemed also to have seen the fountain playing in the darkness of death, he decides that though exact knowledge of something outside the self, in this case an afterlife, is not to be had, nonetheless its existence and its outlines, if not its exact nature, its "texture" if not its "text," can be confidently inferred:

> Life Everlasting—based on a misprint!
> I mused as I drove homeward: take the hint,
> And stop investigating my abyss?
> But all at once it dawned on me that *this*
> Was the real point, the contrapuntal theme;
> Just this: not text, but texture; not the dream

But topsy-turvical coincidence,
Not flimsy nonsense, but a web of sense,
Yes! It sufficed that I in life could find
Some kind of link-and-bobolink, some kind
Of correlated pattern in the game,
Plexed artistry, and something of the same
Pleasure in it as they who played it found.
(ll. 803–15)

There are other instances in the novel in which a message however misunderstood in its details, its text, nonetheless conveys a "web of sense" to the receiver, some "correlated pattern" of the original. The translations of Shakespeare made by Conmal, Kinbote's Zemblan uncle, who learned English only from the lexicon and could not understand the spoken language, nevertheless still give off some pale reflected fire of the original when retranslated into English by Kinbote; and Sibyl Shade's translations of Andrew Marvell into French get something of the tone. But the most remarkable, and amusing, case of a garbled message which nonetheless makes sense comes when the assassin Gradus calls his headquarters in Zembla:

> Under the assumption that it would attract less attention than a BIC language, the conspirators conducted telephone conversations in English—broken English, to be exact, with one tense, no articles, and two pronunciations, both wrong. Furthermore, by their following the crafty system (invented in the chief BIC country) of using two different sets of code words—headquarters, for instance, saying "bureau" for "king," and Gradus saying "letter," they enormously increased the difficulty of communication. Each side, finally, had forgotten the meaning of certain phrases pertaining to the other's vocabularly so that in result, their tangled and expensive talk combined charades with an obstacle race in the dark. Headquarters thought it understood that letters from the King divulging his whereabouts could be obtained by breaking into Villa Disa and rifling the Queen's bureau; Gradus, who had said nothing of the sort, but had merely tried to convey the results of his Lex visit, was chagrined to learn that instead of looking for the King in Nice he was expected to wait for a consignment of canned salmon in Geneva.
>
> (n. 469)

But when the people from headquarters break into the Queen's house they find an envelope which gives them the needed information about the King's whereabouts in New Wye.

If we follow these tracks, they take us to the possibility that Kinbote's Zemblan interpretation of Shade's poem—whether it be the hallucinations of a madman or the history of an unfortunate royal refugee ceases to matter—though it misses the exact text, may somehow get the context right. On the face of it this at first seems impossible, not only because the Zemblan romance is so radically different from Shade's ironic and somewhat matter-of-fact autobiographical poem, but also because Shade, while aware that Kinbote wants him to write a Zemblan epic, specifically rejects the idea, though again in one of the cancelled variants. There are, of course, topsy-turvical coincidences between "Pale Fire" and Kinbote's romance, and Kinbote makes as much as he can out of these points of crossing. The word "Zembla" occurs at line 937 of the poem, but only as a metaphor taken from Pope's *Essay on Man* for Shade's gray beard. A reference to "killing a Balkan king" (l. 822), and the description of the brave death of a king at the hands of "some uniformed baboon" (l. 600) raise Kinbote's hopes that at least portions of the matter of Zembla he fed to Shade are still present in the text. At other times he shows extraordinary ingenuity in finding it encoded in the text, as when the words "Tanagra dust" (n. 596), yield him "Gradus," the name of the assassin who kills Shade. But press as he will, Kinbote and his Zembla are as literally excluded from Shade's poem as completely as the subject matter of the poem is excluded from Kinbote's story.

But the poem and the commentary, the autobiography and the romance, do finally reverberate in sympathy with one another at a deeper level than the surface of the text. The similarity perhaps first becomes apparent—at least to this reader's ear—in a counterpoint between Shade's sense of the isolation of the self in nature and mortality, and Kinbote's equally radical and fearful sense of danger and alienation from the world. Whatever kind of delusions Kinbote may have, he genuinely sweats with terror at the thought of the thugs who are coming to kill him, groans with excruciating migraine headaches, feels that the dark evenings are destroying his brain, prays for forgiveness for burrowing "in filth every day" (n. 493). "I cannot describe," he writes, "the depths of my loneliness and distress" (n. 62). At times an involuntary gasp of existential fear escapes him, "Dear Jesus, do something" (n. 47–48). Like Shade, too, Kinbote tries desperately to escape from this terrifying solipsism. In Kinbote's case these attempts at escape first take the form of trying to imprint himself and his reality on Shade, even as Shade has sought to validate his images of the transcendental world in the mind of the woman who had died and seen the mountain. The efforts are at least as comical as they are pitiful as Kinbote spies on Shade from every point of vantage, peering out of his windows, standing upon garbage cans to peep under shades, inventing excuses to drop in and go for walks, bursting into the bathroom while Shade is bathing, always trying to enter the life of another and thus validate the self in the other, thereby escaping the terror of total loneliness. But, though Shade is a genial and extraordinarily tolerant and understanding man, the shades are always ultimately drawn against this intruder who is himself much too dense or self-preoccupied to understand what really is going on in the Shade household, an unusually tight nuclear family of poet-husband and protective wife. But Kinbote is not merely seeking companionship to lighten his loneliness, he is trying to get the poet John Shade to confirm his identity, to validate the Zemblan reality which is his hope of salvation by making it into a poem.

There was once in the town of New Wye a mad railwayman who thought he was God and began redirecting trains on that basis. Shade—perhaps with a glance at Kinbote?—argues that one should not apply the word *mad* "to a person who deliberately peels off a drab and unhappy past and replaces it with a brilliant invention" (n. 629). This is perhaps the way Kinbote has used the story of Zembla, but whether his story is true or invented, it is equally necessary to Kinbote's sanity that it become real, be believed, and he is unable by himself to achieve this necessary validation through objectification. So Kinbote tries to plant Zembla in Shade's mind, as the subject of a poem, trying to get him to fulfill the poetic contract as Wordsworth fulfilled it for Mill, and as the Imaginary Library had fulfilled it for generations of readers:

> "Once transmuted by you into poetry, the stuff *will* be true, and the people *will* come alive."
>
> (n. 433–34)

"We all are, in a sense, poets" (n. 629), says Kinbote, but his Zemblan story needs another better poet to authenticate it, in the way all the many poets who are incorporated in Shade's poem are needed by him to make his own poetic dreams real. But Shade, like many modern poets, disappoints his reader for "Pale Fire" is about the poet, not about Zembla, and so Kinbote must try in his notes to tell his own story, be his own poet. And he is not nearly so powerful a poet, for where Shade faces his solipsism directly, and still manages a wry detachment, Kinbote patches together a musty old romance and smuggles it into the notes attached to the greater poem to insure its being read and thereby becoming real.

One of Nabokov's many ironies is that the good gray sensible American poet Shade with his simple autobiographical poem is really far more daring in his search for an ultimate reality, more aware of his own aloneness, and more visionary in his simplicity, than Kinbote with his seemingly wild but extremely conventional romance of faraway kingdoms, secret passages, hair-breadth escapes, exotic landscapes, and secret band of murderers. But both, to put it most simply, tell in different terms the same story of fearsome isolation within the self and the attempt to break out of it: in the case of the poet into the metaphysical reality of finding some meaning in the abyss, in the case of the neurotic critic in telling the story of Zembla which gives substance and form to the justifying dream. So there are, it would finally seem, correspondences, some communication between people as isolated and different as Shade and Kinbote, poet and critic, realist and romantic, even though they do not speak the same language. This perhaps is the meaning of the title of the poem and the novel, *Pale Fire,* taken from Shakespeare's *Timon of Athens:*

> The sun's a thief, and with his great attraction
> Robs the vast sea. The moon's an arrant thief,
> And her pale fire she snatches from the sun.
> The sea's a thief, whose liquid surge resolves
> The moon into salt tears.
>
> (4.3.437–41)

In Shakespeare the lines are spoken by Timon, himself an exile from the city of men, living as a hermit in the desert, and the words express his misanthropic conviction that all things in the world live in total selfishness, robbing from others. The lines obviously bear on the situation in the novel: Shade's poem "steals" from all the other poetry echoed in it and only palely reflects the metaphysical confidence of those earlier poets; Kinbote's Zemblan story is a retelling of a standard romance, and it steals Shade's poem by parasitically attaching the story to the poem in the form of notes, as all criticism steals the original works on which it feeds. But in the context of Nabokov's novel, the lines he has robbed from Shakespeare, lines which reflect so palely in Conmal's Zemblan translation retranslated into English—"The sun is a thief: she lures the sea and robs it"—take on a secondary meaning latent in the original: that communication, however weak and indirect, is possible, that light still reflects from one point to another. The possibility of this positive meaning in the lines is strengthened by the fact that the Zemblan translation does catch something of the basic sense of the original, though it does not contain the words "pale fire," and that

Kinbote, although he has with him only "a tiny vest pocket edition of *Timon of Athens*—in Zemblan"—is reminded of the correct scene in *Timon* by some cancelled variants of lines 39–40, although in his note to line 962—"Help me, Will. Pale Fire"—he cannot identify the Shakespeare play from which the words come. The pulses of the signal fade in and out in both sender and receiver, but they continue to flicker. A copy of *Timon* in Zemblan, perhaps the one Kinbote carries, was lying in the closet leading to the secret passage through which King Charles made his escape, passing under Timon Alley and Coriolanus Lane on his way to a hidden exit in the theater. *Pale Fire* seems to have picked up a Shakespearean subtext suggesting interaction and communication, however palely, in the universe, and to have developed it by connecting *Timon* with escape, freedom, breaking out of imprisonment.

Nabokov has, of course, purposely placed his readers in a most difficult position, forcing them to face the fact that any reading of his work may be simply a reflection of the reader's own subjective needs from within a prison house of self as confined as Shade's or Kinbote's. The interpretation I have offered may well be as self-serving a story as Kinbote's, though not nearly so interesting or amusing. By setting up the Kinbote misreading of the Shade poem, Nabokov involves us as readers in an awareness of the full extent of human subjectivity and its causes, and at the same time warns us against detective-story types of interpretations which arrive at some absolute truth to the exclusion of all other possibilities. But the novel does not seem finally to deny the possibility of any correspondence whatsoever between writer and reader, text and understanding. Indeed, it seems deliberately to tempt us by its own elaborately wrought internal form, to follow up the possibility of some overall meaning in the work, even as Shade followed up the hints of some overall meaning, however faint, in the cosmos.

For the reader of Nabokov's novel that meaning must come not from Shade's poem "Pale Fire" alone, or from Kinbote's Zemblan story told in the notes, but from the larger image of poem and story in relation to one another, and both in the context of events during the winter and spring of 1959 in New Wye. And such meaning as appears will be not of a factual kind, precisely pinpointed, but only a possibility created by hints, coincidences, suggestions. The reader must finally be like the "good Zemblan Christian" who "is taught that true faith is not there to supply pictures or maps, but that it should quietly content itself with a warm haze of pleasurable anticipation" (n. 493). Approached in this way, seeking not the text but the context, "events, strange happenings, that strike / The mind as emblematic," as Shade puts it in a cancelled variant printed in the note to line 70, appear. For example, the Vanessa butterfly appears at several crucial points in the poem in such a way as to tease us with the possibility that it may have some meaning beyond its immediate presence. Shade refers to his beloved wife Sibyl as "My dark Vanessa" (l. 270); on the night before he dies and just as he finishes his poem, he looks out his window where,

> A dark Vanessa with a crimson band
> Wheels in the low sun, settles on the sand
> And shows its ink-blue wingtips flecked with white.
> (ll. 993–95)

And Kinbote tells us that as he and Shade were walking toward his house, one minute before Shade's death, a Vanessa or "Red Admirable . . . came dizzily whirling around us like a colored flame."

> One's eyes could not follow the rapid butterfly in the sunbeams as it flashed and vanished, and flashed again, with an almost frightening imitation of conscious play which now culminated in its settling upon my delighted friend's sleeve. It took off, and we saw it next moment sporting in an ecstasy of frivolous haste around a laurel shrub, every now and then perching on a lacquered leaf and sliding down its grooved middle like a boy down the banisters on his birthday. Then the tide of the shade reached the laurels, and the magnificent, velvet-and-flame creature dissolved in it.
>
> (n. 993–95)

A reader inescapably responds to this butterfly, even as Shade responded to the white fountain, particularly because of its appearance at the moment of death and the verbal associations with "shade" and the poet's laurels, as a manifestation of some transcendental force in the universe moving in correspondence with human life, something like, perhaps, the powers Shade himself believed to play through human life:

> It did not matter who they were. No sound
> No furtive light came from their involute
> Abode, but there they were, aloof and mute,
> Playing a game of worlds.
> . . . .
> Coordinating these
> Events and objects with remote events

And vanished objects. Making ornaments
Of accidents and possibilities.
(ll. 816–29)

The possibility of meaning, however tenuous, is strengthened by long threads of association spreading throughout the novel from the Vanessa butterfly, the "Red Admirable," to Swift's Vanessa and her associations of love, poetry, and madness, and the red waxwing, with whom Shade identifies, which dies trying to fly through the reflected world on the window pane. Every event in Shade's world of New Wye has its correspondence in Kinbote's Zemblan world, and so the waxwing and the Vanessa have their Zemblan correspondents, the *sampel* or "silktail" and *harvalda,* "the heraldic one," and the red color common to both leads on to King Charles who makes his escape from Zembla dressed in bright red, and his many loyal subjects who risk their lives to aid his escape by also dressing in red to confuse the police.

In this "link-and-bobolink" way, everything in the "plexed artistry" of the novel seems to lead on to everything else and to tease us with the possibility of a completely articulated structure which if understood will allow us to fly through the barrier of the text into a meaning beyond. Shade's epileptic attack, which gives him for an instant the oceanic sense, begins when he is playing with a mechanical toy man pushing a wheelbarrow, and the last line of his poem, written just before his death, describes Kinbote's gardener "Trundling an empty barrow up the lane." His killer, now approaching, who uses an *automatic* pistol, is the mechanical man, Jakob Gradus, alias Jack Degree, in the Zemblan story, Jack Grey in the New Wye version. In the Zemblan version his automatism is that of the modern proletarian revolutionary, a "degraded" rootless childhood, work in the *mirror* factory, blind obedience to party discipline, the gray dull life of cheap hotel rooms, buses, and stale sandwiches, and the emotionless killing on command of a king or a poet. In the New Wye version the automaton is a compulsive maniac who had been committed to a hospital for the criminally insane and has now escaped—a link with all the other attempted escapes?—and returned filled with hatred to kill the judge who sentenced him. He blindly fires at the man who looks like the judge and is standing on the steps of the judge's house. Shade is killed, in either version, of revolutionary assassin or compulsive maniac, by the same total solipsism, the automatism of the given, which he spent his life and wrote his poetry trying to escape.

Escape cannot finally be for the poet or the reader, as the death of Shade indicates, from the uncertainties of self to a sure knowledge of some transcendent reality beyond the self, figured or mapped by the text, whether world or poem. Nabokov includes in his novel a Zemblan parable of the false art of the Zemblan painter Eystein, "a prodigious master of the *trompe l'œil,*" who in his paintings of the old kings and queens of Zembla had only managed to make them look more dead by his incredibly detailed, realistic renderings of the objects surrounding them, the flowers, the cloth, the panelling:

> But in some of those portraits Eystein had also resorted to a weird form of trickery: among his decorations of wood or wool, gold or velvet, he would insert one which was really made of the material elsewhere imitated by paint. This device which was apparently meant to enhance the effect of his tactile and tonal values had, however, something ignoble about it and disclosed not only an essential flaw in Eystein's talent, but the basic fact that "reality" is neither the subject nor the object of true art which creates its own special reality having nothing to do with the average "reality" perceived by the communal eye.
>
> (n. 130)

The complete failure of this kind of art is portrayed in the efforts after the revolution of two Russian investigators, acting like readers or critics searching for solid meaning, to locate the crown jewels which they believe lie concealed behind one of Eystein's pictures. In their search they come at last to a metal plate which Eystein has inserted in a portrait of a royal treasurer as the cover of his strong box, but upon prying the plate off the picture they find only the shell of a walnut, the kernel of which had been painted in beautiful perspective lying on a plate resting on top of the safe. Eystein's art and the investigator's criticism offer another image of that mirror situation of imprisonment and solipsism in world and self which is the existential fact of the novel. But Shade, and Kinbote, and Nabokov offer a very different kind of art which does not try to find the kernel of truth by literally representing some absolute reality, but rather by palely reflecting the light of some distant sun, in an elaborate play of correspondences and possibilities which suggest, but do not prove, some ultimate pattern of meaning, some elaborate game of complex moves. The truth that art offers is thus not in its literal picturing of the world, or in the rendering of some ideal truth perceived by the imagination, but in a provisional truth constructed by the mind to satisfy its own necessities. This is what Shade partly discovers after his failure to validate the existence of the ghostly fountain:

A feeling of fantastically planned,
Richly rhymed life.
                    I feel I understand
Existence, or at least a minute part
Of my existence, only through my art,
In terms of combinational delight;
And if my private universe scans right,
So does the verse of galaxies divine
Which I suspect is an iambic line.
                    (ll. 969–76)

This is also what Kinbote dimly knows in his desperate belief that his Zemblan story will become real if only Shade can somehow be persuaded to give it poetic form.

Powerful as Shade's statement about the value of art is, the old romantic certainty that the poet is a man speaking to men is gone, and in its place is an image of each of us, poet and reader, Shade and Kinbote, the citizens of New Wye and the murderer Grey, sitting in isolation staring into the mirrors of ourselves, unable to understand the messages sent us by the other and unable to send clear messages to others, despite a desperate need to communicate. Shade experiences this condition in its extreme metaphysical form, as befits the traditional poet, trying to penetrate the barriers of the universe itself, trying to fly through the sky reflected on the windowpane. Kinbote experiences it in its most terrifying and absurd human form in which his understanding of himself and his place in the world may be either an implausible truth or an insane man's elaborate delusion put together to justify himself and escape an unbearable reality. We as readers experience it by trying to find an absolute, fixed meaning in a novel which reveals each of our strategies of interpretation as the reflection of our own desire for self-justification.

But there is still in Nabokov's novel a glimmer of pale fire in the darkness, reflected dimly from the sun of some possible ultimate meaning, to the poet Shade, and from him to Kinbote, and from him, perhaps, to the readers. However different the players in the game may be—and they could hardly be more different—Kinbote's situation does correspond in certain crucial ways to Shade's, and the poem "Pale Fire," however mangled and misunderstood by Kinbote, does evoke in him an expression of his own kindred existential loneliness and fear. Some communication at the most basic level is still possible. And in both Shade and Kinbote, and ultimately in Nabokov—who identifies himself with Kinbote in various ways—the act of poetic creativity with its order and coherence suggests the possibility, nothing more, of corresponding qualities in the universe. The structure may be right even if the facts are wrong, the context right, if not the text. But even if the many suggestions that this belief too may be mere illusion, that Shade and Kinbote are equally deluded in different ways, are rejected, *Pale Fire* still puts the matter of poetic communication in a very different light than do more traditional poetics. The distance between poet and reader is as vast as it has become in the twentieth century, the languages as garbled, the solipsism as deep, and the need for validation through communication as desperate. The poem is no longer a bridge between the writer and the reader, no longer a hard statement of an absolute meaning, no longer a validation of truths the reader desperately needs to have made real for him by the poet. Instead, each poem and each reading are merely projections of ourselves, fictions constructed to save ourselves in our loneliness by making our world seem real. If there is any communication it is only a sharing of nameless fear and an attempt to deal with it by creating stories which name it, shape it, and give it a context of possible meaning.

THOMAS R. FROSCH

Parody and Authenticity in Lolita

It has been said that *Lolita* is simultaneously "a love story and a parody of love stories" and that its parody and its pathos are "always congruent." In this article I wish to explore what such a condition—that of being both parodic and authentic at the same time—may mean.

First, however, I suggest that we best describe *Lolita* generically not as a love story or a novel of pathos but as a romance. The plot itself is composed of a series of typical romance structures, each one a version of the quest or hunt and each one an embodiment of a specific type of suspense or anxiety. We begin with the pursuit of Lolita, and the anxiety of overcoming sexual obstacles. Next, once Humbert and Lolita are lovers, we have a story of jealousy and possessiveness, as Humbert is beset by fears of rivals and by Lolita's own resistance. Finally, in Humbert's dealings with Quilty, we have a third and fourth type, each with its attendant style and anxiety: the double story and the revenge story. Furthermore, these plot structures are infused with the daimonic (that is, a quality of uncanny power possessed originally by beings, whether good or evil, midway between gods and people), which is a primary characteristic of romance as a literary mode. Lolita is an inherently unpossessable object; her appeal consists partly in her transiency—she will only be a nymphet for a brief time—and partly in her status as a daimonic visitor to the common world. The quest is thus an impossible one from the outset; it is variously presented as a quest for Arcadia, for the past, for the unattainable itself; it is nympholepsy. Even in the rare moments

From *Nabokov's Fifth Avenue*, edited by J. E. Rivers and Charles Nicol.

when Humbert is free from his typical anxieties, he is not totally satisfied; he wants to "turn my Lolita inside out and apply voracious lips to her young matrix, her unknown heart, her nacreous liver, the sea-grapes of her lungs, her comely twin kidneys." Humbert is a believer in the enchanted and the marvelous. Like Spenser's Red Cross Knight, he rides forth on his quest adorned by the image of his guiding principle, in his case a blue cornflower on the back of his pajamas—the blue cornflower being Novalis's symbol of infinite desire. *Lolita* contains numerous parodic allusions to other literary works, especially to Mérimée's *Carmen* and Poe's "Annabel Lee," but the real anti-text implied by the allusions and parodies together is the romantic sensibility in general from Rousseau to Proust.

But exactly how seriously are we meant to take Humbert and his quest? The book's complexity of tone and the question of Humbert's reliability as a narrator are the first issues in an investigation of the relationship between the parodic and the authentic.

Nabokov takes great delight in rapid and unpredictable changes in tone; we are never permitted to rest for long in the pathetic, the farcical, the rapturous, or the mocking. One of the clearest examples of tonal complexity is the novel's "primal scene," the seaside love scene with Annabel Leigh. After a buildup of high erotic suspense during which the two children are repeatedly frustrated in their sexual attempts, the famous episode concludes as follows: "I was on my knees, and on the point of possessing my darling, when two bearded bathers, the old man of the sea and his brother, came out of the sea with exclamations of ribald encouragement, and four months later she died of typhus in Corfu." We misread this little roller-coaster ride from the impassioned to the hilarious to the poignant if we take any one of its tonalities as definitive. Certainly this is not simply a satire of the romantic; its effect comes rather from the coexistence of its three tonalities in a single moment. In such a passage, we might expect the romantic to go under, partly because of its inherent vulnerability and partly because, as the dominant tone of the long buildup, it is apparently punctured by the intrusion of the burlesque. Yet the paragraphs that follow return to a tone of erotic rapture in a scene that is chronologically earlier than the seaside scene. The second scene, describing another frustrated tryst, concludes as follows: "That mimosa grove—the haze of stars, the tingle, the flame, the honeydew, and the ache remained with me, and that little girl with her seaside limbs and ardent tongue haunted me ever since—until at last, twenty-four years later, I broke her spell by incarnating her in another." If Nabokov had intended to puncture Humbert's rhapsody, it would have been more appropriate for him to arrange the two scenes chronologically so that the ribald bathers would appear at the end of the entire sequence, instead of in the middle. As it is, nothing is punctured; if anything, the romantic has found a new energy after the interruption. It is as if, in the following paragraphs, the romantic has been given the bolstering it needs to be able to hold its own with the jocular.

The novel's narrative point of view is as elusive as its tone. Clearly, when Humbert tells us, as he does repeatedly, that he has an essentially gentle nature and that "poets never kill," he is belied by the destruction he wreaks on Charlotte, Quilty, and Lolita. And when Humbert accuses Lolita of "a childish lack of sympathy for other people's whims," because she complains about being forced to caress him while he is spying on schoolchildren, Nabokov is being sarcastic. Humbert also fails to see things that the reader can pick up; for example, he misses the name Quilty ("Qu'il t'y") concealed in a friend's letter to Lolita. Just as clearly, though, Humbert is sometimes Nabokov's champion, as for example in Humbert's satirical comments about psychoanalysis and progressive education. At other points, Nabokov's attitude toward his persona is quite intricate: Humbert says of his relationship with Annabel that "the spiritual and the physical had been blended in us with a perfection that must remain incomprehensible to the matter-of-fact, crude, standard-brained youngsters of today"; and Humbert does serve as a serious critic of modern love from the standpoint of a romantic exuberance of feeling, even if his criticism is undercut by his own divided love, in which what he calls his "tenderness" is always being sabotaged by what he calls his "lust."

But if we compare Humbert to another demented storyteller in Nabokov, Hermann in *Despair,* we see how Nabokov operates when he really wants to make a dupe out of his narrator. *Despair* is a take-off on the doppelgänger theme, in which the hero, Hermann, takes out an insurance policy on himself and then murders his double in order to collect; it doesn't work, however, because he's the only one who sees the resemblance. Hermann is among other things a Marxist, a sure sign that Nabokov is using him ironically, and Nabokov puts into his mouth frequent and obvious reminders of his unreliability. "I do not trust anything or anyone," he tells us. His wife's hero-worship of him is one of his constant themes, and yet his self-satisfaction and blindness are such that he can find her undressed in the apartment of a man who is her constant companion and not experience a moment's doubt of her fidelity. Nabokov himself, calling both Humbert and Hermann "neurotic scoundrels," does make an important distinction between them, when he writes that "there is a green lane in

Paradise where Humbert is permitted to wander at dusk once a year; but Hell shall never parole Hermann."

Even Hermann, however, at times seems a stand-in for Nabokov, as, for instance, whenever he speaks of outwitting or playing games with the reader. Much has been written of Nabokov's own fondness for game-playing, such as the use of the *Carmen* parallel in *Lolita* to tease the reader into believing that Humbert will kill his nymphet. In fact, it's difficult to find a Nabokov hero or narrator, however antipathetic, who doesn't at times sound like the author in his nonfiction. Even John Ray, the fool who introduces *Lolita,* asserts a prime Nabokov theme when he says that every great work of art is original and "should come as a more or less shocking surprise." And many readers have noticed the relationship between the desperate nostalgia of Humbert or that of the crazed Kinbote in *Pale Fire* and Nabokov's own commitment to the theme of remembrance. Conversely, Van Veen in *Ada*—who is the Liberated Byronic Hero, among other things, as Humbert is the Enchanted Quester and Hermann the Metaphysical Criminal—although he has been taken as almost a mouthpiece for Nabokov himself, has been condemned by his creator as a horrible creature. The fact seems to be that Nabokov in his fictional and nonfictional utterances has created a composite literary persona, just as Norman Mailer has. His heroes, like Mailer's D. J. and Rojack, tend to be more or less perverse or absurd inflections of his own voice. In two of his own favorite works, *Don Juan* and *Eugene Onegin,* we have narrators who keep intruding on their heroes to deliver speeches and who also are at pains to differentiate themselves from those heroes. Nabokov behaves similarly, except that he does so within the range of the single voice. As in the case of tone, we discover an interplay of engagement and detachment, an interplay that is most active and subtle in the most memorable of the characters, like Humbert and Kinbote.

With this general sense of the status of tone and narrator in *Lolita,* we can turn now to consider what Humbert actually says. Humbert subtitles his story a confession. More accurately, it is a defense. Portraying himself as a man on trial, Humbert repeatedly refers to his readers as his jury. "Oh, winged gentlemen of the jury!" he cries, or, "Frigid gentlewomen of the jury!" But he also frequently addresses us directly as readers; in the middle of a torrid sequence he speculates that the eyebrows of his "learned reader . . . have by now traveled all the way to the back of his bald head." And late in the book, in a parody of Baudelaire's "Au lecteur," he addresses the reader as his double: "Reader! *Bruder*!" The reader is sitting in judgment on Humbert; the purpose of his story is to defend what he calls his "inner essential innocence"; and the rhetoric of the book as a whole, its strategy of defense, is proleptic, an answering of objections in advance. Humbert's self-mockery, for example, has to be understood as a proleptic device, and, indeed, to follow the style of *Lolita* is to track the adventures of a voice as it attempts to clear itself of certain potential charges. As we will see, in many ways the defense is Nabokov's, even more than Humbert's.

At the end of the novel, Humbert sums up his defense by passing judgment on himself; he would give himself "at least thirty-five years for rape" and dismiss the other charges, meaning chiefly the murder of Quilty. But there are further accusations that the novel strives to evade. As a whole, the book defends itself against a utilitarian concept of art. This charge is rather easily evaded by the use of John Ray, who introduces the novel as an object-lesson in the necessity of moral watchfulness on the part of "parents, social workers, educators." Nabokov's obvious satire here is intended to remove the allegation of his having a conventional moral purpose. Other accusations are handled within the text itself. In addition to conventional moralists, Nabokov detests psychiatrists and literary critics, and it is against these types of readers—or these metaphors for the Reader—that Humbert wages constant war. Anti-Freudianism is one of Nabokov's pet themes, and Humbert is a man who, in his periodic vacations in insane asylums, loves nothing more than to take on a psychiatrist in a battle of wits. His chief defense against a psychoanalytic interpretation of *Lolita* is to admit it readily and dismiss it as trite and unhelpful. When he describes his gun, he says, "We must remember that a pistol is the Freudian symbol of the Ur-father's central forelimb"; Humbert beats the analysts to the draw and says, in effect, "So what?" At another point, he anticipates a Freudian prediction that he will try to complete his fantasy by having intercourse with Lolita on a beach. Of course he tried, Humbert says; in fact, he went out of his way to look for a suitable beach, not in the grip of unconscious forces but in "rational pursuit of a purely theoretical thrill"; and when he found his beach, it was so damp, stony, and uncomfortable that "for the first time in my life I had as little desire for her as for a manatee."

Ultimately, we have to understand Nabokov's anti-Freudianism in the context of a hatred for allegory and symbolism in general. In *Ada,* Van Veen says of two objects that both "are real, they are not interchangeable, not tokens of something else." Nabokov is against interpretation; an image has no depth, nothing beneath or behind or beyond; it is itself. Discussing Hieronymus Bosch, Van tells us, "I mean I don't give a hoot for the esoteric meaning, for the myth behind the moth, for the masterpiece-baiter who makes Bosch express some bosh of his time, I'm allergic to allegory and am quite sure he was just enjoying himself by crossbreeding casual fancies just for the fun of the contour and color." Another of Nabokov's heroes, Cincinnatus in *Invitation to a Beheading,* is a man whose mortal crime is to be opaque, or inexplicable, while everyone else is transparent. To be inexplicable is to be unrelatable to anything else; Humbert refers to the "standardized symbols" of psychoanalysis, and Hermann, a bad literary critic, points out a resemblance that nobody else can see. Nabokov's hero-villains are often allegorists, like Humbert, who imposes his fantasy of Annabel Leigh on Lolita and turns her into a symbol of his monomania.

Allegory, as Angus Fletcher has shown, is daimonic and compulsive; it is a spell, enchanted discourse. Nabokov, on the contrary, tries to create structures that defy interpretation and transcend the reader's allegorism, Freudian or otherwise; like Mallarmé, he dreams of a literature that will be allegorical only of itself. Thus, Humbert evades our attempts to explain him according to prior codes or assumptions. First of all, he insists that women find his "gloomy good looks" irresistible; therefore, we can't pigeonhole him as someone forced into perversion by his inability to attract adult women. Then, too, Lolita is not "the fragile child of a feminine novel" but a child vamp, who, furthermore, is not a virgin and who, even further, Humbert claims, actually seduces him—a claim that is at least arguable. And finally, when we are forced to compare Humbert to Quilty, a sick, decadent, and cynical man, a man who is immune to enchantment, it becomes impossible simply to categorize Humbert as a pervert like all others. In all these ways, Humbert is not only made to look better than he otherwise would; he is also made difficult to explain and classify, and his uniqueness is a crucial theme of his defense. In *Ada,* Van Veen acclaims the "individual vagaries" without which "no art and no genius would exist." In *Despair,* Hermann the Marxist longs for the "ideal sameness" of a classless society, where one person is replaceable by another, while his rival, the artist Ardalion, believes that "every face is unique." In fact, even Hermann admits that his double resembles him only in sleep or death; vitality is individuation. It is a favorite theme of Nabokov. We are told in *Pnin* that schools of art do not count and that "Genius is non-conformity." The author himself always hates being compared to other writers: "Spiritual affinities have no place in my concept of literary criticism," he has said. In light of this, it is worth noting that the alienation and linguistic eccentricity of a character like Pnin are, in addition to being poignant and comical, the valuable signs of his singularity. Whatever else they are, heroes like Pnin, Humbert, and Kinbote are recognizable; they are rare birds. Humbert tells us that he is even singular physiologically in that he has the faculty of shedding tears during orgasm.

Humbert's chief line of defense is that he is no "brutal scoundrel" but a poet. Nympholepsy is aesthetic as well as sexual; the nymphet in the child is perceived by the mind. Humbert does not wish merely to tell us about sex, which anyone can do; he wants "to fix once for all the perilous magic of nymphets"; he wants to fix the borderline between "the beastly and beautiful" in nymphet love. He calls himself "an artist and a madman, a creature of infinite melancholy"; he is an explorer of that special romantic domain of sensation, the feeling of being in paradise and hell simultaneously; and he is a sentimentalist who revokes the anti-romantic bias of modernism in a sentimental parody of Eliot's "Ash Wednesday." The problem is that in portraying himself as a romantic dreamer and enchanted poet, rather than as a brutal scoundrel, he leaves himself open to another charge: literary banality. He recognizes his position as a spokesman for values that no one takes seriously anymore and says that his judges will regard his lyrical outbursts and rhapsodic interpretations as "mummery," so much hot air to glorify his perversion. His nymphet, on the other hand, is at best bored by his mummery, and the two often operate as a vaudeville team, in which he is the alazon and she the eiron:

> "Some day, Lo, you will understand many emotions and situations, such as for example the harmony, the beauty of spiritual relationship."
>
> "Bah!" said the cynical nymphet.

Humbert fears Lolita's "accusation of mawkishness," and his madcap and mocking humor defends him against any such accusation by the reader. So too does the presence of Charlotte, a trite sentimentalist whose mode of expression he mocks and against which his own appears unimpeachable. Yet he says, "Oh, let me be mawkish for the nonce. I am so tired of being cynical."

If the book's central rhetorical figure is prolepsis, its central structural figure is displacement, or incongruity. Often cultural or geographical, incongruity appears in such local details as Charlotte's calling her patio a "piazza" and speaking French with an American accent; but more generally it appears in Humbert's old-world, European manner—aristocratic, starchy, and genteel—set in a brassy America of motels and movie magazines, and in his formal, elegant style of speaking posed against Lolita's slang. But Humbert is not only out of place; he is also out of time, since he is still pursuing the ghost of that long-lost summer with Annabel Leigh. The incongruity is also erotic, in the sexual pairing of a child and an adult, and, in the application of romantic rhetoric to child-molesting, it appears as a problematic relation between word and thing. The geographical, linguistic, and temporal aspects of Humbert's dislocation are often related to Nabokov's own exile; but I wish to emphasize here another primal displacement, Humbert's status as a nineteenth-century hero out of his age. In this literary dislocation, a romantic style is placed in a setting in which it must appear alien and incongruous. Humbert's problem is to defend his romanticism in a de-idealizing, debunking, demythologizing time.

In *Eugene Onegin* Tatiana wonders if Onegin is a mere copy of a Byronic hero:

> who's he then? Can it be—an imitation,
> an insignificant phantasm, or else
> a Muscovite in Harold's mantle,
> a glossary of other people's megrims,
> a complete lexicon of words in vogue? . . .
> Might he not be, in fact, a parody?
> (ellipses in original)

Humbert, in his displaced and belated romanticism, must prove that he is not an imitation. Nabokov's use throughout his work of various doubles, mirrors, anti-worlds, and reflections has been much documented and explored. His heroes are typically set in a matrix of doubleness: the condemned man Cincinnatus in *Invitation to a Beheading,* for example, is doubled both by his secret inner self—his freedom or his imagination—and by his executioner. Among its many functions, the double serves as a second-order reality, or parody. The double Quilty parodies Humbert who parodies Edgar Allan Poe. Humbert is referred to many times as an ape, and an ape is not only a beast but an imitator. Nabokov has written that the inspiration of *Lolita* was a story of an ape who, when taught to draw, produced a picture of the bars of his cage. So Humbert, the ape, the parody, gives us a picture of his emotional and moral imprisonment and enchantment. To be free is to be original, not to be a parody.

"I am writing under observation," says the jailed Humbert. Once upon a time, observers walked out of the sea to destroy the best moment of his life; before their arrival, he and Annabel had "somebody's lost pair of sunglasses for only witness." Fear of discovery is Humbert's constant anxiety; he feels that he lives in a "lighted house of glass." The observer, the jury, the brother in the mirror represent the reader and also the self-consciousness of the writer. Robert Alter has pointed out in his excellent study *Partial Magic* that an entire tradition of the "self-conscious novel," stemming from *Don Quixote,* employs a "proliferation of doubles" and mirror-images to present a fiction's awareness of itself as fiction and to speculate on the relation between fiction and reality. *Lolita* certainly participates in this tradition, but the sense of time expressed by its displacements and its literary allusions suggests that we understand its self-consciousness as specifically historical, as in the theories of Walter Jackson Bate and Harold Bloom. Humbert's jury is the literary past, which sits in judgment over his story. Humbert is both a mad criminal and a gentleman with an "inherent sense of the *comme il faut*"; self-consciousness figures here as the gentleman in the artist, his taste or critical faculty, his estimation of what he can get away with without being condemned as an imitator, a sentimentalist, or an absurdly displaced romantic.

What is on trial, then, is Humbert's uniqueness and originality, his success in an imaginative enterprise. To what judgment of him does the book force us? Quilty is the embodiment of his limitations and his final failure. He first appears to Humbert in the hotel where the affair is consummated; thus as soon as the affair begins in actuality, Humbert splits in two; and later, practicing to kill Quilty, he uses his own sweater for target practice. Described as the American Maeterlinck, Quilty is a *fin-de-siècle* decadent and thus the final, weak form of Humbert's romanticism; his plays reduce the themes of the novel to the sentimental and the banal: the message of one of them is that "mirage and reality merge in love." Quilty, who is worshipped by Lolita and who couldn't care less about her, incarnates the ironies of Humbert's quest: to possess is to be possessed; to hunt is to be hunted. In addition, to be a parody, as Humbert is of a romantic Quester, is to be defeated by doubleness: Quilty is an ape who calls Humbert an ape.

In relation to Lolita, Humbert accepts complete guilt. The end of the book is filled with outbursts against himself for depriving her of her childhood. A poet and a lover of beauty, he finishes as a destroyer of beauty. At one point, learning how to shoot, Humbert admires the marksmanship of John Farlow, who hits a hummingbird, although "not much of it could be retrieved for proof—only a little iridescent fluff"; the incident aptly characterizes Humbert's actual relationship to his own ideal. At the end, he recognizes that "even the most miserable of family lives was better than the parody of incest, which, in the long run, was the best I could offer the waif." All he can achieve is parody. When he calls himself a poet, the point is not that he's shamming but that he fails. Authenticity eludes him, and he loses out to history. What he accomplishes is solipsism, a destructive caricature of uniqueness and originality, and he succeeds in creating only a renewed sense of loss wherever he turns: of his first voyage across America with Lolita, he says: "We had been everywhere. We had really seen nothing. And I catch myself thinking today that our long journey had only defiled with a sinuous trail of slime the lovely, trustful, dreamy, enormous country."

Humbert is finally apprehended driving down the wrong side of the road, "that queer mirror side." This is his last dislocation and is symbolic of all of them. We can now address one further form of displacement in Humbert's quest, the displacement of the imagination into reality. The mirror side of the road is fantasy, and Humbert has crossed over. Lolita was a mental image, which Humbert translated into actuality and in so doing destroyed her life and his; but his guilt is to know that she has a reality apart from his fantasy. The narrator of Nabokov's story " 'That in Aleppo Once,' " measuring himself against Pushkin, describes himself as indulging in "that kind of retrospective romanticism which finds pleasure in imitating the destiny of a unique genius . . . even if one cannot imitate his verse." So Humbert is proud to inform us that Dante and Poe loved little girls. Hermann, in *Despair,* treats the artist and the criminal as parallels in that both strive to create masterpieces of deception that will outwit observers and pursuers; it is Hermann's failure not only to be found out but to be told that his crime, an insurance caper, was hopelessly hackneyed. Kinbote too confuses imagination and reality in *Pale Fire,* for he thinks he has written a critique and a factual autobiography, whereas he has really produced a poem of his own. Crime and mythomania are parodies of art; Humbert parodies the novelist who attempts to displace the imagination into actuality, and this would seem to be the judgment of him handed down by the novel itself. Note, however, that this is the way romantic heroes—for example, Raskolnikov, Frankenstein, Ahab—typically fail. Perhaps it is Humbert's deeper failure to think, not that he could succeed, but that he could achieve the same kind of high romantic failure as those heroes of a lost age.

In any case, at the end, Humbert—who was a failed artist early in his career, who tried to translate art into life and again failed, and who then turned a third time to art, now as a refuge, a sad compensation, and a "very local palliative"—sees art as a way to "the only immortality" he and Lolita may share. Having in effect destroyed her, he now wants to make her "live in the minds of later generations." A new idea of art does begin for him in his own imaginative failures. Then, too, he now claims to love Lolita just as she is, no longer a nymphet and now possessing an identity, dim and gray as it may be, that is separate from his private mythology. Thus, unlike

Hermann, who will never be paroled from Hell, Humbert is finally able to see beyond the prison of his solipsism.

At this point I wish to turn from Humbert's engagement with the parodic and the romantic to Nabokov's, and I will begin with several points about parody in general. Parody is representation of representation, a confrontation with a prior text or type of text. The mood of the confrontation varies with the instance. We can have parody for its own sake; for example, in *TLS* (21 January 1977), Gawain Ewart translated an obscene limerick into two prose passages, one in the style of the *OED,* the second in the style of Dr. Johnson's dictionary. Then we can have parody for the purpose of critique—satirical parody, such as J. K. Stephen's famous takeoff on Wordsworth and his "two voices": "one is of the deep . . . And one is of an old half-witted sheep." *Lolita* includes examples of both types: for instance, the roster of Lolita's class with its delightful names (Stella Fantazia, Vivian McCrystal, Oleg Sherva, Edgar Talbot, Edwin Talbot . . .) and the Beardsley headmistress's spiel about her progressive school ("We stress the four D's: Dramatics, Dance, Debating and Dating"). But as a whole the novel participates in a third type, parody that seeks its own originality, what Robert Alter would call metaparody: parody that moves through and beyond parody.

When Alter calls parody "the literary mode that fuses creation with critique," he is saying something that is strictly true only of satirical parody. What is common to all three types is that they fuse creation with differentiation. Parodists use a voice different from their own in such a way as to call attention to themselves. Parody is at once an impersonation and an affirmation of identity, both an identification with and a detachment from the other. This sense of displaced recognition, this incongruous simultaneity of closeness and distance, is a primary source of the delight and humor of parody, although it should be noted that parody is not inevitably comic, as in the case of John Fowles's *The French Lieutenant's Woman,* for example. Some parody, such as Stephen's, emphasizes the distance, but we also need to remember John Ashbery's idea of parody to "revitalize some way of expression that might have fallen into disrepute." It may be true that some aggression is inherent in all parody, no matter how loving, but it is an aggression that is more primal than intellectual critique: it is the kind of aggression that says, "This is me. This is mine."

Page Stegner has said that Nabokov uses parody to get rid of the stock and conventional, and Alfred Appel, Jr., that he uses parody and self-parody to exorcise the trite and "to re-investigate the fundamental problems of his art." I think it is finally more accurate to say that he uses parody to evade the accusation of triteness and to elude the literary past in the hope of achieving singularity. Nabokov's parodism is an attempt to control literary relations, a way of telling his jury that he already knows how his book is related to prior work. More than that, it is a way of taking possession of the literary past, of internalizing it. Nabokov has repeatedly noted and critics—most vividly, George Steiner—have often stressed the idea that he writes in a borrowed language. But in his difficult condition of personal and linguistic exile, Nabokov also points to another, more general kind of displacement. Irving Massey has suggested that many works of literature deal with the problem that "*parole* is never ours," that we all speak a borrowed idiom in expressing ourselves in the public medium of language. It is also relevant that a writer inevitably speaks in the borrowed language of literary convention. Like so many other writers of the nineteenth and twentieth centuries, Nabokov dreams of detaching his representation from the history of representations, of creating a *parole* that transcends *langue*.

In relation to romance, parody acts in *Lolita* in a defensive and proleptic way. It doesn't criticize the romance mode, although it criticizes Humbert; it renders romance acceptable by anticipating our mockery and beating us to the draw. It is what Empson calls "pseudo-parody to disarm criticism." I am suggesting, then, that *Lolita* can only be a love story through being a parody of love stories. The most valuable insight about *Lolita* that I know is John Hollander's idea of the book as a "record of Mr. Nabokov's love-affair with the romantic novel, a today-unattainable literary object as short-lived of beauty as it is long of memory." I would add that parody is Nabokov's way of getting as close to the romantic novel as possible and, more, that he actually does succeed in re-creating it in a new form, one that is contemporary and original, not anachronistic and imitative. Further, it is the book's triumph that it avoids simply re-creating the romantic novel in its old form; for Nabokov to do so would be to lose his own personal, twentieth-century identity.

Nabokov has tried to refine Hollander's "elegant formula" by applying it to his love affair with the English language. His displacement of the formula from the literary to the linguistic is instructive. Indeed, both in theory and practice, he is always moving the linguistic, the stylistic, and the artificial to center-stage. "Originality of literary style . . . constitutes the only real honesty of a writer," says Van Veen, who characterizes his own literary activities as "buoyant and bellicose exercises in literary style."

Language that calls attention to itself relates to romance in one of two ways. Either it becomes—as in Spenser or Keats—a magical way of intensifying the romance atmosphere, or—as in Byron with his comical rhymes and his farcical self-consciousness—it demystifies that atmosphere. As in *Don Juan,* language in *Lolita* is used to empty out myth and romance. The novel opens with Humbert trilling Lolita's name for a paragraph in a parody of incantatory or enchanted romance language and proceeds through a dazzling panorama of wordplay, usually more Byronic than Joycean: zeugmas, like "burning with desire and dyspepsia"; puns, such as "We'll grill the soda jerk"; alliterations, such as "a pinkish cozy, coyly covering the toilet lid"; unexpected and inappropriate condensations, such as the parenthetical comment "(picnic, lightning)" following Humbert's first mention of his mother's death; instances of language breaking loose and running on mechanically by itself, as in "drumlins, and gremlins, and kremlins"; monomaniacal distortions of diction: "adults one dollar, pubescents sixty cents."

Certainly, verbal playfulness for its own sake is an important feature of Nabokov's art; certainly, too, we ought not underestimate the way in which Nabokov's linguistic exile has contributed to his sense of language as an objective presence, not merely a vehicle. It may also be that wordplay is used to overcome language: in *Despair,* Hermann says that he likes "to make words look self-conscious and foolish, to bind them by the mock marriage of a pun, to turn them inside out, to come upon them unawares." But I would suggest that language is finally a false clue in Nabokov's work unless we see that his centering of language and style chiefly has the value of a poetic myth. A literature of pure language and convention is a dream, congruent with the dream of a literature beyond interpretation; it is a dream of literature as a word game with no depth, a manipulation of conventions, a kind of super-Scrabble. The function of this poetic myth, or "bellicose exercise," is here proleptic; it detaches the writer from the romantic so that he may then gain for the romantic an ultimate acceptability.

This is also true of the idea of games in Nabokov and of all the devices of self-consciousness that Alfred Appel, Jr., has valuably described, such as the kind of coincidental patterning that runs the number 342 into the novel in different contexts to emphasize the artificiality of the fiction. Humbert and Quilty share with their creator a love for the magic of games, as do so many other of Nabokov's characters; and sometimes that magic can assume diabolical form, as it does in the case of Axel, a forger of paintings and checks in *Laughter in the Dark.* The vicious Axel completely identifies creativity with game-playing; for him, "everything that had ever been created in the domain of art, science or sentiment, was only a more or less clever trick." Parody, Nabokov has said, is a game, while satire is a lesson.

A game is a matter of manipulating conventions; it is also a matter of play, a little Arcadia; and it is also a matter of competition. We can look at the idea of the game as a trope, a clinamen in Harold Bloom's sense, by which Nabokov swerves from the dead-seriousness of typical romance. But I see it ultimately, like parody and the centering of style, as an enabling poetic myth, the I-was-only-joking that permits us to get away with shocking utterances, like romantic rhapsodies in the mouth of an urbane, sophisticated, literate person like Humbert. It is the fiction that permits fiction to occur.

We might say that Nabokov must kill off a bad romantic and a bad artist in Humbert in order for his own brand of enchantment to exist. Nabokov's recurrent fascinations are romantic ones; he writes about passion, Arcadia, memory, individualism, the ephemeral, the enchanted, imagination, and the power of art. Indeed, his problem in *Lolita* is essentially the same as Humbert's: first, to be a romantic and still be original, and, second, to get away with being a romantic. *Lolita* has been taken as a critique of romanticism, and I am not arguing that it should be read as a romantic work. Rather, in its final form it is a work of complex relationship to romanticism, a dialectic of identification and differentiation. Like Byron in *Don Juan,* Nabokov in *Lolita* is divided against himself, although in a different way: Byron is a poet struggling against his own romantic temperament, while in Nabokov we see a romantic temperament trying to achieve a perilous balance in an unfriendly setting. But the results do illuminate each other: in *Don Juan* a romantic lyricism and melancholy are achieved through mocking parody and farce; in somewhat similar fashion, Nabokov uses the energies of his style—its parody, its centering of language, its flamboyant self-consciousness—first against the spirit of romance and then in behalf of it. This, then, is the status of style in *Lolita,* and this is why style is elevated to such prominence; perhaps this is even why it must be a comic style: it functions as a defensive strategy both against the romanticism of the material and against the anti-romanticism of the "jury."

Indeed, the tradition of romance continues most interestingly and convincingly today in writers, such as Thomas Pynchon and John Fowles, who are ambivalent about it and often present it negatively. In such teasing and parodic works as *V.* and *The Magus* we see an attempt to gain the literary power of romance without falling under its spell. These are romances for a demythologizing age. The phenomenon of the romantic anti-romance is hardly new; *Don Quixote, The Odyssey,* and *Huckleberry Finn,* in addition to *Don Juan,* are also works of enchantment that simultaneously reject enchantment. All of them create a language which, in Marthe Robert's description of *Don Quixote,* is both "invocation and critique"—indeed, Alter applies this phrase to the self-conscious novel as a tradition. What may be new, however, is the anxiety created by novels like *V.* and *The Magus* in their skeptical and modernistic perspective on the daimonic. That anxiety—our uncertainty about how we are meant to take the daimonic—is the source of the suspense in such works. In *Lolita,* the comedy considerably mitigates this anxiety; it is, however, produced to an extent by the dizzying narcissism of Kinbote in *Pale Fire* and, even more, by the celebratory tone of *Ada,* that incestuous love story with a happy ending.

Writing of Spenser, Harry Berger, Jr., has said that advertised artificiality in Renaissance art functioned to mark off an area in which artist and audience could legitimately indulge their imaginations. Today similar techniques of self-consciousness serve to keep our imaginations in check by telling us that what we are offered is only a fiction, merely a myth. Yet these cautionary measures, even when—as in *V.*—they seem to constitute the major theme of the work, may, once again, serve chiefly to allow us to enter a daimonic universe with a minimum of guilt and embarrassment. In sophisticated art we can consent to romance only after it has been debunked for us.

In *The Magus,* Fowles tells a fable of a young man who learns that the only way to avoid being victimized by magical illusions is to be a magician oneself. This is also true of Nabokov. In *Invitation to a Beheading,* everyone in Cincinnatus's totalitarian society appears to him to be a parody, a shadow of a reality, a copy. To be a parodist is one way of not being a parody. In *Despair,* Hermann, who seeks originality and hates and shuns mirrors, falls prey to a fake doubleness; Kinbote and Humbert are also trapped by reflections and doubles. But uniqueness resides in being able to manipulate doubleness; the inability to do this seems to be one of Nabokov's central criticisms of his failed artists. As for *Lolita* itself, it does beyond a doubt achieve singularity; however, singularity is not, as Nabokov would have it, to transcend literary relations but to be able to hold one's own among them.

Appel points out that Jakob Gradus, the assassin of *Pale Fire,* is an anagrammatic mirror-reversal of another character in that novel, Sudarg of Bokay, described as a "mirror-maker of genius," or artist. Both death and the artist create doubles of life, and each struggles against the other. For the writer the assassin comes from many directions: previous literature, current critical standards, the expectations of the audience, the resistance of language, the writer's own self-consciousness. Nabokov has spoken of the artist as an illusionist trying to "transcend the heritage" with his bag of tricks. This is the magic of sleight-of-hand, and Nabokov is referring to matters of style, technique, and language. But we are really dealing in works such as *Lolita* with the magic of the shaman, and, in this case, parody—together with the other features of a proleptic comic style—is perhaps his most powerful spell.

LUCY MADDOX

Pnin

Timofey Pnin, annotator par excellence, might have had a field day with the novel *Pnin* had he taken any interest at all in contemporary fiction. A meticulous scholar who delights in details, Pnin can straighten out the chronology of *Anna Karenina* for an acquaintance who is reading the book for the seventh time, and pinpoint for him the inconsistencies in it; he knows the birth and death dates of his favorite writers; he can give an ex tempore dissertation on the confusion between *vair* and *verre* in the evolution of the Cinderella story; he can document the first mention of various sports in literature; as a researcher, one of his greatest pleasures is finding and correcting errors in the documentation of others. Pnin, in short, cannot abide imprecision and inconsistency. "It was the world that was absent-minded," the narrator observes, "and it was Pnin whose business it was to set it straight."

Surely, then, Pnin would have had something to say about the carelessness with which the narrator of *Pnin* handles details. For example, the narrator mentions that in the spring of 1911 Pnin was thirteen years old and he, the narrator, was twelve; yet five years later in the summer of 1916 he was only sixteen, while Pnin was properly eighteen. In addition, he first gives 1925 as the year Pnin met his wife, Liza, yet later he speaks of that meeting as occurring "in the early twenties." He cannot be any more specific about the beginning of his acquaintance with Pnin's good friend Chateau than to place it in the summer of 1935 or 1936. Pnin would certainly have footnoted and cross-referenced some other oddities in the narrator's account, such as the appearance of that ubiquitous couple, Christopher and Louise Starr of the fine arts department, who turn up later as the psychologists Louis and Christine Stern, then as the analyst's dolls Lou and Tina, and finally as Chris and Lew, "a pair of twittering young Englishmen." Or the appearance of two apparently unrelated minor characters with the same name, the American Bob Horn and the Russian Robert Karlovich Horn.

Pnin might very well have been able to sort out these matters for us, or perhaps to explain them as gracefully as he explained Tolstoy's inconsistent chronology as an instance of the difference between Lyovin's spiritual time and Vronsky's physical time, "the best example of relativity in literature that is known to me." For our part as readers, these matters are troublesome enough, but less troublesome than the more difficult problem of how to suspend disbelief and accept the veracity of the narrator's very intimate portrait of a man with whom he has only a slight acquaintance. The problem is compounded because we would like very much to believe in the reality of this gentle, vulnerable, unselfconscious Pnin, who feels sorry for thirsty squirrels and hungry dogs, frequents a failing restaurant purely out of sympathy, despises gossip and intrigue, and is capable of completely selfless, lifelong devotion to the things he loves. Yet we resist putting full faith in the account of this character because the narrator keeps intruding to remind us that it is *his* account and thus, indirectly, that Pnin—at least Pnin in his private moments, and there are many in the book—is his invention. We would prefer an invisible narrator to whom we could willingly grant the privilege of omniscience, who would allow us to maintain our aesthetic double standard and acknowledge the fictiveness of *Pnin* but not of Timofey Pnin, to delight in the real toad we find in the imaginary garden. The narrator seems almost to warn us not to take his story too seriously, or at least not too literally. He confesses that his recollections of the few encounters he has had with Pnin are hazy and that he and Pnin disagree on some of the details of those encounters; Pnin even accuses him in public of being a "dreadful inventor." Two of his sources of information about Pnin are clearly unreliable—Eric Wind, the psychiatrist for whom Liza left Pnin, and Jack Cockerell, who sees Pnin as a buffoon, the campus character who lends himself well to comic imitation.

The narrator also drops enough clues for the alert reader to recognize that he played a major part in the events that led to Pnin's ill-fated marriage to Liza. He and Liza had a brief affair in Paris that left the narrator unmoved and Liza so moved that she attempted suicide when the affair ended. She married Pnin, on the advice of her analyst friends and after warning the narrator that she would marry someone else if he didn't come through with a proposal immediately, as therapy for her depression. Liza is vain, shallow, histrionic, and flighty—and Pnin loves her devotedly. She leaves Pnin for Eric Wind, a man who "understood her 'organic ego,' " returns to Pnin briefly on two occasions when she needs his help, leaves Wind for an American named Church, then leaves him for an Italian art dealer. The narrator is thus indirectly responsible for a large part of Pnin's sadness and sense of loss. When the narrator notes on one occasion that a remark Pnin happened to hear but paid little attention to "now bothered and oppressed him, as does, in retrospection, a blunder we have made, a piece of rudeness we have allowed ourselves, or a threat we have chosen to ignore," the reader begins to suspect that the narrator's motives for writing about Pnin are not disinterested, that he may be trying to rid himself of a lingering regret that now bothers and oppresses him. He protests, almost too much, that Pnin is his friend; he points out that the letter to the editor of the *New York Times* that Pnin proudly carries in his wallet was written with his help, and that the lady at the American consulate in Paris who helped facilitate Pnin and Liza's departure for America was a relative of his. The narrator's account of Pnin is, it appears, a demonstration of the "amazing fact" that V in *The Real Life of Sebastian Knight* found so hard to understand, "that a man writing of things which he really felt at the time of writing, could have had the power to create simultaneously—and out of the very things which distressed his mind—a fictitious and faintly absurd character."

The unusual narrative strategy of *Pnin* eventually lures the reader into a characteristically Nabokovian trap by refusing to conform to his expectations and jostling his preconceptions at every turn: what in the world are we to do with the paradox of an unreliable first-person omniscient narrator? This elaborate, carefully laid trap—baited with the most appealing character in Nabokov's novels—in the end offers the reader an object lesson in the nature of the Nabokovian art of fiction. The first and most elementary precept of that lesson is that a character who distorts some details and invents others is no more unreliable than the author who created the character and the details in the first place. The narrator of the story of Pnin is in fact imitating the creator of *Pnin,* a man he strongly resembles. Both are Anglo-Russian writers who emigrated to America, both were born in Saint Petersburg in the spring of 1899, both are named Vladimir Vladimirovich, and both are amateur lepidopterists. These similarities do not lead us to conclude, as some readers have done, that the narrator *is* Vladimir Nabokov. Rather, they serve to nudge us into the recognition that both are "dreadful inventors" whose fictions, rooted and grounded though they are in the real, take whatever liberties with the real these inventors may choose, in order to make of it an aesthetic whole that satisfies their own whims. Each of them is, as Nabokov has said of another, hypothetical artist, a "forger . . . constructing a mosaic out of genuine odds and ends with his own mortar."

The clearest example of the narrator's capricious imagination at work occurs in what is, significantly, the most sentimentally weighted scene in the book. This scene culminates a series of events that have conspired first to give Pnin the greatest happiness and emotional security he has had since coming to America, and then to snatch them away again. Pnin is content with his job at Waindell College and delighted with the progress of his research, and he has finally, after years of being a nomad, found the house of his dreams. He invites his friends to a "house-heating" party to celebrate his good fortune; the party also gives him a chance to display the splendid new punch bowl he has received as a gift from Liza's son, Victor. The marvelous bowl was "one of those gifts whose first impact produces in the recipient's mind a colored image, a blazoned blur, reflecting with such emblematic force the sweet nature of the donor that the tangible attributes of the thing are dissolved, as it were, in this pure inner blaze, but suddenly and forever leap into brilliant being when praised by an outsider to whom the true glory of the object is unknown."

After the party, the success of which provides the capstone to Pnin's happiness, Pnin's friend and ally Professor Hagen remains behind with an unenviable task to perform: he must tell Pnin that he is going to be fired from Waindell and thus will lose not only his job but his beloved house as well. Hagen delivers the cruel message and departs, leaving Pnin alone with his shocked disappointment, a stack of dirty dishes, and the new bowl:

> He prepared a bubble bath in the sink for the crockery, glass, and silverware, and with infinite care lowered the aquamarine bowl into the tepid foam. Its resonant flint glass emitted a sound full of muffled mellowness as it settled down to soak. . . . He groped under the bubbles, around the goblets, and under the melodious bowl, for any piece of forgotten silver—and retrieved a nutcracker. Fastidious Pnin rinsed it, and was wiping it, when the leggy thing somehow slipped out of the towel and fell like a man from a roof. He almost caught it—his fingertips actually came into contact with it in mid-air, but this only helped to propel it into the treasure-concealing foam of the sink, where an excruciating crack of broken glass followed upon the plunge.
>
> Pnin hurled the towel into a corner and, turning away, stood for a moment staring at the blackness beyond the threshold of

> the open back door. A quiet, lacy-winged little green insect circled in the glare of a strong naked lamp above Pnin's glossy bald head. He looked very old, with his toothless mouth half open and a film of tears dimming his blank, unblinking eyes. Then, with a moan of anguished anticipation, he went back to the sink and, bracing himself, dipped his hand deep into the foam. A jagger of glass stung him. Gently he removed a broken goblet. The beautiful bowl was intact. He took a fresh dish towel and went on with his household work.

The narrator lingers over this intense moment, exposing defenseless, pitiful Pnin to the strong glare of his narrative, and toying with both the reader's emotions and Pnin's in the terrible interval between the crack of broken glass and the discovery that the bowl was safe. (Pnin is caught in this passage from the very perspective that Eliot's Prufrock feared so, exposing to prying eyes his baldness and his vulnerability.) It is as if the narrator also pauses during that interval, lifting his pen while he decides the fate of his helpless character. Having chosen to leave Pnin and his bowl intact, the narrator can then return, like Pnin, to the business at hand: he can take a fresh sheet of paper, begin a new chapter, and go on with his work.

This scene in which Pnin is saved from complete despair is similar in its effect to the closing scene in *Bend Sinister,* in which Adam Krug is saved from too much awareness: in both cases we are permitted to see the narrator-as-anthropomorphic-deity at work, creating the private world of a character for whom, at times, he feels pity. In that world fate is much kinder and more sympathetic to the emotional needs of the character and the reader than it is in the "real" world, because it is determined by the forces of imagination, which, Nabokov once said, "in the long run are the forces of good." The kindness of the narrators in *Pnin* and *Bend Sinister* is arbitrarily bestowed, in defiance of both logic and the tendencies of their own narratives. But in both cases the manipulating narrator offers a justification for his choice of emotional consonance over logic by contrasting his arbitrary kindness with the wanton cruelty that the other deity permits in *his* created world—cruelty that is represented in both books by the slaughtering of innocents that goes on under totalitarian governments. Pnin's first sweetheart, Mira Belochkin, died in a German concentration camp, and the painful knowledge of her fate has since threatened to undermine Pnin's sanity:

> In order to exist rationally, Pnin had taught himself, during the last ten years, never to remember Mira Belochkin—not because, in itself, the evocation of a youthful love affair, banal and brief,

> threatened his peace of mind (alas, recollections of his marriage to Liza were imperious enough to crowd out any former romance), but because, if one were quite sincere with oneself, no conscience, and hence no consciousness, could be expected to subsist in a world where such things as Mira's death were possible. One had to forget—because one could not live with the thought that this graceful, fragile, tender young woman with those eyes, that smile, those gardens and snows in the background, had been brought in a cattle car to an extermination camp and killed by an injection of phenol into the heart, into the gentle heart one had heard beating under one's lips in the dusk of the past. . . . She was selected to die and was cremated only a few days after her arrival in Buchenwald, in the beautifully wooded Grosser Ettersberg, as the region is resoundingly called. It is an hour's stroll from Weimar, where walked Goethe, Herder, Schiller, Wieland, the inimitable Kotzebue and others.

In his descriptions of Pnin's private moments, such as the dishwashing scene, the narrator is providing his invented character with an alternative world in which beautiful, adored things do not have to be destroyed. The proximity of the poets' Weimar to Buchenwald is a reminder that, while the very real horrors of Buchenwald cannot be denied, there can and do exist what Nabokov once described as "other states of being where art (curiosity, tenderness, kindness, ecstasy) is the norm."

Nabokov's self-conscious, involuted novels frequently contain analogues of their own themes and methods—which in an art so insistent on its artifice become almost indistinguishable. *Pnin* provides an analogue of its method in Pnin's pet project, the "great work on Old Russia, a wonderful dream mixture of folklore, poetry, social history, and *petite histoire,*" in which "a choice of Russian Curiosities, Customs, Literary Anecdotes, and so forth would be presented in such a way as to reflect in miniature *la Grande Histoire*—Major Concatenations of Events." Pnin's opus is to be a commentary, a sustained footnote that fleshes out the skeleton of historical fact and gives it life. The narrator also begins with the bare bones of personal history—major concatenations of events in the life of Timofey Pnin, himself a Russian Curiosity—and then supplies his own commentary, a dream mixture of fact and fiction. As frequently happens with Nabokov's commentators (including Pnin himself), however, eventually "the quest overrides the goal, and a new organism is formed, the parasite so to speak of the ripening fruit." For Pnin the parasite is the intellectual pleasure of research, while for the narrator it is the psychological pleasure of creating an aesthetically and emotionally satisfying mosaic out of genuine odds and ends.

Pnin is studded with reminders that in the special world of Nabokov's fiction truth is compounded of the actual and the imaginary, and that the desire to distinguish between the two is an impulse that is sometimes best left outside the door. Within that world life imitates art as often as art imitates life. For example, the two "identically framed" pictures on the wall of the art teacher Lake's studio contain figures with identical facial expressions, although one picture is a photograph and one is a reproduction of the head of Christ from a Rembrandt drawing. Similarly, the paintings of the sentimental émigré artist Gramineev closely resemble the photographs taken by Mira Belochkin, Pnin's Russian sweetheart. Gramineev was a "well-known, frankly academic painter, whose soulful oils—'Mother Volga,' 'Three Old Friends' (lad, nag, dog), 'April Glade,' and so forth—still graced a museum in Moscow." Some of Mira's "artistic snapshots" are of the same subjects: "pets, clouds, flowers, an April glade. . . , a sunset skyline, a hand holding a book." The painter, the sunset skyline in Mira's photograph, and the actual people surrounding Pnin in the present eventually merge into an image in which even the narrator cannot, or will not, separate the real from the contrived: "On the distant crest of the knoll, at the exact spot where Gramineev's easel had stood a few hours before, two dark figures in profile were silhouetted against the ember-red sky. They stood there closely, facing each other. One could not make out from the road whether it was the Poroshin girl and her beau, or Nina Bolotov and young Poroshin, or merely an emblematic couple placed with easy art on the last page of Pnin's fading day."

The two clearest examples of the merging of art and actuality are Laurence Clements's discovery of an exact likeness of himself in Jan van Eyck's painting of Canon van der Paele, and Jack Cockerell's imitation of Pnin. Cockerell has worked at his performance so long and so successfully that not only can he impersonate Pnin to perfection, he has also in the process "acquired an unmistakable resemblance to the man he had now been mimicking for almost ten years." Hidden in the names of these two characters, Clements and Cockerell, are allusions to two plays by Arthur Schnitzler, author of *Libelei,* the play the narrator recalls seeing Pnin perform in back in 1916. Clements takes his name from the character Clemens in *Literature,* and Cockerell (whose wife is named Gwen) takes his from the title of *The Green Cockatoo.* Both plays share themes with *Pnin,* since both are about the impossibility of distinguishing between what Schnitzler calls "pretense" and "truth." *Literature* contains a very Liza-like character named Margaret who writes (as Liza does) bad love poetry. Her fiancé, Clemens, objects to Margaret's aspirations as a writer on the grounds that the poet or novelist is an emotional exhibitionist who shamelessly exposes his most intimate secrets to the public gaze. Margaret retorts that the writer does not always tell the truth: "We write of things we've never experienced, things we've dreamed or only invented." By the end of the play, however, it has become clear that Margaret's novel is in fact a true account of her life—which has been a series of carefully contrived gestures designed to make good material for a novel. In this sense, Margaret's novel tells the truth, and her life tells a lie.

The Green Cockatoo is set in Paris on July 14, 1789—the day the Bastille was stormed. A café owner has discovered that he can attract a wealthy aristocratic clientele to his café by hiring down-and-out actors to pose as exaggerated versions of themselves for the entertainment of the customers. As part of their act, they boast that the day is soon coming when they and their audience will have exchanged places. When news reaches the café that the Bastille has been taken and that members of the government are being killed, the audience is thrown into confusion, not knowing whether they are still watching a performance or not. The import of all this confusion is summarized by one member of the audience, the poet Rollin: "Reality—acting—can you always tell the difference, Chevalier? . . . I cannot—and what I find so remarkable here is that the apparent differences are done away with. Truth dissolves into pretense, pretense into truth."

The apparent differences are also done away with in *Pnin,* so that it is ultimately impossible to determine how much of the narrator's account of Timofey Pnin is "truth" and how much is pretense. Even when he seems most honest and straightforward, relating an event he himself has witnessed, his perspective frames the event and his imagination colors it, so that what we are given is always an image compounded of reality and imagination. At the end of the novel, for example, the narrator describes his last glimpse of his "good friend" Pnin. By an especially cruel twist of fate's knife, the narrator has been hired to fill the vacancy created at Waindell by the firing of Pnin; he is to launch his career there with a public lecture. Arriving in town a day early, he spends the night with the Cockerells and is treated to a great deal of Scotch and the famous impersonation. This drunken hilarity at Pnin's expense leaves the narrator with "the mental counterpart of a bad taste in the mouth"; he sleeps badly and slips out early the next morning in search of breakfast. In the course of his walk he spots Pnin speeding out of Waindell, all his possessions and the stray dog he couldn't leave behind loaded into the car. "From where I stood I watched them recede in the frame of the roadway, between the Moorish house and the Lombardy poplar. Then the little sedan boldly swung past the front truck and, free at last, spurted up the shining road, which one could make out narrowing to a thread of gold in the soft mist where hill after hill made beauty of distance, and where there was simply no saying what miracle might happen."

Pnin, who has lost his job to a rival and had to give up his beloved house on Todd Road, who has absolutely no place to go, and whose departure is of interest only to Cockerell, who wanted one more chance to mock Pnin with a drunken midnight serenade, thus departs in a framed picture, up a golden road into the soft mist of a future of miraculous possibilities. One clear sign, then, of how much manipulating the narrator is up to in this passage is that there is simply no way to justify its rosy—or golden—optimism. But there are other signs of the made-up quality of the entire passage that appear when we pay close attention to the details of the scene.

Most readers have seen little irony in this concluding passage, finding instead that it "evokes and affirms Pnin's continued vitality"; that it is a sign of Pnin's having sloughed off his roles of exile and alien to become a kind of existential hero, "the man, free and at home in his homelessness"; that even in this passage the narrator "does not appear to be a distorting refractor of the events he relates"; or that the narrator's dismissal of Pnin is a positive moral choice, a sign of his refusal to play the Pninian role of victim. Other readers have described Pnin's departure as a successful flight from the prying of the narrator, and certainly this is a logical explanation of why Pnin chooses to leave early in the morning of the very day—Pnin's birthday, incidentally—he expects the narrator to arrive in Waindell. But the framed picture is not of a defeated man in flight; it is of a confident adventurer setting out to seek the fortune that lies just beyond those lovely hills. The narrator's description of Pnin's departure is very similar to the account of Chichikov's departure from the town of N—— in Gogol's *Dead Souls.* (I might note that the narrator is accompanied on his early morning walk by a four-footed clue—the Cockerell's dog Sobakevich, who shares his name, which means "son of a bitch" in Russian, with a character in *Dead Souls.*) As Chichikov speeds out of town, "everything is flying by: the mileposts fly, merchants fly by on the boxes of their carriages. . . ; the entire highway is flying none knows whither away into the dissolving distance." Nabokov's comment on this lyrical passage, and I have quoted from his translation of it, is suggestive: "Beautiful as all this final crescendo sounds, it is from the stylistic point of view merely a conjuror's patter enabling an object to disappear, the particular object being—Chichikov." Pnin's exit, like Chichikov's, is a matter of style, the narrator's dismissal of the Pnin he has created.

While we know very little about this narrator, what we do know suggests that in several important respects he and Pnin are opposites, and that in filling in the outlines of Pnin's personality he has attributed to Pnin the very qualities he lacks himself. Early in the novel he indicates that he is a realist with a strong streak of pessimism: "Some people—and I am one of them—hate happy ends. We feel cheated. Harm is the norm. Doom should not jam. The avalanche stopping in its tracks a few feet above the cowering village behaves not only unnaturally but unethically. Had I been reading about this mild old man, instead of writing about him . . ." But he *is* writing about Pnin the incurable romantic, creating out of the things that distress him a faintly absurd character who nevertheless is able to cope with those very sources of distress. His anxieties grow out of his consciousness of what Van Veen calls "the direction of Time, the ardis of Time, one-way Time, . . . the irreversibility of Time." The narrator is on the one hand tormented by the inexorable backward glide of all things into the past; in recalling his childhood visit to Pnin's father (an eye specialist) to have a speck removed from his eye, he wonders "where that speck is now? The dull, mad fact is that it *does* exist somewhere." On the other hand, he visualizes the only future awaiting all living things as "a kind of soundlessly spinning ethereal void."

Out of this anxiety he creates Pnin, a man for whom all that is most dear has been buried in the past and whose faulty heart should keep him constantly aware of the proximity of death, yet who is so undisturbed by the passage of time that he never even takes note of his own birthday. Pnin has several defenses against despair at the treasonableness of time. One is his spontaneous and unabashed delight in living: "He was alive and that was sufficient." His psychological resilience is strong enough to defeat the efforts of his treacherous hearts (the real one and the metaphoric one) to lead him into despair—sufficient even to save him from his hopeless, suffocating love for Liza. "If people are reunited in Heaven," Pnin muses, "(I don't believe it, but suppose), then how shall I stop it from creeping upon me, over me, that shriveled, helpless, lame thing, her soul? But this is the earth, and I am, curiously enough, alive, and there is something in me and in life—." Pnin is interrupted before he can complete this thought by an urgent request: a thirsty squirrel is asking him to turn on the water fountain. Pnin accedes to this demand as naturally as he accedes to the more difficult demands that life—and Liza—make on him. He keeps the fountain on long enough for the squirrel to drink its fill; then, "its thirst quenched, the squirrel departed without the least sign of gratitude." Liza too has just departed from Pnin without a sign of gratitude, after having secured his assent to *her* urgent request that he send her son Victor some money each month.

Joan Clements, the most sympathetic and sensible of the secondary characters in the book, is used on occasion as a convenient, reliable mouthpiece for the narrator. After Liza's brief visit to Waindell, which finally convinces Pnin that he has lost her forever, Joan attempts to distract the disconsolate Timofey by showing him magazine pictures. She tries to interest him in a cartoon drawing of a desert island with palm tree, shipwrecked sailor, and mermaid, but Pnin refuses to be amused:

> "Impossible," said Pnin. "So small island, moreover with palm, cannot exist in such big sea."
>
> "Well, it exists here."
>
> "Impossible isolation," said Pnin.
>
> "Yes, but—Really, you are not playing fair, Timofey. You know perfectly well you agree with Lore that the world of the mind is based on a compromise with logic."

Joan's homiletic remark contains one of those puns that the practiced reader of Nabokov learns not to overlook. "Lore" is her nickname for her philosopher husband Laurence, but the word also suggests the "paradise of Russian lore" that is Pnin's refuge and chief delight as a scholar, and the source of material for his book. This kind of lore makes its own compromise with logic and with the sterile facts and chronologies of history.

The events of the recent past have confirmed Pnin's belief that "the history of man is the history of pain." But the *grande histoire* that records human pain is only half the story; Pnin's *petite histoire* will tell the other half. His book will complete the sentence that Pnin began, at a moment when he was feeling acutely the painfulness of his own life: "But this is the earth, and I am, curiously enough, alive, and there is something in me and in life—." (A similar situation occurs in *Ada;* there Van Veen writes a very long book to complete one of Ada's similes.) Pnin's alternative history will document man's persistent, irrational belief that harm is not the norm, that doom will eventually jam. The lore that fascinates Pnin—like the Green Week ceremony he reads about in a book on Russian myth, still practiced "in the margins of Christian ritual" in the nineteenth century, in which peasant maidens floated wreaths of spring flowers on the Volga—is a celebration of continuity, recurrence, and eternal return. Pnin himself, in spite of the fact that each new year seems to bring new losses and new disappointments, still can look forward eagerly to the "springtime splendor, all honey and hum," of the lilacs in his yard. When Pnin discovers his Green Week maidens he immediately associates them with Shakespeare's Ophelia; the folk ceremony, Shakespeare's fictions, and the narrator's inventive history of Pnin are all artificial, stylized forms—art forms, in short—which preserve the kind of irrational, subjective truths, verifiable only by the strength of their attraction on human thought and feeling, that offer an alternative to the historian's approximations.

Pnin has another saving quality which the narrator lacks, the ability to relinquish fully those things that are irretrievably lost and to delight in the novelty of the replacements that are provided. Pnin is, as Yeats says all men are, in love and loves what vanishes. The most valuable of the many things Pnin has "lost, dumped, shed" is the beloved Russia of his youth. Rather than remaining an exile mourning his homelessness, however, Pnin, after a transitional interval in Paris, chooses a new home—"America, my new country, wonderful America which sometimes surprises me but always provokes respect." Pnin is even willing to make difficult concessions to his new country, struggling with its unwieldy language and consenting to be called "Tim" rather than the "Timofey Pavlovich" he prefers. When he has to have all his teeth pulled, Pnin spends the first few toothless days "in mourning for an intimate part of himself. It surprised him to realize how fond he had been of his teeth." But once he gets his false teeth, Pnin characteristically stops regretting and rejoices in his discovery of something new, even if it is a substitute for the beloved original. Suddenly the new gadget, his plate, is "a revelation, it was a sunrise, it was a firm mouthful of efficient, alabastrine, humane America."

The Russia that Pnin loved died in the civil war of 1918–22. In the America of the 1950s Pnin is surrounded by evidence of the residue left by the turmoil of Russia's recent past: McCarthyism; his intellectual émigré friends, liberals and libertarians in prerevolutionary Russia, who now belong to American anticommunist organizations; the Starrs' modish interest in Dostoyevski and Shostakovich; President Poore's charitable commencement-speech reference to "Russia—the country of Tolstoy, Stanislavski, Raskolnikov, and other great and good men"; the student who hopes after a semester of Russian grammar to be able to read *Anna Karamazov* in the original; the 1940s Russian propaganda film including shots of a happy worker's family and the unanimous nomination of Stalin as candidate from the Stalin Election District of Moscow. These attitudes and postures underscore the isolation of the greatest and most apolitical Slavophile of them all,

Timofey Pnin, for whom Russia is a wrenching memory of things he loved and has lost—parents, friends, the beautiful Mira Belochkin, and the birches and bird cherries of the Russian woods.

Pnin has trained himself not to think of these things too often, but he has moments when time collapses for him, when something in the present brings the past back in an unexpected rush, so that Pnin for a moment lives simultaneously in the past and the present. The park between Waindell and Cremona, with its rhododendrons and oaks, brings back a childhood delirium in which he became obsessed with the pattern of rhododendron and oak on the wallpaper of his room; facing the audience at the Cremona Women's Club brings back an evening on which schoolboy Pnin recited a Pushkin poem before an audience that included his parents and Mira Belochkin; watching and listening to his Russian friends gathered for tea on the porch of Al Cook's country house brings back an evening in the summer of 1916 when he and Mira met in the garden while their families had tea on the porch of the Belochkins' country house.

These visions that come upon Pnin unexpectedly fuse past and present into a single image which juxtaposes the banality of Pnin's current surroundings with memories of the most intensely felt experiences of his past. In the few moments before he begins delivering his address to the Cremona Women's Club, for example, Pnin sees his audience undergo a strange transformation:

> In the middle of the front row of seats he saw one of his Baltic aunts. . . . Next to her, shyly smiling, sleek dark head inclined, gentle brown gaze shining up at Pnin from under velvet eyebrows, sat a dead sweetheart of his, fanning herself with a program. Murdered, forgotten, unrevenged, incorrupt, immortal, many old friends were scattered throughout the dim hall among more recent people, such as Miss Clyde, who had modestly regained a front seat. Vanya Bednyashkin, shot by the Reds in 1919 in Odessa because his father had been a Liberal, was gaily signaling to his former schoolmate from the back of the hall. And in an inconspicuous situation Dr. Pavel Pnin and his anxious wife, both a little blurred but on the whole wonderfully recovered from their obscure dissolution, looked at their son with the same life-consuming passion and pride that they had looked at him with that night in 1912 when, at a school festival, commemorating Napoleon's defeat, he had recited (a bespectacled lad all alone on the stage) a poem by Pushkin.

> The brief vision was gone. Old Miss Herring, retired Professor of History, author of *Russia Awakes* (1922), was bending across one or two intermediate members of the audience to compliment Miss Clyde on her speech, while from behind that lady another twinkling old party was thrusting into her field of vision a pair of withered, soundlessly clapping hands.

The mention of old Miss Herring and her book on Russia is not gratuitous; the images stored in Pnin's unconscious memory, this passage suggests, give a truer and more resonant picture of the past than the historian's chronicle of events and movements can give.

Proust says of the personal past that "it is a labour in vain to attempt to recapture it: all the efforts of our intellect must prove futile. The past is hidden somewhere outside the realm, beyond the reach of intellect." The narrator of *Pnin,* who once boasts of "the unusual lucidity and strength of my memory," becomes confused in his recollections of actual events in the past because his memory is an effort of the intellect, subverted by his anxieties about the past. For example, the guilt he apparently feels for his part in bringing about Pnin's marriage to Liza causes him to misremember Pnin's part in the performance of *Libelei.* He recalls that Pnin took the part of the cuckolded husband who avenges himself by killing his wife's young lover in a duel; Pnin, on the other hand, insists that he played the part of the old father who is left alone and distraught at the end of the play when his daughter leaves him, apparently to commit suicide. Paradoxically, we are by the end of the novel convinced of the reliability of Pnin, who is largely a creature of the narrator's imagination, and of the unreliability of the narrator who creates him. Like Schnitzler's Margaret, the narrator fabricates, with the aid of imagination, a convincing fictive truth out of the approximations and half-truths of the real.

The narrator's subject, Timofey Pnin, is also his model. Like Pnin's work on Old Russia, the narrator's book about Pnin is a commentary that serves as a necessary adjunct to the "real" life. While we grant the fictiveness of the narrator's account, we also recognize that it is no less "true" than Pnin's *petite histoire;* both define a life—one the life of a country, the other the life of a man—in terms of its texture, rather than in terms of a series of actions. In both instances those actions provide the text, but it is the commentary that gives the text authenticity, authority, and meaning.

DAVID RAMPTON

The Gift

The Gift is a key novel for anyone interested in Nabokov. Its detailed and provocative discussion of Russian literature and culture provides us, as one critic has said, with "basic insights into Nabokov's views on the uses of literature and literary criticism and contains an explanatory key to many of Nabokov's controversial literary, political and social opinions." This, combined with the fact that it is usually described as the best of his Russian novels, might lead one to suppose that a considerable amount of criticism devoted to the issues raised in the novel already exists. Yet surprisingly little has been written about *The Gift*. While it was still coming out in serial form in *Sovremennye Zapiski* (1937–38), Khodasevich predicted that there would be a stormy response to things like the presentation of the nineteenth-century radical critics in the novel: "All disciples and worshippers of the progressive thought police, watching over Russian literature since the 1840s, will fly into a rage," he wrote in *Vozrozhdenie*. But few of them did, at least in print. By refusing to publish chapter 4, the biography of Chernyshevsky which raises so many crucial questions about the role of Russian literature and the role of its "thought police" in the last century and in our own, the editors of the most important émigré journal effectively stifled the debate before it got started. The novel did not receive any substantial critical attention until 1963, when Simon Karlinsky published his brief but penetrating analysis of it. Since then various summaries of *The Gift*'s contents have appeared, and many interesting observations about it have been made in

---

passing; but only Field and Hyde, in their studies of Nabokov, have made important contributions to our understanding of the novel, and we still have no comprehensive account of the literary and social questions raised by Nabokov in it. What follows is an attempt to fill part of this gap, and in so doing to make a case for laying the emphasis squarely on the novel's content. Inevitably, it has been reread in the light of Nabokov's late fiction. Julia Bader calls it one of "the most apparently 'artificial' of his novels." John Stark says that of the novels written between *Mary* and *Lolita, The Gift* most closely resembles *Pale Fire, Ada,* and *Transparent Things.* And Alfred Appel, Jr. has stressed its self-reflexive qualities, noting that it begins on April Fool's Day, and that certain aspects of its structure call into question our most basic assumptions about fiction and reality: "If it is disturbing," he writes, "to discover that the characters in *The Gift* are also the readers of Chapter Four, this is because it suggests, as Jorge Luis Borges says of the play within *Hamlet,* 'that if the characters of a fictional work can be readers or spectators, we, its readers or spectators, can be fictitious.' " My interests are rather different.

This essay is divided into three parts. In the first [not reprinted here], I examine the portrayal of Nikolay Chernyshevsky and the discussion of his ideas. Chapter 4 of *The Gift* provides us with another opportunity for observing how Nabokov the novelist deals with real historical people and events. In the second part, I explore some of the ramifications of the debate about the Russian literary tradition, with specific reference to the discussion in the novel of "committed" and "uncommitted" literature. In the final section, I discuss some of the things that *The Gift* has to tell us about Nabokov's own relation to Russian literature. . . .

In the second part of this essay I want to focus on one of the principal issues raised in *The Gift:* the whole question of artistic freedom in the 1850s and 60s, and the effect of the critical views formulated in this period on the subsequent development of Russian literature. Nabokov deals with this question in two different ways, comic and serious. The following excerpt from a discussion of "the epoch" is a good example of the first way:

> At this point sparks flash from our pen. The liberation of the serfs! The era of great reforms! No wonder that in a burst of vivid prescience the young Chernyshevski noted in his diary in 1848. . . : "What if we are indeed living in the times of Cicero

> and Caesar, when *seculorum novus nascitur ordo,* and there comes a new Messiah, and a new religion, and a new world? . . ."
>
> The fifties are now in full fan. It is permitted to smoke on the streets. One may wear a beard. The overture to *William Tell* is thundered out on every musical occasion. . . . Under this cover Russia is busily gathering material for Saltikov's primitive but juicy satire.

Here Nabokov sees the whole period as gathering material for his purposes. His parodic version of newsreel history sets the hyperbolic tone, and the spirit of 1848, and the reforms, and the social unrest, and the revolutions, all float away in the hot-air balloon he has prepared for them. The epoch with all its important issues becomes a mere simulacrum. The radical critics, the men who along with Chernyshevsky played such an important role in the debate about these issues, are treated just as irreverently. Think of the images we are left with. Belinsky: "that likeable ignoramus, who loved lilies and oleanders, who decorated his window with cacti (as did Emma Bovary)"; Dobrolyubov: wrestling with Chernyshevsky, "both of them limp, scrawny and sweaty—toppling all over the floor, colliding with the furniture—all the time silent, all you could hear was their wheezing"; Pisarev: his "perverted aestheticism," "unbearable, bilious, teeth-clenching phrases about life being beautiful," and "completely insane" letters. With the opposition in this kind of farcical disarray, Nabokov presses home his advantage by allowing them to put their case for committed literature in only its most unconvincing and exaggerated forms. The argument might almost be won by default.

It isn't, because the issues involved are so momentous that they cannot be mocked into nonexistence. But before I take up the serious things Nabokov has to say about the status of literature at this crucial point in Russian history, I want to give someone else a chance to present his view of just what was at stake for Russia and its culture in the 1850s and 60s. I am thinking of Dostoyevski. He mistrusted the radical critics as much as Nabokov did, but he too thought their ideas about literature needed to be discussed. Of course he fares rather badly in *The Gift*. His work is dismissed in two delightful one-liners: "Bedlam turned back into Bethlehem," and "a room in which a lamp burns during the day." And he makes a personal appearance in chapter 4 as a panic-stricken supplicant, come to plead with Chernyshevsky to stop the St. Petersburg fires. Nevertheless, concerning this question of the obligations of the literary artist in mid nineteenth-century Russia, his analysis is a model of clarity and good sense.

In 1861 Dostoyevski wrote an article called "G. —bov i Vopros ob

Iskusstve" ("Mr —bov and the Art Question"), an overview of contemporary criticism (the figure alluded to in the title is Dobrolyubov), in which he discusses the debate between the advocates of pure and committed art. He asks the reader to imagine himself in eighteenth-century Lisbon just after the great earthquake. Half the city's population has been destroyed; its buildings lie in ruins; dazed survivors wander the streets. A newspaper appears, and, eager for information about the catastrophe that has befallen them, the people rush to see what it contains. What, asks Dostoyevski, are they to think if featured prominently on the front page they find the following poem by Fet?

> A whisper, timid breathing,
>   A nightingale's trills,
> The silver and flutter
>   Of a somnolent brook,
> Night's light, night's shadows,
>   Endless shadows.
> A series of magical changes
>   Of a dear face,
> In smoky clouds the purple of roses,
>   The reflection of amber,
> And kisses, and tears,
>   And the dawn, the dawn!

His answer is that the distraught citizens, outraged at the very idea of this kind of poetry's being written in the midst of their agony, would seize the author and summarily execute him in the public square for his inhuman and antisocial act. But he goes on to suggest that fifty years later they would erect a monument to the poor poet, for his wonderful verse in general and for "the purple of roses" in particular. Dostoyevski concludes that it was not the subject matter of the poem that was at fault but the poet's insensitivity. Once the public issues that so occupied the people are forgotten, the value of the poet's work can be assessed at its true worth. The message for critics like Dobrolyubov is plain. Yet having made clear that the demand for literature which addresses itself to certain social problems can only encroach upon the writer's freedom, Dostoyevski is careful to point out that the writer's inspiration can come as easily from a political or social issue as from anything else. And he takes it for granted that when any nation finds itself on the edge of an abyss, every citizen, writers included, should work together for the common good. They cannot be coerced into doing it; but if literature is allowed to develop freely, it will become the powerful weapon the utilitarians want it to be.

The existence in Dostoyevski's Russia of a large body of literature that is related to the major social and political issues of the day suggests that Russian writers felt themselves to be caught up in events as potentially destructive as any earthquake, and that at this time, in this place, they had the most fundamental contribution to make to their country. Chernyshevsky asserted quite unequivocally that this was the Russian tradition: while great writers in other countries at other times had worked with the perfection of their art in mind and for the benefit of their country only indirectly, Russian society, because of its relative immaturity, intellectual history and (though this could not be said openly) its political history, had always relied on literature, and for some time to come must continue to do so, in a way that other nations did not. Literature *was* Russia's political and social history. Most writers, more conscious of the problems created for their art by this tradition, and more aware of the contradictions inherent in their situation, wanted to write about social problems without producing the social tracts that Chernyshevsky often advocated. Yet even the "aesthetes," whom Fyodor so roundly condemns, sound more than a little like their progressive enemies at times. Druzhinin argued that all art was linked to the moral development of society, extolled the merits of practical experience in the working world for the aspiring writer, and insisted that if poetry was "the flower of life," it must be much more firmly rooted in the national soil than it was. And Turgenev, classified as an aesthete in *The Gift* for his "much too elegant 'visions' and misuse of Italy," wrote in one letter that "There are epochs when literature cannot remain *merely* art, when there are interests higher than poetic interest"; and in another that a novel like *Fathers and Sons* had been written at the right moment, had been of some "benefit" to the nation, and that this was the only thing that had any ultimate significance.

Nabokov really has three answers for all this talk about a Russian writer's social obligations. The first involves him in a detailed and subtle parody of these very sentiments in *The Gift* itself. Both A. Y. Chernyshevsky and Vasilev make respectful noises about "the epoch" and "national life" in relation to Fyodor's book at the end of chapter 3, but the main attack is saved for the reviews of the biography at the start of the last chapter. These show Nabokov at his best, brilliantly imitating a type of criticism that he knew well. The sentiments expressed above are brought up to date in the remarks of someone like Mortus, who combines civic concerns with a trendy apocalypticism in his denunciation of *Chernyshevsky:* "The fact that it is precisely now, precisely today, that this tasteless operation is being performed is in itself an affront to that significant, bitter, palpitating something which is ripening in the catacombs of our era." But this comedy is deadly serious. In the long review of the book by Professor Anuchin, Nabokov works at exposing the whole notion of an era or epoch as a concept that inevitably leads to all sorts of intellectual dishonesty. The critic argues:

> What is important is that, whatever Chernyshevski's views may have been on art and science, they represented the *Weltanschauung* of the most progressive men of his era, and were moreover indissolubly linked with the development of social ideas, with their ardent, beneficial, activating force. It is in this aspect, in this sole true light, that Chernyshevski's system of thought acquires a significance which far transcends the sense of those groundless arguments—unconnected in any way with the epoch of the sixties—which Mr Godunov-Cherdyntsev uses in venomously ridiculing his hero.

Anuchin is not just a Nabokov straw man, to be knocked over with a casual backhand when he has served his purpose, but a Trojan Horse wired for sound, spouting all sorts of "truths" that, if accepted, turn out to be absolutely fatal for the enemy camp. His argument that Chernyshevsky's ignorance of aesthetics is unimportant because it comes wrapped up with many nobler sentiments in a big progressive lump is the kind of reckless defence Nabokov wants his opponents to advance. The same goes for Anuchin's contention that there is only one humanitarian tradition in Russian literature, from which all "non-progressive" writers are excluded. For it was critics like Chernyshevsky, with their arbitrary judgments about what kinds of literature were in step with the progressive movement, that made their own case so vulnerable to attack, and actually deflected attention from the genuinely radical arguments they had to put forward.

Nabokov's second answer is: "Look what happened"—when the Chernyshevskys came to power in Russia, when their ideas about what literature should be became the only acceptable ones. When Vasilev's *Gazeta* refuses to publish Fyodor's book, Nabokov forces the reader to think about what kind of freedom-loving tradition would deny freedom of expression to those who happen to disagree with the traditional view. And several unobtrusive comparisons between Chernyshevsky and Lenin remind us of the consequences for literature in the Soviet Union of some of Chernyshevsky's ideas. Nabokov notes that, according to Lunarcharsky, Chernyshevsky shared with Lenin "breadth and depth of judgment" and the same "moral make-up," and that he was the Russian leader's favourite novelist and critic, leaving the reader to draw his own conclusions. Here a distinction should be made between Chernyshevsky's aesthetic views, which do lead directly to socialist realism and the like if one adheres to them more strictly than he himself did, and his "moral make-up." Unlike Lenin, he would not have welcomed the starvation of peasants in the famine of 1891, or advocated the censorship of literature in 1921, because both events were in keeping with the logic of history or helped "the Cause." Nevertheless, the persecution of Soviet writers fills in the gaps in Nabokov's argument about the importance of artistic freedom, and helps him to point an accusing finger at anyone who sets out to limit it.

The third argument should be the clincher. What do we find, Nabokov asks, when we look at the literary works of those who believe that the writer's primary obligation is to his age and country, as compared to the works of those who view their tasks as writers differently? And what happens when we read the whole of Russian literature as something other than a commentary on contemporary affairs? His answers are found in the many passages devoted to literary matters in *The Gift*. The remarks on the formal aspects of literary art alone—Pushkin's prose style, narrative transitions in different novelists, Bely's scansion of Russian verse, Chernyshevsky's attempted scansion of Russian verse, the extraordinarily rich account of how a poem actually comes to be written—are enough to justify the claims made for the novel as an important study of Russian literature. The parodies and the evocative details chosen from the works of various authors (and here Nabokov cuts across party lines) show us what a sensitive reader its author was. But it is the evaluations which effectively rewrite Russian literary history and form the centre of the argument in *The Gift* about committed and uncommitted art.

The most audacious and controversial of these evaluations occurs in the first imaginary conversation between Fyodor and Koncheev. In their discussion only four prose writers, Pushkin, Gogol, Tolstoy, and Chekhov, are admitted to the first rank. Their brilliant colloquy on these figures raises certain questions: Why does Fyodor forbid Koncheev to say anything negative about Pushkin? Why does he follow up this admonition with an unqualified acceptance of Chekhov's work as well? Why are minor criticisms of the great Tolstoy allowed? Why is Dostoyevski so pointedly excluded from this group? A cogent and suggestive response to these questions is found in Simon Karlinsky's "Nabokov and Chekhov: the Lesser Russian Tradition" (in Appel and Newman), in which he argues that Nabokov's own art can be traced back in a direct line that runs through Chekhov to

Pushkin. These three writers, unlike Dostoyevski or Tolstoy, refuse to subordinate their art to some social or ideological purpose, and yet each is a committed writer in a different sense. Their approach involves a cool diagnosis of social and human problems, biological as opposed to social humanitarianism. A writer in this tradition uses "precision of observation and restraint in evaluation"; he "describes what he sees and refrains from sweeping conclusions or generalizations." This helps explain some of Nabokov's assessments, but if we move to the novelists he places in the second rank there is still a problem. Goncharov, we are told, is a poor writer because *Oblomov* is a committed novel. Fyodor calls its hero, who happens to share a patronymic with Lenin, "that first 'Ilyich' who was the ruin of Russia." This is a witty dismissal that occurs during some rapid-fire repartee, but it does suggest the link in Nabokov's mind between writing "useful" literature and decreeing that nothing but "useful" literature can be written. Now any objective appraisal of Goncharov's novel would have to acknowledge that, although the author has chosen to represent certain aspects of contemporary Russian society, he has not subordinated his art to some social or ideological purpose, and that the "Oblomovism" he describes was a more important factor in the "ruin" of Russia than his description of it. Here we can see the problem with Karlinsky's formulation. Not because there is no room for Goncharov in his schema—he can easily be placed between the two tendencies outlined above—but because Nabokov, with this impetuous and undiscriminating condemnation of socially relevant literature, commits his own to all the things that are supposed to characterize the "other" tradition, to "sweeping conclusions," "generalizations," even "ideological purpose," if campaigning against those with an ideology is itself an ideological commitment. Throw out Goncharov's most important novel in this way, and you have to throw out Aksakov, Leskov, and a host of other novelists who have a variety of social and political views and use their fiction to discuss them, without becoming excessively dogmatic or didactic. Nabokov seems to be on the brink of doing just that, if we are to judge by the decidedly mixed reception given these authors in *The Gift*. Twenty years later he warned Edmund Wilson to steer clear in his Russian studies of the "Goncharov–Aksakov–Saltïkov–Leskov porridgy mass." He had decided to throw them out. Unfortunately, he never convinces us that we should take such judgments seriously.

This kind of dismissal is misleading in another way. It threatens to obscure the very real resemblances between Nabokov and the writers he characterizes so arbitrarily. The Aksakov who wrote lengthy and detailed accounts of the pleasures of hunting butterflies, and who created a world in which memory and nostalgia are at the very centre of human experience, is more important to the Nabokov reader than the one dismissed as "wretched" by Fyodor for the blunders in his descriptions of nature. The pointed criticism of Turgenev can also distract us from more significant matters. Accusing the author of *Rudin* and *Smoke* of appeasing the radicals, or dismissing *Fathers and Sons* for its "inept tête-à-têtes in acacia arbours"—these claims are so unusual that they may have the desired effect and actually make us reconsider Turgenev's work. But when we hear his descriptions of nature being ridiculed for their "howlers," we may well begin to feel that the "novelist's novelist" is being deliberately misrepresented by one of his old admirers, now overly anxious to assert his independence. Consider the following passage from chapter 5 of *The Gift* (Fyodor is lying on his back in a forest, looking upward):

> And still higher above my upturned face, the summits and trunks of the trees participated in a complex exchange of shadows, and their leafage reminded me of algae swaying in transparent water. And if I tilted my head back even farther, so that the grass behind (inexpressibly, primevally green from this point of upturned vision) seemed to be growing downward into empty transparent light, I experienced something similar to what must strike a man who has flown to another planet.

Now compare it with a passage from *A Sportsman's Sketches:*

> It is an extremely agreeable occupation to lie on your back in the woods and look upwards! It seems that you are looking into a bottomless sea, that it is spreading itself out far and wide *beneath* you, that the trees are not rising from the ground, but, like the roots of huge plants, dropping perpendicularly down into those glass-clear waves; and the leaves on the trees are now transparent as emeralds, now condensed to a goldish, almost blackish green.

A coincidence perhaps, but a more promising field of inquiry for someone interested in Nabokov and his relations with Russian novelists of the mid nineteenth century than the territory so zealously fenced off in *The Gift.*

Nabokov anticipates and forestalls some of this criticism by including his own auto-critique in the second dialogue imagined by his hero, when Koncheev tells Fyodor that he sometimes says things in *Chernyshevsky* "chiefly calculated to prick your contemporaries." Another possibility is that the novel's iconoclastic excesses are the mark of Fyodor's immaturity, something he must leave behind him if he is to become a full-fledged novelist like his creator. But this desire to "prick" contemporaries becomes more prevalent in Nabokov as he gets older; and even if we agree to accept these judgments as mere youthful exuberance, the main point remains unchanged: Nabokov's insistence on the necessity of the literary artist's freedom is eloquent and persuasive, but the view of literature that results when this single criterion is applied in an idiosyncratic and dogmatic way is not very convincing. He has not dealt successfully with the special problems of the writer in the Russia of the 1850s and 60s, and he is so determined to ridicule what he imagines to be the opposition that he misrepresents the epoch and the literature he knew so well.

Of course Nabokov's discussion of nineteenth-century Russian writers takes him beyond the arguments about committed and uncommitted literature at a given period in the nation's history. In the final part of this essay, I want to explore in more detail his search for his antecedents and his attempt to establish the exact nature of his relationship with them. I am specifically interested in why he calls chapter 2 "a surge toward Pushkin," and why he says at the end of that chapter that his hero is moving from "Pushkin Avenue to Gogol Street." The search for some answers to these questions takes us to the heart of what being a Russian writer means to Nabokov.

First Pushkin. It is clear from the commentary on Pushkin's art that the lucidity of his prose and the precision of his observations are what most impress Fyodor when he reads Pushkin to help him prepare for his own literary tasks. Karlinsky's attempt to place Nabokov in a tradition of Pushkinian objectivity is not confirmed by the literary criticism in *The Gift*, but perhaps it is borne out by this quality in other parts of the novel. One of the works Nabokov singles out for special praise is *Journey to Arzrum*, Pushkin's account of his experiences in the Caucasus in 1829. A comparison between this short work and Nabokov's novel turns out to be instructive.

Pushkin's work is especially rich in simple allusions to small details: the graffiti on a minaret, the special rites used by the Georgians to open their casks of wine, the way the sky changes as a storm approaches. Opening *The Gift* at random, we find something like "the sound of hooves had been heard on the bridge (a swift wooden drumming which was immediately cut off)," something as simple and real as these details in Pushkin, something which, although we have always known about it, becomes more clear to us because it has been recorded in this way. Pushkin's special kind of lucid objectivity takes other forms as well. Interested in seeing what a military engagement is actually like (he is with a Russian army which is in the

Caucasus to fight against the Turks), he is sent by a Russian general "to the left flank." The poet rides on a little and then wonders to himself: "What does left flank mean?" This simple question and the descriptions of the disorderly skirmishes that follow are a perfect example of Shklovsky's famous *ostranenie,* the device that forces the reader to look at what is actually happening instead of merely putting it in a conventional frame of reference. Nabokov's use of the device is different but the effect is the same. The branches of a poplar "resembling the nervous system of a giant," "the radiance of a lawn-sprinkler that waltzed on one spot with the ghost of a rainbow in its dewy arms," a caterpillar "checking the number of inches" between two people—Nabokov uses metaphors in this way to add strangeness to beauty, and to reveal that strangeness in phenomena that most people look at but never see. Few novels are as rich as *The Gift* in this kind of detail, and this is particularly true of Nabokov's act of homage to Pushkin in chapter 2, Fyodor's biography of his father, with its splendid evocations of the natural world and its mysteries in the countries visited by the lepidopterist.

But these resemblances are not what is finally most important. As we read *Journey to Arzrum* we are struck by a fundamental difference between Pushkin and Nabokov in so far as a third kind of objectivity is concerned, the desire to describe what one sees and refrain from "sweeping conclusions or generalizations." Pushkin's account of an incident that occurred while he was stopped by the side of the road, waiting for a military convoy to go by, will help illustrate what I have in mind:

> While the carriages were passing, the officer of the convoy informed us that he had a poet from the Persian court with him, and, at my request, presented me to Fazil-Khan. With the aid of an interpreter I began a bombastic eastern greeting, but how ashamed I was when Fazil-Khan answered my inappropriate intricacies with the simple, wise politeness of a decent human being! "He hoped to see me in Petersburg; he regretted that our acquaintance would be short-lived," and so on. Embarrassed, I was obliged to forgo my pompously humorous tone and to adopt ordinary European phrases. Here is a lesson for our Russian derisiveness [*nasmeshlivost'*]. In future I won't judge a man by his sheepskin cap and his painted fingernails.

It is this kind of objectivity that is often quite foreign to Nabokov's art. He needs this "Russian derisiveness" for satiric bite, and he doesn't shirk from making the peremptory judgments it gives rise to. The most obvious example in *The Gift* is the treatment of the Germans. Many passages highlight the traits of various individual Germans, but their national characteristics are summed up at the beginning of the "surge toward Pushkin" chapter. Among other things, Fyodor hates them for their

> love of fences, rows, mediocrity; for the cult of the office; for the fact that if you listen to his inner voice (or to any conversation on the street) you will inevitably hear figures, money; for the lavatory humour and crude laughter; for the fatness of the backsides of both sexes . . .; for taking pains with dirty tricks, for the abominable object stuck carefully on the railings of the public gardens; for someone else's live cat, pierced through with wire as revenge on a neighbour, and the wire cleverly twisted at one end; for cruelty in everything, self-satisfied, taken for granted.

But the man who prompts this outburst by bumping into Fyodor on a tram turns out to be a Russian, and Fyodor, who has "seen" all these characteristics in the physical features of the man, is forced to face up to the dangers of generalizing about the moral character of national types. So it is tempting to see this, as some critics have done, as a first step in the process of Fyodor's maturation. But what are we to make of the passage near the end of the book in which Nabokov describes a "typical" group of German bathers?

> Old men's grey legs covered with growths and swollen veins; flat feet; the tawny crust of corns; pink porcine paunches; . . . the pimply shoulder blades of bandy-legged girls; the sturdy necks and buttocks of muscular hooligans; the hopeless, godless vacancy of satisfied faces . . . And over all this, especially on Sundays when the crowding was vilest of all, there reigned an unforgettable smell, the smell of dust, of sweat, of aquatic slime, of unclean underwear, of aired and dried poverty, the smell of dried, smoked, potted souls a penny a piece.

He thought this particular passage so important that, when he published excerpts from *Dar* in *Poslednie Novesti,* he added it to the end of the third one, "A Walk in the Grunewald," omitting the eight paragraphs that join Fyodor's "walk" and his discovery of the Germans by the lake. I do not want to wax morally indignant here. Nabokov often includes such passages because he knows how much readers enjoy reading lists of energetic insults, watching all the obnoxious details pile up like the bodies on the beach. But this was how he felt about Germans, and the derisiveness Pushkin warns us about obviously does have some unfortunate effects. Here it speaks the language of snobbery and prejudice, and prevents the observer from seeing what he is supposed to be looking at. It can even lead to foolish ranting, as when Fyodor describes the Germany of the 1920s as a country "where a novel about incest or some brash trash, some cloyingly rhetorical, pseudo-brutal tale about war is considered the crown of literature; where in fact there is no literature, and hasn't been for a long time." (*The Magic Mountain* was published in 1924, *Steppenwolf* in 1927, etc.) In the foreword to *The Gift,* Nabokov does the noble thing and admits that there is something wrong with these anti-German diatribes. He attributes it to the influence of the Nazis: "history shows through artistry" here, he says. I think it makes more sense to see it as art flouting history, savage comic caricature winning out over objective representation.

What Nabokov means by taking up residence on "Gogol Street" has already been explained by G. M. Hyde. He notes that "The style of the novel at once becomes more comic and devious, more fanciful and "metaphysical," yet at the same time more grotesquely involved with the minutiae of Berlin life," adding that "the resources of baroque Gogolian wit will be stretched to the utmost by being applied to such an apparently unsuitable subject as Chernyshevsky." I think this is essentially true; but the relation between the two authors is more complex than this formula suggests. Berlin as seen through Nabokov's eyes and the Chernyshevsky biography often do remind us of Gogol, but great chunks of both these sections of *The Gift* also remind us that the two writers differ in a fundamental way. It is perhaps best summed up by saying that Nabokov is more personal than Gogol: he makes us conscious of his presence in a way that the author of *Dead Souls* does not. To read Gogol on *poshlost'* is to learn about the crude, the vulgar, the corny. To read Nabokov on the same subject is to learn about all that, and about him and the long list of things he loathes. Gogol is as merciless in his exposure of human absurdity, but he travels along the roads his heroes take; and when he eludes us, he does so by disappearing into the world he has created. When Nabokov ridicules someone or something, we feel the unbridgeable gap between him and the object of his contempt.

We can see the difference clearly if we look at the portrayal of the Russian people in *The Gift*. In the retrospective sections of the novel, they appear as a collection of ignorant outsiders, mostly servants, who are totally out of place in the special world inhabited by the hero. Think of them gawking uncomprehendingly at the mysterious rites of the elite Entomological Society, whose members are huddled together studying a rare species in the woods. Fyodor describes the scene, and adds: "to this day I am wondering what the coachmen waiting on the road made of all this," a remark that constitutes at least a muted recognition of the gulf separating the classes. But instead of developing this insight, Nabokov proceeds to exploit the comic consequences of such a gap. An orderly borrows Fyodor's butterfly net and brings home to the young master all sorts of things that strike him as worth collecting in the countryside, only to have his offering rejected with disdain. We get the distinct sense that we are reading about the self-satisfied snobbery of callow youth which the author is about to expose and condemn. But Nabokov's aims are quite different. He concludes with a sarcastic "The Russian common people know and love their country's nature." Gogol has a great deal of fun with the ignorance of his "common people," but he never deals with them quite so sharply as this.

The point is that Nabokov's Russia, like his Germany and his Chernyshevsky and his history of Russian literature, is a very personal thing. Field tells us that the Nabokov family regarded itself as "a little nation." Nabokov himself said in an interview that his Russia was "very small": "A road here, a few trees there, a sky. It is a treasure chest to which one returns again and again." For all the memorable portraits of Russian people that Nabokov created, what he remembers here is a Russia with no people in it. Of course one can find similar musings in Gogol. In some of his letters he says practically identical things about a Russia seen from the vantage-point of exile. But once again there are some important differences. Gogol worked in a country that had hailed him as a great Russian writer and criticized him for what it took to be his shortcomings, a country that had linked its destiny with his. His exile was self-imposed; his works, despite the censorship, were published; he could say "we Russians" in a way that Nabokov could not. Gogol actually says as much in *The Gift* itself: "Longer, longer, and for as long as possible, shall I be in a strange country. And although my thoughts, my name, my works will belong to Russia, I myself, my mortal organism, will be removed from it," quotes Fyodor in the "Gogol Street" chapter. Although Nabokov is certain that he too will one day be thought of as one of the great Russian writers, he is not bound in the same way to his native land, and he is not so sure about where that recognition will come from.

He deals with this question in *The Gift* by means of a seemingly casual allusion to a poem by Pushkin which sets up associations that eventually include the entire Nabokov *oeuvre*. Fyodor and Koncheev are discussing the problem of a readership for the émigré writer. "Who knows my poems?" asks Koncheev. The answer in *Dar* is: "One hundred, one hundred and fifty, at most, at most, two hundred intelligent expatriates, of whom again ninety per cent don't understand them. That's provincial success, but not fame." These figures increase by a factor of ten in the English translation, and Nabokov adds the sentence: "Two thousand out of three million refugees!" He regularly helps the English reader out with bits of information of this kind, but only very rarely changes actual points of detail in a translation that is not a substantial reworking of the original. No doubt he did so here because he thought the second set of figures more realistic. But the point about a paucity of receptive readers is essentially the same in both versions, and Koncheev makes it again when he says that only ten people (a dozen in *The Gift*) among the émigrés will be able to appreciate Fyodor's book. That is the situation as it stands, declares Koncheev, and "a great deal of time will have to elapse before the Tungus and the Kalmuk of Pushkin's '*Exegi monumentum*' begin to tear out of each other's hands my 'Communication,' with the Finn looking enviously on." In that poem, Pushkin announces that his literary achievement is a monument more impressive than the Alexandrine Column in St Petersburg and more durable than flesh, and that his greatness will eventually be appreciated by all the Russian people, because he "exalted freedom" in his "cruel age" and "called for mercy toward the downfallen." The arrogant sound of this is qualified by the fact that the four stanzas which contain these sentiments are actually a delicate parody of Derzhavin's "I've set up to myself a monument," which is itself based on Lomonosov's translation of Horace. The fifth stanza adds more qualification:

> To God's command, O Muse, obedient be,
> offense not dreading, and no wreath demanding;
> accept indifferently praise and slander,
> and do not contradict a fool.

When he wrote *The Gift,* knowing that he would not be going back to Russia, uncertain about the chances of being published there during his lifetime, and already contemplating abandoning Russian for English, Nabokov must have been wondering what kind of monument he had erected and how long it would last. Presumably he alludes to Pushkin here because this poem gets the balance about right: it is written by a poet who really does care how he will be remembered but who knows that the expression of a desire to be immortalized by his own verse must be, at least in part, a conventional rhetorical exercise, and that he can't do anything about it anyway.

The analogy between Pushkin's situation and that of the émigré writer is picked up again in another allusion to "*Exegi monumentum*" in a

Nabokov poem called "Slava" ("Fame"), written in 1942, which turns out to have an important link with *The Gift.* The speaker of the poem has a debate with a nasty and pessimistic inner voice that insists he renounce any hope of an admiring posterity. Once again Pushkin's "monument" is contrasted with the exile's lack of one:

> "No, never will anyone in the great spaces
> make mention of even one page of your work;
> the now savage will dwell in his savage ignorance,
> friends of steppes won't forget their steppes for your sake."

But the poet triumphs over such gloomy predictions because he has a "secret" that makes him immune to this "empty dream / about readers, and body, and glory." He can't give it away but he can hint at what it is: "A book's death can't affect me since even the break / between me and my land is a trifle"; and: "I've read in myself how the self to transcend." In her introduction to *Stikhi,* a collection of Nabokov's verse published two years after her husband's death, Vera Nabokov suggests what the secret is. She defines it as *potustoronnost',* "the hereafter," the "chief theme" of the Nabokov *oeuvre,* the one that all the critics missed. Knowing this secret gave Nabokov his "imperturbable cheerfulness" and made him "invulnerable to all the very stupid or malicious attacks" made on him. She directs readers interested in learning more about this secret to a specific passage in *The Gift,* the paragraph in chapter 2 where Nabokov describes a mysterious, indefinable quality that Fyodor notices in his father, a special, inviolable solitude, a knowledge that cannot be shared with anyone else.

There is certainly no need to worry about posterity if you've got the hereafter on your side, and W. W. Rowe's remarkable book, *Nabokov's Spectral Dimension,* has convincingly demonstrated the importance of spirits and the "other world" in Nabokov's work; but I cannot help thinking that the Nabokov secret has little to do with some mysterious knowledge of an ineffable beyond, that it is really an open secret, lying there like the purloined letter in Poe face up on the table. The intensely subjective view of Chernyshevsky, of Russian literature, of the role that literature is to play in society, of the writer's "gift" as something the special individual is entrusted to keep safe from the "malicious hags and crooked hucksters" of the general populace who would like to steal it from him—what are all these but versions of Nabokov's "secret," the possession of a creative imagination so powerful that it remakes every aspect of the world it comes into contact with? This is why he doesn't have to worry about his "monument." If

Russia is lost, Fyodor will create a new Russia, revisit his country "with pen in hand," look up from his writing, and "see a Russian autumn." The country estate at Leshino? Re-created in the play of sun and shadow in the isolated paths of Fyodor's private Grunewald. The romance with a girl before the revolution? Fyodor even tries to create his new love out of the shadows of the Berlin streets; and when he finally meets her, he gives her the name of his muse, "Mnemo*zina*," and decides to write a novel about how "fate" has brought them together. It is no good objecting that all this does not happen in real life. Nabokov thought otherwise. Andrew Field once asked Nabokov's wife what she thought her life would have been like had the Revolution not occurred and she not emigrated and met a young Russian writer in Berlin. Her husband interrupted her response with: "You would have met me in Petersburg, and we would have married and been living more or less as we are now!" A man born on Shakespeare's birthday whose grandfather might have been the son of a tsar cannot help but feel that he was born to create his own tradition and his own destiny.

When Nabokov published the English translation of *The Gift* in the early sixties, he had done just that. His books were being read; his reputation was made; his mastery had been acknowledged. Yet the foreword to the novel is not full of the exultant self-assertion one might expect. The doubts expressed there are related, not to his own work, but to the communal enterprise of which they once formed a part: émigré literature, one of his links with Russia, is gone, and he feels its loss. Not the émigré literature so amusingly demolished in the novel: the frauds and schemers of the Writers' Union, spending all their time in endless wrangling and petty intrigues, the mediocrities who frequent the poetry readings, the critics fussing about ineffectually in a world circumscribed by their own ignorance and prejudice. Not this, but the other émigré literature, the one represented by the names Nabokov intones in the foreword: Bunin, Aldanov, Remizov, Khodasevich. All but Aldanov are from the older generation of exiles; all have strong links with the Russian literature of the past. They and Russian intellectuals like them were the representatives of a whole world. That world is now a "phantasm," Nabokov tells us, and its history reads like "the wanderings of some mythical tribe." Elsewhere he talks about the air of "fragile unreality" in which the émigré writers found themselves, "hardly palpable people" trying to hold on to Russian culture in order to pass it on to the next generation. Nabokov does not seem entirely convinced of their success. Yet seen from another point of view, this ghostly wandering of Russian culture and its representatives may actually constitute a living link with the past, and some kind of hope for the future. Perhaps it was always thus. In 1841, Belinsky wrote to a friend: "We are men without a country—no, worse than without a country, we are men whose country is a phantom—is it any wonder then that we ourselves are phantoms, that our friendship, our love, our aspirations, our activities are phantoms?" This feeling may be the very essence of Russian literary culture and its history.

ROBERT ALTER

Ada, *or the Perils of Paradise*

Ada occupies a problematically dominant place among Nabokov's novels. Twice as long as any other work of fiction he wrote, this ambitious, formally elaborate, fantastically inventive novel of his seventieth year was clearly intended as a culmination of the distinctive artistic enterprise to which he devoted half a century. In it he sought to incorporate and reach beyond the achievement of his two English masterpieces, *Lolita* and *Pale Fire* (both of which are abundantly alluded to in *Ada*). Or, to invoke a painterly analogy specifically brought to our attention several times in the novel, *Ada* is the third panel in a Boschean triptych, a novelistic garden of Earthly Delights that began with *Lolita* in 1954. In it there is a paradoxical fusion of lyricism and the grotesque, of uninhibited invention and scrupulous attention to familiar reality. Beauty flowers from perversion, a radiant dream of happiness rises from the shadow of loneliness and exile.

Lolita was the most brilliant in the line of books that since the 1920s had studied the vertiginous intercrossings of imagination and reality, the artist and his world, through athletically allusive, involuted, and parodic forms. These concerns were then given even more original and intricate formal expression in *Pale Fire,* while the new central emphasis in *Lolita* on the quest for a paradisiac past (Humbert Humbert's golden "princedom by the sea") appeared in oblique refraction through Kinbote's longing for his lost kingdom. In *Ada,* as we shall see in detail, Nabokov moved boldly from a vision of paradise lost to one of paradise regained—or retained—for the

---

first time in his fiction, though following the precedent of the autobiographical *Speak, Memory;* and he also produced the most capaciously encompassing of all his parodic forms.

The result of this consciously culminating effort was, of course, greeted with catcalls by the anti-Nabokovians as a supreme monstrosity of literary narcissism, and hailed with jubilation by the Nabokov loyalists as a climactic masterpiece. Rereading *Ada* a decade after its publication, I find it a dazzling, but at times also exasperating, near-masterpiece that lacks the perfect selectivity and control of *Lolita* and *Pale Fire*. At the book's weaker moments, one feels that the novelist permits himself too much, inadvertently unraveling threads in his own rich tapestry through his eagerness to pursue every linguistic quibble, every gratuitous turn of a sexual or literary double meaning. In this last major work, Nabokov invented a hypothetical antiworld where everything culturally precious to him—the Russian, English, and French languages, the vanished graces of his parents' aristocratic estate—could be harmoniously combined; and it may be that this embarrassment of riches encouraged a certain softness, made it more difficult for him to distinguish between imaginative necessity and private indulgence. But these recurrent capitulations to the temptations of mere byplay are the defect of a virtue; for the exuberance of the novel's more meaningful playfulness in fact brings it close to the crowning achievement Nabokov sought. Through many extraordinary passages and in its larger design, *Ada* succeeds in illuminating in new depth and breadth the relation between art, reality, and the evanescent ever-never presence of time past; and it is that illumination that chiefly deserves our attention.

The dimension of parody, established with the first words of the text, has to be kept clearly in perspective; for nowhere else in Nabokov's writing is the parodic mode made so pervasive and so deliberately obtrusive as here. Because parody is intrinsic to Nabokov's method, and because he more often parodies plot, situation, and motif than style and narrative technique, a plot-summary of any of his novels is bound to be thoroughly misleading, but perhaps more so for *Ada* than for any other work. (To mislead the unsuspecting, of course, is precisely what he always intends: thus, the four concluding paragraphs of *Ada* are a pitchman's synopsis of the book, the prose of the novel followed by what the narrator, tongue in cheek, calls "the poetry of its blurb.") *Ada,* which, when it is going well, manages to be one of the sunniest works of fiction written in this century, sounds, to judge by the bare outlines of its plot, like a dark drama of fatal, incestuous passion. Van Veen, the retrospective nonagenarian narrator, has an ecstatic affair at the age of fourteen with twelve-year-old Ada, ostensibly his cousin, later discovered to be his sister. Irresistibly drawn to each other by their inner nature, the two are separated by social taboo and the course of outward events. The lovers enjoy four fleeting periods of illicit ardor together in the two decades from early adolescence to mature adulthood, but each time the subsequent separation is longer. While Van seeks the simulacrum of his Ada in a thousand whores and mistresses, both he and she are physically thickened and coarsened by the passing years, until at last they come together in late middle age, all passion not spent but certainly muted. In the background, moreover, of their partings and joinings, as the third, unequal angle of a thoroughly incestuous triangle, is the pathetic figure of Lucette, their mutual half-sister, who loves Van relentlessly body and soul, loves Ada, periodically, in a more strictly bodily sense, and finally destroys herself when she is rejected by Van.

All this may sound like rather lurid stuff, especially when one adds that there is a much higher degree of descriptive specification about sexual matters here than anywhere else in Nabokov's fiction. And it must be conceded that there are moments when the writer's sense of freedom in treating sexual materials leads to a certain gloating tone—most evidently, in the repeated evocation of an international network of elite whorehouses to which Van Veen becomes habituated.

In any case, the actual tenor of the novel as a whole is, of course, precisely the opposite of what this summary suggests. On a stylistic level, the seeming paradox is easy enough to explain: Nabokov's intricately wrought, elaborately figurative style, with its painterly effects and its perspectivist mirror-games, transmutes objects of description, even the most pungently physical objects, into magical *objets d'art.* When, for example, the narrator, in a spectacular set piece, describes all three siblings in bed together (surely a parody of the *ménage à trois* grapplings that are stock scenes of pornographic literature), he invites us to view the action as though it were reflected in the ceiling mirror of a fancy brothel, and then proceeds to convert the rampant eroticism into a formal contrasting and blending of colors and movements. Physical details are not spared—"the detail is all," Van Veen had affirmed earlier about the reality of all experience and memory; but, to cite a strategic instance, the exposed sexual fluff of redheaded Lucette and black-haired Ada becomes here a new-fledged firebird and an enchanting raven, varicolored birds of paradise in a poet's Wonderland.

Nabokov has often been celebrated for his brilliance as a stylist; but it is important to recognize that this brilliance, perhaps most centrally in *Ada,* is not ornamental, as in some of his American imitators, but the necessary instrument of a serious ontological enterprise: to rescue reality from the bland nonentity of stereotypicality and from the terrifying rush of mortality by reshaping objects, relations, existential states, through the power of metaphor and wit, so that they become endowed with an arresting life of their own. An incidental samovar, observed in passing, "expressed fragments of its surroundings in demented fantasies of a primitive genre." Lucette drowning sees her existence dissolve in a receding series of selves and perceives that "what death amounted to was only a more complete assortment of the infinite fractions of solitude." Van Veen, driving through the Alps to his first rendezvous with Ada after a separation of fifteen years, sees from his flesh (to borrow an apposite idiom from Job) the palpable reality of time as his recent telephone conversation with Ada and his view of the landscape around him are transformed in the alembic of consciousness into a summarizing metaphor: "That telephone voice, by resurrecting the past and linking it up with the present, with the darkening slate-blue mountains beyond the lake, with the spangles of the sun wake dancing through the poplar, formed the centerpiece in his deepest perception of a tangible time, the glittering 'now' that was the only reality of Time's texture." As a vivid commentary on what he aspires to achieve through style, Nabokov likens the youthful Van's astonishing agility in walking on his hands to the function of metaphor in Van's later work as a writer: "It was the standing of a metaphor on its head not for the sake of the trick's difficulty, but in order to perceive an ascending waterfall or a sunrise in reverse; a triumph, in a sense, over the ardis of time . . . Van on the stage was performing organically what his figures of speech were to perform later in life—acrobatic wonders that had never been expected from them and which frightened children." We shall devote further attention later to those acrobatic wonders when we consider Nabokov's rendering of Ada and the paradisiac world of youth with which she is inextricably associated.

When one moves from effects of style to the larger narrative patterns of the novel, it is difficult to make full sense of the incestuous complications without attention to the ubiquitous use of literary allusion. In order to talk about the allusions, something first must be said about the setting. The principal action of *Ada* takes place, one recalls, in the late nineteenth and early twentieth centuries of a world alternately referred to as Antiterra and Daemonia, which has the same geography as our world but a teasingly different though parallel history. The area we call Russia having been conquered some centuries earlier by the Tartars, America has been settled by Russian as well as English and French colonists; and so Nabokov's own three native languages and literary traditions are able to flourish side by side, as complementary parts of a single national culture. From a terrestrial viewpoint—Terra the Fair, by the way, is a supposedly celestial place believed in mainly by the deranged on Antiterra—historical periods as well as cultural boundaries have been hybridized; the daemonian nineteenth century combines the quiet country houses of Chekhov and Jane Austen with telephones, airplanes, skyscrapers; a mock-Maupassant figure is contemporaneous with the author of a *Lolita*-like novel masquerading (anagrammatically) as J. L. Borges.

This device of a fictional antiworld gives Nabokov a free hand to combine and permute the materials of culture and history in piquant and suggestive ways, though perhaps, as I have already proposed, it also sometimes tempts him into self-indulgence. One begins to feel he is playing his games of anagrams, trilingual puns, coded hints, and conflated allusions for their own sake, not because they have any imaginative necessity in a larger design. Vladimir Nabokov, that is, at times rather too closely resembles his anagrammatic double in the novel, Baron Klim Avidov, bequeathing ornate sets of super-Scrabble to the characters and, implicitly, to the readers. It must be admitted, though, that some of the incidental games, especially those involving literary figures, are amusing enough in themselves that one would hesitate to give them up. My own favorite is the treatment of T. S. Eliot, who appears as a truncated version of his own ape-necked Sweeney, "solemn Kithar Sween, a banker who at sixty-five had become an *avant-garde* author; . . . had produced *The Waistline,* a satire in free verse on Anglo-American feeding habits"; and who is seen, in most poetic justice for a versifier on anti-Semitic innuendoes, in the company of "old Eliot," a Jewish real-estate man.

The most important advantage, in any case, that Nabokov gains through the freedom he allows himself to shuttle across temporal and cultural boundaries is that he is able to compress into the lifespace of his protagonist a parodic review of the development of the novel. The story begins in the classic age of the novel; and, really, everything that happens occurs in purely novelistic time and novelistic space. Ardis Manor, where young Van Veen will meet Ada, is glimpsed for the first time, characteristically, in the following fashion: "At the next turning, the romantic mansion appeared on the gentle eminence of old novels." The narrative is frequently punctuated with such notations to remind us that everything is taking place against a background of familiar and perhaps jaded literary conventions, as the view shifts quickly, and not necessarily chronologically, from romantic *récit* to Jane Austen, Turgenev, Dickens, Flaubert, Aksakov, Tolstoy, Dostoyevski, the pornographic novel, the Gothic novel, Joyce, Proust, and Nabokov beyond them. The "plot," in fact, is from one point of view composed of a string of stock scenes from the traditional novel—the young man's return to the ancestral manor; the festive picnic; the formal dinner; a midnight conflagration on the old estate; the distraught hero's flight at dawn from hearth and home as the result of a misunderstanding; the duel; the hero's profligacy in the great metropolis, and so forth.

Though the technique of allusion is common to all Nabokov's novels, there is a special thematic justification for this recapitulation in parody of the history of a genre; for what Van Veen's story represents is a reversal of the major thematic movement of the novel as a genre. The novel characteristically has concerned itself with lost illusions—the phrase, of course, was used as a title by Balzac in a central work—from the quixotic knight who finally abandons his pursuit of a Golden Age, a broken man renouncing his chivalric vision and dying; to Flaubert's Emma, spitting out her daydreams of a blue Beyond in the last hideous retches of an arsenic suicide; to Anna Karenina—the first sentence of her story is quoted, in reverse, in the first sentence of *Ada*—ending her tortured love under the wheels of a locomotive. What "happy endings" one finds in the classic novel are generally a matter of mere acquiescence to convention (Dickens) or sober accommodation of the protagonists to society (Jane Austen, George Eliot). *Ada,* in direct contrast, is an attempt to return to paradise, to establish, in fact, the luminous vision of youth and love's first fulfillment as the most intensely, perdurably *real* experience we know. It bears affinities both to Molly Bloom's great lyric recall of first flowering love at the end of *Ulysses* and to Proust's triumph over time through art in the last volume of his novel; but it is a more concerted frontal attack on Eden than either.

Two key allusions are especially helpful in understanding what Nabokov is up to with his incestuous lovers. One is simple, a mere negative parallel to serve as a foil; the other is complex, being a kind of imaginative model for the whole book and ramifying into other related allusions. Several passing references are made to Chateaubriand: Ada jokingly calls Van her "René"; and the first half of the novel's title, *Ada or Ardor,* looks suspiciously like a parody of that most Romantic title, *René ou les Effets des Passions.* René, like Van, is a singular man with an artist's soul who enjoys the rare delights of bucolic ambles with his dear sister until the incestuous nature of her attachment to him forces them to separate. So much for the parallels; all the rest is pointed contrast. *René* is a book suffused with Romantic *mal du siècle;* and René and Amélie, unlike the Veen siblings, are anything but "children of Venus"; the paradisiac fulfillment of premoral desire is quite unthinkable for René and his sister, so that the very existence of such desire drives Amélie into a convent and ultimately leads to martyrs' deaths for both of them. In *Ada,* one can see from the sunlit River Ladore near the Ardis estate a view of Bryant's Castle (gallicized, *Château-Briand*), "remote and romantically black on its oak-timbered hill." The chief quality of Van Veen's world, by contrast, is brightness and intimate closeness, social and sexual, tactile and visual; and its oak trees, as we shall see, are part of a landscape very different from the dark romantic wood. René actively longs for death, even before the revelation of his sister's passion; he sees in it a hazy, alluring *ailleurs,* as though the concrete objects of this world could not conceivably satisfy the needs of his own swoon of infinite desire. *Ada's* hero and heroine, on the other hand, delight in observing the concrete particulars of this world—Ada is a naturalist, Van an artist—and recall them with tender meticulous care; and they both passionately love existence in this world, each being the other's ultimate point of anchorage in it, Van's male V or arrowhead (*ardis* in Greek) perfectly fitting into its inverted and crossed female mirror-image, the A of his sister-soul (ideogrammatists take note; Freudians beware).

The mirror play of Van's and Ada's initials—underscored at one point when Nabokov finds dramatic occasion to print the A upside down—suggests that the two are perfect lovers because ultimately they are complementary halves of one self. Indeed, Van's book is really "written" by the two of them, one imagination called "Vaniada" expressing itself in two antiphonal voices. The birthmark on the back of Van's right hand reappears in exactly the corresponding spot on Ada's left hand, for both physically and psychically the lovers are really the two halves of that androgynous pristine human zestfully described by Aristophanes in Plato's *Symposium* and at one point explicitly alluded to by Nabokov. According to rabbinic legend, Adam in the Garden before the creation of Eve was androgynous; and it is clear that Nabokov, like the rabbis, has conjoined the Greek and the Hebrew myths, creating in his deliciously intertwined sister and brother an image of prelapsarian, unfragmented humanity.

A major clue to Nabokov's intention in this respect is the repeated allusion, especially in the Ardis section of the novel, to one of the most splendidly realized experiences of paradise in English poetry, Marvell's "The Garden." Adolescent Ada tries to translate the poem into French—in her version, an oak tree stands prominently at the beginning of the second line; after the lovers' first separation, the poem, most appropriately, serves as a code-key for the letters in cipher that they exchange. (The other code-key is Rimbaud's *Mémoire,* another ripely sensual poem of bucolic repose, rich in color imagery, presided over by "the gambol of angels.") The second stanza of Marvell's poem, not quoted in the novel, begins as follows: "Fair quiet, have I found thee here, / And Innocence thy Sister dear! / Mistaken long, I sought you then / In busie Companies of Men." The lines are, of course, applicable point for point to the novel, a kind of adumbration of its plot, though both "sister" and "innocence" are given rather different meanings. Marvell's poem is a vision of bliss beyond the raging of physical passions. The solitary garden-dweller, however, does revel in the pleasures of the senses, luscious fruit dropping from the trees to delight his palate, while his mind withdraws into the happiness of self-contemplation where it—like the author of *Ada*?—"creates, transcending these, / Far other Worlds, and other Seas."

In *Ada*'s ardisiac setting, luscious fruit also comes falling from the branches, when the tree-climbing young Ada slips and ends up straddling an astonished Van from the front, thus offering him an unexpectedly intimate first kiss. In a moment Ada will claim that this is the Tree of Knowledge, brought to the Ardis estate from Eden National Park; but her slip from its branches clearly enacts a Happy Fall; for in this garden, as in Marvell's, no fatal sin is really possible. Marvell's poem also gives us a comic image of a Fall with no evil consequences: "Stumbling on Melons, as I pass, / Insnar'd with Flow'rs, I fall on Grass." The interlaced limbs of ardently tumbling Van and Ada are similarly assimilated to the premoral world of vegetation, likened to tendril climbers; and Van, rushing away from a last embrace of Ada at the moment of their first separation, is actually described as "stumbling on melons," an allusion which would seem to promise that he will eventually return to his Ada-Ardis-Eden.

It is the concluding stanza, however, of Marvell's "The Garden" that offers the most suggestive model for what Nabokov seeks to achieve in *Ada*. After the garden-dweller's soul, whetting and combing its silver wings among the branches, has experienced ecstasy, the poet glances backward at the first Adam's paradise, and then returns us to the "real" world of time; but it is time now transfigured by art, nature ordered by "the skilful Gardener" in a floral sundial to measure time. The industrious bee, then, no less than man, "computes its time" (a pun on "thyme" and thus a truly Nabokovian word-play) with herbs and flowers; time the eroder has been alchemized in this artful re-creation of paradise into a golden translucence, delighting palate and eye. Nabokov means to create just such an inter-involvement of art and pleasure transcending time, or rather capturing its elusive living "texture," as Van Veen calls it; and this, finally, is the dramatic function of the novel's unflagging emphasis on erotic experience.

The point is made clearer in the novel by yet another allusion. Marvell's "The Garden" modulates into several other poems in the course of the narrative; but the most significant is Baudelaire's "Invitation au voyage," which is burlesqued in the novel with an oak tree inserted in the second and third line, to establish the cross-link with Marvell. Baudelaire's poem is also a ravishing dream of a perfect world, a world saturated with both generally sensual and specifically erotic delight, but realized, as such bliss can only be realized, through the beautiful ordering of art. Against the background of the novel, the famous opening lines of the poem become an evocation of Ardis, Van addressing Ada: "Mon enfant, ma soeur, / Songe à la douceur / D'aller là-bas vivre ensemble! Aimer à loisir / Aimer et mourir / Au pays qui te ressemble!" It is noteworthy that fragments of these lines are bandied about by Ada at the point in the narrative when their first sexual intimacy is recollected; significantly, this is the one moment in the novel when Ada actually says to Van that they are not two different people.

Baudelaire's poem, then, suggests what is also clear in the novel in other ways, that *Ada* is formed on the paradox of rendering the perfect state of nature through a perfect state of art, self-conscious, allusive, and exquisitely ordered. In this respect, Nabokov also follows the model of Milton (who is burlesqued in tetrameters at one point) in the fourth book of *Paradise Lost,* where prelapsarian Eden is described through the most finely ostentatious artifice—a natural garden full of sapphire founts, sands of gold, burnished fruit, crystal-mirror brooks, in which the preceding literary tradition of envisioned paradises is incorporated through the cunning strategy of negation ("Not that fair field / Of Enna," and so forth). It may be that *Ada* pays a price as a novel for being an extended poetic vision of Eden: Van and Ada sometimes seem to be more voices and images in a lyric poem than novelistic characters; the excess of formal perfection they must sustain makes them less interesting individually, less humanly engaging, than many of Nabokov's previous protagonists. In compensation, the expression in *Ada* of a lover's consummated delight in life and beauty is an achievement that has few equals in the history of the novel. Here is one brief but representative and thematically central instance, in which the lovers' present is juxtaposed with their ardisiac past.

> Her plump, stickily glistening lips smiled.
>
> (When I kiss you *here,* he said to her years later, I always remember that blue morning on the balcony when you were eating a *tartine au miel;* so much better in French.)
>
> The classical beauty of clover honey, smooth, pale, translucent, freely flowing from the spoon and soaking my love's bread and butter in liquid brass. The crumb steeped in nectar.

The honeyed bread-slice here is very much a Nabokovian equivalent of Proust's *petite madeleine* and, especially, of that more erotic tidbit, the ambrosial seedcake Molly Bloom puts from her mouth into her young lover Leopold's. Through its sweetness past and present fuse; or, to speak more precisely, they fuse through its sweetness minutely observed and recollected, then distilled into the lucid order of a poem that moves in alliterative music through a poised choreography of dactyls and trochees to the culminating metaphorical paradox of the honey as liquid brass and the final substitution of nectar for the honey, now become "literally" food for the gods.

It is really for the experience of such moments—and there are many of them in the course of the novel—that *Ada* exists. To state this in generic terms, *Ada* is, in a rather precise sense of the word, Nabokov's most lyric novel. Characterization, certainly when compared with his own earlier fiction, tends to be abstract or schematic; and the operation of plot, always a source of fascination for Nabokov the ingenious craftsman, is somewhat problematic here, especially in the long, telescoped period after Van's and Ada's youth. This is a novel about time, Van Veen repeatedly reminds us, which means that it is a novel about memory, a faculty that in Nabokov's view can serve us vitally only if we exercise the finest, fullest attentiveness to the life of each moment, and, ideally, the control of language required to focus the moment recalled. Nearly halfway through the novel, one character is described trying "to *realize* (in the rare full sense of the word), . . . to *possess* the reality of a fact by forcing it into the sensuous center," and a page later, the narrator, with continuing italic emphasis, goes on to say that such realization can be effected only through "that *third sight* (individual, magically detailed imagination) which many otherwise ordinary and conformant people may also possess, but without which memory (even that of a profound 'thinker' or technician of genius) is, let us face it, a stereotype or a tearsheet." *Ada* is a series of verbal experiments in making one *realize* in the rare full sense of the word, and the success of those experiments is ample compensation for the flaws of the book.

In order to understand more concretely how this process of realization works in the novel, let us consider two further images of young Ada recalled (by her lover, of course, almost eight decades after the fact) to set alongside the moment of the *tartine au miel* we have already observed. Van remembers watching Ada during an evening game of "Flavita" (Baron Klim Avidov's super-Scrabble) in the halcyon year of 1884: "The bloom streaking Ada's arm, the pale blue of the veins in its hollow, the charred-wood odor of her hair shining brownly next to the lampshade's parchment (a translucent lakescape with Japanese dragons), scored infinitely more points than those tensed fingers bunched on the pencil stub could ever add up in the past, present, or future." This is beautiful; and it is also wittily complicated in a peculiarly satisfying way. The verbal portraitist is attentive to the fine modulations of color, texture, and odor in his subject, with the oddly adverbial "shining brownly" intimating the suggestively kinetic sense of hue that a gifted colorist can produce in a subtle composition. (Ada's hair is actually black; but Nabokov is aware of the way colors assume different values when orchestrated together and depending on the source of the light.) Thus, through individual, magically detailed imagination, Ada at the game-table, otherwise elusive as all objects of memory are elusive, is forced into the sensuous center. What she means to the imagination of her enraptured beholder infinitely transcends the arithmetic scores of the anagrammatic game they have been playing; and the reference to past, present, and future is strategically important, because Ada as a luminous image treasured in the memory of the artist becomes an eternal present, beyond the ravages of time; she is the fulfilled quest of the novel as a whole.

This evocation of Ada is not only artful but, like most of what happens in the novel, it is set against another artwork—the translucent lakescape of the parchment lampshade with its Japanese dragons. The most immediate function of this detail is to contribute to the scenic realization of the moment; but it is also, like so many other artworks that Nabokov introduces, an analogue and an inverted reflection of the world of the novel. The lampshade painting is executed, one assumes, with reticent Oriental brushstrokes quite unlike the Boschean descriptive vividness of the novel's technique. Instead of the serpents of Ada's Eden, there are Japanese dragons; instead of Ardis's rural streams, a lake. A more elaborate instance of Ada's being set off against serpentine art occurs earlier in the novel, when she is a still virginal, though already distinctly nubile, twelve-year old:

> His sentimenal education now went fast. Next morning, he happened to catch sight of her washing her face and arms over an old-fashioned basin on a rococo stand, her hair knotted on the top of her head, her nightgown twisted around her waist like a clumsy corolla out of which issued her slim back, rib-shaded on the near side. A fat snake of porcelain curled around the basin, and as both the reptile and he stopped to watch Eve and the soft woggle of the bud-breasts in profile, a big mulberry-colored cake of soap slithered out of her hand, and her black-socked foot hooked the door shut with a bang which was more the echo of

> the soap's crashing against the marble board than a sign of pudic displeasure.

As in the scene of Ada by the lamp, painterly attention is given to shading and color, with that wonderful mulberry-colored soap somehow bringing the whole scene into bright focus and, at the same time, introducing a delicate suggestion of gustatory delight into the vision of soapy Ada in her ritual of ablution. But, while Ada at the game-table was a static portrait, movement dominates this passage, from the scrubbing hands of the beginning through the soft woggle of the breasts in the middle to the door kicked shut at the end. Indeed, even what should logically be static begins strangely to move. Ada's slim back "issues" from her pulled-down nightgown like a object in fluid motion; and the "nightgown twisted" is a noun with a participle ambiguously turning itself into an active verb; so that the "clumsy corolla" of the garment can provide a perfect compositional parallel, in floral imagery, to the fat porcelain snake curling around the basin. The snake's movement is then imparted to the bar of soap, which "slithers" out of Ada's hand. The rococo serpent, an item of aristocratic bric-à-brac, is permanently frozen as a piece of decorative sculpture, but seems to possess (or to have possessed) movement, it being in the nature of plastic art to create the illusion of kinesis out of perfect stasis. The enamored Van, then, can wittily recruit the snake as a fellow-admirer of Ada's beauty, imagining that the reptile observer like himself has momentarily stopped in its tracks with amazement over what it beholds. A snake observing Eve obviously points back to that forever fateful moment at the beginning of Genesis; but this fat fellow seems more a jovial attendant to the young woman's loveliness than a sinister seducer. The question of where or whether evil enters the Veens' Eden, a place paradoxically rich in demonic nomenclature, is not easy to resolve; and we shall try to sort out some of the main elements of that issue in a moment.

First, however, I should like to point out how traditional this whole enterprise of realizing experience is, at least in one crucial respect. For the moments Van Veen recreates for us are not taken from indifferent topics. Almost all the truly memorable ones, like the three we have just considered, are sensuous meditations on the image of Ada. If he and she are two halves of a primal self, there is complementarity rather than equality between them, because he is the artist, she the subject, model, muse. Nabokov had at first thought of calling the novel *The Texture of Time,* a title he then relegated to a metaphysical work by Van Veen; but his book had to be called *Ada* for the same reason that the sundry sonnet-cycles of the English

Renaissance were emblazoned with titles like *Delia, Diana, Phyllis, Celia.* Art, to borrow the vocabulary of the "Viennese quack" Nabokov never tired of mocking, is a flow of libidinous energy toward the world, a formally coherent reenactment—perhaps more intensification than compensation—of the pleasure the artist has known in the world. And for the male-dominated Western tradition, at least as far back as Dante, the emblem, talisman, or goal of this pleasure is the figure of a beloved woman; it is through her that the artist comes to realize the fullness of life. "He saw reflected in her," Van says of himself and Ada just before the end, "everything that his fastidious and fierce spirit sought in life."

Nabokov had played with this tradition once before in his other English novel bearing a woman's name as title; but *Lolita* is, of course, in many respects a highly ironic version of the myth of the Muse or eternal Beloved, shrewedly raising all sorts of psychological and epistemological questions about what is involved in a man's addiction to such a myth. *Ada,* less novelistic and more lyric than its predecessor, attempts to renew the myth without ironic subversion, which may explain some of its weaknesses, but is also the reason for its distinctive beauty. At one point, Van is unsettled to learn that his love for Ada has become the subject among the inhabitants of the Ardis region of a whole cycle of romances, epics, folk songs, and ballads sung to the strum of seven-stringed Russian lyres. His own task is to present a more scrupulous version that will not falsify the sensuous truth of his lifelong love, in a literary art that is in turn lyrical, painterly, wittily playful, scientific, aphoristic, self-reflective. The result of this effort will be the "real" Ada, and a 589-page poem called *Ada.*

All this still leaves unexplained the lurking elements of shadow in Nabokov's large sunny picture. At several points in the novel the narrator takes pains to inform us that "Ada" is the genitive form of the Russian word for hell. This makes Ada an exact etymological antithesis of the Renaissance poet's fair beloved, Celia, a name formed from the Latin for heaven. The main point, I would assume, is that Ada and Van in their Eden are in a state before the knowledge of good and evil, when heaven and hell cannot be distinguished. This also suggests, however, that there could be an ambiguous underside of evil in the edenic fulfillment offered Van by his sister-soul; and the suicide to which the two of them inadvertently drive Lucette may indicate that a paradisiac love can have evil consequences when it impinges on the lives of others outside the Garden, that there may be something essentially destructive in a passion that is so relentlessly an *égotisme à deux.* An oddly grim fatality accompanies the long history of Ada's and Van's raptures. All four of their putative and actual parents come to a bad end, two of them being quite mad at the end, and one of them, Dan Veen, actually dying "an odd boschean death" under the delusion that he is being ridden by a huge rodent, a detail he remembers from Bosch's *The Garden of Earthly Delights.* Nabokov's invocation of that painting as one possible model for his own project in *Ada* is itself an indication that his notion of the representation of Eden had its darker aspects. Bosch is praised by Demon Veen for the sheer freedom of fantasy he exercised, "just enjoying himself by crossbreeding casual fancies just for the fun of the contour and the color, . . . the exquisite surprise of an unusual orifice"; and presumably Nabokov means to emulate that uninhibited exuberance of invention in his novel. But *The Garden of Earthly Delights* is not merely, as Demon Veen contends, an expression of an artist's delight in freely manipulating the medium; it is also a disturbingly ambiguous conception of the terrestrial paradise. Its central panel, "In Praise of Lust," is a panoramic representation of polymorphous perversity in which the actors look more often like doomed souls than gleeful sybarites. The right panel of the triptych, moreover, is no garden at all, but a vision of damnation against a black background, crowded with the usual Boschean monsters and eerie images of dismemberment, and entitled, because of the huge musical instruments in the foreground, "Musical Hell."

Did Nabokov mean to suggest that there is something ultimately monstrous about the artistic imagination itself; that, given absolute freedom, it will conjure up not only beautiful birds of paradise but the most fearful monstrosities as well? (Here, as in other respects, there might be a moment of convergence between Nabokov's view of the mind and Freud's, however great the polemic distance the novelist placed between himself and psychoanalysis.) Certainly Van Veen as the exemplary artist within the world of the novel gives one pause for thought. He may even be intended, as Ellen Pifer argues in a forthcoming book on the moral dimension of Nabokov's fiction, as another in the series of manipulative, sinister artist-figures that goes back to Axel Rex in *Laughter in the Dark.* There is something distinctly chilling about Van Veen's relation to everything and everyone except Ada and his own writing. Outside his private garden-world and his literary lucubrations, he is a snob, a cold sensualist, and even on occasion a violent brute (as when he blinds the blackmailer Kim by caning him across the eyes). But if it was Nabokov's intention somehow to expose Van Veen, it is an intention not held in steady focus; for it is clear that the author shares many aspects of Van's sensibility and imaginatively participates in Van's dearest artistic and metaphysical aspirations, inviting us as readers to do so as well. The perilous closeness of beauty and monstrosity is manifestly an idea Nabokov conjures with in this most ambitious, and most avowedly

Boschean, of his novels; but it remains uncertain whether he actually succeeded in defining the relationship between those antitheses in fictionally cogent terms.

In any event, the ultimate sense that the novel means to project is of all threats of evil, including the evil of the corrosive passage of time, finally transcended by the twinned power of art and love. One last clue encodes this idea as a signature of affirmation at the end of the novel. Moving around mysteriously in the background of the concluding section is an unexplained figure named Ronald Oranger. Since he marries the typist responsible for Van's manuscript, and since he and his wife, according to a prefatory note, are the only significant persons mentioned in the book still alive when it is published, one may assume that his is the final responsibility for the text of *Ada,* and that he is the presiding spirit at the end. All we really know about him is his name, "orange tree" in French. No orange trees are explicitly mentioned in Marvell's "The Garden," though they are spectacularly present in "Bermudas," another remarkable poem by Marvell about a garden-paradise. In any case, "Ronald Oranger" in a Nabokov novel has a suspiciously anagrammatic look, and could well be rearranged as a reversal of the book's title, "angel nor ardor"—which is to say, the fixative force of art, working through the imagination of love, has extracted heaven from hell, Eden from Ada, has established a perfected state that originates in the carnal passions but goes quite beyond them.

Fortunately, the code-games and allusions in *Ada* are merely pointers to the peculiar nature of the novel's imaginative richness, which does not finally depend on the clues. Despite its incidental annoyances and even its occasional *longueurs,* few books written in our lifetime afford so much pleasure. Perhaps the parody-blurb at the end is not so wrong in proffering the novel as a voluminous bag of rare delights: Nabokov's garden abounds with the pleasurable visions whose artful design I have tried to sketch out here, and, as the blurb justifiably concludes, with "much, much more."

GARRETT STEWART

Death Bequeathed

In his penultimate novel, *Transparent Things* (1972), Nabokov puts into the words of a mental patient a notion Nabokov himself shares with Beckett. This is his understanding of the widespread mistake in thinking that the question of "survival after death," once settled, would go far toward solving "the riddle of Being. Alas, the two problems do not necessarily overlap or blend." Nabokov repeatedly courts the "blended" moment in rhetoric only to expose its metaphysical elusiveness. His is a style of elision and overlap exempt from the pressure of explanation, a hymn to the mystery of the textual intervals it enacts. Ending the first verse line with a nagging idiom straight out of Beckett, Nabokov elsewhere writes, "A Poet's death is, after all / A question of technique, a neat / Enjambment, a melodic fall." The assonant "neat" is slanted off from an internal near rhyme with "-nique" toward the neatly timed run-on, and eased from there into the cannily unsaid "dying cadence" for "melodic fall." Existential death seems at times in Nabokov not only a dead but a decomposed metaphor in the stylistics of closure.

The comparably prominent relation between textuality and mortality in Beckett and Nabokov turns out in many ways to be contrastive, measuring their divergence on the postmodernist spectrum. Death in Beckett lays claim to its full viciousness and intimidation, however much palliated by word play and gentled in the event by equivocation. In Nabokov style tends to elide death into mere figure, all terminus merely a transposition of terms.

Beckett channels his obsession with death as absence and negation so as to deconstruct progressively the whole play of signification that shapes the referential gestures of narrative. Nabokov never stops this play and this playing; the fantasy of presence incarnated by text is no sooner seen through than put back into play as heuristic illusion. Where Beckett succumbs to the textual status of the narrative endeavor, Nabokov summons the specter of exclusive textuality only to model all narratology on some new verbal cosmology. With Beckett deploying the full range of verbal effects at his disposal to approximate the intractable fact of death, we find Nabokov's style contriving to talk its way out (the other side) of dying. A single instance might help elucidate the difference between them. The closed rectangle of the fictional page is only intermittently projected by Beckett as a three-dimensional world, and at that only as the cramped world of a single book's dimensions. He has his hero Malone decline toward death at the voided center of a space defined by "these eight, no, six, these six planes that enclose me" (*Malone Dies*). They are, among other things, the six sides of the narrative volume that describes them, a geometrical containment that gradually erodes as its sustaining consciousness breaks down. By contrast, Nabokov closes *Transparent Things* by imagining death's "ultimate vision" centered on a kindred but distinct geometry, the three-dimensional "incandescence of a book or box"—read: its capacity for illumination—"grown completely transparent and hollow." It is a transparent coffin perhaps, but also the shape of fiction itself. The barely habitable cell of signifiers which Beckett manufactures and then dismantles burns to become in Nabokov a space lit from within and delimited by magic margins, invisible limits.

If in Nabokov a poet's death is only "a neat / enjambment," let us turn to the death of a poet's own issue, his daughter rather than his poetry. Such a death, by drowning, occurs at the exact enjambed midpoint of the poem called "Pale Fire" at the heart of the novel by that name, a poem which is a long meditation on the death that centers it: "A blurry shape stepped off the reedy bank / Into a crackly, gulping swamp, and sank" (ll. 499–500). The metrics step off their own tread across the run-on at the pivotal turn of the entire poem, proceeding then to the dying cadence of the final rhyme, "and sank," with any further momentum toward chaos or void belied by the orderly heroic couplet. The human victim is relegated to a "shape," the swamp personified as "gulping," yet the fine tuning of the whole transition betrays a stylistic finesse at odds with the blank event. Drowning as a yielding of identity to materiality, a swallowing of self by the impersonal, is carried by the metaphors of the passage without being transported to new meaning by them. The rather amorphously defined daughter of the great poet, Haze(l) to his Shade, is in a sense epitomized as a "blurry shape" in death. Yet the interest of the passage rests not with the metaphysics of drowning it might evoke but with the verbal transition, the multiple enjambment as it were, through which the human story achieves its displacement into pure style. In this sense the couplet is a microcosm for the whole textual allegory of death in *Pale Fire,* as in Nabokov's fiction both before and after it.

Death, Nabokov closes *Bend Sinister* (1947) by saying, is "but a question of style . . . a question of rhythm." He then glosses as well as enlarges the thought in his 1963 preface, insisting that "death is but a question of style, a mere literary device, a musical resolution." Such a claim could stand as motto for this book, especially when Nabokov's point is seen not to rarefy so much as clarify death as a novelist's challenge. Less the aestheticizing sidestep than it at first appears, Nabokov's remark would acknowledge that inevitable stylizing of death whose consideration began these chapters. Death again stands forth as that absolutely elusive narrative moment which, all words and no action, is always lettered rather than lived, a figure or specter of sheer speech—always, that is, less evidenced in words than "devised" creatively by them. Later in *Pale Fire,* between the drowning of his daughter and his own death in mid-rhyme, falls the poet's near encounter with death after a heart attack. Again enjambment manages to bridge the interval it cannot wholly portray: "I did know that I had crossed / The border" (ll. 699–700). Meter itself becomes the measure of eternity. At one level of generality this is the familiar myth of immortality through art. But this is not a level at which the novel *Pale Fire* has much abstract business. It is rather within the syntax and prosody, the lexical pliability and high varnish of style itself that the transgressed limit of temporality takes its definition. Style in Beckett, enfeebled to a lone cry as the whole bottom drops out of the novel as genre, falls through in Nabokov to a wilder freedom yet, autonomous and autotelic in an opportunism of pure beauty. His rhetoric abdicates from the reality it then refabricates, and death becomes a touchstone of strange centrality. Since mimesis has always bowed at death to the freely imagined, the death moment becomes more than ever before paradigmatic. It is an instant of undeniable fictive will. Yet if death is only a "question of style," what about life? Such a rhetorical question, animated by the lambent play of his language, is the extravagant gambit that valorizes the maze and dazzle of Nabokov's fictions. Though not always the focal subject, death remains the vantage of all such stylistic elaborations.

This was true from early in Nabokov's career, long before *Pale Fire* or his later novel *Transparent Things*. We may begin by looking at *The Real Life of Sebastian Knight* (1941), appearing only a decade after *The Waves*. The title figure is a famous novelist, recently deceased, whose last novel is described in minute detail by the narrator as the Beckett-like death scene of a text itself. As with Beckett's glamorless and vulgarized version of the Woolfian stream of consciousness in "gurgles of outflow," nominally describing the sea which threatens to reclaim his characters, so in *Sebastian Knight* it is the welter, surge, and abatement of prose in its own right that becomes the medium of finality. The novel is "itself . . . heaving and dying" along with the hero, who is "sinking throughout the book . . . now rolling up this image, now that, letting it ride in the wind, or even tossing it out on the shore, where it seems to move and live for a minute on its own and presently is drawn back again by grey seas where it sinks or is strangely transfigured." The unulant conjunctive grammar of this sentence eddies, even in the retelling, with its own congruence between subject and descriptive mode.

Beyond the metaphors associated with this death as a wavering delineation at the "shore of consciousness," the rhythms of build and dip also attach specifically to "the swell and fall of uneven breathing," and in turn to the breath of utterance in the contours of its own inscription. But psychological mimesis is still firmly in office. The dying man comes to realize what the deathbed tradition in literature might have taught him: how interval and rehearsal rather than prophetic vision delimit the capacities for representation at death. He knows "that only one half of the notion of death can be said really to exist: *this* side of the question, the wrench, the parting, the quay of life gently moving away . . . the beach receding." It is from within this interval of withdrawal that revelation, such as it is, must unfold. Only by "an incredible feat of suggestive wording" can the author infer without referential directness "that he knows the truth about death and that he is going to tell it." Since this can only be the truth about life seen from the point of view of finality, it amounts to the textualization of the world as a suddenly legible narrative. Prose style becomes the very model of order and cogency. The world's topography is now like "the page in a book where these mountains and forests, and fields, and rivers are disposed in such a way as to form a coherent sentence: the vowel of a lake fusing with the consonant of a sibilant slope." The last is a self-exampling sibilance followed by the alliteration and assonance of another case in point: "the windings of a road writing its message in a round hand, as clear as that of one's father," an original and authorizing speech. Here is the exaggerated legibility of the given. Death in fiction, as well as the death of fiction in the sense of its closure, is the stuff of elusive artifice converted to revelatory pattern.

As in most novels, so in *Sebastian Knight* the revelation is entirely retrospective, addressing this side of last things. It italicizes the texture of life at the verge of unconsciousness. What Nabokov sets about to suggest later in his career is that the very discovery of pattern within the process of life's story or text is the uncovering not of life's truth in the act of death but of death's finality in the work of a summarized life. Every "coherent sentence" thus seems gathered from flux into an orderly death sentence of a sort. *Pale Fire* not only suggests this but allegorizes it at every level of its manifold fantasy. When the waters into which Hazel's figure vanishes, in the interval of enjambment, are given their true geographical coordinates, they do not provide a mappable path of meaning rendered legible at death so much as a linguistic parable of death itself as the gaping interstices of language. As if she emerges out of one of Rhoda's nightmares in *The Waves,* the introverted and neurotic Hazel Shade takes her life in an icy lake (or lacuna) between "Exe and Wye"(l. 490), between two consecutive letters of a punning alphabet where there is no scriptive footing, only void. Rhoda too, we recall, feared those same "white spaces" where Derrida perceives annihilation in the gap(e) between all letters, death a manifested function of difference.

Charted as if the lay of reality's land were merely the surface of a poem, Hazel's ironically textualized death is thus a linguistic counterpart to the stalking of her father by the assassin, Gradus, until the last line of Shade's fatally truncated poem. Devious incarnation of the gradual, this personification of fatality in the name Gradus seems to lurk between letters, words, and lines, which is not to say in the absence of text but within the scriptive differentiations from absence that make text possible. The annihilating Gradus thus makes his way "through the entire length of the poem, following the road of its rhythm, riding past in a rhyme," even "hiding between two words" and "breathing with the caesura" as an aspect of cancellation en route rather than merely *ad quem.* "Steadily marching nearer in iambic motion" on the "escalator of the pentameter," Gradus is seen "stepping off" in a double sense—both marking and departing—the metrical unit into the next line's "new train of thought." He is secreted there within the pun on "train" as vehicle, gaining on whatever final word will double for the onset of silence.

The formal allegory of *Pale Fire* has to do with the way it dramatizes the inherence of death in writing itself, drives death out of hiding into a visible condition of all textuality. For a sense of this we need to stand back and consider the organizing structure of the book's self-embedding nest of texts. Nabokov's novel, so-called, once introduced to us through a foreword by Charles Kinbote, émigré pedant from a mythical European state of mind called Zembla, is then primarily composed of an unfinished poem in four cantos, one line short of its five hundred rhyming couplets, by American poet John Shade, followed by Kinbote's extensive, testy, and fanatical annotations. But this is only as it seems. Between the lines of poem and prose we begin to perceive that Charles Kinbote, who fancies himself the exiled King Charles of Zembla—as we are always exiled from the glories of our daydreams—may be in fractured fact the mad Professor Botkin, colleague of Shade's at Wordsmith College and editor of his posthumous verses. If we can suppose with many critics, indeed the majority, that Shade has invented the character of Kinbote to explicate his own poem for him, we should also be able just as readily to imagine Kinbote as a maestro of prose puzzles who has projected himself into the persona of a doomed poet in an ingrown game of mouse and cat.

The latter role is closer, for one thing, to Nabokov's in writing the book, at least as close as the two names, Kinbote and Nabokov, approach to anagram. Kinbote emerges from such a recognition as a feverish fabulator who has devised his alter ego's accidental assassination so as to give irrevocable finality to his (their) text. Shade (as *his* name would adumbrate) is devised simply to be annihilated, a subhuman assassin's bullet taking him forever beyond Kinbote's reach: "I felt—I still feel—John's hand fumbling at mine, seeking my fingertips, finding them, only to abandon them at once as if passing to me, in a sublime relay race, the baton of life." Akin to Malone's pencil, the imagined baton is ultimately the pen of art which has given Shade what life he has in the first place. It is the penned art of the poem itself, putatively by Shade, as well as of the appended and deviously preemptive endnotes by Kinbote. Every character seeks his or her continued life at the "fingertips" of the author, which might suggest, of course, Kinbote's receiving not just better expression but life itself from Shade, rather than the other way around. Yet, conversely, every maker of texts may feel the artist he knows he has in him fumbling at his fingertips to get free, to become immortal—and so to give himself over in turn, as Thackeray has hinted, to the holding hand of the reader. As Kinbote says in the final sentence of his foreword, again recalling the editorial parable at the end of *The Newcomes,* "For better or worse, it is the commentator who has the last word." In a later "stage play" which Kinbote has in mind to create out of this death scene, the poet hero will perish in the "line of fire" between two lunatics, returning us by another pun to the death lurking from line to line, just waiting to be dramatized, in the present state and status of the text.

To tell of his Zemblan adventures of power and dispossession, otherwise understood as his wildest dreams, Kinbote creates Shade as a poetic offshoot who should be able to transmute them to beauty, but who does so only by fitful glimpses here and there in a poetic text otherwise engaged. A novel, Nabokov suggests, is not just prose compared to poetry but some coalition, some composite form, that goes forward both at the pace of narrative and with the charge of poetic symbol. By the defiantly hybrid shape of the book bound under the title *Pale Fire*—half elegant verse, half prose gloss, to be read interchangeably as per instructions, the one after and in the light of the other—Nabokov's creation, though seemingly not a novel at all, announces itself as both the quintessence of the genre and an exegesis upon it. Bringing the rhapsodic and the prosaic into commentary on each other, the beautiful and the mimetically dutiful (however deranged the latter's "reality"), *Pale Fire* becomes in essence every great novel's transparent imposition of verbal harmony upon the frustrations of identity, song upon quest for self, mastered creation upon the degrading record of loss, attrition, deposition, exile. The condensation of elegiac verse faces off the rawer material of supposed gloss, undigested nostalgia, and obsession to define in their very interchange the genius of fiction as life under pressure of art, art of life.

Kinbote, without his voiced fantasies of Shade and other shadows, might be only a diarist dying, another version of the Beckett persona. But if Malone, all alone, could really believe in his Sapo and Macmann, could release his own wit to them, liberating rue into amusement, then he would come at least a little closer to the confidence of Nabokov's narrators and their easy way with finalities. We may recall here the typifying exit of Conmal, the Russian translator in *Pale Fire,* whose "last words in his last delirium" were, "*Comment dit-on 'mourir' en anglais?*"—"a beautiful and touching end." This linguist's epitomizing wish to end in a transaction between spheres of purely textual reference may even suggest a motive for the close of *Malone Dies,* the hero's secondary creations left adrift somewhere between the mainland, their fatherland, and an unspecified island—as if between their native French and their English incarnations, dead of the very idea of transposition into another set of terms.

To return to *Pale Fire* and that plot's largest argument, it would seem to be Nabokov's point that any persona, whether musing aloud at his desk or being hunted down by a mad assassin, as Kinbote thinks he too is at the end—that any first person in fiction is always caught halfway between an autonomous "I" and the murderous impulse of all art to enshrine identity in permanence. For days after the shooting, Kinbote "wore" Shade's poetic draft about his person in the form of "ninety-two index cards," feeling himself "armoured with rhyme." It is this same draft that he had tried with allegorical futility to hold up as a protection for Shade in the moment of the assassination. Shade stands all along for that aspect of genius which inevitably dies out of life into text, while Kinbote, still talking at the end, represents that deathproof aspect of art as the displacement of self and voice into book. Fiction cannot save, it can only preserve. William Burroughs has made much this same postmodernist point. Asked in an interview if it were possible to suggest "in your own writing where your death is reflected," Burroughs replied, "I would say in every sentence." For Kinbote, every line of Shade's poem sentences to death that half of the creative self willing to delve into the realm of elegy. In Melville's phrase "an author from the dead," in other terms the sacrificial agent in the Orphic recovery of all narrative poetry (all the poetry of narrative), Shade bears as his very name an anagram of that Hades which metaphorically designates in Thackeray, for instance, the entire region of retrospective plot. The art of this Shade (in the dictionary sense of his name as a dweller among the dead) having been willed either by or to Kinbote—or in some sense both—is raised from the very death which is the native domain of commemoration. Shade's text is thus the record of descent into some more openly visionary configuration not so much of his name as of his identity and his dreams.

In the first paragraph of *Transparent Things* (1972), the most provocative speculation on death and textuality in Nabokov's work following *Pale Fire,* it is Hugh Person whom we hear hailed by the narrator, a character whose first name identifies him by near-homonym as the almost (but not quite) second person of any fictional address. Hugh, all but "you," stands between the "I" of the narrator and the reader thus indirectly addressed, half within the plot as character, half identified with the recipient of plot. As sacrificial victim of the death destined to close the novel, he is thus, in Woolf's terms, a perfect "border case" for the illustration of death's transactive style in the interval, both invisible and atemporal, between the scene of annihilation and the scene of reading. As hero, "You" Person is always equidistant from the author who pens him and the reader whose silent voice enunciates him as a cathartic second self. When he is later called by the narrator "our Person," the triangulation of author, character, and reader is complete in an editorial as well as regal plural. It is through just this sacrificial surrogate, standing in for the author (almost as his own person) by way of creative empathy, that death is brought to life for the receiving consciousness of the reader.

Check Out Receipt

BPL- Brighton Branch Library
617-782-6032
http://www.bpl.org/branches/brighton.htm

Monday, Jun 17 2013 3:14PM

Item: 39999006381832
Title: Strong opinions
Material: Book
Due: 07/08/2013

Item: 39999062019318
Title: The ascent of money : a financial h
istory of the world
Material: Book
Due: 07/08/2013

Item: 39999055570699
Title: Vladimir Nabokov
Material: Book
Due: 07/08/2013

Total items: 3

Thank You!

Transparent Things can be seen to reverse only so as to restate the allegory of *Pale Fire*. Here Hugh Person is the humble proofreader assigned to edit the later works—including the posthumous novel—of the renowned author R., an obvious avatar of the Nabokovian style. Shade is to Kinbote as R. is finally to Hugh, an already dead writer who is nevertheless (indeed therefore) the guarantor of his satellite's immortality. This is true in *Pale Fire* because Shade has supposedly imported Kinbote's story into his capacious and memorable art, or at least seems to have evoked it there as coded undersong. In *Transparent Things,* as we shall see, R. lifts Hugh beyond mortality by actually appearing at his death, in the last paragraph of the novel, as confessed omniscient overvoice, easing the decedent across the stylistic and metaphysical interval to disembodiment, reembodiment, or call it textual finality. As much as R. shares in the thematic and stylistic preoccupations of Nabokov, so does Hugh, in his undeveloped talents, fantasies, even lovers, share too in the rich biography of the novelist whose aesthetic dreams in fiction he is assigned to proof—to prove true. When the deathless voice of narration, apparently R.'s own from beyond the grave, hails Hugh at the end, we hear the perfected artist inviting the fallible human (side of himself) to rest. The narrator of *Transparent Things* at one point uses a suggestive textual metaphor for the relation of dreams to life, calling them the "anagrams of diurnal reality." Hugh's wild dreams are also the anagrams of that transmutation of reality known as R.'s art. They are as Kinbote's fantasies to Shade's poem, or say as Shade to Hades, and so in one of Hugh's wildest nightmares we find an early version of some recurrent dream motif called a "first rough draft." The ambiguous, repetitive nightmare of this dreaming proofreader, within which he dies finally in a hotel fire, goes, the tables turned, through a final redrafting in R.'s own voice at the end.

On our way to this last scene of the novel, we must pause over the inset text, comparable to Shade's posthumous published poem, which prepares for the redefined terms of the novel's closural fatality. This is the posthumously received last letter written by R. to his publisher, which, as much as Decoud's last letter to his sister in *Nostromo,* is a concerted study in the relationship of textuality to death. This deathbed letter occupies the whole twenty-first chapter of the novel, and more than any other compressed stretch of fiction I know manages to catalogue, investigate, and then divest itself of a whole range of mortal platitudes and textual formulas. R. explains that he expects either to be "proofread by cherubim—or misprinted by devils," the last a pun on typesetting apprentices. It is a tried and tested turn. Authors have frequently enjoyed, by the logic of epitome, thinking of themselves as perfected at death like their own texts in press, redeemed ineffaceably by record from the vicissitudes of experience, *bound* in every sense for remembrance. John Donne offers an early instance of this trope of textual eternity which would be dear to the heart of Nabokov's translator, Conmal: "All mankind is of one author, and in one volume; when man dies, one chapter is not torn out of the book, but translated into a better language . . . some pieces are translated by age, some by sickness, some by war, some by justice; but God's hand is in every translation, and his hand shall bind up all our scattered leaves again, for that library where every book shall lie open to one another." Before he became an autobiographer Benjamin Franklin had as a young printer sketched out his own epitaph in this same mode: "The Body of B. Franklin. Printer; Like the Cover of an Old Book, Its contents torn out, And stript of its Lettering and Gilding, Lies here, Food for Worms. But the Work shall not be wholly Lost; For it will, as he believ'd, appear once more, in a new and more perfect Edition, corrected and amended by the Author." In a quite different agnostic mood, Keats passed on to his publisher this in-joke and double pun just before he died: "Tell Taylor I shall soon be in a second Edition—in sheets—and cold press." The poet is perfected by, and textually displaced into, the paradox of a dead but deathless volume.

R.'s next broadside at the mortuary tradition in his last letter is also a play on the linguistic epitomization in which certain kinds of vocabulary find their true validation only in finalities. Told by an Italian doctor that his "*Operazione* had been *perfetta,*" R. quips that "it had been so in the sense Euler called zero the perfect number." "It is comic," R. continues, but "I used to believe that dying persons saw the vanity of things, the futility of fame, passion, art, and so forth. I believed that treasured memories in a dying man's mind dwindled to rainbow wisps." He had a belief akin to the overarching instincts of Thackeray's *Vanity Fair,* say, "but now I feel just the contrary: my most trivial sentiments and those of all men have acquired gigantic proportions." As time runs out on the living man, the smallest things of this world seem a microcosm of an eternity by which they are no longer dwarfed: "The entire solar system is but a reflection in the crystal of my (or your) wrist watch." Human life ticks to the greater rhythms of the timeless, or vice versa, and even the signifying configurations on a private timepiece wheel in the shape of vaster orbits, infinite renewals.

R. now describes the miracle of his own serenity in death with a writerly play on "composure" (its scriptive overtones of "composition" already familiar from the more obvious punning in *The Waves*) as in particular an author's articulate dispensation at the end: "Total rejection of all religions ever dreamt up by man and total composure in the face of total death!" Would that he could compose it into portable form: "If I could explain this triple totality in one big book, that book would become no doubt a new bible and its author the founder of a new creed." The moment of revelation is, however, deflected by the text, resistant to scripted form, "not merely because a dying man cannot write books but because that particular one would never express in one flash what can only be understood *immediately.*" Italicized into prominence, this adverb marks the intensive moment that has no room for extension. It will always in the "mediation" of narrative require that "so many consecutive words" violate or deny in their own verbal duration the attempted paradox of the instantaneous interval. It is a composure, in short, that has no room in which to be composed.

There ends the letter, apparently with no time for subscript or signature, as if that italicized word, *immediately,* was itself tilted forward into the epiphanic instant about which it despaired of speaking. The chapter closes with a "note added by the recipient," followed by this addendum: "Received on the day of the writer's death. File under Repos—R." Redolent of the financial term for "repossessed property," the abbreviation for a repository of correspondence stands also, by scriptive synonymy, for the "repose" of the soul which this writing constitutes. As one might suspect from such verbal dexterity, the supposed recipient's shorthand "—R." seems almost to be the signature of the writer himself posthumously overseeing the disposition of his last written work, in all the anonymity of its masked subscript. Like Decoud's letter offering up the truth of events as he sees them to the vessel of his memory in a loving sister, R. gives himself up to the secular creature upon whom his immortality as writer is fashioned, the "greater Publisher" of eternal reissue and renown. In writing, the novelist R. had always secured his withdrawal from the immediate present—as if all letters, all words, were his last, but also his immortality. By the most elusive reflexive logic of the whole novel, R. outlives himself in any text, fictional or epistolary, at least long enough to sign and seal his fate within that text.

What are the consequences of suspecting R. to have signed off for himself this particular last missive, the internal text of this brief chapter? It might well be that we are helped in this way to imagine him as writing the whole present novel as well as that one posted text, and chapter, within it. His admitted posthumous novel, the one we hear referred to at least, is to appear under the title *Tralatitions,* meaning "metaphors," unless the publisher changes it. Yet what is *Transparent Things* but another name, indeed a metaphor, for metaphors as such, for words translucent to similitude, windows upon likeness? Beginning to suspect at some point that novelist R.

may be, by a homonym no more lazy or irrelevant than Hugh for "you," *our* novelist, that he may have written as his last fiction the book we are now reading, we realize why the intonations and sprung idioms in which the narrative voice speaks to the dying Hugh in the last paragraphs of *Transparent Things* seem drawn from the bastard locutions of the naturalized English speaker R. His immortality, proven by the book, can extend as fictive gift to his created hero and proofreader. In the last novel by Nabokov before *Transparent Things* there is a similar conclusion, though not as inventively dramatized. In *Ada* (1969) it is stated outright of hero and heroine that "if our time-racked, flat-lying couple," supine like an open book, "ever intended to die they would die, as it were, *into* the finished book, into Eden or Hades, into the prose of the book or the poetry of its blurb" (Nabokov's emphasis). More recently than *Transparent Things*, in his own devious reversal of the usual figurative relation of ephemeral living author to immortal if phantom character, John Fowles closes *Daniel Martin* (1977) by having the narrator declare himself in the final sentence as the title character's "ill-concealed ghost." That feeble shrouding of the author's status as effectually posthumous—and so in a sense already immortal—is rendered in Nabokov even more deliberately flimsy by the structural "transparency" of his earlier novel.

Earlier yet in Nabokov's work the closural death scene has repeatedly collided with a rescuing confession of fictional artifice. What *Transparent Things* adds to *Ada* and its Nabokovian predecessors in this vein is primarily the dramatized death of the narrator himself. Its plot enacts the inevitable removal of its own articulation from the imagined world of the novel to the scene of its writing, where narrating voice can subsequently be discovered to await coincidence with the hero at his and the novel's own last moment. At the end of *Bend Sinister* the hero, Adam Krug, is spared one kind of "execution" by the confession of another, redeemed from assassination by stylistic assignation. "I felt a pang of pity for Adam," writes the narrator, "and slid towards him along an inclined beam of pale light," a pale fire of transfiguration just before the hero faces the firing squad. Narrator appears to his character through the manifestation of the book's heraldic title in a slant of strange light—that is, in the definitive medium of the text itself that constitutes, presumably along the angle of a moving pen, such an oblique illumination of the world.

This novel's prefacing definition of death as mere style, the rhetoric of sheer "literary device," returns now in a passage which succumbs to a forced periodic interval in the very conception rather than the enactment of death, putting a strain on the prose more violently suspensive than any comparable parallel grammar of overarched discontinuity in Woolf: "I knew that the immortality I had conferred on the poor fellow was a slippery sophism, a play upon words. But the very last lap of his life had been happy and it had been proven to him that death was but a *question of style*. Some tower clock which I could never exactly locate, which, in fact, I never heard in the daytime, struck twice, then hesitated and was left behind by the smooth fast silence that continued to stream through the veins of my aching temples; *a question of rhythm*" (my emphasis). The "question of rhythm" is the very question begged by the disorienting sprung rhythm of this passage. The hero having been put to, and at the same time beyond, death, that dying is now displaced into the narrator's closural metacommentary on the creative pulse of his own performance. Recalling the role of apposition as a primary impetus in the Lawrencian style of trespass, and bearing in mind the threefold appositive phrase from the preface to *Bend Sinister* describing death as "but a question of style, a mere literary device, a musical resolution," one is at least tempted to detect in this closural passage death's appositional redefinition (as italicized) distended across an interval of some forty words in a grammatical test case for the very limits of the apposite, the proximate, the approachable. Pressing the natural rhythms of syntax to the farthest stretch of coherence—across not only stylistic time but the invoked clock-tower symbolism of time as prosodic measure—this prolonged mortal interval, replayed and participated in by the discursive voice, transposes the preceding narrative solution of death toward its "musical resolution" as prose style in extremis. Prose contorts its way inward from the bloodless efficacy of a "literary device" for death to the very lifeblood of the devising mind in the "aching" pulse of its invention. The final cadence of closure then becomes the accepted silence on the other side of creative expenditure. And yet again the apparent aestheticism is held in check, for the very word "question," beneath its meaning as mere "matter," preserves also the suggestion of death's irreducible mystery and its interrogation by narrative.

Even earlier in his career, it is a similar benign annihilation of hero into character to which Nabokov consigns the executed protagonist of *Invitation to a Beheading* (1934; translated 1959). At the moment of his decapitation by the guillotine in a Paris square, the hero is retrieved from this three-dimensional end into a cardboard apocalypse. In this outdoor theater of death, suddenly the "spectators" are "quite transparent now," and the "dust, rags, chips of painted wood," further on the "pasteboard bricks, posters" into which this stage-set world reverts, call up the two-dimensional paper surface of the text upon which this mortal backdrop has after all been rendered. The fate that would level, indeed sever, the hero instead flattens the world to page. The site of execution has thus become the scene of reading, the fated city "square," of which little now "[is] left," being transfigured to the rectangle of its novelistic inscription. In the metatextual economy by which death is rescued and recompensed by style, the encircling trees are said to lie "flat and reliefless," a sculptural as well as vegetative pun (worthy of Hopkins's "Goldengrove unleaving") on the contrasting "relief" of the hero's reprieve from death. As at the end of *Transparent Things* too, it is finally utterance alone, the presumed ventriloqual projection of the narrator, which not only ushers the dying character out but summons him from beyond; in the very last sentence of the *Invitation,* the protagonist makes "his way in that direction where, to judge by the voices, stood beings akin to him."

Like this early hero, invited not only *to* but out *through* a beheading; like the protagonist in *Bend Sinister,* not falling to his death but cadenced to closure; like the "flat-lying" couple in *Ada,* dying into rather than out of the book; like Fowles's Daniel Martin, hero and book by his name, survived by an admitted spectral originator—so too the proven hero of *Transparent Things,* himself a proofer of texts, finds himself resurrected into the transcribed voice of his always and already "ghostly" progenitor and double. As his dutiful proofreader is in the process of being composed and composited, the omniscient R. speaks to him in a fatherly, authorizing tone whose verbal tics we have heard him use before: the paternalistic and patronizing "son," the familiarizing filler "you know," incorporated here into the whole scrambled syntax of the novel's last sentence, "Easy, you know, does it, son." Grammar, like life, is coming apart at the seams. Just before, Hugh is in the middle of an erotic dream of reunion with the wife he accidentally murdered years earlier, also in his sleep, completing now the closed circle of his "uncorrected" dream world, when a hotel fire, mysteriously set, immolates him at the moment of pity and terror while *translating* him into proofread final copy: "Person, *this* person, was on the imagined brink of imagined bliss when Armande's footfalls approached—striking out both 'imagined' in the proof's margins (never too wide for corrections and queries!)" At this moment authorship tips its hand, retrieves the hero for continued narrative, validates and preserves him, but only as an invention within an epiphany of the book's own formal and formative energy: "This is where the orgasm of art courses through the whole spine with incomparably more force than sexual ecstasy or metaphysical panic." The very pun on the spine of a book bursts with the *jouissance* it asserts. The textualized, corrected Hugh has undergone a transposition from a quoted and qualified "imagined" to the thing itself unhedged, and this in a joint epitome of his prodigious dream life and his profession as corrector of texts. It is fitting that his attempted escape from the flames is blocked by a "fatal draft," a final pun combined of textual revision itself and the afflatus of original inspiration that has motivated it. At the same time, whereas Kinbote in an editorial pun admits his desire to be "bullet-proof at last" by hiding behind Shade's poem, Hugh might paradoxically be seen in the very moment of his narrative immolation to be fireproofed by the text for future readers.

It is at this point that the narrative voice, given a second wind, intervenes with an elaborated language of displacement across an interval from life to text which prose attempts to conjure with an absolute minimum of rhetoric. It is an effort at displacement with no temporal bearings: the deathbed interval become the mere space of differentiation. Calling to "our own Person" across the liminal border of death, narrative in R.'s tone and tongue offers a mere demonstrative, "it," that turns out to be a reflexive self-demonstration, stalled momentarily by the grammatical intrusion of the language of faith or "belief" in lower case. "This is, I believe, *it:* not the crude anguish of physical death but the incomparable pangs of the mysterious mental maneuver needed to pass from one state of being to another." Character partakes in a displacement of state rather than a temporal transition, while that last pronoun, "another," its antecedence determined, could never in any conceivable secular grammar become an adjective shoving off into a new descriptive phrase, there being nothing sayable to which it might refer forward. The style of dying involves not only a rhetoric but a grammar of retrospect. Remembering R.'s emphasis on the "*immediately*" which any consecutive text of death would have to belie, we may well take the italicized "*it*" to stress the simple here and now of the conclusive "this." The text would thus refer in a reflexive manner to the very demonstrative phrase that names the finality of death. After the clobbered grammar at the end of *Malone Dies,* this is the language of fiat revindicated by a specification of the text itself, not Hamlet's "let be," but "let this" (here: this textual moment) "be it." Dying for the hero is no more than the naming of death for him by the narrative voice. And so, though peremptory, how anguishing can it be? For this is his perfection too, a displacement from imagined presence into textual memorial that is the only labor of dying in this fictive universe, epitaph and apotheosis in the same phrase, a dying *into* rather than out of the book.

One six-word monosyllabic sentence after an indentation—"Easy, you know, does it, son"—and this novel, like *The Waves,* comes to an end by ceding its drama to omniscience in its own bizarre, inbred sense. Jauntily choppy, periodic, halting but confident, bordering on a Beckett-like grammatical entropy but suggesting instead an infinite gentleness in the displacement of ended presence into rendered text, this is Nabokov's closure at its most assured. Shade made it possible for Kinbote, and vice versa, the unnamed narrator for the heroes of *Invitation to a Beheading* and *Bend Sinister*. Now the immortal R. secures such closure for his second person, You. Yet it was Malone who said it: "My story ended I'll be living yet. Promising lag." In Nabokov, too, this lag is textually ingrown, atemporal. Its interval is simply the definitive, the inevitable space—mediated but laboring for the power of immediacy—between story and discourse, imagined event and its report when plotted to closure. Besides identifying the voice as R.'s, that garbled vernacular of the death sentence seems also to raise questions about the very capacities of language when confronting a death scene. Tmesis (syntactic cutting) replaces mimesis in an attempt to break open, to discompose the interval long enough for the "flash" of recognition. Such normative syntax as, for instance, "You know, son, easy does it," once transposed (in both the typographical sense and that of the special mortal terminology of this study) becomes the transfiguring truth Hugh knows on his own "I's" behalf, on Ours, on R.'s. "There exists an old rule," writes Nabokov in *Look at the Harlequins!* (1974), "—so old and trite that I blush to mention it. Let me twist it into a jingle—to stylize the staleness: The I of the book / Cannot die in the book." But if the "I" can confer some part of itself upon a dying effigy, and by deferral or deflection name that second self's death without having further to effect it, then that promising lag becomes the work of textuality itself in the ever-suspended scene of death.

The novel that opens in direct address—"Here's the person I want. Hullo person!"—closes upon another jostled apostrophe to the "son." It does so in a language of disarrangement whose balked syntax generates the delays and reemphases of a periodic grammar gone piecemeal. The master stylist renowned for the syllabic brocade and sensuous folds of his syntax ties up this narrative with the simplest of crossed stitches: "Easy, you know, does it, son." With even euphony eschewed, it remains a question what kind of style death is a "question of." In the shuffling vocative register of this last cockeyed apostrophe, such mainstays of the verbal interval as elision and punning, anaphora and apposition are all excluded. Absent is the grammar of Forsterian connection, of Lawrencian trespass, or of Woolfian fluidity, even the syntactic disengagement and disintegration of Beckett's closure. Instead of eased dissipation or transit, there is contortion from within, a transfiguring torque on the idiomatic mold of the language's deep structure. The mortal formula of transposition, by syntax or metaphor, has, as mentioned, become in its other sense the internal flip-flop of language, a slippery grip and spin on utterance, as if by force of will it can be twisted into new writ. It is indeed a "mysterious mental maneuver" in which the mortal interval has grown entirely hermetic: the internal relation of syllables and words. The grammatical metathesis (or syntactic transposition) accords with the rhetorical metastasis (the rapid "remove" from one frame of reference to another discussed in connection with Dickens and phrased by Nabokov as a transit from "one state of being to another"). What results is a metatextual furthering of this elusive "maneuver," a transformation prose both declares and in its own formulation endows.

After more than two centuries of the English-language novel, the fictional death scene has transparently purified itself to a revelation about the very scene of fiction. Against the precedents of postmodernism, the motivating force of transposition in Nabokov has become the writer's epitomizing dream of release from "so many consecutive words" into an undeferred vision of stylistic essence without reference, a displacement from the secondariness of transcribed content to the state of sheer form. If, as suggested in the second chapter, death as a stylistic challenge must in some sense play both sides against the middle, with the far side always inexpressible, here is a whole posthumous text that stands confessed within this limbo and this bliss, holding firm on the paper-thin threshold between imaginative articulation and imagined (re)incarnation.

Not only does this closure sum up the threefold structure and rhetoric of the traditional death scene as an acknowledged textual maneuver, but *Transparent Things* further serves for review here by epitomizing in this passage its own attempted compromise between a phenomenological and a deconstructive imagination of the text. With his fiction conceived now as trace, now habitable space, now the one inscribing our entrance to the other, Nabokovian deconstruction would rebuild our faith in presence within the contours of a story's entirely invented world. For R., for Kinbote before him, for the narrator of *The Real Life of Sebastian Knight* earlier yet, a text is the regally privileged "state of being" where a phenomenal world available somehow through words carries through on its promise and grows noumenal. Unwilling, even or especially in death, to relax his faith in the credibility of such a world, N.'s surrogate specter R. can certify it anew by incorporating into its bordering consciousness a "real" person, his Hugh, at the last instant when character is able to be transfigured from independent figment of the text to an admitted verbal fixture in it.

If as the dying mind approaches the point of revelation the world itself turns to a "coherent sentence," with (again from *Sebastian Knight*) the "windings of a road writing its message in a round hand, as clear as that of one's father," then that inscribed road is also the only route of access to the space it crosses. This is the disclosed topography of the Logos, where every authored world is as clearly turned out as that of any First Cause or Universal Father, indeed as that of the "anthropomorphic deity" (*Bend Sinister*) behind the verbal metamorphoses of any text. Speaking *ex nihilo* to his "son," R. in his last utterance offers up the disconnected nonsequiturs of his broken English segued to finis like the "translation" of the dying linguist, Conmal, in *Pale Fire*. These last words testify to an unattributed but indubitable state of being cogently invoked simply by coinciding with the textual security of closure and containment. Brought to limit and illumination by death, and this through the virtuoso opacity of his word play, the phenomenological *jeu d'esprit* of Nabokov's fiction is to render a whole world transparently accessible through the things of the text that openly confect it.

EDMUND WHITE

Nabokov's Passion

Nabokov is the high priest of sensuality and desire, the magus who knows virtually everything about what is at once the most solemn and the most elusive of all our painful joys—the stab of erotic pleasure, that emblem of transitory happiness on earth. As Proust observed, ardor is the only form of possession in which the possessor possesses nothing.

But if passion is the treasure (that is, the absence) that lies at the heart of the great pyramid of Nabokov's art, he has been careful to protect it from the vulgar, the prying, the smug; he has surrounded his secret riches with a maze of false corridors, of precariously balanced, easily triggered, almost lethal megaliths. These are the notorious traps, the crushing menhirs of Nabokov's wit, his scorn, his savage satire. Nonetheless I'd insist that passion, not brilliance or cruelty or erudition or the arrogant perfection of his craft, is his master motif, that his intelligence is at the service of the emotions.

In a superb story, perhaps his best, "Spring in Fialta," first written in Russian and published in 1938, the love between the narrator and the heroine, Nina, is contrasted with—I'm tempted to say safeguarded by—the contempt directed at her husband, Ferdinand. Nina is an impulsive, generous, but negligent woman who has often given herself to the narrator (and to many other men along the way); just as suddenly and often she has forgotten the gift she's conferred on them. The narrator first meets Nina in Russia "around 1917," as he says with an eerie casualness, and they exchange their first embrace outdoors in winter:

From *The New York Review of Books* (29 March 1984).

> Windows light up and stretch their luminous lengths upon the dark billowy snow, making room for the reflection of the fan-shaped light above the front door between them. Each of the two side-pillars is fluffily fringed with white, which rather spoils the lines of what might have been a perfect ex libris for the book of our two lives. I cannot recall why we had all wandered out of the sonorous hall into the still darkness, peopled only with firs, snow-swollen to twice their size; did the watchmen invite us to look at a sullen red glow in the sky, portent of nearing arson? Possibly. Did we go to admire an equestrian statue of ice sculptured near the pond by the Swiss tutor of my cousins? Quite as likely. My memory revives only on the way back to the brightly symmetrical mansion towards which we tramped in single file along a narrow furrow between snowbanks, with that crunch-crunch-crunch which is the only comment that a taciturn winter night makes upon humans. I walked last; three singing steps ahead of me walked a small bent shape; the firs gravely showed their burdened paws. I slipped and dropped the dead flashlight someone had forced upon me; it was devilishly hard to retrieve; and instantly attracted by my curses, with an eager, low laugh in anticipation of fun, Nina dimly veered toward me. I call her Nina, but I could hardly have known her name yet, hardly could we have had time, she and I, for any preliminary; "Who's that?" she asked with interest—and I was already kissing her neck, smooth and quite fiery hot from the long fox fur of her coat collar, which kept getting into my way until she clasped my shoulder, and with the candor so peculiar to her gently fitted her generous, dutiful lips to mine.

When the narrator sees Nina indoors a minute later, he is astonished "not so much by her inattention to me after that warmth in the snow as by the innocent naturalness of that inattention."

In this passage, the visual memory turns instantly into visual invention, when the lit doorway nearly becomes an ex libris. The seemingly innocent description soon enough resolves itself into an emblem—"out of books," indeed, since the scene that follows is reminiscent of Chekhov's "The Kiss"—the same mansion, a similar party, the same passionate kiss between strangers. Moreover, the quality of the narrator and Nina's intermittent affair is always novelistic and the language used to recount it is invariably the language of literature: "Again and again she hurriedly appeared in the margins of my life, without influencing in the least its basic text."

If this marginal romance—lusty, a bit sentimental, not quite honest, genuinely moving but also tinged with *poshlust*—is related by a narrator who is a writer *manqué,* then the ghastly Ferdinand, Nina's husband, is nothing but a writer—diabolic, coldly technical. In fact, he is one of those many grotesque versions of himself Nabokov planted throughout his fiction, a sort of signature not unlike Hitchcock's fleeting appearances in his own films. This particular double is particularly unappetizing, driven as he is with a "fierce relish" for ugly things and woebegone people: "Like some autocrat who surrounds himself with hunchbacks and dwarfs, he would become attached to this or that hideous object; this infatuation might last from five minutes to several days or even longer if the thing happened to be animate."

In "Spring in Fialta," which is just twenty-one pages long, Nabokov manages to generate as dense a sense of lived-through time as can be found in many novels. He achieves this narrative density by two means: a complex but rigorous time scheme; and the juxtaposition of highly contrasted moods. I won't dwell on the time scheme now except to mention that the story progresses on two planes: connected episodes at Fialta in the present that alternate with memories of past trysts with Nina in many cities over the years. Both the present and the past are told sequentially and the last flashback to be presented is the narrator's most recent memory of Nina. In other words, these two systems of time converge to produce the final scene, in which Nina is killed when her car crashes into a traveling circus company, whose arrival has been heralded throughout the tale by dozens of tiny details, as at sea the approach of land is promised by a quickening flux of grass, twigs, and land birds. The two time schemes and the payoff of the circus's appearance at the end tie together everything.

But the actual sense of time passing also depends on the rapid alternation of contrasted scenes, a technique perfected by Tolstoy. These scenes are either satirical or romantic. Some of the romantic scenes are not scenes at all but instead beautifully rendered telescopings of time:

> Once I was shown her photograph in a fashion magazine full of autumn leaves and gloves and windswept golf links. On a certain Christmas she sent me a picture post card with snow and stars. On a Riviera beach she almost escaped my notice behind her dark glasses and terra-cotta tan. Another day, having dropped in on an ill-timed errand at the house of some strangers where a

> party was in progress, I saw her scarf and fur coat among alien scarecrows on a coat rack. In a bookshop she nodded to me from a page of one of her husband's stories.

The tone of these passages is elegiac, tender, and sensual; it is Nabokov's genius (as one might speak of the genius of a place or of a language) to have kept alive almost single-handedly in our century a tradition of tender sensuality. In most contemporary fiction tenderness is a sexless family feeling and sensuality either violent or impersonal or both. By contrast, Nabokov is a Pascin of romantic carnality. He writes in "Spring in Fialta": "Occasionally in the middle of a conversation her name would be mentioned, and she would run down the steps of a chance sentence, without turning her head." Only a man who loved women as much as he desired them could write such a passage.

What makes the narrator of this tale a writer *manqué* is his uncritical—one might say his uninjured—ease in the world of the sentiments. There is no bite, no obliqueness, no discomfort in his responses, and though he is in no danger of becoming vulgar, he is close to that other Nabokovian sin, philistinism. No wonder he is repelled by the real writer, Ferdinand, the center of the satirical scenes with their passages that send up the culture industry, the fatiguing milieu of art groupies. Ferdinand sounds a bit like a combination of the sardonic Nabokov and, improbably, a naive Western European devotee of Russian communism. But instead of focusing on Ferdinand's bad politics, let us concentrate instead on his peculiarities as a writer:

> Having mastered the art of verbal invention to perfection, he particularly prided himself on being a weaver of words, a title he valued higher than that of a writer; personally, I never could understand what was the good of thinking up books, of penning things that had not really happened in some way or other; and I remember once saying to him as I braved the mockery of his encouraging nods that, were I a writer, I should allow only my heart to have imagination, and for the rest rely upon memory, that long-drawn sunset shadow of one's personal truth.
>
> I had known his books before I knew him; a faint disgust was already replacing the aesthetic pleasure which I had suffered his first novel to give me. At the beginning of his career, it had been possible perhaps to distinguish some human landscape, some old garden, some dream-familiar disposition of trees through the stained glass of his prodigious prose . . . but with every new

> book the tints grew still more dense, the gules and purpure still more ominous; and today one can no longer see anything at all through that blazoned, ghastly rich glass, and it seems that were one to break it, nothing but a perfectly black void would face one's shivering soul.

In this remarkable, and remarkably sly, passage, the narrator's relationship to the reader (and to the writer Nabokov) becomes intricate. We know that Nabokov's own art is not autobiographical in the simple photographic sense, and we resist the narrator's assumptions about the sufficiency of memory to art. The narrator sounds too sincere, too Slavic, to our ears, although his objections to Ferdinand are phrased with all the suavity and eloquent conviction at Nabokov's command. Since we, the readers, know that a figure much like the diabolical Ferdinand has written even this argument for sincerity, our relation to the text is slippery. The nastiness of these passages contrasts vividly with the tenderness of the alternating scenes to produce an almost topographical sensation of traveling through time, as though the landscape below the tip of the wing were either a mountain peak or a shadowed gorge, never a flat plain.

Many writers proceed by creating characters who are parodies of themselves or near misses or fun-house distortions, or they distribute their own characteristics across a cast of characters, and some especially like to dramatize their conflicts and indecisions by assigning them to different personages. One thinks of Proust, who gave his dilettantism to Swann, his homosexuality to Charlus, his love of his family to the narrator and his hatred of his family to Mlle. Vinteuil, his hypochondria to Aunt Leonie, his genius to Elstir and Bergotte, his snobbism to the Guermantes, his Frenchness to Françoise. In this sense (but this strict sense only) every novel, including Nabokov's, is autobiographical. Indeed the notion of a parallel life that does, impossibly, converge with one's own may have suggested the concept of two worlds and two histories slightly out of sync—the moiré pattern of Terra and anti-Terra woven by *Ada.*

But it was Nabokov's particular delight to invent sinister or insane or talentless versions of himself, characters who are at least in part mocking anticipations of naive readers' suspicions about the real Nabokov. For all those innocents who imagined that the author of *Lolita* was himself a nympholept, Nabokov prepared a hilarious response in *Look at the Harlequins!*, in which the narrator's biography is composed from nothing but such crude suppositions: "As late as the start of the 1954–55 school year, with Bel nearing her thirteenth birthday, I was still deliriously happy, still seeing nothing wrong or dangerous, or absurd or downright cretinous, in the relationship between my daughter and me. Save for a few insignificant lapses—a few hot drops of overflowing tenderness, a gasp masked by a cough and that sort of stuff—my relations with her remained essentially innocent." *Essentially* innocent—that's the kind of essence that lubricates our villainous society.

Nabokov's model for inventing such characters, the author's disabled twin or feebler cousin, mad brother or vulgar uncle, was surely Pushkin among others, for it was Pushkin, following Byron's lead in *Don Juan,* who fashioned a distorted portrait of himself in Eugene Onegin, the young man of fashion whose attitudes and deeds sometimes draw a crude outline of the poet's own silhouette and just as often diverge completely. Of course Pushkin scrupulously disowns the resemblance (I use Nabokov's translation):

> I'm always glad to mark the difference
> between Onegin and myself,
> lest an ironic reader
> or else some publisher
> of complicated calumny,
> collating here my traits,
> repeat thereafter shamelessly
> that I have scrawled my portrait
> like Byron, the poet of pride.

Before Pushkin establishes their differences he points out the similarities. He tells us that he likes Onegin's "sharp, chilled mind" and explains their friendship by saying, "I was embittered, he was sullen."

Wit, scorn, and the parody of romance can be a way of rescuing romance. Just as Schoenberg remarked that only the extreme recourse of his twelve-tone system was able to provide German romantic music with another fifty years of life, so Nabokov might have asserted that only by casting *Lolita* into the extreme terms of a Krafft-Ebing case study, the tale of a European nympholept and his gum-snapping, wise-cracking, gray-eyed teen-age enchantress—that only by making such a radical modulation could he endow the romantic novel with new vitality.

That vitality is attributable to obsession, the virtue that is shared by vice and art. As Adorno observes in the *Minima Moralia:* "The universality of beauty can communicate itself to the subject in no other way than in an obsession with the particular." The lover, like the artist, loathes the general, the vague, the wise, and lives only for the luminous singularity of the beloved or the glowing page. Everything else is insipid.

Lolita, as all the world knows, is full of parodies—parodies of literary essays, of scholarly lists of sources, of scientific treatises, of psychiatric reports, and especially of the confession and the legal defense. It is also a compendium of sometimes serious, but usually jocular, allusions to key works of nineteenth-century romanticism, especially French fiction and verse (Humbert's first language is French, of course, and *Lolita* is more Gallic than American or Russian, at least in its explicit references and models). But the function of this brilliant panoply of literary allusions is not to disown romanticism but to recapture it. As Thomas R. Frosch remarks in "Parody and Authenticity in *Lolita,*"

> In relation to romance, parody acts in *Lolita* in a defensive and proleptic way. It doesn't criticize the romance mode, although it criticizes Humbert; it renders romance acceptable by anticipating our mockery and beating us to the draw. It is what Empson calls "pseudo-parody to disarm criticism." I am suggesting, then, that *Lolita* can only be a love story through being a parody of love stories.

To be sure, the entire history of romantic verse and fiction has been self-consciously literary. One could go further and insist that romantic passion itself is literary; as La Rochefoucauld said, no one would ever have fallen in love unless he had first read about it. Humbert and Lolita's mother, Charlotte Haze, represent two quite distinct romantic traditions, the courtly versus the bourgeois. For the courtly lover love is useless, painful, unfulfilled, obsessive, destructive, and his very allegiance to this peculiar, seemingly unnatural ideal is proof of his superiority to ordinary mortals. As Frederick Goldin has remarked about the origins of courtly love in the Middle Ages:

> Ordinary men cannot love unless they get something in return—something they can get hold of, not just a smile. If they do not get it, they soon stop loving, or, if the girl is from one of the lower orders, they take it by force. But usually, since ordinary men love ordinary women, they get what they want; and then, their mutual lust expended, they go their separate ways, or else, if they are restrained by some vulgar decency, they mate and settle down. In this wilderness of carnality and domesticity, nobility declines; there is no reason, and no chance, for the longing, exaltation and self-discipline of true courtliness. This is one of the basic creeds of courtly love.
>
> (*The Mirror of Narcissus in the Courtly Love Lyric*)

One of the most amusing paradoxes of *Lolita* is that the satyr Humbert Humbert becomes the minnesinger of courtly love for the twentieth century. To be sure, before he can fully exemplify the "longing, exaltation and self-discipline of true courtliness" Humbert must lose Lolita and kill his double, Quilty. If Humbert and Quilty have mirrored each other in the first half of the book, in the second half they turn into opposites, as Humbert becomes leaner, older, more fragile, more quixotic, and Quilty grows grosser, drunker, fatter, and more corrupt; the murder of Quilty expiates Humbert of everything base.

If Humbert embodies courtly love, Charlotte comes out of the more recent tradition of bourgeois marriage. It is a sign of Nabokov's compassion that he is so gentle in his treatment of the ridiculous Charlotte, who in spite of her constant smoking, her bad French, her humorlessness, her middle-brow cultural aspirations, and her cruelty to her daughter he also shows is lonely, touching, decent: "To break Charlotte's will I would have to break her heart. If I broke her heart, her image of me would break too. If I said: 'Either I have my way with Lolita, and you help me to keep the matter quiet, or we part at once,' she would have turned as pale as a woman of clouded glass and slowly replied: 'All right, whatever you add or subtract, this is the end.' " Even Humbert describes her, poetically, as a creature of "clouded glass," an impression denoting nothing but connoting beauty.

Charlotte has been shaped by reading women's magazines and home-decoration manuals and popular novels. Her pious expectations of the monogamous and "totally fulfilling" marriage in which sex, sentiment, and even religious faith coincide is at odds with Humbert's stronger emotions and more desperate aspirations. The best Humbert can do by way of a domestic fantasy is to imagine marrying Lolita, fathering a daughter, and living long enough to indulge in incest not only with that child but with *her* daughter as well: "—bizarre, tender, salivating Dr. Humbert, practicing on supremely lovely Lolita the Third the art of being a granddad." Even when he attempts for a moment to abandon his own brand of romantic literature, the script of his courtly and obsessive passion, for Charlotte's kind of pulp, the attempt fails: "I did my best; I read and reread a book with the unintentionally biblical title *Know Your Own Daughter*."

Nabokov wrote in *The Gift* that "the spirit of parody always goes along with genuine poetry." If "genuine poetry" is taken to mean romantic literature about passion, one can only concur, since passion is parody. *Don Quixote* is a parody of tales of knightly adventure; in Dante the lovers Francesca and Paolo discover their mutual passion when they read "of Lancelot, how love constrained him." The pump of Emma Bovary's ardor has been printed by her reading of cheap romantic magazine stories. In *Eugene Onegin,*

> Tatiana is besotted by romantic fiction:
> With what attention she now
> reads a delicious novel,
> with what vivid enchantment
> drinks the seductive fiction!

But her reading, alas, is different from Onegin's, for Tatiana reads Rousseau's fiction and Goethe's *The Sorrows of Young Werther* (as Nabokov comments in his notes, "Werther weeps on every occasion, likes to romp with small children, and is passionately in love with Charlotte. They read *Ossian* together in a storm of tears"). Immersed in her own brand of Lachrymose Lit, Tatiana

> sighs, and having made her own
> another's ecstasy, another's melancholy,
> she whispers in a trance, by heart,
> a letter to the amiable hero.

That letter sounds like Charlotte Haze's avowal:

> "I am nothing to you. Right? Right. Nothing to you whatever. *But* if, after reading my 'confession,' you decided, in your dark romantic European way, that I am attractive enough for you to take advantage of my letter and make a pass at me, then you would be a criminal—worse than a kidnaper who rapes a child. You see, *chéri. If* you decided to stay, *if* I found you at home . . ."

and so on. Charlotte's letter seems a parody of Tatiana's far more touching but no less fervent appeal:

> My fate
> henceforth I place into your hands,
> before you I shed tears,
> for your defense I plead
> . . . .
> I'm waiting for you: with a single look
> revive my heart's hopes,
> or interrupt the heavy dream,
> alas, with a deserved rebuke.

Humbert may fake his acceptance of Charlotte's avowal, but Onegin rejects Tatiana in rolling Byronic phrases:

> But I'm not made for bliss;
> my soul is strange to it;
> in vain are your perfections;
> I'm not worthy of them.

This understanding, fatal to the future happiness of both characters, is not so much owing to character differences as to different reading lists. Whereas Tatiana has read of lovers given to sacrifice, duty, and devotion, Onegin has been coached by Byron's egotistical and disabused Don Juan:

> My days of love are over; me no more
>   The charms of maid, wife
> . . . .
> Can make the fool
> . . . .
> The credulous hope of mutual minds is o'er.

Years go by, Tatiana suffers, becomes stoic, and then one day is drawn to Onegin's deserted country house. She enters his library, reads the books he once read, and in a stunning passage she wonders whether Onegin might not be "a glossary of other people's megrims, / a complete lexicon of words in vogue? / . . . Might he not be, in fact, a parody?" Just as Charlotte recognizes Humbert's criminal passions for Lolita once she reads his diary, so Tatiana understands Onegin is a fraud once she peruses his books.

The Byronic hero could, in his most degraded form, become coldly indifferent to women and with men murderously touchy on points of honor. If the calculating seduction is the way the Byronic monster approaches women, his characteristic exchange with other men is the duel. Here again Humbert executes a grotesque parody of the duel in stalking down Quilty; this is the final sorry end to the already shoddy, senseless business of the Lenski-Onegin duel.

So it is not surprising that *Lolita* is a parody of earlier works of romantic literature, including not only *Onegin* but much more obviously a succession of French novels devoted to the anatomy of the passions—that line that runs from *La Princesse de Clèves* through *Les Liaisons dangereuses, Adolphe, Atala,* and *René* and on to *Mademoiselle de Maupin, Carmen,* and *Madame Bovary*—a tradition, moreover, that Humbert specifically alludes to again and again. His mind is also well stocked with French poetry from Ronsard to Rimbaud. Whereas some Russian Formalists (I'm thinking of

Tynyanov's *Dostoevski and Gogol: Remarks on the Theory of Parody*) argued that parody is a way of disowning the past in an act of literary warfare, in Nabokov's case we see that parody can be the fondest tribute, the invention of a tradition against which one's own originality can be discerned, a payment of past debts in order to accrue future capital.

In his treatment of love, Nabokov points the way beyond parody and convention. At their best his characters act out of character, transcend their roles. The most sublime moment in *Lolita,* of course, occurs when Humbert sees the "hugely pregnant" Lolita after searching for her for several years.

> There she was with her ruined looks and her adult, rope-veined narrow hands and her goose-flesh white arms, and her shallow ears, and her unkempt armpits, there she was (my Lolita!), hopelessly worn at seventeen, with that baby, dreaming already in her of becoming a big shot and retiring around 2020 AD—and I looked and looked at her, and knew as clearly as I know I am to die, that I loved her more than anything I had ever seen or imagined on earth, or hoped for anywhere else.

Here the pervert breaks through the narrow confines of his perversion, the connoisseur of *le fruit vert* looks longingly at the no-longer-ripe apple in a now vanished Eden. Passion—fastidious, tyrannical, hostile—has given way to compassionate love. Correspondingly, Lolita shrugs off her own grudges and forgives Humbert for having taken away her youth; when Humbert asks her to leave with him, she says, "No, honey, no." In a heartbreaking line, Humbert writes "She had never called me honey before."

A similar moment when love transcends passion, when sentiment exceeds sexuality, occurs in *Pale Fire.* The exclusively homosexual Kinbote—who had always treated his wife with "friendly indifference and bleak respect," while drooling after "Eton-collared, sweet-voiced minions"—begins to *dream* of Disa, his queen, with throbbing tenderness:

> He dreamed of her more often, and with incomparably more poignancy than his surface-like feelings for her warranted; these dreams occurred when he least thought of her, and worries in no way connected with her assumed her image in the subliminal world as a battle or a reform becomes a bird of wonder in a tale for children. These heart-rending dreams transformed the drab prose of his feelings for her into strong and strange poetry.

The transcendent virtue of love is seen again in *Ada* when the aged rake Van Veen is reunited after many years with his now plump and no longer appealing Ada: "He loved her much too tenderly, much too irrevocably, to be unduly depressed by sexual misgivings." *This* from the great sensual purist! Of course this very passage, in which love goes beyond its conventional limits, is, paradoxically, itself a parody of the end of *War and Peace* and the marriage of Natasha and Pierre.

Andrew Field writes, "All of his novels, Nabokov told me once, have an air—*not quite of this world, don't you think?*" Field didn't take the remark seriously; he thought it was just more leg-pulling. But I think the hint that his novels are "not quite of this world" should be taken seriously. After boyhood Nabokov was not conventionally religious, although the poetry of his early twenties continued to rely occasionally on religious imagery. Nevertheless, he retained within his pages a quick, visceral sense of disturbing spiritual presences. His is a haunted world, and to prove it W. W. Rowe recently published an entire volume to that effect: *Nabokov's Spectral Dimension.* Inspiration itself is such a specter, of course; in *The Gift* when Fyodor begins to write, he is conscious of "a pulsating mist that suddenly began to speak with a human voice." Vera Nabokov, the writer's wife and the dedicatee of virtually every book from his pen, has said that a main theme in all of Nabokov's writing is "the hereafter." Of Fyodor's father, the boy thinks: "It was as if this genuine, very genuine man possessed an aura of something still unknown but which was perhaps the most genuine of all."

The luminous unknown, this aura of the ghostly genuine, is always bordering the picture Nabokov presents to his reader. The narrator of his last novel, *Look at the Harlequins!,* is afflicted with recurrent bouts of madness. His perception of space is so personal and so harrowing that at one point he becomes paralyzed. "Yet I have known madness not only in the guise of an evil shadow," he tells us. "I have seen it also as a flash of delight so rich and shattering that the very absence of an immediate object on which it might settle was to me a form of escape."

It is in those flashes of delight, which illuminate almost every passage, that Nabokov's glimpses of another world can be detected. Lolita's smile, for instance, "was never directed at the stranger in the room but hung in its own remote flowered void, so to speak, or wandered with myopic softness over chance objects." In *The Gift,* the hero imagines returning to his ancestral home in Russia: "One after another the telegraph poles will hum at my approach. A crow will settle on a boulder—settle and straighten a wing that has folded wrong." That straightened wing—the precision of an imagined imaginary detail—is worthy of a Zen master. In "Spring in Fialta," we encounter "that life-quickening atmosphere of a big railway station where everything is something trembling on the brink of something else"—a phrase that might well serve as Nabokov's artistic credo (and that recalls Quine's notion that a verbal investigation of language is akin to building a boat while sailing in it).

Mythology in Nabokov does not (as it does in Joyce's *Ulysses*) limit the neural sprawl of a stream of consciousness. Nor is it there to provide a plot (as in the neoclassical drama of Anouilh and Giraudoux). Nor is it there to lend unearned dignity to an otherwise dreary tale, as in the plays of Archibald MacLeish or Eugene O'Neill. In Nabokov the vocabulary of religion, fairy tales, and myths is the only one adequate to his sense of the beauty and mystery of the sensual, of love, of childhood, of nature, of art, of people when they are noble. It is this language that metamorphoses the comic bedroom scene in *Lolita* into a glimpse of paradise. Once they're in the hotel room, Lolita

> walked up to the open suitcase as if stalking it from afar, in a kind of slow-motion walk, peering at that distant treasure box on the luggage support. (Was there something wrong, I wondered, with those great gray eyes of hers, or were we both plunged in the same enchanted mist?) She stepped up to it, lifting her rather high-heeled feet rather high, and bending her beautiful boy-knees while she walked through dilating space with the lentor of one walking under water or in a flight dream.

Nabokov's novels are not of this world, but of a better one. He has kept the romantic novel alive by introducing into it a new tension—the struggle between obsessive or demented characters and a seraphic rhetoric. Given his inspired style, no wonder Nabokov chose to write not about the species or the variety but about the mutant individual. Such a subject gives his radiant language something to overcome. In one story, "Lance," Nabokov relaxed this tension and indulged in his verbal splendors with chilling abandon. In that story the young hero, Lance Boke, ascends into the heavens as his old parents watch through field glasses: "The brave old Bokes think they can distinguish Lance scaling, on crampons, the verglased rock of the sky or silently breaking trail through the soft snows of nebulae." I like to think of Nabokov himself, the supreme alpinist of the art, ascending those new heights.

He must be ranked, finally, not with other writers but with a composer and a choreographer, Stravinsky and Balanchine. All three were of the same generation, Russians who were clarified by passing through the sieve of French culture but were brought to the boiling point only by American informality. All three experimented boldly with form, but none produced "avant-garde trash," as Nabokov called it, for all three were too keen on recuperating tradition. In a work such as the *Pulcinella* ballet score, the baroque mannerisms of Pergolesi are aped, even insisted upon, but baroque squares are turned into modernist rhomboids and scalenes, and mechanical baroque transitions, the yard goods of that style, are eliminated in favor of a crisp collage built up out of radical juxtapositions. Everything is fresh, new, heartless—and paradoxically all the more moving for the renovation. Similarly, Balanchine eliminated mime, a fussy port de bras, story, and decor to make plotless ballets that distill the essence of the Petipa tradition. As parodists, all three artists loved the art they parodied and make it modern by placing old jewels into new settings.

Most important, all three men had a vision of art as entertainment, in the sense of wooing shrewder, more restless though robust, sensibilities. Sartre once attacked Nabokov for his lack of political content, but one could reply to that charge without hesitation that the paradise Balanchine, Stravinsky, and Nabokov have made visible to us is one of the few images of happiness we have, that very happiness politics is working to secure, the promise of harmony, beauty, rapture.

In "Fame," a poem he wrote in Russian in 1942, Nabokov bitterly echoed the 1836 poem *Exegi monumentum* of Pushkin, which in turn echoed the poem by Horace and those of many other poets. Whereas Horace and Pushkin could well consider their verse a monument they had raised to their own eternal glory, Nabokov, writing in exile for a tiny Russian-speaking audience that would soon be dying out, could only imagine a fantastic, garrulous visitor:

> "Your poor books," he breezily said, "will finish
> by hopelessly fading in exile. Alas,
> those two thousand leaves of frivolous fiction
> will be scattered."

As we know now, and know with gratitude, the prophecy was not fulfilled. More glorious and surprising in his metamorphosis than any butterfly he ever stalked, Nabokov, the Russian master, turned himself into a writer in English, the best of the century.

D. BARTON JOHNSON

Look at the Harlequins!: *Dementia's Incestuous Children*

Look at the Harlequins! (*LATH*), Nabokov's incest-suffused last novel, is a retrospective of its author's favorite themes and a meditation on the identity of its own narrator. In *Ada,* the theme of sibling incest, if not its degree or extent, is readily apparent to the reader. In *LATH*, perhaps owing to the involuted narrative, the tangled web of consanguinity enmeshing the narrator, his wives and lovers is thoroughly obscured. The novel is cast in the form of the autobiography of the distinguished Anglo-Russian writer Vadim Vadimovich N. (b. 1899). Composed in the aftermath of a mysterious paralytic stroke, VV's memoir is no ordinary one and is perhaps best described in the words of the narrator himself:

> In this memoir my wives and my books are interlaced monogrammatically like some sort of watermark or *ex libris* design; and in writing this oblique autobiography—oblique because dealing mainly not with pedestrian history but with the mirages of romantic and literary matters—I consistently try to dwell as lightly as inhumanly possible on the evolution of my mental illness. Yet Dementia is one of the characters in my story.

We shall see that Dementia is not merely "one of the characters" in the story but that she is the leading lady. The narrator's works and women (apart from the last) are, in the form he sees and describes them, the offspring of his Dementia who is both Mistress and Muse. The autobiography deals quite literally with "mirages of romantic and literary matters."

The narrator, Prince VV, is the putative son of an aristocratic Russian couple who assertedly abandon him to the care of relatives thanks to the frenetic pace of their divorces, remarriages, redivorces, and so on. Their neurasthenic, dreamy son is left in the custody of a grand-aunt, who resides on one of the family estates called Marevo, a Russian word appropriately meaning "mirage." It is this aunt who advises her morose seven- or eight-year-old charge to "Look at the harlequins!" "Play! Invent the world! Invent Reality!" This is just what VV does, starting, he confesses, with his grand-aunt.

Following the Bolshevik revolution, VV shoots a Red Army sentry and steals across the Polish border. He then makes his way to London where, funds soon exhausted, he discovers a patron, the Anglophilic Count Nikifor Nikodimovich Starov. The Count, who had "graced several great Embassies during a spacious span of international intercourse," is a quondam lover of VV's "beautiful and bizarre" mother. In fact we shall learn that Count Starov, by virtue of his "spacious span of international intercourse," is the progenitor of several of the characters of *LATH*. He is also the head of an anti-Soviet spy network, the White Cross, that passes itself off as a charitable organization for Russian refugees.

It is through the grace of Count Starov that his protégé attends Cambridge where, in his final term in the spring of 1922, he is invited to the newly inherited Riviera villa of his classmate, Ivor Black. Here he meets Ivor's twenty-year-old sister, Iris, who becomes the memoirist's first wife. The parentage of the fond brother and sister is no less murky than that of VV himself. Their mother, Iris says, was "American and horrible," while the businessman father had "good connections" in London diplomatic circles. This becomes strangely portentous when VV and Iris, newly married unbeknownst to the Count, visit him at his summer Villa on the Côte d'Azur. Upon being introduced to Iris (whom he assumes to be Vadim's fiancée) the old Count gazes at her for a time and then somewhat ambiguously tells his protégé that his fiancée "is as beautiful as your wife will be." After Iris leaves the room to have tea in "an adjacent alcove (illuminated by a resplendent portrait by Serov, 1896, of the notorious beauty, Mme. de Blagidze, in Caucasian costume)," the newly enlightened Count asks VV his wife's maiden name. Slowly shaking his head, he then inquires the name of Iris's mother. Vadim's reply is greeted by the identical response and the conversation moves on to talk of the couple's financial future.

VV and Iris move to Paris where, during the seven years of their marriage, the narrator embarks upon his literary career, rapidly publishing three Russian volumes—*Tamara* (1925), *Pawn Takes Queen* (1927), and

Plenilune (1929). Iris, not knowing Russian, is somewhat excluded from her husband's literary milieu and it is through her unsuccessful effort to learn Russian that she becomes the (unwilling?) object of the amorous attentions of Lt. Wladimir Starov-Blagidze, the husband of her tutoress. The lieutenant, VV learns, is another "protégé" of Count Starov at whose funeral the two half-brothers first meet as pallbearers. Starov-Blagidze, three or four years senior to VV, is apparently the result of a liaison between Count Starov and the "notorious St. Petersburg courtesan" depicted in the Serov portrait mentioned above. The lieutenant, already half-mad from a Russian Civil War head wound and now spurned by Iris, runs amok and on the night of April 23, 1930, shoots Iris and himself in the presence of VV and Ivor, one of whom, and possibly both, are likewise offspring of the mysterious Count Starov.

After his wife's death, VV submerges himself in his writing, finishing his fourth and fifth Russian novels, *Camera Lucida* and *The Red Top Hat.* The narrator meets his second wife, Annette (Anna Ivanovna Blagovo), when he hires the long-necked Botticellian beauty as the typist for his longest, last and best Russian novel, *Podarok otchizne* (*Gift for the Fatherland*), later known in English as *The Dare.* Notwithstanding her inept typing, her thoroughly philistine tastes and her frigidity, VV is so strongly attracted to her that he enters into his second and longest marriage. In 1939, VV, who has now completed his first English-language novel, *See under Real,* emigrates with Annette to the United States where he joins the faculty of Quirn University (Quirn = kernel = Cornell). Here VV adds to his modest reputation as an English novelist with *Esmeralda and Her Parandrus* (1942), *Dr. Olga Repnin* (1946), and the short story collection *Exile from Mayda* (1947). Meanwhile, Annette conceives, and a daughter, Isabel, is born on New Year's Day 1942. The marriage, never more than marginally adequate, comes under the blighting influence of their ex-Soviet landlady Ninel (a palindrome of Lenin) who befriends and carries off Annette and the four-year-old Isabel to her lakeside cottage while VV dallies with Dolly von Borg. The brief affair with Dolly, who successfully schemes to break up her lover's marriage, is the long delayed consummation of a series of furtive fondlings with the compliant eleven-year-old Dolly while VV had been a house guest of her Russian émigré grandparents in prewar Paris.

The covert kinship pattern that characterizes VV's first marriage is quite possibly, if obscurely, present in the second. Anna Blagovo is the daughter of a Tsarist army surgeon, who in 1907 married a provincial belle in the Volgan town of Kineshma a few miles from one of VV's most romantic estates—presumably Marevo. It may well occur to the reader that

Count Starov, the long-time lover of VV's mother, was quite possibly a visitor to the estate and its environs. Further, there are hints that Annette herself may have been acquainted with the late Lt. Starov-Blagidze. This becomes apparent in her responses to VV's questions at the time of his proposal. Although the status-conscious Annette hesitantly agrees to marry her titled suitor, she finds him strange—unlike other men she has met. In answer to VV's query as to whom she had met: "trepanners? trombonists? astronomists?" she blandly replies "mostly military men . . . officers of Wrangel's army." That Lt. Starov-Blagidze, who served under Wrangel, has been subject to trepanning is quite probable (possibly at the hands of Annette's father) for we know he suffers a "terrifying tic" as a result of his head wound. Still more curious is VV's choice of "astronomist," for the initial syllable is the Latin root for "star" while the first five letters form an anagram corresponding to the first five letters of the name Starov. In short, Anna Blagovo, like Iris Black, may be the half-sister, as well as the wife, of the narrator. Again like Iris, she is (possibly) acquainted with Lt. Starov-Blagidze.

In 1953, some seven years after Annette flees VV, she and Ninel perish in a flood, and Isabel, now eleven and a half and called Bel, returns to live with her father. For two blissful years Bel and her adoring father are inseparable companions, spending their summers idyllically wandering from motel to motel in the Far West. The intimacy of father and daughter as well as brilliant Bel's precocity lead to ugly rumors which Professor N. seeks to counter by marrying Louise Adamson, the fast young widow of the former head of the Quirn English Department. Beautiful Louise, a sexually and financially avaricious celebrity collector, is all too ready to wed the novelist who is reportedly the leading candidate for "the most prestigious prize in the world." She is, however, equally quick to cool when the prize is not forthcoming. Her relationship with Bel is abysmal, and the daughter is soon packed off to a Swiss finishing school from which she eventually elopes with an American student who defects to Russia. VV finds solace for the loss of Bel by reliving their life and travels in the transmuted form of what will become his most successful (and sensational) novel, *A Kingdom by the Sea* (1962).

Louise, VV's third wife, is also implicated in the incestuous network of the author's life. She too is not without family ties to her husband's tangled past. Shortly before his marriage proposal, VV spends an evening with a number of guests including Louise and her cousin Lady Morgain, the fat and fiftyish daughter of a former American Ambassador to England. Fay Morgain informs VV that she had been acquainted with Iris Black in London around 1919 when she herself was "a starry-eyed American gal." Louise's obscure connection with Count Starov is also hinted in another anagrammatic reference. As VV and Louise leave the gathering, she agrees to marry him: "She was gone before I could enclasp her slender form. The *star*-dusted sky, usually a scary affair, now vaguely amused me . . . I made water into a sizzle of *asters*" (my italics). Thus Louise too may be a member of the Count Starov's consanguineal brood.

VV meets his fourth and final grand love in September 1969 on the day when the now notorious author submits his resignation to the overjoyed administration of Quirn University. As VV is leaving campus, a bulky folder under his arm spills, and he is aided in gathering up its contents by a young woman coming from the library. As the girl helps VV collect his scattered papers she inquires about Bel (now in Russia). The narrator suddenly remembers her name and "in a photic flash of celestial memory" sees her and her schoolmate Bel "looking like twins, silently hating each other, both in blue coats and white hats, waiting to be driven somewhere by Louise." This young woman, who is throughout referred to only as "you" and who shares Bel's birthday (January 1, 1942), becomes VV's lover during his final year at Quirn while he writes his last novel, *Ardis*. At the end of the academic year they move to the Continent.

VV is markedly reluctant to speak of the details of his relationship with "you" in his autobiographical account, saying that "Reality would only be adulterated." In consequence we learn very little about the background and identity of VV's last love. She speaks a "lovely, elegant Russian," has studied Turgenev in Oxford and Bergson in Geneva, and has "family ties with good old Quirn and Russian New York." She also knows butterflies and her lover's complete *oeuvre*. The question we are approaching is, of course, that of her place, if any, in the intricate network of Count Starov's progeny. The only clue to her identity is connected with her Russian background. This, together with her family association with Quirn, points to Marion Noteboke, the daughter of Professor Noteboke, the head of the Quirn Russian Department. Marion, however, seems to be slightly too old to be "you" who is known to be eleven years and four-odd months of age in May 1953 when Marion is described as being twelve. Also against Marion's candidacy is VV's passing reference to her (circa 1954) as "a depraved and vulgar nymphet" who carries tales of Bel's relationship with her widowed father home to Mrs. Noteboke. In sum it must be concluded that VV's final love, "you," remains both anonymous and outside the Starov family orbit. This assumption is strengthened by VV's persistent association of "you" and

"Reality," an association strikingly absent from his account of his previous loves.

It is a curious and significant fact that at least two of VV's wives have the letter sequence "BL" in their names: Iris *Bl*ack and Anna *Bla*govo. The writer's much loved daughter *Bel* also enters into this alphabetic series. The family name of Louise is unknown but one of the names from her past is *Bl*anc. Also of note is that Starov's other son (and Iris Black's lover) bears his mother's family name *Bl*agidze and that, on occasion, the narrator refers to himself as *Bl*onsky. All of these characters are related to Count Starov and it is their incestuous consanguinity that is denoted by the alphabetic emblem "BL" in their names. The sound sequence is, moreover, not randomly chosen. As we have noted [elsewhere] in connection with *Ada,* Nabokov denies any deep meaning in his use of the incest theme, saying merely that he likes "the 'bl' sound in siblings, bloom, blue, bliss, sable." "BL" is Nabokov's private emblem for the incest theme. That VV's last love is in no way associated with the "BL" incest emblem is additional evidence of her unique reality in his "autobiography."

It is now time to consider the other "real" character in VV's autobiography—Dementia, which is the source of the other "characters." Dementia appropriately attends both the beginning and ending of VV's tale of love and prose. Indeed it predates the narrative which begins with the youthful narrator's meeting his first wife. In the memoirist's earliest reference to himself—as a child of seven or eight—he already harbors "the secrets of a confined madman," something he in fact becomes at various times in his life. At nine or ten, he says, his morbid childhood terrors were supplanted "by more abstract and trite anxieties (problems of infinity, eternity, identity, and so forth)" which he believes to have saved his reason. This belief is, as we shall see, open to question, for it is these more abstract anxieties of space, time, and identity that seem to be at the root of his psychotic episodes. In their acute phase these episodes last from several weeks to several years, and seven are severe enough to require hospitalization.

VV's mental condition, vaguely described as "a nervous complaint that skirted insanity" and as "flayed consciousness," displays a number of symptoms among which the more mundane are severe headaches, dizziness, neuralgia, and confusion about his surroundings. Attacks are sometimes occasioned by a faint ray of light that awakens the sleeper into a state of madness. Along this narrow beam descends a row of bright dots "with dreadful meaningful intervals between them." We shall see that sanity ultimately reestablishes itself in a not dissimilar pattern.

The most peculiar manifestation of the writer's madness is his inability to visualize left/right reversals. The problem is entirely psychological for VV is physically able to reverse his tracks and the corresponding vista without difficulty. It is the mental effort of imagining the left/right reversal of vista accompanying any such about-face that induces stress so acute that VV is literally immobilized. He likens the effort of such inversions to trying to shift the world on its axis. The "paralysis motif" is prefigured in VV's account of earlier fits of total cramp while swimming—fits which he describes as the physical counterpart of "lightning insanity." Mental transpositions of any sort induce severe trauma for the narrator. So acute, for example, is VV's distress arising from the change of languages entailed in the composition of his first English-language novel that it "almost led to the dementia paralytica that I had feared since youth." It is, however, the purely spatial dimension of his abberation, the mental inability to translate left into right (and right into left), that most troubles VV. So obsessed is he by this seemingly inconsequential aspect of his mental state that he feels honor bound to confess it—to the exclusion of the seemingly more serious aspects of his illness—to each of his four brides-to-be. These set scenes have an almost ritualistic quality.

Vadim Vadimovich's psychological malaise is rooted in his troubled sense of dual identity. He is haunted by the feeling that he is a pale shadow, an inferior variant, of another, vastly more gifted Anglo-Russian writer. On one level the plot of *LATH* consists of the accumulation of evidence that this is so. The reader must regard VV's statements about his identity with suspicion for VV is yet another example of Nabokov's use of the unreliable narrator. A telling example occurs in the narrator's contradictory statements about his father. Early in the narrative VV notes he was raised by a great-aunt (upon whose reality he immediately casts doubt) and saw his parents only "infrequently" due to their frenzied cycles of divorce and remarriage. This "infrequently" is a considerable overstatement for later VV avers that his father, Vadim, a reactionary gambler and rake nicknamed Demon, died in a duel following a card table fracas in Deauville some six months before the narrator's (and Nabokov's) birth in April of 1899. Thus VV could never have seen his "official" father. Such contradictions (quite apart from the previous strong insinuation that Count Starov is VV's father) are among those that must lead us to question the veracity of all of the narrator's account of his life.

The name of the narrator remains obscure throughout his autobiography. In the London psychiatrist's report of his case, the patient is identified as "Mr. N. a Russian nobleman" although, to VV's intense irritation, the doctor lumps his case history with that of "another" patient, a Mr. V. S., whom the reader (but not the narrator) might reasonably associate with Nabokov's Russian pen name, Vladimir Sirin. At a later point the tipsy narrator rhetorically addresses himself as Prince Vadim Blonsky but shortly thereafter disavows the surname as a false one used for a surreptitious trip to Russia in search of his daughter. His Cambridge friend, Ivor Black, once refers to him as "McNab" because he resembles an actor of that name and on a later occasion calls him Vivian—the latter evoking for the reader Nabokov's own sometime anagrammatic pen names of Vivian Calmbrood and Vivian Darkbloom.

The narrator's unease about his name and identity is, of course, symptomatic of his aberrant mental condition which *au fond* seems to partake far more of schizophrenia than dementia paralytica. Even the most casual reader of Nabokov will have noted that most of VV's books, in title, content, and serial order, are transparent variants and blends of Nabokov's own novels. For example, Nabokov's *Kamera Obskura,* which becomes the English, *Laughter in the Dark,* underlies the mad narrator's *Camera Lucida* and its English counterpart *Slaughter in the Sun.* It is VV's unseen and nameless double who is obviously the source of the narrator's intuition that he is a "non-identical twin, a parody." He feels that a demon is forcing him to impersonate "that other writer who was and would always be incomparably greater, healthier, and crueler than your obedient servant." This feeling is reinforced in VV's conversation with Oksman, the Russian bookman, who mistakenly welcomes the author of *Camera Lucida* to his shop as the author of *Camera Obscura* and then blunders again by confusing VV's *Tamara* with a book entitled *Mary.* To make matters worse the amiable bookseller reminisces that he twice saw the narrator's father, a prominent liberal member of the First Duma. On one occasion VV's father was at the opera with his wife and *two* small boys and once again, later, at a public meeting where his English *sangfroid* and absence of gesticulation was in sharp contrast to that of his fiery friend Alexander Kerenski. These recollections from the period between 1905 and 1917 postdate the 1898 death of VV's "father." Oksman, like a number of other characters, is seemingly party to the widespread confusion of the narrator with another, unnamed novelist. This unnerving experience further intensifies VV's lurking dread that "he might be permanently impersonating somebody living as a real being beyond the constellation of . . . tears and asterisks." This is of course precisely what VV is doing within the anagrammatic constellation of Count Starov's *tears* and *asterisks.* The "real" person (or, more accurately, persona) is "Vladimir Vladimirovich." So distraught is VV that he returns home and makes a detailed record of the meeting in cipher. He even contemplates repatterning his entire life, abandoning his art, taking up chess, becoming a lepidopterist, or making a scholarly Russian translation of *Paradise Lost* that would cause "hacks to shy and asses to kick." Realizing, however, that only his writing, his "endless re-creation of his fluid self" keeps him "more or less" sane, he finally contents himself with dropping his *nom de plume,* V. Irisin, in favor of his real (but unrevealed) name. V. Irisin, of course, evokes Nabokov's Russian-language pseudonym, V. Sirin, the initials of which we remarked in the London psychiatrist's report.

In spite of this shift from pseudonym to real name, the narrator continues to be plagued by his shadowy nemesis. Some dozen years later while motor touring in the American West, VV is overcome by a "dream sensation of having come empty-handed—without what? A gun? A wand? This I dared not probe lest I wound the raw fell under my thin identity." The same page also contains an oblique reference to butterflies and it is obviously a butterfly net that VV's empty hand longs to enclasp. The wonder-working wand is also, however, the omnipresent symbol of the autobiography's title motif, the Harlequin, the madcap prankster of the commedia dell-arte—another of the guises of the mysterious double. It is appropriate that the harlequin is traditionally invisible to some of the other commedia characters.

Vadim Vadimovich's sense of duality persists throughout the narrative, even manifesting itself at a particularly radiant moment in his life shortly after he has moved to Switzerland with his last love. The seventy-one-year-old author has just completed the fair copy of his last novel, *Ardis.* Louise has been blackmailed into agreeing to a divorce, and VV is contemplating a proposal of marriage to his new love. Before doing so, however, he feels once again honor bound to confess his bizarre inability to mentally invert right and left. To accomplish this painful chore he hits upon the idea of giving "you" an early manuscript-chapter of *Ardis* in which the hero discusses his own (and VV's) aberration. While his love reads his "confession," VV goes for a pre-prandial stroll. He is in a rare euphoric state that nothing can mar, not even "the hideous suspicion that *Ardis,* my most private book, soaked in reality, saturated with sun flecks, might be an unconscious imitation of another's unearthly art, *that* suspicion might come later." And indeed it does. VV reaches the far end of his stroll, stands before a low parapet, and gazes at the setting sun. As he attempts to turn about and retrace his steps, he finds he cannot: "To make that movement would mean rolling the world around on its axis." VV's psychological inability has become a physical reality. The dementia paralytica he has feared from youth has overtaken him.

VV awakens in a hospital, his mind racing but his body and senses all but lifeless. As he gathers his thoughts he first tries to establish his own identity. He is fairly certain that his first name *cum* patronymic is Vadim Vadimovich but is troubled by the thought that in rapid, indistinct speech the name Vladimir Vladimirovich degenerates into something very like Vadim Vadimych (the slurred form of Vadim Vadimovich). Of his family name the narrator is at first certain only that it contains the letters N and B. After trying and rejecting several possibilities such as Nebesnyy, Nabedrin, Nablidze, Naborcroft, Bonidze, and Blonsky, his "sonorous surname" finally bursts into his consciousness.

The questions of identity and reality are closely coupled. The theme of "reality" in *LATH* is, in turn, closely linked with VV's nameless fourth love. The narrator even declines to identify her or speak of their relationship for fear that it would contaminate "the reality of your radiance." "Yet," he writes, " 'reality' is the key word here; and the gradual perception of that reality was nearly fatal to me." As the reader knows, it is just as VV wishes to go back to his newly enlightened love with his proposal of marriage that his near-fatal seizure occurs. As VV emerges from his deathlike coma and at last recalls his surname, the door of his hospital room opens and he becomes aware of "a slow infinitely slow sequence of suspension dots in diamond type. I emitted a bellow of joy, and Reality entered." Reality in the person of his ideal love has entered the room.

The identity of the narrator is that of the nameless "other" author who is the prototype of which VV and his books are flawed copies. The identity of this original has long been obvious to the reader. It has remained a secret only to the mad narrator who has vaguely sensed but not known the truth. It is only during VV's mysterious paralysis that his speeding mind has attained certain insights from its brief intimacy with non-being and "Problems of identity have been, if not settled, at least set."

Vadim Vadimovich is now consciously aware of both halves of his dual schizoid being. Vadim Vadimovich and "Vladimir Vladimirovich," mad and sane, left and right, have been reintegrated. If we adopt this interpretation, and it seems fully warranted, a new question poses itself. The narrator is now whole and between his seventy-first and seventy-fourth years composes *LATH*. This "autobiography" is, however, patently fantastic. If VV is no longer mad, why does he write a largely fantastical autobiography? There would seem to be only one perspective from which all of the pieces fall into place. *LATH* is an account of the delusional world of the narrator during his existence as Vadim Vadimovich told entirely and consistently from that point of view.

In the fictional universe of Nabokov's *LATH,* there exists a Nabokovian persona who shares much, but far from all, of the biographical background of the real, extra-fictional Nabokov and who has written a series of books—*Mary, Camera Obskura, The Gift, Lolita, Ada,* etc. This Nabokovian persona whom we have termed "Vladimir Vladimirovich" suffers from periods of schizophrenia in which he is Vadim Vadimovich, the author of *Tamara, Camera Lucida, The Dare, A Kingdom by the Sea, Ardis,* etc. None of these works exist outside the mind of the mad narrator. They are simply distorted variants of the real works written by the sane half of the narrator's personality—"Vladimir Vladimovich." The other characters know that the narrator is mad and has periods in which he is the "other" personality. The Stepanovs, for example, with whom VV stays after one of his breakdowns, refer to him as mad. Oksman, the book dealer, also knows this and humors VV by pretending that his reference to *Camera Lucida* as *Camera Obscura* is a slip of the tongue. Note that none of the characters seem *ever* to have read any of Vadim's books—only those of the "other" author.

Vadim's incestuous wives and lovers (with the exception of the last) are no more real than his books, although like the books they are presumably delusional variants of real women in the world of "Vladimir Vladimirovich." The unreality of this aspect of Vadim's life is attested by the gross improbability of the fiction that the multifarious bastards of the mythical Count Starov meet, mate, and murder. Still more implausible is that their diverse names all include the emblematic "BL." The almost ritualistic patterning in the presentation of the women is strikingly artificial. With minor variation three events must precede each new relationship. The obligatory butterfly must appear. There must be a scene in which the nude VV stands before a mirror and takes stock before making his declarations to his future brides. Finally, there is the bizarre left/right confession which assumes a modicum of meaning only in the context of the narrator's schizophrenic dual identity. All this bespeaks the artifice of art rather than the chaos of reality or even fictional realism. Vadim's "autobiography" is so neatly patterned because it never happened. It is entirely the product of his disordered (or possibly his over-ordered) imagination during periods in which "Vladimir Vladimirovich" is supplanted by Vadim Vadimovich.

VV has taken the advice of his invented great-aunt in the creation of his "oblique autobiography" with its "mirages of romantic and literary matters." In obeying the injunction to "Look at the Harlequins!" the narrator is looking at the left-handed world of Vadim Vadimovich's "motley madness" as it is set within the right-hand world of "Vladimir Vladimirovich." VV has invented his own delusional "reality" through inversion.

The incest theme that suffuses *LATH* has obvious congruity with several aspects of the narrative. The incestuous brother-sister relationship (actually half-brother/half-sister) mirrors several crucial aspects of the narrative: the relationship of Vadim Vadimovich and "Vladimir Vladimirovich" and their respective worlds, the relationship of their respective novels, the relationship of the Russian and English parts of their careers to each other, and the left/right aberration of the narrator. In each case one half of the pairing is a reflected inverted version of the other half, a distorted mirror image, a simulacrum of the forbidden brother-sister relationship.

Ada and *LATH* are united by much more than the theme of hidden sibling incest. The events of each novel take place on an inverted antiworld. In *Ada,* with its Anti-Terra, this is literally the case, while in *LATH* the antiworld seemingly consists of the hero's delusional world which coexists with the "real" world. In each case, the antiworld hero has obscure intimations of a parallel world which is a distorted mirror-image of his own. Although the heroes take their own worlds as the "real" ones, they are troubled by secret patterns that hint that their worlds are but imperfect copies of an original prototype. Much of the data testifying to the existence of the other world comes from the delusions of madmen. Vadim Vadimovich is mad, and Van Veen, a psychologist, derives much of his information about Terra from the delusions of his patients.

Each novel has a shadowy character who is a source of signs and portents: *Ada*'s Baron Klim Avidov who supplies the vatic Scrabble set that foretells the incestuous relationship of Van and Ada, and *LATH*'s Count Nikifor Nikodimovich Starov who sires Vadim and his half-sister brides. In both novels the secret pattern of sibling incest is one of the clues to the controlling presence of another world. Just as the narrators seek out covert patterns suggesting another world, the reader of Nabokov's two novels must decipher the secret labyrinth of sibling incest that lies at their center. For the voyager who discovers "What the Sailor Has Hidden," the intricate patterns of sibling incest testify to the controlling presence of Nabokov, the mazemaker.

MICHAEL SEIDEL

Stereoscope: Nabokov's Ada *and* Pale Fire

FALSE PASSPORTS

Of all novelists who have lived in exile and written its traumas and its imaginative opportunities into the texture of their fiction, Vladimir Nabokov reigns, in his way, supreme. As the poet John Shade puts it in *Pale Fire,* the old exile "suffocates and conjures in two tongues." The agonies and ecstasies of the exilic state for Nabokov—what he calls, borrowing a line from Melville, the life of a flower exiled by a weed—are emotionally and aesthetically connected to the retrospective imagination, to the search and Proustian *recherche* for the nostalgic source that locates the wonder and combinatory powers of the creating mind.

When Nabokov writes in *Speak, Memory* of his long-cherished exilic recollections of Russia, he means those that he associates with the special memories of his youth:

> Nowadays, the mental image of matted grass on the Yayla, of a canyon in the Urals or of salt flats in the Aral Region, affects me nostalgically and patriotically as little, or as much as, say, Utah; but give me anything on any continent resembling the St. Petersburg countryside and my heart melts. What it would be actually to see again my former surroundings, I can hardly imagine. Sometimes I fancy myself revisiting them with a false passport, under an assumed name. It could be done.

From *Exile and the Narrative Imagination.* Yale University Press, 1986.

Nabokov goes on to say he shall never do it—"I have been dreaming of it too idly and too long"—but the exiled writer, no matter where he is, travels with a false passport all his life. Or, to put it another way, his passport may be false in the eyes of literalists like the border police, but valid enough in the realm of memorial retrospect. An exile's passport is the license to travel, like Blake's mental technician, inside the head. Such travel could take place, must take place, and does take place for Nabokov under a variety of names in a variety of places.

To comprehend more fully the effect and resonance of exile in Nabokov's life and art, it makes sense to begin at the place where Nabokov begins: with the origin of imagination in the familiar and marked domain of childhood. The exilic imagination in its maturity tries to recapture not only remembered space but nostalgic time. Whenever Nabokov writes, as he does so often, of the loss of Russia, he separates it from any notion of real material loss, the loss, say, of a family fortune, and turns instead to family memories: "the nostalgia I have been cherishing all these years is a hypertrophied sense of lost childhood, not sorrow for lost banknotes." At home, or *in time,* a child's first imaginative efforts are phenomena "of orientation rather than of art, thus comparable to stripes of paint on a roadside rock or to a pillared heap of stones marking a mountain trail." To move into the world of art is to project into a world of possibilities, a world beyond those traditional boundary markers setting out the contours of familiar territory.

In Nabokov's early, partially autobiographical novel, *The Gift,* Fyodor Cherdyntsev, the émigré poet and novelist, contemplates the supplementing powers of the imagination and draws a comparison with those extraordinary moments of childhood when "he could see all sorts of distant and interesting things, just as, when a little boy, his father used to lift him by his elbows thus enabling him to see what was interesting over a fence." The word *interesting* is pivotal here in the sense of focusing originary perspective. Recall and vision, a rush of orienting memories and extravagant projections, position the imagination. Nabokov always relies on positioning to measure the poetic or artistic moment. He notes that "in a sense, all poetry is positional: to try to express one's position in regard to the universe embraced by consciousness, is an immemorial urge. The arms of consciousness reach out and grope, and the longer they are the better. Tentacles, not wings, are Apollo's natural members."

For the child "all forms of vitality are forms of velocity, and no wonder a growing child desires to out-nature nature by filling a minimum stretch of time with a maximum of spatial enjoyment." This gesture remains in essence what Nabokov offers as formal design in his later fiction, whether accomplished by sequences of exquisitely formulated sentences or by the splendor of invented kingdoms and reformulated continents. Artistic positioning begins at the boundary or meeting place between that which already exists as accessible information or sensation and that which requires the projection of images: "There is, it would seem, in the dimensional scale of the world a kind of delicate meeting place between imagination and knowledge, a point . . . that is intrinsically artistic." When Nabokov grappled later in his career with the difficulties of capturing America imaginatively for *Lolita,* he worried about his own positioning: "My private tragedy, which cannot, and indeed should not, be anybody's concern, is that I had to abandon my natural idiom, my untrammeled, rich, and infinitely docile Russian tongue for a second-rate brand of English, devoid of any of those apparatuses—the baffling mirror, the black velvet backdrop, the implied associations and traditions—which the native illusionist, frac-tails flying, can magically use to transcend the heritage in his own way."

Perhaps because Nabokov's sensibility encouraged it, he began to consolidate from his knowledgeable world his imaginative world, what he called his "unreal estate," even before he needed it. Looking back upon his childhood, he writes of his first memory of returning to Russia once from abroad: "In result, that particular return to Russia, my first *conscious* return, seems to me now, sixty years later, a rehearsal—not of the grand homecoming that will never take place, but of its constant dream in my long years of exile." Later, in England, Nabokov felt himself able to deal with the condition of exile when his imagination freed itself to present his homeland to him complete; he crammed himself full of Russian literature for "fear of losing or corrupting, through alien influence, the only thing I had salvaged from Russia—her language." He writes of the immense relief he experienced at Cambridge when he also finally felt at home in England, and "this state of harmony had been reached at the very moment that the careful reconstruction of my artificial but beautifully exact Russian world had been at last completed." There could be no clearer example of the exilic projection serving as exilic supplement, a replica serving as replacement.

Politically, Nabokov tried to think in similar ways—to make the supplemental reconstruction of Russia his memorial reality so he could beneficially accommodate his exilic perspective. Nabokov writes in an essay on the tenth anniversary of the 1917 Russian Revolution that the best of what remains to be imagined about the homeland is precisely what can be imagined in exile:

> In that particular Russia which invisibly surrounds, quickens, and supports us, nourishes our souls, adorns our dreams, there

> is not a single law except the law of love for her, and there is no power except that of our own conscience. We may say everything about her, write everything, for we have nothing to hide, and there is no censorship to limit us—we are free citizens of our dreams. Our far-flung state, our nomadic empire has its strength in this freedom, and someday we shall be grateful to the blind Clio for the way in which she allowed us to taste this freedom and in emigration to understand thoroughly and develop a deep feeling for our native land.
>
> (*Nabokov: His Life in Art,* translated by Andrew Field)

The gratefulness, of course, reserved itself for intellectual and literary memory because time took its toll on the political element of that dream. Nabokov writes in the 1962 foreword to the English translation of *The Gift* of that saving Russian remnant whose memorial status becomes almost mythical in exile, "at present as much of a phantasm as most of my other worlds":

> The tremendous outflow of intellectuals that formed such a prominent part of the general exodus from Soviet Russia in the first years of the Bolshevist Revolution seems today like the wanderings of some mythical tribe whose bird-signs and moon-signs I now retrieve from the desert dust. We remained unknown to American intellectuals (who, bewitched by Communist propaganda, saw us merely as villainous generals, oil magnates, and gaunt ladies with lorgnettes). That world is now gone. Gone are Bunin, Aldanov, Remizov. Gone is Vladislav Khodasevich, the greatest Russian poet that the twentieth century has yet produced. The old intellectuals are now dying out and have not found successors in the so-called Displaced Persons of the last two decades who have carried abroad the provincialism and Philistinism of their Soviet homeland.

What Nabokov carries abroad is the consciousness of where he has been. In *Speak, Memory,* he describes his exilic experience upon settling in New England and wonders

> what I am doing in this stereoscopic dreamland? How did I get here? Somehow, the two sleighs have slipped away, leaving behind a passportless spy standing on the blue-white road in his New England snowboots and stormcoat. The vibration in my ears is no longer their receding bells, but only my old blood

> singing. All is still, spellbound, enthralled by the moon, fancy's rear vision mirror. The snow is real, though, and as I bend to it and scoop up a handful, sixty years crumble to glittering frost-dust between my fingers.

In aesthetic terms, the stereoscopic blood song of memory in fancy's rear vision mirror is so strong it seems to enter even when not exactly invited. In *The Gift,* Fyodor considers the layering of reaction to the sighting of a face and the distant, former home place takes strange, if irrelevant, hold. Merely by looking at a person the many valences of art and exile enter in:

> You look at a person and you see him as clearly as if he were fashioned of glass and you were the glass blower, while at the same time without in the least impinging upon that clarity you notice some trifle on the side—such as the similarity of the telephone receiver's shadow to a huge, slightly crushed ant, and (all this simultaneously) the convergence is joined by a third thought—the memory of a sunny evening at a Russian small railway station; i.e., images having no rational connection with the conversation you are carrying on while your mind runs around the outside of your own words and along the inside of those of your interlocutor.

ZEMBRE ON THE MINDER

If we turn now to the way Nabokov constructs the special worlds and special places of his fiction, we begin to see the centrality of exilic projection as a principle of narrative design. To bring into imaginative scope what Nabokov calls in *Ada* the "whereabouts and whenabouts" of memorial space is to draw on the alliance between exile and nostalgia, a key alliance in his fiction and one, as Van Veen says in *Ada,* that measures "the blood current coursing through my brain, and thence through the veins of the neck heartward, back to the seat of private throes." Van knows the process well; he is a psychiatric writer of what Nabokov calls "physics fiction," visionary treatises on mental landscapes embedded in the texture of time: "Time is a fluid medium for the culture of metaphors." He theorizes that the present lasts at best a tenth of a second, during which time the impostor space makes its only impression on the eye. Futurity is at best a guess. Time is what one desires and "to give myself time to time Time I must move my mind in the direction opposite to that in which I am moving." Van has a special term for past as a product of memory—he calls it a construction, a "Deliberate Present" as opposed to the "Specious Present" of living life as unreconstructed "nowness." And he asks a question whose answer approximates the form, shape, and temporal overlap of *Ada,* not only as childhood chronicle, but as exilic space-romance, a narrative genre that transverses inconvenient space and collapses oppressive time: "Has there ever been a 'primitive' form of Time in which, say, the Past was not yet clearly differentiated from the Present, so that past shadows and shapes showed through the still soft, long, larval 'now'?"

Van goes on to expound on the process of imaginary spatialization, which is at the heart of the exilic imagination and which implies transforming geography into a species of temporal metaphor: "Not for the first time will Space intrude if I say that what we are aware of as 'Present' is the constant building up of the Past, its smoothly and relentlessly rising level. How meager! How magic!" Van had already proposed an illustration in which memorial nostalgia actually becomes physical reconstruction, the imagined restoration of an original town named Zembre on the river Minder—a natural enough space-place—that during the decades of the Industrial Revolution experienced a bad case of urban sprawl. The architectonics here provide a parallel for the deliberate present of exilic reconstruction:

> Today, after years of subtle reconstruction, a replica of the old Zembre, with its castle, its church, and its mill extrapolated onto the other side of the Minder, stands opposite the modernized town and separated from it by the length of a bridge. Now, if we replace the spatial view (as seen from a helicopter) by the chronal one (as seen by a retrospector), and the material model of old Zembre by the mental model of it in the Past (say, around 1822), the modern town and the model of the old turn out to be something else than two points in the same place at different times (in spatial perspective they *are* at the same time in different places). The space in which the modern town coagulates is immediately real, while that of its retrospective image (as seen apart from material restoration) shimmers in an imaginary space and we cannot use any bridge to walk from one to the other.

The imaginative, restrospective space, the one that admits of no real bridge to real state, is, of course, the space of Nabokov's supreme fictional supplements, Humberland in *Lolita,* Zembla in *Pale Fire,* and the North American Estoty on the planet Antiterra of *Ada.* Of *Lolita,* for example, he writes: "It had taken me some forty years to invent Russia and Western Europe, and now I was faced by the task of inventing America." Nabokov does so before he writes *Lolita*, but he also does so between parts one and two of the novel. The transition from part one to part two is a neat Nabokovian fold that first brings the object of obsession into the sphere of the obsessed and then widens the sphere to an inscriptive or mental place, an exilic territory. As Lolita comes to Humbert, part one ends: "You see, she had absolutely nowhere else to go." Humbert and his Lo, after a couple of compulsory text-dividing blank pages, initiate the trajectory that makes up much the rest of the book: "It was then that began our extensive travels all over the States." Humbert, the maniac of the map, seems to sense that he is nothing but itinerary: "She had entered my world, umber and black Humberland."

Nabokov also rewrites America in *Ada* by projecting it as exilic space. Backing up a century in its putative time scheme while still allowing its inhabitants to live as if in a different version of the twentieth century, *Ada* provides the perfect reconstructive supplement for the cosmopolitan Russian genius-cum-exile. It is as if the circumstances for exile never existed in Russia, indeed, as if centuries of worldwide geopolitical contingencies are rearranged for the benefit of the imagining mind. Not only does Nabokov's exilic event, the Russian Revolution, fail to occur, but most of the historical conditions for centuries past that might have proven threatening to the aristocratic, liberal Western world are altered on Antiterra. What remains is a world of extended European and American civilization that has marginalized rather than centralized violence and political uprootedness. *Ada* takes place primarily on a continent called Amerussia, leaving European and Asian Russia for the hordes of Tartary (as if these throwbacks from the realm of darkness held Russia in her hyperborean prehistory and never lost her). Home for *Ada* in the nineteenth and twentieth centuries is an amalgam of the Yukon, French and British Canada, and northern America, where culture's separate imprints produce a fictionally unified country, Estoty, coincidentally served by virtually interchangeable languages, Russian, French, and English, Nabokov's native and exilic tongues.

The temporal-spatial axis of *Ada*'s world is based on a complicated conceit where, in a reversal that befits the exilic reconstruction, history as we might know it from perusing the front pages of the *New York Times* or *Pravda* is represented only by a bizarre and remote projection on a planet or plane called Terra, accessible only to presumed lunatics and visionaries. Terra, of course, is a place where Russia still is Asian and European, where "Russian peasants and poets had not been transported to Estotiland. . . .

they were dying, at this very moment, in the slave camps of Tartary." Since the inhabitants of Antiterra deal with Terra only as a fantasy, facts get garbled, but experts (or madmen) have a sense of what its history looks like—the English Empire has broken up into small pieces, somebody called Athaulf the Future has thrown Europe into a terrible turmoil, Tartarian Russia is called, as far as Van mishears or misconstrues, the Sovereign Society of Solicitous Republics. Like many exiles whose imaginative spirit strikes home no matter where their bodies, Nabokov undermines the devalued homeland by keeping his characters well out of it.

The represented world of Antiterra—the pun is idyllic as well as nostalgic—denies the reality of Terra precisely because its historical fantasy is too terrible. Antiterra, which Van seems to require as an intermediate world to his true desire, the young girl Ada at Ardis, takes on personal dimension, which is why it exists aesthetically. It is also known by family names that center Van's chronicle, making it sound slightly mad and demonically supplemental: Demonia, Vandemonia, Desdemonia. As is the case for Kinbote's evocation of Zembla in *Pale Fire,* a symptomatic kind of artistic insanity lurks in the full geographical supplement. Van Veen seems to sense as much—it is not just Terra that projects a mad world: "He also gave a minute's thought to the sad fact that (as he well knew from his studies) the confusion of two realities, one in single, the other in double, quotes, was a symptom of impending insanity." Antiterra is the verbal and visual imposition that allows him to make *Ada* out of his artistic treatise, *The Texture of Time.* The entire planet becomes that memorial space, a Neverland, "where artists are the only gods." Indeed, the only named god is the appropriate figure for an exilic place filled with and by what Nabokov calls "word dreams": God Log, a parodic form of the word, or logos. Again, as in *Pale Fire,* Nabokov adds an exilic signatory to the imaginative Shakespearean compact among lunatics, lovers, and poets.

For Van, Antiterra makes over the historical rift by literally remembering over it or remembering it over. We can gain a sense of the two worlds of the novel by listening to a distinction Van makes early between the supposedly real Antiterra and the fantastic Terra, a "distortive glass of our distorted glebe":

> *Ved'* ("it is, isn't it") sidesplitting to imagine that "Russia," instead of being a quaint synonym of Estoty, the American province extending from the Arctic no longer vicious Circle to the United States proper, was on Terra the name of a country, transferred as if by some sleight of *land* across the ha-ha of a doubled

> ocean to the opposite hemisphere where it sprawled over all of today's Tartary, from Kurland to the Kuriles! But (even more absurdly), if, in terrestrial spatial terms, the Amerussia of Abraham Milton was split into its components, with tangible water and ice separating the political, rather than poetical, notions of "America" and "Russia," a more complicated and even more preposterous discrepancy arose in regard to time—not only because the history of each part of the amalgam did not quite match the history of each counterpart in its discrete condition, but because a gap of up to a hundred years one way or another existed between the two earths; a gap marked by a bizarre confusion of directional signs at the crossroads of passing time with not *all* the no-longers of one world corresponding to the not-yets of the other. It was owing, among other things, to this "scientifically ungraspable" concourse of divergences that minds *bien rangés* (not apt to unhobble hobgoblins) rejected Terra as a fad or a fantom, and deranged minds (ready to plunge into any abyss) accepted it in support and token of their own irrationality.

The language here boasts of word modules such as "sidesplitting," which, like Nabokov's imp Split, makes exilic imagining into a "preposterous" temporal-spatial rupture. The mitosis of the supplement (a fabulous birth if not strictly Caesarean) allegorizes the joke of projection, spatialized in the figure of the landscape trompe l'oeil, the "ha-ha," where space is an aesthetic surprise, the projection that at once seems an illusion and a prospect, a disjunct and an adjunct, a joke and a doubling. Beyond Nabokov's delicate spatial magic, however, is the process of exilic imagining at its most robust. Van's throwaway for the governor of Amerussia, Abraham Milton, hints at a mythic territory that is both originary and structuring, since Abraham begins and Milton records the great founding and exilic experiences of Western tradition.

EXILIC DESIRE

Having artfully and laboriously constructed, named, and overlapped two worlds in *Ada,* one the exilic idyll, the other a newsreel artifact, an "actuality" as a fantasy of the remote, Nabokov also augments the spaces of the nostalgic supplement, associated, as is so often the case in his writings, with the sexual fixations of youth: "*One* wonders if *any* art could do without that erotic gasp of schoolgirl mirth." If this sounds either perilously or generatively close to the center of the earlier *Lolita,* one should not be surprised. Very little of *Lolita* as well makes sense without an understanding of the allegorization of nostalgia as original nymphette desire and the subsequent displacement of desire into the spatial diaspora of lust. The pathos of *Lolita* is that Humbert's inscription of desire is all exilic velocity without the imaginative innocence left behind on the Riviera of his youth. In the beginning was the original nymph, Annabel on the beach:

> I leaf again and again through these miserable memories, and keep asking myself, was it then, in the glitter of that remote summer, that the rift in my life began; or was my excessive desire for that child only the first evidence of an inherent singularity? When I try to analyze my own cravings, motives, actions and so forth, I surrender to a sort of retrospective imagination which feeds the analytic faculty with boundless alternatives and which causes each visualized route to fork and refork without end in the maddeningly complex prospect of my past.

When Nabokov has Humbert say that "in a certain magic and fateful way Lolita began with Annabel," he is saying that the girl and the book derive from the same retrospective overplus. The difficulty for Humbert Humbert is that his world, like his name, is indeed double; it comprises both the America of his odyssey and the Nabokovian "elsewhere" of nostalgia reflected erotically in *Lolita.* Even Humbert recognizes the "maddeningly complex prospect" where the projection of his own childhood desire both sustains him and imposes upon him, so "that the search for a Kingdom by the Sea, a Sublimated Riviera, or whatnot, far from being the impulse of the subconscious, had become the rational pursuit of a purely theoretical thrill."

From the experience of reading *Lolita* it would appear that there are two entirely different circuits of an American odyssey taking place. One is a criss-cross country ramble of perversion and pathos: "We had been everywhere. We had really seen nothing. And I catch myself thinking today that our long journey had only defiled with a sinuous trail of slime the lovely, trustful, dreamy, enormous country that by then, in retrospect, was no more to us than a collection of dog-eared maps, ruined tour books, old tires, and her sobs in the night—every night, every night—the moment I feigned sleep." The other journey is an authorial reconstruction by the Nabokovian exile in awe of the territory he inscribes, the wordsmith who marvels at Painted Canyons because, in a way, he has painted them, who delights in places like Crystal Chamber, Conception Park, and Shakespeare, New Mexico, because he can, after a fashion, admire their aesthetic resonance, admire his having imagined them. Perhaps that is why Nabokov later in *Pale Fire* named a hurricane Lolita and in *Ada* named one of his imagined places on an imagined American mainland Lolita, Texas. The book, in a sense, derives the land. Lo may have been oblivious to the landscape, but Humbert finally saw something out in the West, the traditional literary place for exilic wandering and resettlement, and, in this instance, a place that seems to exist as an inspiration for the writing of it:

> Distant mountains. Near mountains. More mountains; bluish beauties never attainable, or ever turning into inhabited hill after hill; southeastern ranges, altitudinal failures as alps go; heart and sky-piercing snow-veined gray colossi of stone, relentless peaks appearing from nowhere at a turn of the highway; timbered enormities, with a system of neatly overlapping dark firs, interrupted in places by pale puffs of aspen; pink and lilac formations, Pharaonic, phallic, "too prehistoric for words" (blasé Lo); buttes of black lava; early spring mountains with young-elephant lanugo along their spines; end-of-the-summer mountains, all hunched up, their heavy Egyptian limbs folded under folds of tawny moth-eaten plush; oatmeal hills, flecked with green round oaks; a last rufous mountain with a rich rug of lucerne at its foot.

Though Humbert's verbal diorama here has the feel of a made-up spectacle, it is at least nominally descriptive of a real America. It is in *Ada* that Nabokov takes the next inevitable step and makes America up as part of a new geography for an Amerussian continent, a geography conforming to the desire and dementia of exilic consciousness. The same "maddeningly complex prospect" that faces Humbert is also structuring in *Ada;* the place and the girl sustain the back action of the novel. Nabokov even provides a book reviewer who mistakenly thinks that Van's *Letters from Terra* (described, by the way, right after a series of letters from the girl, Ada) is "a fancy novel about a girl called Terra," as if all Nabokov's books within books are about the twin supplements of nostalgic place and ardent desire.

There are always two actionable phenomena going on in Nabokov's fiction, described similarly in *Lolita* and again in *Pale Fire:* the viewing of action with open eyes, where events play out in the present, and the viewing of that same action on the nether lids, where present action plays out, almost in a theatric sense, actionable desire. As is the case with the homeland, the desire for the object of love grows in proportion to the distance placed between it and the disorienting, displaced mind. For example, in *Pale*

Fire Charles Kinbote recreates, while in exile, emotions attendant upon his Queen Disa that never existed within the borders of his own imagined Zemblan kingdom:

> He dreamed of her more often, and with incomparably more poignancy, than his surface-life feelings for her warranted; these dreams occurred when he least thought of her, and worries in no way connected with her assumed her image in the subliminal world as a battle or a reform becomes a bird of wonder in a tale for children. These heart-rending dreams transformed the drab prose of his feelings for her into strong and strange poetry, subsiding undulations of which would flash and disturb him throughout the day, bringing back the pang and the richness—and then only the pang, and then only its glancing reflection—but not affecting at all his attitude towards the real Disa.

Love seems more necessary as an exilic and literary solace than as a represented experience. As we remember years before from Nabokov's *Despair:* "To begin with, let us take the following motto (not especially for this chapter, but generally): Literature is Love. Now we can continue." The actual experience of love for Nabokov entails an imaginative fecundity that results in an unending compulsion to supplement. As he says in a passage from *Speak, Memory* about his love for his wife, Vera: "I have to have all space and all time participate in my emotion, in my mortal love, so that the edge of its mortality is taken off, thus helping me to fight the utter degradation, ridicule, and horror of having developed an infinity of sensation and thought within a finite existence."

It is a recurring condition of Nabokov's imaginative life that what seem the intrinsic velocities of consciousness and memory also seem the velocities of love, maddening velocities when beyond the merely nostalgic "erotic gasp of schoolgirl mirth." Love follows the course of the exilic imagination, both centripetally and centrifugally. In that same passage on the immensity of his love for his wife, Nabokov describes love's dimensions and the riot of its explosion inside his heart and brain. The process resembles the emergence of a literary consciousness but lacks the curtailing, reining, proportioning principles of aesthetic design:

> Whenever I start thinking of my love for a person, I am in the habit of immediately drawing radii from my love—from my heart, from the tender nucleus of a personal matter—to monstrously remote points of the universe. Something impels me to

> measure the consciousness of my love against such unimaginable and incalculable things as the behavior of nebulae (whose very remoteness seems a form of insanity), the dreadful pitfalls of eternity, the unknowledgeable beyond the unknown, the helplessness, the cold, the sickening involutions and interpenetrations of space and time.

Love represents at various times and in various places the two great frozen territories of exilic supplements: paradisal memories and hellish, eternal voids. In *Ada,* to know the one is to experience the other: "Eros, the rose and the sore"; or the "horror and ardor of Ardis." Ada's name in Russian means, as she is fond of letting us know, Hades: "I know there's a Van in Nirvana. I'll be with him in the depths *moego ada,* of my Hades." Too much of love in the supplemental state is always degenerative, even unreciprocated love as in Queen Disa's letter to the captive Zemblan king from Villa Paradisa in *Pale Fire,* which gets translated from "I want you to know that no matter how much you hurt me, you cannot hurt my love" to the Zemblan "I desire you and love when you flog me."

Love may induce consciousness for Nabokov, but it also induces pain. In *Ada,* the recapturing of childhood is the recentering of actual, fervent, and abundant desire at the still point of the Antiterrestrian globe, the ancestral estate, Ardis, of both hero and heroine, which means " 'the point of the arrow'—but only in Greek, alas." The estate is cupidic, directional, bullseyed, and, beyond the ecstasy of the primal point of contact, piercing and painful.

Ada, spoken with *ardor* by Van, gathers emotions around her—she is desire at its most desirable time, paradisal love in the paradisal place. Ada's Van is described as "her Adam," while her name seems born of the originary name as well, with two syllables of the first generating male principal in her. Van retains the pelvic consonant of Eve to start him off—but, then, she is the one with "a pink scar between two ribs" and he is the one who gets pregnant: "When in early September Van Veen left Manhattan for Lute, he was pregnant." The split narration in the novel produces a form: "Vainiada." And the collaborative effort of the book is the sexuality of childhood revisited. In Ardis, as "lovers *and* siblings," Ada cried, "we have a double chance of being together in eternity in terrarity. Four pairs of eyes in paradise!"

As is invariably the case with love, the promiscuous pain begins when Ada and Van are forced by the disjunction of time to leave the paradisal world. Edenic exile is the first nostalgic plot. Like Anna Liffey and HCE in

Finnegans Wake, where primal love also turns promiscuous, Ada ends up loving "only males and, alas, only one man." Van ends up leaving Ardis for relentless immersion in various Venus Villas scattered through the novel like the western motels in *Lolita.* The run of action in *Ada* touches, as had *Lolita,* on the debasing horror that constitutes the unfulfilled retrospective imagination as Van wanders the world in desperate search for the lost idyllic embrace. The weed surely exiles the flower as the botanical Ada recedes in time and Van's lust-rage succeeds her.

Time for Van loses its texture when exile extends beyond the Edenic Ardis of the novel. Ardis, in fact, takes up most of the time chronicled in the book as if inconsequential time requires fewer words. The technical trick resembles the explanation Kinbote provides in *Pale Fire* for concentrating on his and Shade's houses at the expense of the much larger Wordsmith College: "It is probably the first time that the dull pain of distance is rendered through an effect of style and that a topographical idea finds its verbal expression in a series of foreshortened sentences."

So much of Veen time, as Nabokov calls it, is spent at the point of the arrow, at the originary, cupidic home because Van sees the primal, death-defying, madness-thwarting ecstasy and agony of original love:

> What, then, was it that raised the animal act to a level higher than even that of the most exact arts or the wildest flights of pure science? It would not be sufficient to say that in his love-making with Ada he discovered the pang, the *ogon',* the agony of supreme "reality." Reality, better say, lost the quotes it wore like claws—in a world where independent and original minds must cling to things or pull things apart in order to ward off madness or death (which is the master madness).

The Elysian or futuristic supplement, of which Van is eschatologically wary, is a recapitulation of memorial desire: "The transposition of all our remembered relationships into an Elysian life inevitably turns it into a second-rate continuation of our marvelous mortality." All time is a riot of pastness, and even the future palatial domain of the older Van and Ada is named Ex, meaning both "out of" and "former," as if the two properties of the exiled mind unite in the previous place of love.

Nabokov realizes that the places the imagination makes for the range of its exilic experience in *Ada,* Paradise and Hell, seem to originate, as Genesis, too, implies, in a myth of excess desire: "One can even surmise that if our time-racked, flat-lying couple ever intended to die they would die, as it were, *into* the finished book, into Eden or Hades, into the prose of the book or the poetry of its blurb." And that is precisely what happens as Van eases into blurb prose to return himself to Ardis at the end of the novel. His is an alluring parody of *Ada*'s own retrospective romance. The supplemental domain is "the writer's magic carpet" where the perfect reconstruction is forever Ardis, the girl within the grove, "the Ardors and Arbors of Ardis—this is the leitmotiv rippling through *Ada,* an ample and delightful chronicle whose principal part is staged in a dream-bright America." Here lovers forever attempt to reimage and rehear, perhaps in stereoscope, the sounds and accents of an exilic spot, what Nabokov calls their "hopeless, rapturous sunset love." Van and Ada "spend their old age traveling together and dwelling in the various villas, one lovelier than another, that Van has erected all over the Western Hemisphere." The last paragraph of the parodied blurb, like the state of exile itself, is a remembered idyll supplemented by a glut ("much, much more"), the very shape of plot in Nabokov's nostalgic, botanical, lepidopterous imagination:

> Not the least adornment of the chronicle is the delicacy of pictorial detail: a latticed gallery; a painted ceiling; a pretty plaything stranded among the forget-me-nots of a brook; butterflies and butterfly orchids in the margin of the romance; a misty view described from marble steps; a doe at gaze in the ancestral park; and much, much more.

"MIRROR, MIRROR ON THE WALL"

Van Veen, as already noted, confesses to the insanity lurking in the confusion of nostalgic and temporally linear worlds. Nabokov witnessed the phenomenon even as a child when his maternal grandfather, like Humbert Humbert, stopped time in the Riviera of his youth. In *Speak, Memory,* Nabokov describes his mother's creation of a nostalgic mirage adjusted to the pathology of the old man's desire:

> As he gradually regained consciousness, my mother camouflaged his bedroom into the one he had had in Nice. Some similar pieces of furniture were found and a number of articles rushed from Nice by a special messenger, and all the flowers his hazy senses had been accustomed to were obtained, in their proper variety and profusion, and a bit of house wall that could be just glimpsed from the window was painted a brilliant white, so every time he reverted to a state of comparative lucidity he found himself safe on the illusory Riviera artistically staged by my mother.

This is a relatively harmless mirage, but matters get more complicated when other of Nabokov's "characters" negotiate illusory space as a way of deflecting experiential anguish. In *The Gift,* Nabokov narrates instances where "if, according to the Swabian code, an insulted actor was permitted to seek satisfaction by striking the *shadow* of the offender, in China it was precisely an actor—a shadow—who fulfilled the duties of the executioner, all responsibility being as it were lifted from the world of men and transformed into the inside-out one of mirrors." In later Nabokovian fiction, the mirror substitutes are not in every sense desirable shadows, and the victims in mirror worlds take upon themselves a burden of violence not even intended for them. Such is the nature of the action in Nabokov's mad exilic narrative, *Pale Fire,* with its world of mirrors and "zemblances," its revolutionaries in glass factories, its projected assassin, Jacob Gradus, reflected from his ancestral source, a mirror-maker image of himself, Sudarg of Bokay, and its poem that begins with the violent crash of waxwing against windowpane and ends with a bungled assassination in which the wrong Shade or shadow stands in for a hanging judge.

The violence done to and by the mirror images in *Pale Fire* is nowhere better depicted than in the climactic scene at the end of the action. Two or possibly three sets of characters are loosed within the narrative's New Wye and Zemblan reflections. The result is not only a moment of violence but a narrative crisis. A lunatic imagines himself to be in pursuit of a judge named Goldsworth, though he shoots a poet named Shade, who teaches at Wordsmith College. Instead of the judge—the harshest of critics—he kills a poet, a wordsmith, thus completing a chiasmus, or cross up. Not only is Goldsmith crossed with Wordsworth, but poetry in the larger sense is crossed by lunacy, which is what *Pale Fire* is all about. Furthermore, the denouement is interpreted by an annotator, an exilic lunatic, who imagines himself as the implicit text of the action when he "wears" the manuscript of "his" dead poet's poem like a bulletproof vest. The manuscript, not the poet, becomes an "inviolable shade." Charles Kinbote, putative Zemblan king, takes the madman's double dip into literalization to avoid, perhaps, another imagined assassin after the first one hit the wrong man: "I circulated, plated with poetry, armored with rhymes, stout with another man's song, stiff with cardboard, bullet-proof at long last." The poem whose subject did not contain enough of Kinbote's story to please him now contains all of him; whereas the man who wrote the poem admits, willy-nilly, a final reflection upon his life that ends up killing him: "I was the shadow of the waxwing slain / By the false azure in the windowpane."

Without treating the crisis of *Pale Fire* solely as a police procedural—

who did what to whom?—it is enough to say that the crossings of the denouement reflect the relation of supplemental to contingent worlds in the exilic state. Narrative for Kinbote is an extenuation of circumstances. When Kinbote's Zemblan empire, from which he claims he is exiled, is translated to New Wye, the remote, romance kingdom becomes confused with another supplemental world appropriately named by Kinbote as New Wye's Arcady. The Myth of Arcadia represents the final intrusion: Death is let loose in poetic spaces. Death's appearance produces a special and unnerving kind of penetration. Kinbote has to account for Shade's New Wye death in terms of the Zemblan supplement, so he says, as if the band of assassins known as the Shadows compose a kind of mirror faculty, that Gradus "has colleagues in Arcady too." He spirits the poet's immortal poem to a hiding place with other Zemblan artifacts while intoning a self-serving Arcadian lament: "My work is finished. My poet is dead."

Death is a contingency for the contingent world, a fate that strongminded exilic fabulists admit less readily than local chroniclers. At the very beginning of *Pale Fire,* presumably before Kinbote gets his hands on it if we grant that the dedication to Vera and the epigraph are not his, Nabokov reveals the subjective impulse to close off death from life, to avoid the invasions of violence that can shatter insular visions and obliterate domestic security. For its epigraph, *Pale Fire* sports an anecdote about Samuel Johnson and his famous cat, Hodge. Upon hearing the story of a lunatic walking the streets of London and shooting cats, Johnson says, Boswell records, and Nabokov cites: "But Hodge shan't be shot: no, no, Hodge shall not be shot." The power of Johnson's concerned mind cannot admit the seepage of contingency into his own reality. This does not so much make the story of the cat-killer a fiction and Johnson's conviction about Hodge a certainty; rather, it makes Johnson's insistence on Hodge's insularity a symptom of his own anxious imaginative power. Perhaps Hodge is not marked for this particular cat-killer, but there will be some contingencies that even Hodge can't dodge.

In similar fashion, despite the elaborate lengths to which Kinbote goes to seal off his supplemental projection—covering himself with the fair-copy cards of Shade's poem, writing its last line, coaxing the pathetic lunatic, Jack Grey, to admit to the Zemblan scheme, taking refuge with his anxious dementia in the vaults of variants—his very language hints that he is the "ego" that violates Arcady. Of possible lunatics in the neighborhood, Kinbote claims he knows no local madmen personally, but he mixes his pronouns, his allusions, and his sly references to Gradus while ventriloquizing what others say of Kinbote's presence in Appalachia: " 'Even in Arcady, am I,' says Dementia." In the doubling that takes place in the seepages of *Pale Fire,* the killer and his object become linked, just as the word *Kinbote* breaks down etymologically into "kingly destroyer." If Gradus is, like Kinbote, demented, then Kinbote is, like Gradus, an assassin. Kinbote will repay in kind for the violation of his royal, almost divine, sanctity, and Nabokov even manages to mirror his own Russian experiences into Gradus's several reflections, bringing exilic dementia a bit closer to home:

> All this is as it should be; the world needs Gradus. But Gradus should not kill kings. Vinogradus should never, never provoke God. Leningradus should not aim his pea-shooter at people even in dreams, because if he does, a pair of colossally thick, abnormally hairy arms will hug him from behind and squeeze, squeeze, squeeze.

When the supplement becomes too perverse in Nabokov's fiction, when the imaginer doubles as assassin-god, the powerful, mirroring mind of art becomes its own worst enemy. Of the meaning of his own name, Kinbote comments to Shade: " 'Yes, a king's destroyer,' I said (longing to explain that a king who sinks his identity in the mirror of exile is in a sense just that)." Kinbote's head hurts at the end of *Pale Fire* when his dazzling Zembla jostles for space in his brain with the migraines that are driving him crazy. Causes confuse effects as Kinbote reverts to a kind of mock-clarity without supplemental potential, symptom without vision: "I may pander to the simple tastes of theatrical critics and cook up a stage play, an old-fashioned melodrama with three principles: a lunatic who intends to kill an imaginary king, another lunatic who imagines himself to be that king, and a distinguished old poet who stumbles by chance into the line of fire, and perishes in the clash between two figments."

What happens here is not simple; it is not merely a moment of sanity in which Kinbote, inadvertently punning on the key and generative word *fire,* sarcastically provides the actual or imaginatively unadorned plot of the novel; it is also a point where, knowing the wealth of what has gone before in the texture of the commentary, the reader can correctly imagine the poverty of literalness if that is all the projecting imagination has to offer. The orchestrative Kinbote, the misreader, the mad editor who covers himself with Shade's poem, is the exilic artist. When Kinbote comments on the line from Pope's *Essay on Man* struck from Shade's poem, "The sot a hero, lunatic a king," he claims not to know its source and says, without exploring its implications, that Shade struck it because of possible offense to a certain king, not to a certain lunatic. Similarly, when Kinbote forces his own name into the ellipsis of Shade's variant line "Poor old man Swift, poor—, poor Baudelaire," he inserts himself between a mad prose writer and a mad poet, surely hoping to share the genius of the company rather than the agony of lunacy.

The literal, as Nabokov well knew, is a none-too-wholesome refuge for art. Those who are committed literalists, whose sole motivation is thirst for revenge or appetite for destruction, are those "for whom romance, remoteness, sealskin-lined scarlet skies, the darkening dunes of a fabulous kingdom, simply do not exist." Gradus is such a figure; so, too, Sybil Shade, who stands in the mind of the visionary Kinbote with the figment Gradus, as a kind of denier. She is a "domestic anti-Karlist." For Kinbote, the Zemblan king, Sybil is also a "domestic censor," responsible for erasing the traces of Zemblan material from Shade's poem, thus barring the king-commentator from the vision of his history that he imagines Shade has imagined for him or along with him. Gradus is far worse. For creatures such as he, whether conjured or real, artistic power, mental power, even political power are preferably brought to one dead level: "People who knew too much, scientists, writers, mathematicians, crystalographers and so forth, were no better than kings or priests: they all held an unfair share of power of which others were cheated."

Kinbote makes it clear that the literalist, assassinating impulse, cannot even imagine the creative impulse when he says of Gradus: "We must assume, I think, that the forward projection of what imagination he had, stopped at the act, on the brink of all its possible consequences; ghost consequences, comparable to the ghost toes of an amputee or to the fanning out of additional squares which a chess knight (the skip-space piece), standing on a marginal file, 'feels' in phantom extensions beyond the board, but which have no effect whatever on his real moves, on the real play." Ghosts can be the shadows of *Pale Fire,* the supplementing images in the book and products of the imagination's most potent forces, but Gradus, among his other failings, is less a ghost with an afterlife than a corpse masking a mechanical man. He has no life left in him. After an affair with his blind and dropsical mother-in-law, he tries several times to castrate himself "and now, at forty-four, was quite cured of the lust that Nature, the grand cheat, puts into us to inveigle us into propagation."

In the absolute form of Kinbote's dementia, Gradus exists in Kinbote's own head, a migraine-like double whom he would annihilate with a reflexive bear hug: "At times I thought that only by self-destruction could I hope to cheat the relentlessly advancing assassins who were in me, in my eardrums, in my pulse, in my skull." But in the nostalgic aesthetics of

Zembla, Kinbote distinguishes himself from the fretting, soporific Gradus: "How much happier the wide-awake indolents, the monarchs among men, the rich monstrous brains deriving intense enjoyment and rapturous pangs from the balustrade of a terrace at nightfall, from the lights and the lake below." "Monarchs" is plural at this point, as if the kingdom of Kinbote's imagination multiplies sovereign exiles rather than subtracts lost principalities. And it is testimony to the power of the imagining mind in opposition to the literal mind that Gradus the assassin, in Kinbote's version, hits the wrong man. In a way, what he does is take the literal in John Shade down with him, thus succeeding in burying one poet while inadvertently releasing the ghost of Zembla, a more restrained "project" than Kinbote's, "a minute but genuine star ghost of my discourse on Zembla and her unfortunate king."

Shade's poem, whose failing from Kinbote's perspective is its admission of too much that did not memorialize him, becomes a double or a Zemblan supplement only when it is no longer a rival or a Zemblan assassinator. Kinbote must squeeze its body to free its vision. An assassin is thus drawn to New Wye purely by the mechanical, literal nature of Shade's art, the line-to-line movement of the poem, "the very mechanism and sweep of verse, the powerful iambic motor." Kinbote's observation on Gradus's presumed movement comes in a note on lines 131–32, canto 1, lines that repeat with a difference the violent opening lines of the poem: "I was the shadow of the waxwing slain / By feigned remoteness in the windowpane." The art of assassination, in this sense, is the literal collision of Shades and Shadows, and for every ghost that flies a body falls.

STYGIAN SOAKS AND LETHEAN LEAKS

There are two supreme fictions at work in *Pale Fire,* fictions that are based in one way or another on the exilic projections of narrative art and the farcical seepages of Nabokovian wit. Even in the spookiest of otherworld visions, communications through dreams with the dead, the imagination finds itself subject to domestic embellishments, accidental details—like puddles on the basement room floor—that seem to seep into projected worlds. Kinbote comments on a passage in John Shade's poem, "Pale Fire": "We all know those dreams in which something Stygian soaks through and Lethe leaks in the dreary terms of defective plumbing."

In *Pale Fire,* the visionary may get enmeshed in domestic pipings, the magical may touch the pedestrian, romance may surface as parody, but the Stygian experience possesses the remnants of its original, the *Aeneid*'s descent. Like the Roman Aeneas, Kinbote means to project from his present circumstances a full history of past wonder and future poetic promise. His domestic lot as "exiled prince" is a one-man *translatio imperii,* and he requires a history that is providential, just as he insists that the afterlife, "Independence Day in Hades," is not some chaotic "science fiction yarn" but has a real end, a *telos.*

Kinbote's past and envisioned simulacrum, his Zemblan unreal estate, is most manifest when, at the moment of the poet Shade's death in the narrative, Charles clutches the bundle of index cards that make up the manuscript of "Pale Fire": "I was holding all Zembla pressed to my heart." Though the scarcity of reference to his supplemental kingdom disappoints Kinbote, he reinvests himself in Shade's narrative by getting underneath it, becoming its Avernian or Stygian spectacle. As Kinbote says of the variants of "Pale Fire," the supplementary stuff upon which his imagination works: "Actually, it turns out to be beautifully accurate when you once make the plunge and compel yourself to open your eyes in the limpid depths under its confused surface."

In the last phrase of his own index, and thus in the last words of *Pale Fire,* Kinbote describes Zembla as "a distant northern land"; its imaginative, literary, or, if anyone insists, real location, places it in the traditional region of literary magic lands and afterworlds. The Avernian spaces of the *Aeneid* are "up toward the frozen North," and the very name, Zembla, is itself a kind of blank, icy, fantasy or poetic trope, a place named by Shade's favorite poet, Alexander Pope, in the *Dunciad* and in the *Essay on Man.* Zembla for Pope is a figuration, a poetic shorthand, the place for the no place, like the actual place names Kinbote remembers from his northern homeland: Embla Point, Emblem Bay, the Gulf of Surprise.

Pale Fire is steeped with examples of its own supplemental vision-making, rendered in language that reflects back on the narrative's and poem's title. The first mention of the phrase "pale fire" comes with an image of Shade standing next to his incinerator burning the index-card drafts of a poem like "wind-borne black butterflies." Kinbote, too, is a fireside imaginer of sorts—he even offers a parable of the Zemblan creation when, if we believe his fantasy, he falls asleep in front of a farmer's fire during his revolutionary escape while "shadows of his lost kingdom gathered to play around his rocking chair." To sleep, perchance to dream: such a state is something like the imagined death or death-in-life that allows poetry its Lethean vision or Kinbote's supplement its exilic splendor—"even the most demented mind still contains within its diseased mass a sane basic particle that survives death and suddenly expands, bursts out as it were, in peals of healthy and triumphant laughter when the world of timorous fools and trim blockheads has fallen away far behind."

Kinbote says that if "I were a poet I would certainly make an ode to the sweet urge to close one's eyes and surrender utterly unto the perfect safety of wooed death." Here the unreal estate is a kind of Asphodel, and, as a recent commentator on the common gaffe in the transcription of Wordsworth's "Immortality Ode"—"fields of sheep" for "fields of sleep"—points out, the editor may slip into woolly pastoral memories but the poet meant "phantom underworld of the Greeks." As Shade might say, "Life Everlasting—based on a misprint!" In the most famous of underworld descents, of course, the exiled Aeneas reascends through one of the gates of sleep, the one made of ivory:

> There are two gates of Sleep, one said to be
> Of horn, whereby the true shades pass with ease,
> The other all white ivory agleam
> Without a flaw, and yet false dreams are sent
> Through this one by the ghost to the upper world.
> Anchises now, his last instructions given,
> Took son and Sibyl there and let them go
> By the Ivory Gate.
> (book 6, ll. 893–900, translated by Fitzgerald)

In a sense, Aeneas's experience remains unavailable to him or to anyone else except through retelling as a dream, and a potentially false dream in the bargain. Commentators on the descent guess that the gates of ivory have something to do with voicing a vision, as if the hero can only tell his supplemental tale by whistling through his teeth. Nabokov has something of the same notion in mind when he has Kinbote describe his path of escape through a secret tunnel from his fantasy palace at Onhava (which means far away). The big lie passes out through an underworld tunnel. As he exits the world of his self-romance and enters the public theater, moving from fantasy to performance, Charles Rex appropriately meets a deformed statue of "Mercury, conductor of souls to the Lower World." The rest of *Pale Fire* consists of getting someone, namely Shade, to believe in the substance of this vision.

Kinbote's adventure makes poets of the dispossessed, exiles out of kings. Whether he invents the entire sequence or not, dozens of Charles's dispersing retainers appear in royal garb, supposedly to confuse the rebels taking power. The gesture is as imaginative as it is strategic. Exiles by the number assume the guise of kingship to ease the anguish of having no kingdom to call their own. Of course, the signifying king, the king who later wishes his friend John Shade would call the poem about him *Solus Rex,* is in every sense all alone after Zembla.

The narrative of Kinbote's exit from Zembla is itself the longest supplement or annotation in *Pale Fire;* it is also the most irrelevant note to anything in Shade's poem. Kinbote says slyly, as if he knows he has put one over, "I trust the reader has enjoyed this note." Later, he recalls the language of the note at the crucial moment when he has to transfer its rudiments to the whole of his exile; he emerges from his New Wye closet after secreting Shade's manuscript in the hope that it will testify to his vision: "I exited as if it had been the end of the secret passage that had taken me all the way out of my enchanted castle and right from Zembla to *this* Arcady." Kinbote speaks metaphorically here of what he had recorded as actuality; but the exilic fable in *Pale Fire* suggests that his "actuality" is, in fact, all metaphor.

Supplemental places have to be imagined and articulated because, like Aeneas's vision of the "plot" for a future imperial Rome, they do not exist in reachable form. Another of Nabokov's northern exiles, Professor Pnin, mentioned in *Pale Fire* as head of Wordsmith's Russian Department, experiences in a more direct way the Virgilian dream through the gates of ivory. In the novel bearing his name, *Pnin,* the professor finds it difficult to portray and memorialize his supplemental world, his lost Russia, until he replaces his rotten teeth, which become an emblem of the very subject that stymies him. He first goes "into mourning for an intimate part of himself," a teethscape memory of old "familiar rocks," or coves and caves of a "battered but still secure kingdom." With his new ivories, what he calls his "new amphitheater of translucid plastics," Pnin feels like "a fossil skull being fitted with the grinning jaw of a perfect stranger." But soon the dentures give him imaginative life: "It was a revelation, it was a sunrise, it was a firm mouthful of efficient, alabastrine, humane America." At this point the freedom from the throbbing pain of exile, old teeth, allows him to begin work on a "dream mixture of folklore, poetry, social history, and *petite histoire,*" exactly the kind of material that exits through Kinbote's passageway from palace to theater to New Wye's Arcady.

DAVID WALKER

The Person from Porlock: Bend Sinister *and the Problem of Art*

Bend Sinister, the first novel Nabokov wrote after coming to America, is fiendishly complex, and its complexities are perhaps particularly apparent to those self-conscious and technically aware readers Nabokov himself cultivated. Protean in its structure, style, and tone, juxtaposing different voices and veering wildly from farce to philosophical discourse to anguishing pathos, the book often threatens to come apart at the seams. Indeed, it has had more than its share of detractors on these grounds. But the conflicting elements and approaches, and the resulting difficulties—both formal and thematic—they raise for a serious reader, are in fact essential to the intricate design of Nabokov's novel.

Part of the reader's difficulty is in determining precisely what kind of book *Bend Sinister* is meant to be. Its date (1947) and subject—the plight of Adam Krug, a brilliant philosopher trapped in the web of a burgeoning police state—would seem to cast it as obviously a reflection of recent political history. Yet the author's own introduction seems pointedly to reject the idea: "I have never been interested in what is called the literature of social concern. . . . I am not 'sincere,' I am not 'provocative,' I am not 'satirical.' I am neither a didacticist nor an allegorizer. Politics . . . leave me supremely indifferent." Nabokov's imperious dismissal appears to support his familiar image as absolute aesthete, whose works are hermetically sealed off from pragmatic or social concerns. But elsewhere he explicitly counters that notion, referring to *Bend Sinister* and *Invitation to a Beheading* as "absolutely final indictments of Russian and German totalitarianism"

(*Strong Opinions*), and even in the *Bend Sinister* introduction he acknowledges the effect on it of his own personal experience of "worlds of tyranny and torture, of Fascists and Bolshevists, of Philistine thinkers and jackbooted baboons." Indeed, on balance it seems indisputable that *Bend Sinister,* with its swastikas and shreds of Leninist rhetoric, is meant to respond to contemporary political realities. What Nabokov objects to—and what the above disclaimer specifically refers to—are fashionable ("*what is called* the literature of social comment" [my emphasis]) and simple-minded ("I am not 'sincere' ") ways of understanding those realities. The difference is that between "human interest" (a cliché Nabokov abhorred) and human interest (which all his novels of course manifest).

A more complex problem lies in trying to reconcile this serious political intention with the way in which Nabokov carries it out. The prose of *Bend Sinister* is highly mannered, artificial, embellished with literary allusions and complex patterns of images, several of which Nabokov is careful to point out in his introduction. Puns and anagrams abound, and the map of Krug's country is marked with such transparently allegorical names as Lake Malheur and Omigod Lane. Perhaps most strikingly, although Adam Krug himself is a character of considerable complexity, the characters who surround him are on the whole patently two-dimensional, cartoonlike figures at the service of the book's themes. This tendency fits obligingly into Nabokov's general pronouncement that "my characters are galley slaves" (*Strong Opinions*), which he amplifies in the *Bend Sinister* introduction, claiming that all its characters "are only absurd images, illusions oppressive to Krug during his brief spell of being, but harmlessly fading away when I dismiss the cast." It is difficult to know how to reconcile these absurd and harmless images with the real and horrific realities to which they correspond.

One answer is that Nabokov was simply inept at handling a subject inimical to his imagination. Edmund Wilson made this charge in a letter to his erstwhile friend shortly before the book's publication:

> You aren't good at this kind of subject, which involves questions of politics and social change, because you are totally uninterested in these matters and have never taken the trouble to understand them. For you, a dictator like the Toad is simply a vulgar and odious person who bullies serious and superior people like Krug. You have no idea why or how the Toad was able to put himself over, or what his revolution implies. And this makes your picture of such happenings rather unsatisfactory.

> Now don't tell me that the real artist has nothing to do with the issues of politics. An artist may not take politics seriously, but, if he deals with such matters at all, he ought to know what it is all about. . . . Beside the actual Nazi Germany and the actual Stalinist Russia, the adventures of your unfortunate professor have the air of an unpleasant burlesque.

The sort of social-realist analysis Wilson was apparently seeking is certainly absent from the novel; no attempt is made to treat the social causes of Paduk's revolution, and the focus remains resolutely on the protagonist rather than on his society. But Nabokov's strategy for approaching "the issues of politics" was considerably more resourceful than his critics give him credit for, and interestingly enough, Wilson's letter goes on to suggest how: "What you are left with on your hands is a satire on events so terrible that they really can't be satirized—because in order to satirize anything you have to make it worse than it is." Having lost his language and the world of his childhood to the Bolshevists, his father to a political assassin, and, more recently, his brother to a Nazi concentration camp, Nabokov *knew* that it was not possible to invent a world more terrible than his own. The resulting artistic dilemma—how to deal in fiction with a world that already seemed improbably unreal—became in fact the strategic foundation on which he constructed his novel. "I have bridged the 'esthetic distance' in my own way" (*Strong Opinions*), Nabokov said about *Bend Sinister*—and that way was, I believe, paradoxically to focus on the esthetic distance itself. The true subject of this novel is not "the issues of politics" but the incongruity between political realities and their representation in a work of art.

In an early review of the book Diana Trilling advanced a charge that has since become familiar: "I suppose it is Mr. Nabokov's elaborate prose style that persuades his publishers that *Bend Sinister* is so distinguished a work of fiction. . . . But in point of fact, what looks like a highly charged sensibility in Mr. Nabokov's style is only fanciness, forced imagery, and deafness to the music of the English language, just as what looks like an innovation in method is already its own kind of sterile convention." The mannerism of *Bend Sinister* is impossible to ignore, but as Nabokov's best critics have shown, his stylistic eccentricities are never simply a matter of showing off; they always express a serious purpose. It may seem special pleading to argue that *Bend Sinister* is a novel about its own failure, constructed to suggest the ways art is finally inadequate to its intractable subject, but I believe it can be demonstrated. Nabokov himself gives us a clue in his introduction: "Paranomasia is a kind of verbal plague, a contagious sickness in the world of words; no wonder they are monstrously and ineptly distorted in Padukgrad, where everybody is merely an anagram of everybody else." The reader of *Bend Sinister* is made increasingly uncomfortable by its acrobatics, its often glib and artificial jokiness, in the face of its subject; the gap between its matter and its manner is the result not of "deafness" but of Nabokov's careful management of the resources of style. As he suggests, the reduction of human beings to anagrams and cartoons is a symptom of the "verbal plague" that parallels the political sickness infecting Krug's world. *Bend Sinister* is an experimental and finally subversive novel, because what the introduction calls "this crazy-mirror of terror and art" is not only a bitter indictment of the reality of totalitarianism but also a deeply skeptical examination of the power of art to affect that reality.

The peculiarly dislocating quality of the novel may be observed in almost any passage. The early episode in which Krug is forced to cross a guarded bridge on his way home, for instance, presents an uneasy variety of tones. The business whereby the two sets of guards cannot read and do not recognize each other's military codes, thus requiring Krug to shuttle back and forth between them, is played for low comedy: "They shrugged their shoulders as if ridding themselves of the burden of knowledge. They even scratched their heads, a quaint method used in that country because supposed to prompt a richer flow of blood to the cells of thought." But the burlesque is countered by the sense that these clowns serve the brutal and repressive regime of the Toad ("The reader desired to know why he could not accompany the professor across the bridge. He was briskly kicked back into the darkness"), which is in turn played against the backdrop of Krug's personal tragedy: he has just left the hospital where his wife has died, and is reduced to heaving sobs in the middle of the chapter. What is perhaps most distinctive is that no effort is made to integrate or unify these various moods; they are simply layered on top of each other, producing an appropriately hallucinatory atmosphere.

This instability is also expressed through structure. For example, the third chapter begins with Krug's return home and traces his experiences and reflections for several pages, until he telephones his friend Ember. The text immediately shifts to record the letter Ember writes after that conversation, then tracks Ember's musings on Krug and his wife, until the point when he decides to call Krug back, after which conversation the focus is on Krug again. These transitions are not especially difficult to follow, but they seem peculiarly arbitrary, and no particular effort is made to ease the reader from one scene into another. Indeed, the artifice is insisted on, as in this moment when, after trying unsuccessfully to get through to Krug, Ember thinks of working on a translation:

> It would not scan because in his native tongue "rack" was anapaestic. Like pulling a grand piano through a door. Take it to pieces. Or turn the corner into the next line. But the berth there was taken, the table was reserved, the line was engaged.
>
> It was not now.
>
> "I thought perhaps you might like me to come."

This turning back of a metaphor on itself is something of a minor tour de force, and the chapter is studded with them. They serve thematically to underscore the radical instability of Krug's world, but more immediately their function is to call attention to a feat of style. Even more striking are the moments when the narration breaks off entirely for a display of pure lyricism, a sort of prose poem embedded in the text, such as the extravagant paragraph of praise to Padukgrad ("O my strange native town! Your narrow lanes where the Roman passed."), which we learn only later is the meditation of an "anonymous muser" in the back seat of the car in which Krug is riding. And the end of the chapter moves still more boldly out of narration, when Krug and his colleagues reach their destination:

> But they did not have to ring or knock or anything for the door on the topmost landing was flung open to greet them by the prodigious Dr. Alexander who was there already, having zoomed perhaps, up some special backstairs, or by means of those non-stop things as when I used to rise from the twinned night of the Keeweenawatin and the horrors of the Laurentian Revolution, through the ghoul-haunted Province of Perm, through Early Recent, Slightly Recent, Not So Recent, Quite Recent, Most Recent—warm, warm!—up to *my* room number on *my* hotel floor in a remote country, up, up, in one of those express elevators manned by the delicate hands—my own in a negative picture—of dark-skinned men with sinking stomachs and rising hearts, never attaining Paradise, which is not a roof garden, and from the depths of the stag-headed hall old President Azureus came at a quick pace.

The stream of associations here, from the thought of an elevator through a traversal of geological history and the memory of a foreign hotel to a sort of theological pun, is mysterious and unexpected; moreover, we cannot be sure which of the characters is responsible for it. These may be Krug's associations, but they are at least as likely to represent the thoughts of someone else, in the vein of the "anonymous muser." We are not allowed to linger over the point: the chapter ends on a more precise riddle, and if we solve it through the realization that it is President Azureus of whom the head nurse reminded Krug earlier in the day, we feel a sense of satisfied closure. But the elevator passage remains ungrounded and unresolved, a piece of the puzzle that refuses to fit neatly into place, and the many similar passages throughout the novel serve continually to suggest that our grasp of Krug's story may not be as firm as we might think.

One result of these various stylistic mazes and structural puzzles is to make us focus attention on their source, and it is here that I believe the novel has been most misunderstood. Stylistic exuberance and self-consciousness are hallmarks of Nabokov's work, of course, and since the narrator of *Bend Sinister* is not characterized in the manner of Humbert Humbert or *Despair*'s Hermann, most readers have been explicitly or implicitly content to identify him with the book's author. Again here the introduction is at least partly to blame, since in at least two places Nabokov seems to encourage this identification. Referring to the "nameless, mysterious genius" who arranges Krug's dreams in chapter 5, the introduction identifies this "someone in the know" as "an anthropomorphic deity impersonated by me." And Nabokov also claims that the puddle-image that recurs throughout the book, and is pointedly identified with the narrator's world in the final paragraph, "vaguely evokes in [Krug] my link with him." Thus it is not surprising to read Robert Merrill's claim that it is Nabokov who "stops the action of *Bend Sinister* fully nine pages from the end in order to describe the room in which he is writing the book and to comment on the denouement." Similarly, Susan Fromberg Schaeffer comments on a reference to "the magician in our midst": "The author is a magician, but he is also an artist, and hence a stylist. He is free to do anything he thinks justified by the end he hopes to achieve." And Julia Bader sees an equally magus-like Nabokov as the central referent and reality of the novel:

> The involutions of the action constantly direct us toward the dual process of Krug creating his world, encircled by the author creating Krug and his world. . . . The structure of *Bend Sinister* radiates outward from a central consciousness to interlocking patterns. The solace of pattern perceived by Krug is a pattern strategically placed by the author. . . . Politics is shown in perspective as intermittent and minor material for the workings of the author's imagination.

To see *Bend Sinister* as such an ultimately solipsistic enterprise, and Nabokov casting himself in the role of omnipotent protagonist of the book, is to minimize the ambiguities crucial to its exploration of the meaning and value of art. It is worth pointing out that the introduction was written sixteen years after the novel, and that in any case Nabokov's apparent claims about the meaning of his work are often in fact highly ambiguous: to identify the nameless genius of Krug's life as a "deity impersonated by me" is, after all, to suggest a mysteriously oblique relation, not a straightforward designation. Much more importantly, there is considerable evidence in the book itself to suggest that the aesthetic position the narrator represents is to be viewed with substantially more distance than the introduction might indicate.

To understand why, it is necessary to see that *Bend Sinister* presents and examines a number of different aesthetic models and embodies them in a variety of ways. At one extreme is the notion of art as pure and absolute, not contingent or dependent in any way on the life that surrounds it. Krug embodies this ideal in his image of Shakespeare: "Nature had once produced an Englishman whose domed head had been a hive of words; a man who had only to breathe on any particle of his stupendous vocabulary to have that particle live and expand and throw out tremulous tentacles until it became a complex image with a pulsing brain and correlated limbs." For Krug this is an entirely salutary image, a tribute to the poet's power and unique genius, but for the reader there is surely something ominous about seeing Shakespeare's plays as a sort of quivering octopus, a homunculus of the imagination. The idea is attractive to Krug because, if art is autonomous and self-generating, then it becomes a valuable refuge from the circular prison of mortality. His own writing has in the past afforded him this sort of escape:

> When (some fifteen years before) both his parents had been killed in a railway accident, he had managed to alleviate the pain and the panic by writing Chapter III (Chapter IV in later editions) of his "*Mirokonzepsia*" wherein he looked straight into the eyesockets of death and called him a dog and an abomination. With one strong shrug of his burly shoulders he shook off the burden of sanctity enveloping the monster, and as with a thump and a great explosion of dust the thick old mats and carpets and things fell, he had experienced a kind of hideous relief.

Aesthetic distancing comes naturally to him; early in the novel we learn of his extreme self-consciousness:

> As usual he discriminated between the throbbing [self] and the one that looked on: looked on with concern, with sympathy, with a sigh, or with bland surprise. . . . The stranger quietly watching the torrents of local grief from an abstract bank. A familiar figure, albeit anonymous and aloof.

Self-consciousness is for Krug "the last stronghold of the dualism he abhorred"; presumably he would be happier (at least theoretically) if he could achieve absolute autonomy by turning himself into a work of art, a philosophical object.

Certainly he attempts to live up to that image, by insisting throughout the novel on his own invulnerability and superiority. Warned by his friend Maximov to beware of the Toad's power, Krug replies, "I am invulnerable. Invulnerable—the rumbling sea wave [*volna*] rolling the rabble of pebbles as it recedes. Nothing can happen to Krug the Rock." Repeatedly he denies responsibility to anything outside himself and his work; Garbo-like, he snaps, "I want to be left alone," "I do not give a damn for this or any other university," "I am not in the least interested in your government." Faced with unpleasant realities, he attempts to transmute them into the ordered terms of his own art, or to leap beyond them into "the pale starry heavens of untrammelled philosophy." For example, a shopkeeper named Peter Quist describes the hardships involved in his method for smuggling Krug out of the country:

> "My clients," said Quist, "have to do about twenty miles on foot, through blueberry woods and cranberry bogs. The rest of the time they lie at the bottom of trucks, and every jolt tells. The food is scant and crude. The satisfaction of natural needs has to be denied one's self for ten hours at a stretch or more. Your physique is good, you will stand it. Of course, taking your child with you is quite out of the question. . . . Do you visualize the dangers?"
>
> "Vaguely. But I could never leave my child behind."

Having ignored the clues that Quist is in fact a member of the secret police, Krug reveals the secret that will enable the state to gain control over him; moreover, he typically recognizes the dangers only "vaguely." And later he imagines the grim journey Quist has outlined as much more romantically stylized:

> With a pang of impatient desire, he visualized a railway platform and glanced at a playing card and bits of orange peel enlivening

> the coal dust between the rails under a Pullman car which was still waiting for him in a blend of summer and smoke but a minute later would be gliding out of the station, away, away, into the fair mist of the incredible Carolinas. And following it along the darkling swamps, and hanging faithfully in the evening aether, and slipping through the telegraph wires, as chaste as a wove-paper watermark, as smoothly moving as the transparent tangle of cells that floats athwart an overworked eye, the lemon-pale double of the lamp that shone above the passenger would mysteriously travel across the turquoise landscape in the window.

In contrast to the "vaguely" visualized details of the real escape by truck, the images of the fantasy-journey by Pullman are vividly and acutely alive to him. He is "impatient" with the sordid and tedious truth of his world, and if the over-ripe rhetoric here—"away, away, into the fair mist of the incredible Carolinas," "darkling," "evening aether"—betrays some self-consciousness about his flights of fancy, it gradually disappears as he gives himself up to them entirely. And as the lamp-reflection rises before us suggestively transfigured as a watermark, we may well catch a glimpse of another ghostly double—the author's own lamp reflected in his window as he sits at his desk—while Krug figuratively writes himself into his own lemon-and-turquoise world.

The trouble is that it simply doesn't work. "The reader," Douglas Fowler writes, "should never forget to oversimplify along with Nabokov in order to read him accurately: the solitary genius [i.e., Krug] is absolutely good, the group absolutely evil." And while few critics would accept this formula, many would join in seeing Krug as what Fowler calls an "author-equivalent." Julia Bader, for example, says, "Krug and the author are certainly identified. . . . The author as God is god of a pantheistic word world; the dreamer is his own creation. . . . The literary dream will not allow us aesthetic distance: the voice of the dreamer is at our ear, perhaps *in* our ear." But to identify Krug with his creator, and to assent to the ideal he seems to represent, is to ignore the considerable evidence that—to put it plainly—Krug fails as an artist. In the first place, the real world he attempts to deny is a good deal more hostile and powerful than he admits. His sense of presumed invulnerability is largely a myth based on past reality, and as Krug himself has recognized, "to try to map our tomorrows with the help of data supplied by our yesterdays means ignoring the basic element of the future which is its complete non-existence. The giddy rush of the present into this vacuum is mistaken by us for a rational movement." Krug was once a best-selling author, but he now lives in a society that believes "the only true Art is the Art of Discipline" and that "popular common sense must spit out the caviar of moonshine and poetry," and by attempting to ignore it, he puts himself deeply at risk. There is something noble about his refusal to accept the world on the Toad's terms, but there is also something stupidly willful in his failure to recognize the dangers of that position: even when his friends—the Maximovs, Hedron, Ember—are in turn arrested and marched off to prison, he continues to trust "that so long as he kept lying low nothing harmful could happen." As Krug repeatedly fails to see the strands of the web being woven around him—the organ-grinders, Dr. Alexander, Quist, Mariette—his aesthetic distance begins to seem more and more like blindness.

A second reason why Krug's effort to construct a private refuge of pure thought fails is that as a philosopher he is "a slave of images." His attempt to deal rationally with the experience of death leads him to recognize that death is so unimaginable as to be beyond reason, and that all his language, thought processes, and experience are grounded unhelpfully in life: "We speak of one thing being like some other thing when what we are really craving to do is to describe something that is like nothing on earth." In more personal terms, Krug's theoretical argument that death is not to be feared cannot be written because he does not believe it; he has been shattered by Olga's death and is unable to make it conform to theory:

> My intelligence does not accept the transformation of physical discontinuity into the permanent continuity of a nonphysical element escaping the obvious law, nor can it accept the inanity of accumulating incalculable treasures of thought and sensation, and thought-behind-thought and sensation-behind-sensation, to lose them all at once and forever in a fit of black nausea followed by infinite nothingness. Unquote.

The final word is Krug's attempt to use irony to distance himself from his acknowledgment, but he cannot disguise the pain and bewilderment he feels.

Finally, and most simply, Krug's aesthetic autonomy fails because, as both Maximov and (surprisingly) the Toad himself tell him, he is not alone. He would like to imagine himself a solitary aesthete, viewing the world in abstract and amoral detachment, but is prevented from doing so by his deep emotional commitments, most centrally his grief for Olga and his love for his son David, the "handle" by which he is apprehended by the state. This sense of relationship is of course a flaw in the philosopher-artist as measured by the Shakespearean paradigm; paradoxically and crucially, it is also that element through which Krug—otherwise a rather selfish and even cruel man—is made more human, morally responsible, and sympathetic. Nabokov says in his introduction that "the main theme of *Bend Sinister,* then, is the beating of Krug's loving heart, the torture an intense tenderness is subjected to—and it is for the sake of the pages about David and his father that the book was written and should be read," and few readers will fail to understand why this is so. What perhaps does need emphasis is the degree to which Krug's human tenderness is seen as antithetical to his artistic intentions.

Thus throughout the novel he struggles unsuccessfully to construct a philosophical refuge while the country falls to pieces around him. Devoid of inspiration, plagued by the fear that "he was empty, he would never write another book, he was too old to bend and rebuild the world which had crashed when she died," he becomes a sort of automaton, writing in circles. Even in the one evening when he does sense a glimmer of original thought, he seems to recognize that it is only "a rush of second-rate inspiration and somewhat precious imagery" that "kept him going nicely," and he is interrupted when reality breaks in on him in the form of his lust for the sordid Mariette.

Critics have devoted considerable attention to providing explanations for the long central chapter in which Krug and Ember discuss interpretations of *Hamlet,* variously ludicrous and witty, somewhat in the manner of the "Scylla and Charybdis" chapter of *Ulysses;* surely part of the point is that the afternoon does provide them with the sort of aesthetic retreat—from political realities and the pain of Olga's death—that both seek in art: "Krug had recently lost his wife. A new political order had stunned the city. Two people he was fond of had been spirited away and perhaps executed. But the room was warm and quiet and Ember was deep in *Hamlet.*" The chapter allows the reader a similar kind of respite from the political and personal paranoia of the previous chapters; there is considerable relief in giving ourselves up to the sheer verbal pleasure of puns and anagrams, through which the characters assert control over the tragic details of the *Hamlet* plot. But inevitably reality reasserts itself in the ironically theatrical entrance ("If you are not actors") of the villainous Hustov and Linda Bachofen, come to haul terrified Ember off to prison. The intellectual idyll, like all the self-enclosed aesthetic spheres in the novel, is doomed to be vulnerable to the real life outside it. Nabokov's working title for this novel—

The Person from Porlock—simply gives a name to this pattern, the shattering intrusion of reality on the poetic ideal.

The Shakespeare paradigm is strikingly illuminated in an earlier passage where Krug muses on a fanciful idea he and Ember shared:

> One day Ember and he had happened to discuss the possibility of their having invented *in toto* the works of William Shakespeare, spending millions and millions on the hoax, smothering with hush money countless publishers, librarians, the Stratford-on-Avon people, since in order to be responsible for all references to the poet during three centuries of civilization, these references had to be assumed to be spurious interpolations injected by the inventors into actual works which they had re-edited; there still was a snag here, a bothersome flaw, but perhaps it might be eliminated, too, just as a cooked chess problem can be cured by the addition of a passive pawn.

The wonderfully Borgesian notion of having invented the works of Shakespeare outside the culture and context in which he wrote, and simultaneously inventing the history which these works influenced, parallels the pure autonomy of Krug's later conceit. The snag or "bothersome flaw" represents all those various obstacles that reality throws up to the ideal of absolute art; here of course the hoax would not succeed because of history and individual memory, the fact that readers would have memories of Shakespeare (or his absence) before the advent of Krug and Ember's invention, which no amount of textual editing could alter. The bothersome flaw could only be eliminated by removing Shakespeare from his human context. As in the case of Krug's own writing, the attempt to create an autonomous work of art, absolute and sealed off from the world around it, is bound to fail.

A second aesthetic paradigm is provided by Krug's musing on the meaning of Ember's art of translation:

> This process entailed a prodigious amount of labour, for the necessity of which no real reason could be given. It was as if someone, having seen a certain oak tree (further called Individual T) growing in a certain land and casting its own unique shadow on the green and brown ground, had proceeded to erect in his garden a prodigiously intricate piece of machinery which in itself was as unlike that or any other tree as the translator's inspiration and language were unlike those of the original au-

> thor, but which, by means of ingenious combinations of parts, light effects, breeze-engendering engines, would, when completed, cast a shadow exactly similar to that of Individual T.

Bend Sinister expresses a particularly ambivalent attitude toward translation. On one hand, Ember is not a literary hack, producing word-for-word literal equivalents, but a sensitive and accomplished scholar dedicated to communicating the value and effect of important works of art. On the other hand, since those works already exist, attempting to reproduce them exactly is a process "for the necessity of which no real reason could be given." A perfect translation, in Krug's interpretation, would conform in every respect except in the material it is made of to its original; thus the ideal translator would suppress every spark of inspiration or imagination in himself, in order not to distort the shadow of Individual T: "From a practical point of view, such a waste of time and material . . . was almost criminally absurd, since the greatest masterpiece of imitation presupposed a voluntary limitation of thought, in submission to another man's genius." Translation thus becomes a high art of self-suppression, a brilliant but ultimately mechanical act of reproduction.

This is immediately parodied on the next page, when Krug glances out the window and sees two organ-grinders, who effectively cancel each other out: " 'Never in my life,' said Krug, 'have I seen *two* organ-grinders in the same back yard at the same time. . . . An organ-grinder is the very emblem of oneness. But here we have an absurd duality.' " The doubling does not multiply the pleasure one might take in a single organ-grinder; rather, it reduces both to absurdity. The fact that the reader recognizes that they are secret policemen, and that their appearance signals Ember's imminent arrest, adds a malign note to the image. The value of translation is even more deeply questioned when Krug asks himself whether "this suicidal limitation and submission" is only "an exaggerated and spiritualized replica of Paduk's writing machine." The padograph, an invention of the Toad's father, reproduced its owner's handwriting "with repellent perfection"; highly effective in practical jokes and petty forgery, it nevertheless had limited appeal, since "a close examination of the script never failed to reveal the presence of a mechanical medium." This apparently innocuous device also has a sinister dimension, since it reflects the Toad's Ekwilist Party's commitment to rigid, mechanical conformity and to the stamping out of individual differences. The padograph is a symbol "of the fact that a mechanical device can reproduce personality, and that Quality is merely the distribution aspect of Quantity." So far as these two images reflect back on translation, they raise the serious paradox of whether a perfect translation could be considered a work of art at all.

Thus developed, the translation model represents an aesthetic paradigm at the opposite end of the spectrum from the Shakespeare paradigm. Rather than an autonomous and reflexive sphere, the perfect "translation" would be purely mimetic. Rather than being completely self-generating, the translation is completely self-canceling; the first paradigm turns the mirror in on itself, the second turns it outward. And as we have seen, the novel casts serious doubt on the validity and effectiveness of both these kinds of art, both by embodying and parodying them, and by drawing analogies to elements of the book's disturbing political world.

Having identified these two aesthetic paradigms, we may focus on a third by returning to the riddle of the book's narrator. Just as many readers have identified the narrator with Nabokov, a number have wondered whether he is Krug himself: "Who is the 'I' who steps from time to time between the reader and the novel? Is it Mr. Nabokov, or is it the insane Krug himself, breaking from the third person into the first, as children do when they write stories?" [V. S. Naipaul, "New Novels," *New Statesman* 59 (1960):461]. The evidence is presumably the degree to which the narrative style reflects the process of Krug's consciousness, particularly in such passages as chapter 9, when Krug directly addresses the memory of his dead wife. But the theory does not sufficiently account for the passages that reflect other characters' points of view, such as Ember's memories of Olga, or for such complicated transitions as this:

> Krug, semi-intentionally, keeps out of reach. He is a difficult person. Describe the bedroom. Allude to Ember's bright brown eyes. Hot punch and a touch of fever. His strong shining blue-veined nose and the bracelet on his hairy wrist. Say something. Ask about David. Relate the horror of those rehearsals.

While it is clearly the narrator's voice that begins this passage, self-consciously summoning up his narrative strategy, it is Ember, uncomfortable in his first meeting with Krug since Olga's death and struggling to maintain small talk, who addresses himself in the last three sentences. Of course it could be argued that this is Krug-as-narrator imagining what Ember would have been thinking, but there is no evidence to support the hypothesis, and it would be equally logical to presume that the entire scene represents what a third character—Maximov, say—might imagine what Krug and Ember would say and think. Surely it is more reasonable to see the narrator as an independently drawn figure who is fully able to intrude on his characters' thoughts.

But beyond the issue of the narrator's identity lies the more puzzling question of his attitude toward the story he tells. He is so accomplished a shape-shifter, indeed, that it might be thought impossible to identify any consistent narrative stance. The presentation of some scenes of action and dialogue seems entirely objective, the narrator acting simply to record external action or an individual character's musing or memory. In many other places, of course, he is highly self-conscious about his ability to manipulate and direct our sense of Krug's story, pointing out tense shifts ("to switch into a lower past-gear"), talking to himself ("Now he found himself running / by night, ugly? Yah, by night, folks / down something that looked like a railway track"), parodying the clichés of literary technique:

> "Eez eet zee verity," said Beuret, suddenly shifting to English, which he knew Krug understood, and speaking it like a Frenchman in an English book, "eez eet zee verity zat, as I have been informed by zee reliably sources, zee disposed *chef* of the state has been captured together with a couple of other blokes (when the author gets bored by the process—or forgets)."

A reader might conclude that this shuttling between the objective and the subjective represents an alternation between the translation paradigm and the Shakespeare paradigm, and that the narrator's aesthetic constitutes an effective balance between the two. Yet it is possible to identify certain patterns in the novel which cast the narrator in quite a different light.

The narrative technique of *Bend Sinister* is so idiosyncratic, so self-consciously artificial, as to allow us to distinguish between the stylistic surface and the events that lie beyond or beneath that surface. In fact, reading the first half of the novel, I think we have the sense that the dramatic action of Krug's life is fundamentally realistic or mimetic of real experience. The instability of style and structure is a function not of the plot but of the particular way in which that plot is revealed: the narrator is like an eccentric film editor who takes a broadly realistic film and, through the use of assorted filters, cutting, and overlapping, creates a work of cinematic surrealism. Krug's world is not our world, exactly, but it conforms to essentially the same laws of physics, cause and effect, time, and character. If we compare *Bend Sinister* to *Invitation to a Beheading* (1938), we see that the earlier novel is a metaphysical fable set in a prison whose floor plan continually rearranges itself, whose inhabitants are equally abstract and malleable, often melting into or out of existence, and whose clocks measure time in particularly gnomic ways. By contrast, Krug's world feels essentially solid, its central characters more human, its history uncomfortably close to our own. Reading the first ten chapters, we follow the central events of Krug's life—his reaction to Olga's death, his refusal to involve himself in university politics, his visit to the Maximovs, his conversation with Ember—in clear chronology; the narrator chooses to tell his story eccentrically, but he does not appear to control or manipulate the facts of Krug's experience as Krug himself would see them.

The one notable exception to this pattern in the early chapters is the passage introducing Krug's dream at the beginning of chapter 5. This passage is the first to suggest that Krug does not have the moral and psychological independence he prizes; to account for the details of his dream, the narrator reveals "the presence of someone in the know":

> A nameless, mysterious genius who took advantage of the dream to convey his own peculiar code message which has nothing to do with school days or indeed with any aspect of Krug's physical existence, but which links him up somehow with an unfathomable mode of being, perhaps terrible, perhaps blissful, perhaps neither, a kind of transcendental madness which lurks behind the corner of consciousness and which cannot be defined more accurately than this, no matter how Krug strains his brain.

This strikes a mysterious, powerfully resonant note that clearly prefigures the novel's ending, and as previously noted, the introduction links this shadowy figure with the author himself. Yet within the developing context of the novel, the reference remains undefined, an intuition of pattern or meaning which neither Krug nor—at least on first reading—the reader can identify with any precision. And throughout the next few chapters the illusion persists that Krug leads an autonomous existence, independent of the stylistic embellishments the narrator makes in telling his story.

The pattern is abruptly broken in chapter 11, which—not incidentally—recounts Krug's first meeting with the Toad. Theatrical imagery is reintroduced in the first sentence, and as the scene progresses it grows steadily more artificial and surreal. Time begins to collapse in on itself, and the action develops a dreamlike or hallucinatory quality, as when two masked men play hide-and-seek with a vial of sulfuric acid, or when Krug enters a room in which a team of doctors is monitoring the Toad's heartbeat, in a scene straight from *The Wizard of Oz*. Most notably, the narrator begins to assume a much more openly active role, not merely filtering and embroidering the action as he reports it, but self-consciously entering into and controlling it. Paduk is standing at the window with "his back to the reader," and he is described in minute and realistic detail:

> Physically the Toad had hardly changed except that every particle of his visible organism had been expanded and roughened. On the top of his bumpy, bluish, shaven head a patch of hair was neatly brushed and parted. His blotched complexion was worse than ever. . . . His upper lip was disfigured by a scar. A bit of porous plaster adhered to the side of his chin, and a still larger bit, with a soiled corner turned back and a pad of cotton awry, could be seen in the fold of his neck just above the stiff collar of his semi-military coat.

The attention to physical detail rivals that of a naturalistic novel; the narrator seems completely subordinate to his subject, concerned only to provide as clear and accurate a portrait as possible. Then, abruptly:

> In a word, he was a little too repulsive to be credible, and so let us ring the bell (held by a bronze eagle) and have him beautified by a mortician. Now the skin is thoroughly cleansed and has assumed a smooth marchpane colour. A glossy wig with auburn and blond tresses artistically intermixed covers his head. Pink paint has dealt with the unseemly scar. Indeed, it would be an admirable face, were we able to close his eyes for him. But no matter what pressure we exert upon the lids, they snap open again. I never noticed his eyes, or else his eyes have changed.

This is a dazzling moment, and its consequences are considerable. We are asked to accept an entirely different kind of characterization: the character is at one moment apparently realistically perceived, flawed but autonomous, and at the next moment he is a corpse needing a mortician's beautification, and then a dummy with mechanical eyes. The final sentence seems to associate the paragraph with Krug's perspective, and yet the imagination that decides to change the rules, to shift the character's appearance in midstream, must be not Krug's but the narrator's. In a world in which such arbitrary rearrangements are possible, the realist convention which has been sustained throughout the novel is shown to be an illusion subject to the narrator's whim.

The scene that follows seems to revert to the realist model, objectively reporting the dialogue between Krug and Paduk and its interruptions by telephone, letter, and parrot. The conversation is clearly motivated, idiomatic, and "in character." But again, four pages later, there is a sudden break:

"No, it did not go on quite like that. In the first place Paduk was silent during most of the interview. What he did say amounted to a few curt platitudes. To be sure, he did do some drumming on the desk (they all drum) and Krug retaliated with some of his own drumming but otherwise neither showed nervousness." There follows an entirely different version of the meeting, in which Krug is offered the chance to redeem himself by agreeing to become university president. Schaeffer comments: "The second version is the most realistic; the first, the most entertaining. Which should be chosen? By presenting both versions, the author forces the reader to momentarily experience the power of the artist." This is an interesting theory, but it is not persuasive. Surely the point is that we *have* no choice in the matter: we are asked to believe a detailed and credible account, and then are peremptorily told that this account is false and that we must accept another. Rather than being invited to experience the power of the artist, we are virtually bullied by that power, which has been embodied in a narrator entirely free to manipulate the plot of his narrative. As I have said, this represents a considerable change from the dominant convention of the earlier chapters, and as if to emphasize this change, the narrator introduces the issue of perspective:

> Photographed from above, they would have come out in Chinese perspective, doll-like, a little limp but possibly with a hard wooden core under their plausible clothes—one slumped at his desk in a shaft of grey light, the other seated sideways to the desk, legs crossed, the toe of the upper foot moving up and down—and the secret spectator (some anthropomorphic deity, for example) surely would be amused by the shape of human heads seen from above.

From his superior vantage point, the narrator can regard his characters patronizingly, as no longer autonomous but shrunken and doll-like. Similarly, he can direct them in how to play their roles: "It is not a difficult part but still the actor must be careful not to overdo what Graaf somewhere calls 'villainous deliberation.' " The scene continues as if in the earlier convention, but having been alerted to the possibility of the narrator's intervention, we cannot read it with quite the same confidence, and at the end of the interview the narrator again emerges as the controlling figure. Paduk's last speech concludes in suspiciously stagy diction: "Nay, do not speak. . . . Prithee, go." And the narrator proceeds to drain Krug's departure of its realism by referring to the characters as actors and giving them direction:

> The seedy tyrant or the president of the State, or the dictator, or whoever he was—the man Paduk in a word, the Toad in another—did hand my favourite character a mysterious batch of neatly typed pages. The actor playing the recipient should be taught not to look at his hand while he takes the papers *very slowly* (keeping those lateral lower-jaw muscles in movement, please) but to stare straight at the giver: in short, look at the giver first, *then* lower your eyes to the gift.

Throughout this chapter, then, the narrator is for the first time seen to be able to control the novel's world, not simply at the level of style, but also by actual manipulation of character and event.

It seems significant that this sort of manipulation should first become evident in Krug's initial encounter with the Toad, and indeed that his world should become more and more self-evidently artificial as he is drawn more tightly into the dictator's web. In each successive encounter with the Toad or his influence, the narrative stability of time, space, and character is progressively undermined. Thus, for example, Krug's visit to the Toad's agent Peter Quist in a remote corner of the city, reached only by an extended bus ride, ends with his being shown to a secret underground passage that soon deposits him neatly in his own back yard. Similarly artificial is his second encounter with the Toad, who acts the part of a fellow prisoner in an enormous wig, spouting ludicrous dialogue ("My face will be turned to the wall. To the wall my face will be turned. Turned to the wall for ever and ever my face will be"), quoting Schiller and singing Brunnhilde's refrain ("Ho-yo-to-ho! Ho-yo-to-ho!"). The dictator appears to have become another of the narrator's actors, and the serious political world he represents seems—at least for a moment—to descend into vaudeville. Part of the point is simply the degree to which Krug's confident assumptions about the world are shattered ("The nightmare may get out of control"). Perhaps even more important, it is possible to draw a parallel between the brutal totalitarianism of the Toad and the equally authoritarian, if less violent, domination over the novel by its narrator. Not that the narrator is sympathetic to the Toad's regime; although I do not think there is much evidence for speculation about the narrator's motives, his treatment of the country's regime and its ruler is scathing. But simply considered as an exercise of power, his manipulation of the novel's characters and action is strongly parallel to the Toad's, and thus it is striking that they are introduced at precisely the same point in the book's development.

The narrator, in short, represents a third aesthetic paradigm in *Bend*

Sinister. As opposed to the Shakespeare paradigm, the artist who attempts to create a world of pure imagination entirely autonomous of the world beyond it, and the translation paradigm, the artist who attempts to create a duplicate world entirely faithful to the world beyond it, the narrator attempts to superimpose an image of his own making onto the world, thus actually changing the nature of reality by force of will. And for most of the novel, this notion of art seems entirely successful; as in chapter 11, where we are forced to believe one version of events and then to reject it for another, throughout the second half of the book we accept whatever image of experience the narrator chooses to present, however distorted it may be. But as with the first two paradigms, Nabokov presents us with an embodiment of the third that serves to undermine it; in a brilliantly inventive effect, that embodiment is the ending of the novel itself.

Although the final chapter is often discussed as though it presented a single extraordinary manifestation of deus ex machina, the narrator in fact makes two intrusive appearances. In the first, Krug is awakening in his prison cell and about to remember the grotesque circumstances of his son's death:

> It was at that moment, just after Krug had fallen through the bottom of a confused dream and sat up on the straw with a gasp—and just before his reality, his remembered hideous misfortune could pounce upon him—it was then that I felt a pang of pity for Adam and slid towards him along an inclined beam of pale light—causing instantaneous madness, but at least saving him from the senseless agony of his logical fate.

In a single stroke the narrator relieves Krug of the unbearable burden of consciousness, and at the same moment removes his last vestiges of autonomy. However benevolent his motives, the narrator's action is as authoritarian and as absolute as the regime Krug has struggled to resist. The introduction explains the nature of the madness: "Krug . . . understands that he is in good hands: nothing on earth really matters, there is nothing to fear, and death is but a question of style, a mere literary device, a musical resolution." A number of critics have tended to project this into an aesthetic manifesto; Julia Bader, for instance, writes: "Death is disinfected of its horror by being rendered as a problem of fictional representation. . . . 'Death' is 'a question of style' in the sense that it is a problem of description, of representation, of conveying an abstract problem in terms of verbal play and the rotation of images. . . . The solace of language, literature, and allusive texture is a crucial contrast to the restrictive horror of Paduk's regime." But surely it is important to recognize that the notion that death is only a question of style is presented not as an abstract truth but as the manifestation of Krug's madness. Within the narrow boundaries of the work of art, death is of course a mere literary device, and Krug's realization that because he is a literary character he has nothing to fear is a sort of truism. But the fact that this realization comes so soon after we have watched David Krug die in such a particularly horrifying way, and in a world where there is everything to fear, suggests that the narrator's aesthetic solution is effective only in an essentially limited sense. If "the main theme of *Bend Sinister* . . . is the beating of Krug's loving heart, the torture an intense tenderness is subject to," then in freeing Krug of his memory and his anguish—in short, of his ties to life—the narrator has also deprived him of that which gave his life its meaning. The narrator's assertion of control over Krug's life is disturbing both because of the profound loss it represents for Krug, and because we recognize that such instant salvation from suffering is not available to us. For some critics the narrator's self-assertion is reassuring:

> The techniques of self-declared artifice prevent us from identifying with Adam Krug and his world; we have no illusions that such an "invented habitus" is continuous with our own reality. Instead, we share the author's superior vantage point, and are grateful to exist beyond the confines of his created universe.
>
> (Ellen Pifer, *Nabokov and the Novel*)

Such complacency ignores the degree to which Krug's world is uncomfortably like our own, and also the paradoxical implications of the narrator's authoritarian response to the problems of cruelty and pain. Beyond the protective confines of Krug's "blessed madness," the nightmare continues.

The narrator's second major intrusion in the final chapter takes place a few pages later. The mad Krug is taken to a climactic meeting with the Toad and, believing himself back in the schoolyard of his childhood, leads an attack on him, for which he is fired on by the guards:

> He saw the Toad crouching at the foot of the wall, shaking, dissolving, speeding up his shrill incantations, protecting his dimming face with his transparent arm, and Krug ran towards him, and just a fraction of an instant before another and better bullet hit him, he shouted again: You, you—and the wall vanished, like a rapidly withdrawn slide, and I stretched myself and got up from among the chaos of written and rewritten pages, to

> investigate the sudden twang that something had made in striking the wire netting of my window.

It is a masterstroke of inventiveness for the narrator to emerge so openly and unexpectedly, and yet Nabokov has been roundly criticized for the way it seems to trivialize the serious concerns of the rest of the novel:

> The thing has the dimensions of a fantasy seen through the small end of a telescope. Krug, the observer, is real, but not Paduk, not his minions, not his crimes and his victims, not the whole panorama of his evil state. Not even Krug's bereavements, his tears, his fears. . . . And when Nabokov himself steps in deliberately at the end, like the puppetmaster, and draws up his strings and removes Krug, why then the disillusion is complete. Brilliant, brilliant, but after all it was not real, he was not hurt, we need not be concerned, there is the puppet hanging, and here is the master himself, large as life, smiling at us.
>
> (Nathan L. Rothman, "Puppet Under Tyrant," *Saturday Review of Literature* 30, no. 31, 2 August 1947, 33.)

Similarly, Lucy Maddox sees the book as painting itself into a corner:

> Having depicted a brutal police state that is reminiscent of actual totalitarian regimes of the recent past . . . and having worked strongly and deliberately on the reader's sympathies in describing the atrocities committed by the rulers of that state, Nabokov then dismisses the whole sinister business as a fiction. The difficulty, of course, is that real dictatorships are not plays on words or absurd mirages that will go away when we stop thinking about them. By denying that his novel can have any social or political import, Nabokov has also had to deny it any lasting value as art.
>
> (*Nabokov's Novels in English*)

While I agree entirely with the problem she sets out, it would seem here as elsewhere crucial to distinguish between the narrator's aesthetic and Nabokov's. The narrator's aesthetic coup, however logically sufficient, is deeply dissatisfying emotionally, given the degree to which the novel's events have encouraged us to feel about its characters. As we have seen, the history of Krug's country is enough like our own to provoke considerable empathy, and we are moved by the fates of David, the Maximovs, and Ember because they closely parallel tragedies we have ourselves experienced. Even the more artificial second half of the novel is full of realistically conceived examples of suffering ("Mariette sat with closed eyes, in a rigid faint, bleeding gently"). Although we feel relief at Krug's rescue, we also feel cheated. The narrator's attempt to resolve these complex issues by dismissing them and asserting the artificiality of the characters in "the chaos of written and rewritten pages" feels reductive and finally ineffective. It is in some ways analogous to the grotesque film Krug is forced to watch of David's death, which intercuts the horrible filmed record of the boy's torture with unspeakably arch captions ("A Night Lawn Party"); the purpose of the captions is to frame the action "artistically" and thus make it more palatable, even entertaining, but their effect in practice is to accentuate the anguish and make it even more unbearable. The narrator himself admits that "the immortality I had conferred on the poor fellow was a slippery sophism, a play upon words"; in fact his attempt to impose an aesthetic solution on the reality of Krug's life is profoundly unsatisfying, and suggests considerable skepticism—on Nabokov's part—about the power of art to respond to the irrefutable reality of pain.

Some readers might object here that to insist on a substantial distinction between Nabokov and the narrator is problematic, given the degree to which teasing correspondences between them are insinuated. If we are meant to differentiate the narrator's aesthetic stance from the author's, why is the narrator an autocratic, polyglot, pattern-obsessed writer? But this is precisely the point: Nabokov *intends* to implicate himself in the narrator's failure to assert persuasively the priority of life over art. To some extent the narrator is Nabokov's representative in the novel, and *Bend Sinister* is his clearest acknowledgment of the limitations that beset all artists in attempting to respond meaningfully to human predicaments, political or otherwise. Eventually, all the finely distinguished levels of reality, along with all the characters, are collapsed into Nabokov, who still is left with the problem of how to live in a world from which escape is not possible. To say that the narrator, or Nabokov, welcomes Krug back into his bosom can, on the one hand, sound like the aesthetic escapism it has often been taken for; on the other hand, one might say that it is Nabokov's way of acknowledging that Krug's problems are *his* problems, that the terrors of Krug's existence are a metamorphosed representation of the problems that the novelist faces in the world, for which aesthetic solutions are inadequate.

And yet the novel's vision of the power of art is not altogether bleak. If on one level the narrator is representative of all artists, on another he is a character whose own existence is circumscribed by this novel, which is in turn controlled by Nabokov. Following the narrator's powerful intrusion, in the final page of the novel he unwittingly presents considerable evidence that he is not in fact omnipotent, but limited and fallible: he writes with considerable difficulty ("the chaos of written and rewritten pages," "my aching temples"), he has trouble sleeping ("the sleeping tablets"), he is disoriented in his surroundings ("Some tower clock which I could never exactly locate, which, in fact, I never heard in the daytime, struck twice"), his perceptions are imprecise ("the shadow of an arm was combing invisible hair; or perhaps it was a movement of branches"). These details displace the narrator from the center of his narrative; the irony allows us to perceive his function in the structure of the novel as controlled by its author. *Bend Sinister* presents no examples of art which can resist the terrible power of the Toad, and may suggest that such artistic power is impossible; on the other hand, if at the end of the novel we are led to reject the three paradigms, it is the tragic power of the novel itself that has led us this far and caused us to react as we do. The book's intermittently empathetic treatment of its characters, its mysterious and powerful texture of details, and its ability to leave us dissatisfied with the manipulative ending, all testify to art's potency beyond the pattern imposed by the narrator.

Significantly, Nabokov embodies this notion in an appropriate image in the final scene. The narrator is enclosed in the inner sanctum of his study; all the objects in this "comparative paradise," he tells us, "looked with perfect submission into my eyes." But outside not everything is so submissive. Just as he is engaged in his most imperious act of writing Krug out of existence, he is interrupted by a noise at the window and goes to investigate. There he discovers a "big moth" which he does not identify (a last clue that he is not to be simplistically identified with Nabokov), but which we recognize as a hawkmoth, which Krug associates with Olga earlier in the novel. The hawkmoth is an emblem of Krug's loving memory, of those particularly human qualities that make him matter to us and which the narrator would seek to control; here it is attracted momentarily to the narrator's light but then disappears back into darkness and freedom. The novel ends: "Twang. A good night for mothing." The narrator has not caught the moth, but he acknowledges his desire to do so; the moth is free but dangerously drawn to the light. That subtle tension outstrips the absoluteness of the three aesthetic paradigms, and in it lies all the mysterious power of Nabokov's art.

Chronology

1899 Vladimir Vladimirovich Nabokov is born on April 23 in St. Petersburg to the eminent jurist Vladimir Dmitrievich Nabokov and his wife, Elena Ivanovna. In 1906 Nabokov begins his lifelong affair with lepidoptery, first collecting butterflies at Vyra, the Nabokov family summer estate. Until 1911, Nabokov is educated at home by private tutors; from 1911 to 1917, he attends a progressive school in St. Petersburg. In 1916 Nabokov publishes privately his first book of poetry, a work he later disowns.

1919 The Nabokov family escapes Russia, settling eventually in Berlin. Vladimir Nabokov enters Trinity College, Cambridge, on a scholarship.

1922 Vladimir Dmitrievich is assassinated by right-wing Russian terrorists at a political rally in Berlin. Nabokov graduates from Cambridge with Honors in French and Russian literature, then joins his family in Berlin.

1922–37 Nabokov marries Vera Evseevna Slonim in 1925. Under the pen name of "Sirin" he publishes novels, short stories, poems, and chess problems in the émigré press of Berlin and Paris. The novels written during this period are *Mary* (1926), *King, Queen, Knave* (1928), *The Defense* (1929–30), *The Eye* (1930), *Glory* (1932), *Camera Obscura* (1932), *Despair* (1934), and *Invitation to a Beheading* (1935–36). Besides his literary activities, Nabokov helps support his family by teaching French, tennis, and boxing.

1934 Son Dmitri is born.

1937 Fleeing the Nazis, the Nabokovs move to Paris where Nabokov writes *The Gift* (1937–38). His English translation of *Despair* is published in London.

1940–44 With the outbreak of World War II, the Nabokovs leave France for America, sailing shortly before the fall of Paris. Nabokov teaches at Wellesley College (1941–48) and works as a Fellow of the Museum of Comparative Zoology at Harvard University (1942–48). In 1941, he publishes *The Real Life of Sebastian Knight,* his first novel written in English.

1945 Becomes an American citizen.

1947 *Bend Sinister* published in New York.

1948 Appointed Professor of Russian and European Literature at Cornell University, a position he holds until 1959.

1951 Autobiography *Conclusive Evidence* (later to be revised as *Speak, Memory*) is published in New York.

1955 Unable to find an American publisher, Nabokov allows the Olympia Press, a Parisian publishing house specializing in pornography, to bring out *Lolita.*

1956–59 As the first reviews of *Lolita* appear, a controversy erupts over whether it is pornographic literature. In 1957, excerpts from it appear in the *Anchor Review. Pnin* published. The following year, *Lolita* is published in America and quickly becomes a bestseller. Supported by the royalties from American publication, Nabokov retires from teaching. He and Vera move to Montreux, Switzerland.

1962 *Pale Fire.*

1964 Controversial annotated translation of Pushkin's *Eugene Onegin* is published and is attacked by Edmund Wilson in *The New York Review of Books,* beginning a literary feud which eventually ends their friendship.

1965 *Despair* published, thus finishing the project of "re-Englishing," alone or with collaborators, the early Russian novels *Invitation to a Beheading* (1959), *The Gift* (1963), and *The Defense* (1964).

1966 *Speak, Memory,* the revised autobiography, is published.

1969 *Ada.*

1972 *Transparent Things.*

1973 *A Russian Beauty and Other Stories.*

1974 *Look at the Harlequins!*

1977 Dies on July 2 in Montreux while working on a novel provisionally entitled *The Original of Laura.*

1986 *The Enchanter* published, as translated by Nabokov's son Dmitri from the 1939 manuscript.

Contributors

HAROLD BLOOM, Sterling Professor of the Humanities at Yale University, is the author of *The Anxiety of Influence, Poetry and Repression,* and many other volumes of literary criticism. His forthcoming study, *Freud: Transference and Authority*, attempts a full-scale reading of all of Freud's major writings. A MacArthur Prize Fellow, he is general editor of five series of literary criticism published by Chelsea House. During 1987–88 he was appointed Charles Eliot Norton Professor of Poetry at Harvard University.

QUENTIN ANDERSON is Professor of English at Columbia University. His books include *The American Henry James* and *The Imperial Self.*

JULIA BADER teaches English at the University of California at Berkeley. She is the author of *Crystal Land: Artifice in Nabokov's English Novels.*

ELIZABETH W. BRUSS was Professor of English at Amherst College and is the author of *Autobiographical Acts* and *Beautiful Theories.*

ELLEN PIFER teaches English at the University of Delaware and is the author of *Nabokov and the Novel.*

DALE E. PETERSON is Associate Professor of English and Russian at Amherst College and the author of *The Clement Vision: Poetic Realism in Turgenev and James.*

ALVIN B. KERNAN is A. W. Mellon Professor of Humanities at Princeton University and the author, most recently, of *The Imaginary Library: An Essay on Literature and Society.*

THOMAS R. FROSCH is Professor of English at Queens College of the City University of New York. He is the author of *The Awakening of Albion: The Renovation of the Body in the Poetry of William Blake* and *Plum Gut,* a book of verse.

LUCY MADDOX is Associate Professor of English at Georgetown University and the author of *Nabokov's Novels in English.*

DAVID RAMPTON is the author of *Nabokov: A Critical Study of the Novels.*

ROBERT ALTER is Professor of Hebrew and Comparative Literature at the University of California at Berkeley. His books include *Partial Magic: The Novel as a Self-Conscious Genre* and *Motives for Fiction.*

GARRETT STEWART is Professor of English at the University of California at Santa Barbara and the author of *Dickens and the Trials of the Imagination* and *Death Sentences: Styles of Dying in British Fiction.*

EDMUND WHITE has taught writing at The Johns Hopkins University, Columbia University, and Yale University. He is the author of the novels *Caracole, Forgetting Elena,* and *Nocturnes for the King of Naples.*

D. BARTON JOHNSON is Professor of Russian at the University of California at Santa Barbara and the author of *Transformations and Their Use in the Resolution of Syntactic Homomorphy, Prepositional of Constructions in Contemporary Standard Russian,* and *Worlds in Regression: Some Novels of Vladimir Nabokov.*

MICHAEL SEIDEL is Professor of English at Columbia University and the author of *Exile and the Narrative Imagination* and *The Satiric Inheritance, Rabelais to Sterne.*

DAVID WALKER is Associate Professor of English at Oberlin College and the author of *The Transparent Lyric: Reading and Meaning in the Poetry of Stevens and Williams.*

Bibliography

Aldridge, A. Owen. "*Lolita* and *Les Liaisons Dangereuses.*" *Wisconsin Studies in Contemporary Literature* 2 (1961): 20–26.

Alter, Robert. "Nabokov's Game of Worlds." In *Partial Magic: The Novel as a Self-Conscious Genre,* 180–217. Berkeley: University of California Press, 1975.

Appel, Alfred, Jr. *Nabokov's Dark Cinema.* New York: Oxford University Press, 1974.

Appel, Alfred, Jr., and Newman, Charles, eds. "*Nabokov: Criticism, Reminiscences, Translations and Tributes.* New York: Simon & Schuster, 1970. Originally published in *Tri-quarterly* 17 (1970).

L'Arc 24 (1964). Special Vladimir Nabokov issue.

Bader, Julia. *Crystal Land: Artifice in Nabokov's English Novels.* Berkeley: University of California Press, 1972.

Bruss, Elizabeth. *Autobiographical Acts: The Changing Situation of a Literary Genre.* Baltimore: The Johns Hopkins University Press, 1976.

Buell, Lawrence. "Observer-Hero Narrative." *Texas Studies in Literature and Language* 21 (1979): 93–111.

Burgess, Anthony. "Pushkin and Kinbote." *Encounter* 24, no. 5 (May 1965): 74–78.

Butler, Diane. "*Lolita* Lepidoptera." In *New World Writing,* vol. 16, edited by Stewart Richardson and Corlies M. Smith, 58–84. New York: Lippincott, 1960.

Cancogni, Annapaola. " 'My Sister, Do You Still Recall?': Chateaubriand/ Nabokov." *Comparative Literature* 35, no. 2 (1983): 140–66.

Clancy, Laurie. *The Novels of Vladimir Nabokov.* London: Macmillan, 1984.

Couturier, Maurice. *Nabokov.* Lausanne: Éditions l'Age d'Homme, 1979.

Delta, no. 17 (1983). Special Vladimir Nabokov issue.

Dembo, L. S., ed. *Nabokov: The Man and His Work.* Madison: University of Wisconsin Press, 1967. First published in *Wisconsin Studies in Contemporary Literature* 8 (1967). Special Vladimir Nabokov issue.

Dillard, R. H. W. "Not Text, but Texture: The Novels of Vladimir Nabokov." In *The Sounder Few,* 139–91. Athens: University of Georgia Press, 1971.

Dupee, F. W. "The Coming of Nabokov." In *The King of the Cats,* 117–41. New York: Farrar, Straus & Giroux, 1965.

Fiedler, Leslie. *Love and Death in the American Novel,* 325–28, 400. New York: Criterion Books, 1960.

Field, Andrew. *Nabokov: His Life in Art.* Boston: Little, Brown, 1967.

———. *Nabokov: His Life in Part.* New York: Viking Press, 1977.

Fleischauer, John F. "Simultaneity in Nabokov's Prose Style." *Style* 5 (1971): 57–69.

Fowler, Douglas. *Reading Nabokov.* Ithaca: Cornell University Press, 1974.

Gezari, Janet, and Wimsatt, W. K. "Vladimir Nabokov: More Chess Problems and the Novel." *Yale French Studies,* no. 58 (1978): 102–16.

Grabes, H. *Fictitious Biographies: Vladimir Nabokov's English Novels.* Translated by the author and Pamela Gliniars. The Hague: Mouton, 1977.

Grayson, Jane. *Nabokov Translated.* New York: Oxford University Press, 1977.

Harold, Brent. "*Lolita:* Nabokov's Critique of Aloofness." *Papers on Language and Literature* 11 (1975): 71–82.

Hollander, John. "The Perilous Magic of Nymphets." *Partisan Review* 23 (1956): 557–60.

Hyde, C. M. *Vladimir Nabokov: America's Russian Novelist.* New York: Humanities Press, 1979.

Jones, David L. "Dolorès Disparue." *Symposium* 20 (1966): 135–40.

Josipovici, G. D. "*Lolita:* Parody and the Pursuit of Beauty." *Critical Quarterly* 6 (1964): 35–48.

Kazin, Alfred. "A Personal Sense of Time: Nabokov and Other Exiles." In *Bright Book of Life,* 283–317. Boston: Little, Brown, 1973.

Lee, L. L. *Vladimir Nabokov.* Boston: G. K. Hall, 1976.

———. "Vladimir Nabokov's Great Spiral of Being." *Western Humanities Review* 18 (1964): 255–36.

Levine, Robert J. "*Lolita* and the Originality of Style." *Essays in Literature* 4 (1977): 110–21.

Long, Michael. *Marvell, Nabokov: Childhood and Arcadia.* New York: Oxford University Press, 1984.

Maddox, Lucy. *Nabokov's Novels in English.* Athens: University of Georgia Press, 1983.

Mason, Bobbie Ann. *Nabokov's Garden: A Guide to* Ada. Ann Arbor, Mich.: Ardis, 1974.

Megerle, Brenda. "The Tantalization of *Lolita.*" *Studies in the Novel* 11 (1979): 338–48.

Mitchell, Charles. "Mythic Seriousness in *Lolita.*" *Texas Studies in Literature and Language* 5 (1963): 329–43.

Mizener, Arthur. "The Seriousness of Vladimir Nabokov." *The Sewanee Review* 76 (1968): 655–64.

Modern Fiction Studies 25 (1979). Special Vladimir Nabokov issue.

Morton, Donald E. *Vladimir Nabokov.* New York: Ungar, 1974.

Moynahan, Julian. *Vladimir Nabokov.* Minneapolis: University of Minnesota Press, 1971.

Nabokov, Vladimir. *The Annotated Lolita,* edited by Alfred Appel, Jr. New York: McGraw-Hill, 1970.

Naumann, Marina T. *Blue Evenings in Berlin: Nabokov's Short Stories of the 1920's.* New York: New York University Press, 1978.

Packman, David. *Vladimir Nabokov: The Structures of Literary Desire.* Columbia: University of Missouri Press, 1982.

Page, Norman. *Nabokov: The Critical Heritage.* Boston: Routledge & Kegan Paul, 1982.

Pearce, Richard. "Nabokov's Black(Hole) Humor: *Lolita* and *Pale Fire.*" In *The Novel in Motion: An Approach to Modern Fiction,* 66–82. Columbus: Ohio State University Press, 1983.

Pifer, Ellen. *Nabokov and the Novel.* Cambridge: Harvard University Press, 1980.

———. "On Human Freedom and Inhuman Art: Nabokov." *Slavic and East European Journal* 22 (1978): 52–61.

Prioleau, Elizabeth. "Humbert Humbert: *Through the Looking Glass.*" *Twentieth Century Literature* 21 (1975): 428–37.

Proffer, Carl R. *Keys to* Lolita. Bloomington: Indiana University Press, 1968.

———, ed. *A Book of Things about Vladimir Nabokov.* Ann Arbor, Mich.: Ardis, 1974.

Quennell, Peter, ed. *Vladimir Nabokov: A Tribute to His Life, His Work, His World.* London: Weidenfeld, 1979.

Rampton, David. *Vladimir Nabokov: A Critical Study of the Novels.* Cambridge: Cambridge University Press, 1984.

Rivers, J. E., and Nicol, Charles, eds. *Nabokov's Fifth Arc.* Austin: University of Texas Press, 1982.

Rosenblum, Michael. "Finding What the Sailor Has Hidden: Narrative as Patternmaking in *Transparent Things.*" *Contemporary Literature* 19 (1978): 219–32.

Roth, Phyllis A. "In Search of Aesthetic Bliss: A Rereading of *Lolita.*" *College Literature* 2 (1975): 28–49.

———. "The Psychology of the Double in Nabokov's *Pale Fire.*" *Essays in Literature* 11 (1975): 209–29.

———, ed. *Critical Essays on Vladimir Nabokov.* New York: G. K. Hall, 1984.

Rougemont, Denis de. "*Lolita,* or Scandal." In *Love Declared,* translated by Richard Howard, 48–59. New York: Pantheon, 1963.

Rowe, William W. *Nabokov's Deceptive World.* New York: New York University Press, 1971.

———. *Nabokov's Spectral Dimension.* Ann Arbor, Mich.: Ardis, 1981.

Scheid, Mark. "Epistemological Structures in *Lolita.*" *Rice University Studies* 61 (1975): 127–40.

Schultz, N. F. "Characters (Contra Characterization) in the Modern Novel." In *The Theory of the Novel,* edited by J. Halperin, 147–54. New York: Oxford University Press, 1974.

Schuman, Samuel. "*Lolita*—Novel and Screenplay." *College Literature* 5 (1978): 195–204.

Stuart, Dabney. *Nabokov: The Dimensions of Parody.* Baton Rouge: Louisiana State University Press, 1978.

———"*The Real Life of Sebastian Knight*: Angles of Perception." *Modern Language Quarterly* 29 (1968): 312–28.

Tamir-Ghez, Nomi. "The Art of Persuasion in Nabokov's *Lolita.*" *Poetics Today* 1, nos. 1–2 (1979): 65–83.

Tanner, Tony. "On Lexical Playfields (Vladimir Nabokov, Jorge Luis Borges)." In *City of Words,* 33–49. London: Jonathan Cape, 1971.

Trilling, Lionel. "The Last Lover: Vladimir Nabokov's *Lolita*." *Encounter* 11, no. 4 (October 1958): 9–19.

Updike, John. "Grandmaster Nabokov." In *Assorted Prose*, 218–27. London: Deutsch, 1965.

Williams, Robert C. "Memory's Defense: The Real Life of Vladimir Nabokov's Berlin." *Yale Review* 60 (1970): 241–50.

Winston, Matthew. "*Lolita* and the Dangers of Fiction." *Twentieth Century Literature* 21 (1975): 421–27.

Acknowledgments

"Nabokov in Time" by Quentin Anderson from *The New Republic* 154, no. 23 (4 June 1966), © 1966 by The New Republic, Inc. Reprinted by permission of *The New Republic.*

"*Sebastian Knight*: The Oneness of Perception" by Julia Bader from *Crystal Land: Artifice in Nabokov's English Novels* by Julia Bader, © 1972 by the Regents of the University of California. Reprinted by permission of the University of California Press.

"Vladimir Nabokov: Illusions of Reality and Reality of Illusions" by Elizabeth W. Bruss from *Autobiographical Acts: The Changing Situation of a Literary Genre* by Elizabeth W. Bruss, © 1976 by The Johns Hopkins University Press, Baltimore/London. Reprinted by permission.

"Consciousness, Real Life, and Fairy-tale Freedom: *King, Queen, Knave*" by Ellen Pifer from *Nabokov and the Novel* by Ellen Pifer, © 1980 by the President and Fellows of Harvard College. Reprinted by permission of Harvard University Press.

"Nabokov's *Invitation*: Literature as Execution" by Dale E. Peterson from *PMLA* 96, no. 5 (October 1981), © 1981 by the Modern Language Association of America. Reprinted by permission of the Modern Language Association of America.

"Reading Zemblan: The Audience Disappears in Nabokov's *Pale Fire*" by Alvin B. Kernan from *The Imaginary Library: An Essay on Literature and Society* by Alvin B. Kernan, © 1982 by Princeton University Press. Reprinted by permission of Princeton University Press.

"Parody and Authenticity in *Lolita*" by Thomas R. Frosch from *Nabokov's Fifth Avenue*, edited by J. E. Rivers and Charles Nicol, © 1982 by the University of Texas Press. Reprinted by permission of the University of Texas Press.

"*Pnin*" by Lucy Maddox from *Nabokov's Novels in English* by Lucy Maddox, © 1983 by the University of Georgia Press. Reprinted by permission of the University of Georgia Press.

"*The Gift*" by David Rampton from *Vladimir Nabokov: A Critical Study of the Novels* by David Rampton, © 1984 by Cambridge University Press. Reprinted by permission of Cambridge University Press.

"*Ada* or the Perils of Paradise" by Robert Alter from *Motives for Fiction* by Robert Alter. © 1979 by Weidenfeld & Nicolson Ltd., © 1984 by Robert Alter. Reprinted by permission of the author and Weidenfeld and Nicolson Ltd. This essay originally appeared in *Nabokov: A Tribute*, edited by Peter Quennell, © 1979 by George Weidenfeld and Nicolson Ltd. Reprinted by permission.

"Death Bequeathed" by Garrett Stewart from *Death Sentences: Styles of Dying in British Fiction* by Garrett Stewart, © 1984 by the President and Fellows of Harvard College. Reprinted by permission of Harvard University Press.

"Nabokov's Passion" by Edmund White from *The New York Review of Books* (29 March 1984), © 1984 by Nyrev, Inc. Reprinted by permission of *The New York Review of Books.*

"*Look at the Harlequins!:* Dementia's Incestuous Children" (originally entitled: "Dementia's Incestuous Children in *Look at the Harlequins!*") by D. Barton Johnson from *Worlds in Regression: Some Novels of Vladimir Nabokov* by D. Barton Johnson, © 1985 by Ardis Publishers. Reprinted by permission.

"Stereoscope: Nabokov's *Ada* and *Pale Fire* by Michael Seidel from *Exile and the Narrative Imagination* by Michael Seidel, © 1986 by Yale University. Reprinted by permission of Yale University Press.

"The Person from Povlock: *Bend Sinister* and the Problem of Art" by David Walker, © 1986 by David Walker. Published for the first time in this volume. Printed by permission.

Index

Ada, 2, 131, 132, 153, 158, 175–89, 233; Abraham Milton in, 243; Antiterra in, 213, 234, 240, 241, 242, 245; Baron Klim Avidov in, 179, 184, 234; characterization in, 130, 184; death in, 202, 204; exile and nostalgia in, 239–40, 243–49; literary allusions in, 178–79, 180–89, 202; love in, 219; Lucette in, 177, 178, 187; parody in, 176, 179; plot of, 176, 179–80, 184; process of realization in, 184–85; Ronald Oranger in, 189; setting of, 178–79; sex in, 177; sibling incest in, 141, 176–77, 223, 228, 234, 247, 248; style of, 177. *See also* Veen, Van.

Adolphe, 218

Adorno, Theodor, *Minima Moralia,* 214

Adventures of Sherlock Holmes, The (Doyle), 114

Aeneid (Virgil), 254–55, 256, 257

Aksakov, Sergei, 164–65, 179

Alter, Robert, 134, 137, 141; *Partial Magic,* 135

Annotated Lolita, The, 31, 42

Anouilh, Jean, 221

Appel, Alfred, Jr., 31, 35, 42, 137, 139, 141, 158

Aristophanes, 181

Arnold, Matthew, 102

Art: of autobiography, 62–64; and consciousness, 54–56; as entertainment, 222; and fiction, 18, 19, 23, 25, 48, 58, 65–66, 84, 97, 197, 198, 236, 278, 281; freedom in, 163, 188; and immortality, 48, 62, 193, 196, 198; and life, 6, 149, 265; and nature, 182–83; and poetry, 106–7, 124; power of, 278–82; purpose of, 71; and reality, 97, 123, 175, 176, 270, 278; and time, 180, 182, 189; of translation, 270–72, 278; and truth, 98; and women, 187

Ashbery, John, 137

Atala, 218

Austen, Jane, 2, 179, 180

Autobiography, 27–31, 41–42. See also *Speak, Memory*

Bader, Julia, 158, 264, 267, 278

Balanchine, George, 221, 222

Balzac, Honoré de, 8, 180

Bate, Walter Jackson, 135

Baudelaire, Charles, 60, 87, 96, 130, 253; "Invitation au voyage," 183

Beckett, Samuel, 13, 191–92, 193, 194; *Malone Dies,* 192, 196, 197, 205, 206

Belinsky, Vissarion, 88, 159, 174

Bely, Andrei, 163

Bend Sinister, 5, 9, 25, 259–82; aesthetic paradigms in, 265–82; art of

Bend Sinister (*continued*)
translation in, 270–72, 273; David in, 268–69, 272, 279, 280, 281; death in, 193, 203, 204, 206, 208, 265, 268, 278–79; Ember in, 262–63, 268, 269, 270, 271, 272, 274, 277, 280; Mariette in, 269, 281; Maximov in, 266, 268, 272, 274, 280; narrator of, 272–82; Olga in, 268, 269, 272, 274; Paduk in, 11, 261, 262, 263, 271, 275, 276, 278, 280; Peter Quist in, 266, 268, 277; prose style of, 260, 261–62, 264; structure of, 262–64; theme of, 279; Toad in, 262, 266, 268, 271, 274, 275, 277, 279, 282. *See also* Krug, Adam
Benjamin, Walter, 93
Berger, Harry, Jr., 141
Bergson, Henri, 227
Black, Iris (*LATH*), 224–25, 226, 228
Black, Ivor (*LATH*), 224, 225
Blagidze, Mme. de, 224, 225
Blagovo, Anna Ivanovna (Annette, *LATH*), 225, 226, 228
Blake, William, 236
Bloom, Harold, 103, 135, 140
Bloom, Leopold (*Ulysses*), 184
Bloom, Molly (*Ulysses*), 180, 184
Borges, Jorge Luis, 1, 2, 158, 179, 270
Bosch, Hieronymus, 131, 175, 185, 189; *The Garden of Earthly Delights,* 188
Boswell, James, 27, 31, 108, 251
Browning, Robert, 103; "My Last Duchess," 113
Bunin, Ivan, 173, 238
Bunyan, John, 27
Burroughs, William, 13, 198
Bryon, George Gordon, Lord, 30, 138, 139; *Don Juan,* 130, 139, 140, 214, 218; *Manfred,* 30

Cervantes, Miguel de, 66; *Don Quixote,* 135, 140, 141, 216
Chateaubriand, Vicomte de, 180; *René ou les Effets des Passions,* 180–81, 218
Chekhov, Anton, 163, 179; "The Kiss," 210
Chernyshevsky, Nikolay, 11, 157, 158–59, 161, 162, 163, 165, 169, 170, 172
Cincinnatus C. (*Invitation to a Beheading*), 83, 85, 86–99, 132, 134, 141
Conclusive Evidence, 5, 7, 9, 10. See also *Speak, Memory*
Cornell University, 101, 225

Dante, 136, 187, 216
Dar. See *The Gift*
Defense, The, 6; Luzhin in, 9, 11
De Quincey, Thomas, 27, 28
Derzhavin, 171
Despair, 5–6, 8, 10, 12, 129, 136, 141, 264; Ardalion in, 132; Felix in, 6; love in, 246; wordplay in, 139. *See also* Hermann
Dickens, Charles, 179, 180, 207
Dobrolyubov, 159, 160
Dobushinski, M. V., 41
Donne, John, 200
Dostoyevski, Fyodor, 8, 154, 159, 163, 164, 179; "G.—bov i Vopros ob Iskusstve" ("Mr—bov and the Art Question"), 159–61
Dostoevski and Gogol: Remarks on the Theory of Parody (Tynyanov), 219
Dreiser, Theodore, 2
Dreyer (*King, Queen, Knave*), 69–70, 72–80
Dreyer, Martha (*King, Queen, Knave*), 72, 73, 74–80
Druzhinin, 161

Eliot, George, 180
Eliot, T. S., 13, 103, 147, 179; "Ash Wednesday," 133
Emerson, Ralph Waldo, 105

Eroticism, 3, 34, 128, 134, 177, 182–83, 243
Ewart, Gawain, 137
Eye, The, 6, 9, 25

"Fame," 222
Ferdinand ("Spring in Fialta"), 209, 211, 212–13
Field, Andrew, 35, 157, 170, 173, 220; *Nabokov: His Life in Art,* 238
Flaubert, Gustave, 74, 179, 180; *Madame Bovary,* 180, 216–17, 218
Fletcher, Angus, 132
Formalism, Russian, 71, 218
Forster, E. M., 65, 206
Fowler, Douglas, 267
Fowles, John, 140; *The French Lieutenant's Woman,* 137; *The Magus,* 140, 141; *Daniel Martin,* 202, 204
Franklin, Benjamin, epitaph of, 200
Franz (*King, Queen, Knave*), 67–70, 72–73, 74, 76–80
Freud, Sigmund, 1, 2, 3, 8, 32, 112, 131, 132, 181, 188
Frosch, Thomas R., 215
Frost, Robert, 103

Genet, Jean, 13
Gift, The, 8, 9, 10, 11, 157–74, 216, 220, 233; foreword to, 173, 238; Koncheev in, 163, 165, 170, 171; memories of Russia in, 236, 239; mirror substitutes in, 250; portrayal of Germans in, 168–69; portrayal of Russians in, 169–70; Professor Anuchin in, 162; and Russian literature, 157, 159, 160–67; Vasilev in, 161, 162. *See also* Godunov-Cherdyntsev, Fyodor
Giraudoux, Jean, 221
Godunov-Cherdyntsev, Fyodor (*The Gift*), 163, 164, 167, 170, 172, 173, 220, 236, 239; book on Chernyshevsky by, 161–62, 165–66, 171; and Germans, 168, 169
Goethe, 103, 148; *The Sorrows of Young Werther,* 217
Gogol, Nikolay, 3, 28, 163, 166, 169, 170; *Dead Souls,* 16, 151–52, 169
Goldin, Frederick: *The Mirror of Narcissus in the Courtly Love Lyric,* 215
Goldsmith, Oliver, 250
Goncharov, Ivan, *Oblomov,* 164
Gradus, Jacob (*Pale Fire*), 116, 122, 141, 195, 250, 251, 252, 253, 254

Haze, Charlotte (*Lolita*), 2, 35, 45, 129, 133, 215, 216, 217, 218
Haze, Dolores (*Lolita*), 2, 32, 35, 44, 62, 219, 220, 221, 241. See also *Lolita*
Hegel, Georg Wilhelm, 53
Hermann (*Despair*), 5–6, 9, 11, 12, 132, 136, 139, 141, 264; compared to Humbert Humbert, 129–30, 137
Hitchcock, Alfred, 211
Hollander, John, 2, 138
Hopkins, Gerard Manley, 7, 204
Horace, 171, 222
Housman, A. E., 104
Huckleberry Finn (Twain), 140
Humbert, Humbert (*Lolita*), 1, 2, 4, 11, 12, 23–24, 29–35, 39, 40, 42–50, 53; and America, 245; and art, 81, 136; audience of, 59–60, 62, 63; characterization of, 132–33, 135; and Charlotte, 218; compared to Hermann, 129–30, 137; and doubles, 141; and fantasy, 136; and Freudian death drive, 3; and Lolita, 60–61, 127–28, 139, 219, 241, 244; love of games of, 139–40; and memory, 56–57, 59, 175, 249; as narrator, 130–31, 264; and

Humbert, Humbert (*Lolita*) (*continued*)
nymphets, 133; romanticism of, 134, 138, 215, 216
Hunting of the Snark, The (Carroll), 2
Hyde, C. M., 157, 169

Invitation to a Beheading: compared to *Bend Sinister,* 273–74; hero of, 9, 12, 132, 134, 203–4, 206; M'sieur Pierre in, 89, 93–94; as parable, 97; parody in, 141; as political allegory, 83–84, 259; Rodion in, 88, 92. *See also* Cincinnatus C.

Johnson, Samuel, 108, 137, 251
Joyce, James, 1, 8, 13, 139, 179; *Finnegans Wake,* 247; *Ulysses,* 180, 221, 269

Kafka, Franz, 13
Kamera Obskura. See *Laughter in the Dark*
Kant, Immanuel, 28
Karlinsky, Simon, 157, 164, 166; "Nabokov and Chekhov: the Lesser Russian Tradition," 163
Keats, John, 115, 138, 200
Kerenski, Alexander, 230
Khodasevich, Vladislav, 84, 157, 173, 238
Kinbote, Charles (*Pale Fire*), 24, 78, 107–25, 130, 132, 141, 175, 207, 248, 252, 253, 256; as editor of "Pale Fire," 103, 106, 107–8, 111, 117, 136, 196, 205, 250; and Shade, 12, 103, 107, 109, 111, 115, 118, 197, 198, 199, 206; and Zembla, 219, 242, 245–46, 250–51, 254, 255, 257
King, Queen, Knave, 65–81; consciousness in, 73–77, 79–81; detachment from characters in, 65–67, 72, 80; "fairytale freedom" of, 67; murder in, 79; Nabokov's foreword to, 65, 80
Krafft-Ebing, 214
Krug, Adam (*Bend Sinister*), 9, 10, 147, 202, 259, 260, 262–64, 265, 266–81

"Lance," 221
La Rochefoucauld, Duc de, 215
LATH. See *Look at the Harlequins!*
Laughter in the Dark, 6, 7–8, 233; Axel Rex in, 139, 188
Leigh, Annabel (*Lolita*), 32, 128, 132, 133, 134, 244
Lenin, 12, 162, 163, 164, 225, 260
Leskov, Nikolai, 93, 164
Liza (*Pnin*), 143, 144–45, 148, 152, 153, 156
Lolita, 3–4, 6, 9, 19, 28–35, 158, 219, 233, 240–41; and *Ada,* 175, 176, 179, 187, 243–44; anagrams in, 58; as autobiography of Humbert, 29, 31, 37–49, 213; comedy in, 141, 142; and Freud, 3, 32; hereafter in, 220; invention of America in, 240–41, 244–45, 248; Mrs. Holigan in, 31; narration in, 130; parody in, 28, 31, 50, 127–42, 175, 215, 218; Rita in, 33, 34; as a romance, 127, 135, 138, 140, 214, 215, 216; style of, 1–2, 12, 140, 215; vocabulary of, 221, 237; voyeurism in, 31, 34, 35; wordplay in, 139. *See also* Haze, Dolores; Humbert, Humbert
Lomonosov, Mikhailo, 171
Look at the Harlequins!, 206, 213, 220, 223–34; and *Ada,* 234; anagrams in, 226, 227, 228; Dementia in, 223, 228; Dolly von Borg in, 225; Fay Morgan in, 226; incest as theme in, 223, 228, 230, 234; Isabel in, 225, 226, 227, 228; Louise Adamson in, 226–27, 228, 231; Marion Noteboke in, 227; Ninel in, 225, 226; Oksman in,

230, 233; plot of, 224–29; Professor Noteboke in, 227; "reality" as theme in, 232; Stepanovs in, 233. *See also* Vadimovich, Vadim
Love, 2, 215–16, 219, 246, 247, 248
Lunacharsky, Anatoly, 162

McCarthy, Mary, 6, 66, 67, 76
MacLeish, Archibald, 221
Maddox, Lucy, *Nabokov's Novels in English,* 280
Maeterlinck, Maurice, 135
Mailer, Norman, 130
Mallarmé, Stéphane, 132
Malraux, André, 115
Mann, Thomas, 8
Marvell, Andrew, 116; "Bermudas," 189; "The Garden," 181–83, 189
Marx, Karl, 8, 129, 132
Mary, 158, 230, 233
Mashen'ka, 65, 66
Massey, Irving, 138
Maupassant, Guy de, 22, 179
Melville, Herman, 198
Memory, 35–36, 39–41, 46, 50, 58–59, 176, 184–85, 212–13. *See also* Humbert, Humbert, and memory; *Speak, Memory*
Merrill, Robert, 264
Mérrimée, Prosper, *Carmen,* 128, 130, 218
Milton, John, *Paradise Lost,* 104, 183
Murdoch, Iris, 83, 97

Nabokov, Vera, 172, 173, 220, 246, 251
Nabokov, Vladimir, as artist-scientist, 27; compared to Pushkin, 166–67; and English language, 171, 176, 222, 261–62; and exile from Russia, 67, 134, 170, 221–22, 235–38; family of, 52, 53, 55, 63, 236; and Freud, 1, 2, 3, 8, 32, 131, 188; on Germany, 168–69, 170; and lepidoptery, 52, 55, 63, 95; and literary critics, 101, 104, 110–11, 131, 157; and memory, 2, 35–36; on parody, 139, 216; and poetry, 56, 216; and politics, 222, 259–61, 264, 280; pseudonym of, 5, 230, 231; Russia of, 170; and Russian literature, 158, 161–66, 237; as stylist, 1–2; and symbolism, 131; and totalitarianism, 9, 83–84, 92, 259–62, 280; in United States, 52, 54; view of art of, 81, 98, 142, 222; See also *Speak, Memory*
Nabokov's novels: aestheticism in, 13, 84; allegory in, 83–84, 131, 132; America in, 244–45, 249; characters in, 96–97, 145, 183, 213–14, 262; consciousness in, 54–55, 58, 65, 70–81, 84, 90, 91; death in, 191–208, 251, 265, 268, 278–79; exile and nostalgia in, 235–39; "fairytale freedom" in, 67, 76; figures of speech in, 5, 6, 7–8, 178, 184; forewords to, 65, 80, 84, 173, 238; Gnosticism in, 89, 94, 99; hereafter in, 106, 172, 220; and "human interest," 260; imagination and reality in, 175, 184–85; incest in, 223, 228; and language, 13, 138, 221, 261; lepidoptery in, 49, 50, 55–56, 95, 121, 122, 145, 167, 227, 231, 233, 249, 282; and memory, 2, 35–36, 39–41, 46, 50, 184; modernist narrative in, 138; monism in, 25, 75; mythology in, 221; narrators in, 15–16, 18–21, 23, 24, 25, 26, 130, 145, 207, 272–82; naturalism in, 9, 10–11, 12; parables in, 88; parody in, 28, 31, 50, 73, 94, 127–42, 175–77, 215, 216; passion in, 209–22; plots in, 127, 179–80; and politics, 222, 259–61, 264, 280; process of realization in, 184–85; "recastings" of, 83; romantic love in, 138, 215–16, 219; in Russian language, 5, 157, 171; sentimental strain in, 10, 11, 12; social reality in, 66–67,

Nabokov's novels (*continued*) 158–59, 163, 259–61; solipsism in, 45, 46, 84, 104, 115, 117, 118, 122, 123, 125, 135, 137, 265–66; style of, 1–2, 138, 177–78, 261–64; technique of allusion in, 180–81, 215; wordplay in, 139, 182, 226, 260, 261–62. *See also individual works*
Naipaul, V. S., 272
Nina ("Spring in Fialta"), 209, 210, 211
Nostromo (Conrad), 199, 201
Nympholepsy, 3, 32, 46, 127, 133, 213, 214. See also *Lolita*

Odyssey, The, 140
Oedipus, 2
O'Neill, Eugene, 221
Orwell, George H., 84

Pale Fire, 1, 6, 9, 12, 23, 78, 101–25, 130, 136, 141, 158; and *Ada,* 175, 176; allegory of death in, 192, 193, 195–98, 199; Aunt Maud in, 104, 105; Charles Rex in, 256; Conmal in, 115, 116, 197, 200, 208; and exile, 235–36, 239–49; failure to communicate in, 104–7, 111, 124, 125; Gerald Emerald in, 113; mirror images in, 250–52, 253, 255; parody in, 103–4; Professor Botkin in, 196; Queen Disa in, 219, 246, 247; as satire on literature in universities, 101, 104, 110–11; Shade's poem ("Pale Fire") in, 10, 104, 106–9, 118, 119, 120, 136, 192, 250, 255; Sudarg of Bokay in, 141, 250; theme of, 101–2, 250; Zembla in, 103, 107–10, 117–19, 122–24, 196, 197, 240, 242, 246, 247, 250–55, 257. *See also* Gradus, Jacob; Kinbote, Charles; Shade, John
Parody, 17, 163, 216, 218; definition of, 137, 219; and Freud, 1; and poetry, 216; vs. satire, 139. *See also* Nabokov, on parody; Nabokov's novels, parody in; *individual works*
Pascin, Jules, 212
Pergolesi, Giovanni, 222
Person, Hugh (*Transparent Things*), 198–99, 202, 204–5, 207
Petipa, Marius, 222
Pifer, Ellen, 188, 279; *Nabokov and the Novel,* 279
Plato, *Symposium,* 181
Pnin, 9, 12–13, 24, 132, 143–56, 257; and America, 154; Bob Horn in, 144; Chateau in, 143; Eric Wind in, 144, 145; Jack Cockerell in, 144, 149, 150, 151; Joan Clements in, 153; Lake in, 149; Laurence Clements in, 149, 153; Mira Belochkin in, 147–48, 149; Professor Hagen in, 146; Robert Karlovich Horn in, 144; Victor in, 146, 153. *See also* Liza; Pnin, Timofey
Pnin, Timofey (*Pnin*), 24, 143, 144, 148, 150, 152–54, 155–56, 257
Poe, Edgar Allan, 103, 134, 136, 172; "Annabel Lee," 32, 34, 60, 128
Pope, Alexander, 103, 109; *The Dunciad,* 255; *Essay on Man,* 117, 252, 255; *Variorum Dunciad,* 107
Pornography, 2, 177, 179
Poslednie Novesti, 168
Princesse de Clèves, La (La Fayette), 218
Proust, Marcel, 2, 8, 13, 128, 156, 179, 180, 184, 209, 213, 235
Pulcinella (ballet), 222
Pushkin, Aleksandr, 97–98, 136, 155, 163, 164, 166, 170, 214; *Eugene Onegin,* 108, 130, 134, 214, 217, 218; "Exegi monumentum," 171–72, 222; *Journey to Arzrum,* 166–68

"Pushkin, or Verity and Verisimilitude," 97
Pynchon, Thomas, 140; *V,* 140, 141

Quilty, Clare (*Lolita*), 2, 3, 34, 44, 46, 127, 132, 134, 135, 139; and Lolita, 34, 129; murder of, 4, 32, 47, 49, 60, 131, 216, 218

Ray, John, Jr. (*Lolita*), 29, 43, 61, 63, 130, 131
Real Life of Sebastian Knight, The, 5, 9, 10, 15–26, 194, 195; Clare Bishop in, 18, 21; Goodman in, 25; "other woman" motif in, 21–22; parody in, 17, 18, 19, 22; perception and imagination in, 16–17, 23–24; V's narration in, 15–16, 18–21, 23, 24, 25, 26, 145, 207
Realism, 70–71, 75–76, 88, 97, 99
Rimbaud, Arthur, 218; *Mémoire,* 181
Robert, Marthe, 141
Romanticism, 13, 107, 124, 128, 134, 136, 140, 141, 180, 215, 218, 221
Ronsard, Pierre de, 218
Rothman, Nathan L., "Puppet Under Tyrant," 280
Rousseau, Jean-Jacques, 29, 128, 217; *Confessions,* 29
Rowe, W. W.: *Nabokov's Spectral Dimensions,* 172, 220
Russia: and America, 154, 241–43; Bolshevik Revolution in, 2, 224, 237, 238, 241, 261; emigrés from, 66, 67, 83, 154, 170–74, 221, 236–38, 241; literature of, 157, 158–61, 162, 163, 170–74. *See also* Nabokov, Vladimir, exile from Russia

Sartre, Jean-Paul, 222
Schaeffer, Susan Fromberg, 264, 276
Schiller, Johann, 277
Schnitzler, Arthur, 149–50, 156; *The Green Cockatoo,* 149, 150; *Libelei,* 149, 156; *Literature,* 149, 150
Schoenberg, Arnold, 214
Serov, Valentin, 224, 225
Shade, Hazel (*Pale Fire*), 193, 195
Shade, John (*Pale Fire*), 23, 104–25, 193, 250, 251, 257; childhood of, 104–5; death of, 255; on exile, 235; and Kinbote, 12, 107–11, 196, 197, 198, 199, 205, 206, 248, 251, 254; poem of, 10, 103, 106–7, 196, 198, 252
Shade, Sibyl, 106, 108, 116, 121, 253
Shakespeare, William, 173, 242, 265, 269, 270, 272, 273, 278; *Hamlet,* 158, 205, 269; references to, in *Pnin,* 154; *Timon of Athens,* 119, 120; translations of, in *Pale Fire,* 115, 116
Shklovsky, Viktor: "Art as Device," 71; *ostranenie* of, 167
Shostakovich, Dmitri, 154
Sirin. *See* Nabokov, Vladimir
"Slava" ("Fame"), 172
Sorremennye Zapiski, 157
Space, 51, 55–56, 277; and exile, 236, 239, 240; and love, 246; and scientists, 58
Speak, Memory, 17, 28, 31, 35–42, 43, 48–56, 64, 73, 176; childhood recollections in, 36–37, 40, 51–52, 236, 249; index to, 39, 54–55, 56, 63; love for wife in, 246; recollections of Russia in, 235–36, 238–39
Spenser, Edmund, 128, 138, 141
"Spring in Fialta," 8, 209–13, 220
Stalin, Joseph, 154
Stanislavski, Konstantin, 154
Stark, John, 158
Starov, Count Nikifor Nikodimovich (*LATH*), 224, 225, 226, 227, 228, 229, 230, 233, 234
Starov-Blagidze, Lt. Wladimir (*LATH*), 225, 226
Starr, Christopher (*Pnin*), 144, 154
Starr, Louise (*Pnin*), 144, 154

Steiner, George, 138
Stegner, Page, 137
Stendhal, 8
Stephen, J. K., 137
Steppenwolf, Der (Hesse), 169
Sterne, Laurence, 1
Stevens, Wallace, 99, 103
Stikhi, 172
Stravinsky, Igor, 221, 222
Strong Opinions, 259–60, 261
Swift, Jonathan, 253

Thackeray, William Makepeace, 196, 198; *The Newcomes,* 196; *Vanity Fair,* 220
"That in Aleppo Once," 136
Thoreau, Henry David, 105
Through the Looking Glass (Carroll), 2
Time, 5–13, 45–46, 48–49, 50, 55, 144, 152, 178, 277; and art, 56, 176, 180, 182, 189, 213; and exile, 236, 239–40; and love, 51, 246; and memory, 184; and poets, 58
Tolstoy, Leo, 66, 71, 74, 96, 144, 154, 163, 164, 179, 211; *Anna Karenina,* 180; *War and Peace,* 76, 220
Transparent Things, 158; death in, 191, 192, 194, 198, 204, 207; R. in, 199–202, 204, 205, 206, 207, 208. *See also* Person, Hugh
Trilling, Diana, 261
Trilling, Lionel, 2
Turgenev, Ivan, 161, 165, 179, 227; *Fathers and Sons,* 161, 165; *Rudin,* 165; *Smoke,* 165

Vadimovich, Vadim (*LATH*), 223, 224, 225–34
van Eyck, Jan, 149
Veen, Van (*Ada*), 130, 153, 180–82, 184, 234, 242, 245; and Ada, 176–77, 178, 179, 183, 186, 188, 219–20, 247, 248, 249; on allegory, 131–32; on literary style, 138; on Time, 152, 239–40
Vozrozhdenie, 157

Wain, John, 8
Wilson, Edmund, 164, 260–61
Woolf, Virginia, 198, 203, 206; *The Waves,* 194, 195, 200, 205
Wordsworth, William, 103, 105, 137, 250; "Intimations of Immortality from Recollections of Early Childhood," 256; *The Prelude,* 104
Wuthering Heights (E. Brontë), 30

Yeats, William Butler, 103, 154